THE EARLY CHURCH

THE EARLY CHURCH

*Origins to the Dawn
of the Middle Ages*

E. GLENN HINSON

ABINGDON PRESS
Nashville

THE EARLY CHURCH:
ORIGINS TO THE DAWN OF THE MIDDLE AGES

Copyright © 1996 by Abingdon Press

Library of Congress Cataloging-in-Publication Data
Hinson, E. Glenn.
    The early church: origins to the dawn of the Middle Ages/by E.
Glenn Hinson.
        p.   cm.
    Includes bibliographical references.
    ISBN 0-687-00603-1 (pbk.: alk. paper)
    1. Church history—Primitive and early church, ca. 30–600.
I. Title.
BR160.H56   1996
270.1—dc20   95-37832
                                                                CIP

Unless otherwise noted, scripture quotations are from the New Revised Standard Version Bible. Copyright 1989 by the Division of Christian Education of the National Council of the Churches of Christ in the USA. Used by permission.

Scripture quotations noted JB are from *The Jerusalem Bible*, copyright © 1966 by Darton, Longman & Todd, Ltd. and Doubleday, a division of Bantam Doubleday Dell Publishing Group, Inc. Reprinted by permission.

06 07 08 09 10 — 14 13 12 11 10

MANUFACTURED IN THE UNITED STATES OF AMERICA

To
my colleagues
at
Baptist Theological Seminary
at Richmond

Valiant for Truth

CONTENTS

PART ONE

THE BEGINNINGS
TO 70 C.E.

CHAPTER ONE

AN ANCIENT NEW PEOPLE

Christianity began with a history. The first Christians did not consider themselves a new people but an ancient people, Israel, under a new covenant. Stated another way, they thought of themselves as the true Israel having experienced the fulfillment of Jewish messianic hopes through Jesus of Nazareth.

Jesus was a Jew, an heir of centuries of Hebrew history extending from Abraham to his own day. He limited his ministry to the Jewish people and forbade his disciples to witness to any except Jews. He did not intend to begin a new religion. He wanted, rather, to awaken his own people to the dawning of an age of fulfillment of long-nourished hopes in and through him. He failed; yet in failing, he succeeded, for his death and the experience of resurrection that followed it inaugurated a movement that, within a few centuries, spread from Judea and Samaria throughout the civilized world.

Judaism furnished Christianity with both its most salient and central concepts and a well-tilled field in which to plant them. From Judaism came the concept of one God who had sought a people and entered into covenant with them for the purpose of bringing all peoples and nations into relationship with God and with one another. From it came the hopes for a messiah who would redeem a people, a strong ethical sensitivity, a habit of regular worship, and a sense of duty to broadcast the message of one God who offers salvation to all.

The Covenant People

At the heart of Hebrew self-understanding was the conviction that Yahweh had chosen them out of merciful love to be the People of the Covenant. Beyond the more general covenant made with Noah (Gen. 6:8ff.), Yahweh entered into a special covenant first with Abram (Gen. 16:18) and then through Moses (Exod. 19:4-6). The latter, based on God's deliverance of the people from bondage in Egypt, emphasized both favor and demand. "You yourselves have seen what I did with the Egyptians, how I carried you on eagle's wings and brought you to myself. From this you know that now, if you obey my voice and hold fast to my covenant, you of all the nations shall be my very own, for all the earth is mine. I will count you a kingdom of priests, a consecrated nation" (JB).

Much of the story related in the Old Testament concerns Israel's success or failure as the Covenant People, a theme Christians picked up on to establish the validity of Christianity against Jewish claims. When Moses delayed on Mount Sinai, the People demanded a golden calf (Exod. 32:1), symbolic of their subsequent apostasies. During the conquest of the promised land, they regularly went "whoring after other gods"—that is, the Canaanite deities Baal and Astarte. In the period of the Kingdom, the prophets repeatedly thundered warnings against violation of the covenant. Israel's and Judah's collapse, the prophets concluded, resulted from failure to abide by the demands of the covenant for faithfulness and justice and mercy. The eighth-century prophets still held out hopes that a repentant people might avert disaster, but their successors in later centuries saw these hopes dashed on the rock of reality. Jeremiah, rebuffed in his efforts to get his bitter pill swallowed, pointed to the future and to the effecting of a new covenant unlike the one the people broke. "Deep within them I will plant my Law, writing it on their hearts. Then I will be their God and they shall be my people. There will be no further need for neighbour to try to teach neighbour, or brother to say to brother, 'Learn to know Yahweh!' No, they will all know me, the least no less than the greatest—it is Yahweh who speaks—since I will forgive their iniquity and never call their sin to mind" (Jer. 31:33-34 JB). Jeremiah and the prophets in the exile, such as Ezekiel and Deutero-Isaiah (Isaiah 40–55), entertained hopes that a remnant of the people would return. Indeed, Deutero-Isaiah narrowed the remnant to one, the Servant of Yahweh (Isa. 42:1-4; 49:1-6; 50:4-9; 52:13–53:12).

Surprisingly the earliest Christian writers seldom cited the new covenant in their arguments for Christianity. The author of Hebrews excepted, New Testament writers based their case on the older covenant references. The apostle Paul, who deserves more credit than any other for extending the covenant to include Gentiles, cited the covenant with Abraham as being predicated on faith rather than works (Gal. 3:6-14). The author of 1 Peter applied Exodus 19:5-6 directly to Christians with added allusions to Isaiah 43:20-21 and Hosea 1:6-9 and 2:3, 25:

> But you are a chosen race, a royal priesthood, a holy nation, God's own people, in order that you may proclaim the mighty acts of him who called you out of darkness into his marvelous light.
> Once you were not a people,
>   but now you are God's people;
> once you had not received mercy,
>   but now you have received mercy. (1 Pet. 2:9-10)

Christianity, led by the apostle Paul, departed from its parent religion in its incorporation of Gentiles without requiring them first to become Jews by circumcision and the offering of a sacrifice. It continued, however, to insist on baptism as a symbol of entrance into the Covenant People. Letting down certain of these barriers opened the way for this messianic sect to expand in a way its parent religion could not, but it also generated bitter feelings that led to an eventual rupture. In Jerusalem, Christians met opposition to their continuing to worship in the Temple; outside Jerusalem, to their participation in the synagogues. Differing sharply over messianic views, Christianity gradually emerged as a separate religion that, within three centuries, would become the dominant religion of the Roman Empire and in other nations beyond the borders of the empire. As Christianity accommodated itself to Hellenistic culture in the process, the exclusiveness of the covenant was put to the test again and again when masses knocked on church doors seeking admission.

Jewish Corporate Life

In the first century, Jewish corporate life revolved chiefly around two institutions: the Temple and the Law. The Temple had a long history, which endeared it to Jews living in Palestine, but its destruction in 589 B.C.E. and the scattering of the Jewish people undercut its importance even before Jesus' day. To make matters worse, Herod the Great's reconstruction of the Second Temple, begun in 19 B.C.E. was politically unpopular. Nevertheless, the Temple retained a central place in Jewish life until its destruction by the Roman armies in 70 C.E.

In theory, Temple worship entailed the offering of sacrifices symbolic of covenant renewal. The calendar dramatized the "great moments" in the history of the Covenant People when God had acted on their behalf. The sabbath, Passover, New Year's, the Day of Atonement, Pentecost, Purim—all said something about Yahweh mighty to save. Sacrifices offered within the context of liturgical recitals allowed the individual symbolically to renew commitments as the people gathered to renew the covenant. In practice, criticism from ancient times indicate Temple worship often became perfunctory, making little impact on the worshipers. Weightier matters—justice, mercy, peace—had to get attention elsewhere.

As the Temple's importance decreased, the Law's increased. During the exile in Babylon (589–520/19 B.C.E.), for obvious reasons, study of the Law took the place of Temple worship. Such study contributed to the development of synagogues as gathering places for Jewish communities in the Dispersion.

Synagogue worship consisted chiefly of reading and exposition of the scriptures. In Jesus' day, readings from the Torah, the Pentateuch, were prescribed; those from other writings, however, were optional (cf. Luke 4:17). The Old Testament canon did not achieve its present form in Judaism until 99 or 119 C.E., when rabbis at the Jewish school of Jamnia settled the matter.

One other institution played an important role in a society in which religion intersected with everything. In Jerusalem, the Sanhedrin resolved matters of dispute in interpretation of the Torah that synagogues could not settle. Composed of seventy elders presided over by the high priest, it served as a kind of Supreme Court.

The Sects of Judaism

Judaism was by no means monolithic in the first century. It consisted, rather, of numerous parties or sects as well as the "professional" interpreters of the Law, called scribes.

The Sadducees represented the priestly aristocracy, claiming descent from Zadok. As the ruling party, they favored accommodation to Roman hegemony. Religiously, however, they were skeptical of views that came to prominence during the interbiblical period—for instance, resurrection of the dead, judgment, eternal life, and angels or demons. They acknowledged the authority only of the Pentateuch.

The Pharisees were the party most zealous for keeping the Law. Originating during the Maccabean era, they sought "separation" from Gentile customs and the process of Hellenization that Judaism experienced in the third to second centuries B.C.E. In pursuit of this goal, they espoused strict adherence to the oral tradition being developed at the time. They are not to be equated with the scribes, professional interpreters of the Law, but many scribes would have belonged to the party of Pharisees. Unlike the Sadducees, the Pharisees believed in a resurrection of the dead, final judgment, and life in the age to come and accepted other writings besides the Pentateuch.

The Essenes, or Covenanters, entertained the most pronounced messianic hopes of all parties in Judaism. Withdrawing during the Maccabean era in protest of the corruption of the Temple and the priesthood in Jerusalem, they established a monastery near the Dead Sea. Like the Pharisees, they were zealous in study and application of the Law and developed an interpretive method that related scriptures in a particular way to their own experience. They were more strongly influenced, however, by Jewish apocalyptic thought. They conceived of themselves as "the Sons of Light," preparing for the final cataclysmic battle against "the Sons

18

of Darkness," whom they eventually identified as the Romans. In 68 C.E., thinking the end had come, they joined battle with the Romans; most Essenes were either killed or taken captive.

Essene influence on early Christianity was significant but difficult to establish with precision. The Essenes shared with early Christians strong expectations of the coming of a Messiah. They practiced some kind of ritual ablutions related to purification as the Covenant People and observed a messianic meal similar to the Christian Lord's Supper. In addition, they organized in hierarchical fashion similar to the Jerusalem community depicted in Acts. At the top was a Council of Twelve, including Three Priests (sometimes these were in addition to the twelve other members); next came Presbyters or Priests; at the bottom were "the Many." A "Superintendent" (*Mebaqqer*) also played some kind of executive role. The fact that Essenes are never mentioned in New Testament writings has been attributed to familiarity; so many Essenes joined the early church that no one needed to mention them.

Zealots were extreme Jewish nationalists. Impatient to free their homeland and people from Roman domination, they carried on guerrilla warfare. Jesus' ties with Zealots are uncertain, but at least one of his followers, Simon, was called "the Zealot," and Judas may have belonged to the still more radical Sicarii, for the name *Iscariot* can be construed in that way. Efforts to turn Jesus himself into a Zealot, however, require such a vast amount of rewriting of early Christian history as to remain unconvincing.

Herodians supported the royal family, whose Idumean ancestry aroused bitter feelings among the Jews. Herod the Great widened the rift by catering to the Romans and by his brutal rule in the last years of his reign (37–4 B.C.E.). His sons did not fare much better.

Besides these parties or sects, first-century Judaism had guilds of priests, Temple singers, and Levites who attended to Temple functions and a guild of scribes who, from the time of Jesus Ben Sirach (ca. 180 B.C.E.), concentrated on the Law. At the time of Jesus, scribes were divided into two schools—a strict school, called Shammaite, and a liberal one, called Hillelite. Whereas Shammaites emphasized rigorous adherence to the Law, Hillelites stressed love and conciliation.

A New Sect Among the Old

Christianity came to birth in this complex setting. How did it differ from the other religions? One difference was in eschatological expectations. Whereas the other sects looked *forward* to the coming of the Messiah, Christianity looked *backward* from the vantage point of the death and resurrection of

Jesus of Nazareth. The age to come had dawned. The promises had begun to be fulfilled.

This central conviction, however, contained other implications that would push Christianity away from the others. John the Baptist, possibly reared by the Essenes, had become impatient with waiting in the desert and went forth to announce the "coming one." Expectations fulfilled, Christians pressed forth still further. The monotheistic motive that prompted the Jewish mission was heightened to fever pitch. The time within which the message could be proclaimed was short; soon the risen Lord would return to consummate the plan of God for human history.

The urgency with which the mission was pursued, however, soon evoked a third distinction. Zealous to share the "good news" of the inbreaking of the kingdom of God in and through Jesus, Israel's Messiah, Christians soon invited the "godfearers" and marginal people connected with Jewish communities to full membership in the Covenant People without insisting on their receiving the marks of Jews or observing Jewish ritual law. This radical action precipitated a massive debate.

In the words and works of Jesus, Christians found the precedent they needed. Jesus, to be sure, had not extended his ministry beyond the bounds of Judaism. However, he had ministered to the outcasts and earned the reputation of a "friend of tax collectors and sinners." Not the well but the sick need a doctor, he had said in defense. The parables of the lost sheep, the lost coin, and the prodigal son demonstrated God's love for the sinner. God's mercy is wide enough to receive even these.

Like the prophets of old, Jesus also placed human need above observance of the Law. "The sabbath was made for humankind, and not humankind for the sabbath" (Mark 2:27), he argued against rigid interpreters. Those who make a fetish of observance can end up missing the whole purpose of the Law. Tithing mint, dill, and cummin, they neglect the things that really matter (Matt. 23:23f.). Preoccupation with observance may also lead to self-righteousness, which inhibits true justification. Not the self-righteous Pharisee who boasted about his scrupulous observance of the *Halakah* but the lowly tax collector who refused to lift his eyes heavenward and beat his breast in abasement "went home justified" (Luke 18:14).

However much Jesus had done to prepare for the separation of Christianity from other sects of Judaism, the apostle Paul merits the most credit, or blame, for the break. Membership in the Covenant People, the apostle contended, depends on God's grace and the believer's faith, not on doing the Law. Salvation depends purely on God's unmerited favor, for all—Jews and Gentiles alike—have "sinned and fall short of the glory of God" (Rom. 3:23). In Christ, God has opened a way to do what we could not do for ourselves: obey God. By his death on the cross, Christ has taken on himself our condemnation, so that there is now no more condemnation for us (Rom. 8:1). How do we appropriate the benefits of his death? By simple faith. Neither circumcision nor observance of the ritual law will do any good. What is required is simply to trust God. As for Greek, so too for Jew.

Here the apostle undercut the very essence of Jewish piety. Tolerant as Judaism was at many points, on this issue a rift was unavoidable.

CHAPTER TWO

THE WORLD OF EARLY CHRISTIANITY

Judaism gave birth to Christianity, but it did not provide a spawning ground for long. The world of early Christianity was the Roman Empire and its environs—from the British Isles to the Tigris-Euphrates, and from central Europe to northern Africa. By the end of the first century, Christian communities dotted this entire area, in some places rather heavily, in others thinly.

The Roman Colossus

When Jesus was born, Rome dominated the world around the Mediterranean. Still expanding, it reached its greatest extent under Hadrian around 115 C.E. Continuous expansion, however, came at a price. It required increasing concentration of power in the hands of the emperor, constant attention to the strengthening of external boundaries, and the reforming of provincial administration during the succession of emperors from Octavian to Nero (27 B.C.E. to 68 C.E.). In addition, as a means of enhancing imperial authority, the Roman Senate fostered Caesar worship, beginning with Julius. Although Octavian forbade such honors in Rome, he permitted it in the provinces. His successors in the Julio-Claudian line held back few claims, thus setting up a head-on clash with Christianity, which demanded absolute allegiance to Jesus as Lord. Caligula (37–41) was the first emperor to demand universal homage to his statue. Although Domitian (91–96) was the first to use real force, the first clash with Christians came under Nero (60–68).

Roman society in the first century exhibited many features similar to American society today. It was cosmopolitan, a vast melting pot composed of many ancient peoples. The Romans were themselves a composite people. By virtue of their conquests, they absorbed dozens more, everywhere taking captives who would toss their cultures into the pot. The Romans also admired Hellenistic culture, itself cosmopolitan, and spread it wherever they went.

The population of the empire, approximately 70,000,000, was concentrated chiefly in cities. Rome's population numbered about 700,000. Antioch on the Orantes and Alexandria were only slightly smaller. Ephesus, Corinth, Athens, and several other cities vied for third place behind these.

Such cities offered both the opportunities and the disadvantages of modern ones. Rome especially drew hundreds because of its "bread and circuses." Alexandria boasted the world's greatest library and immense cultural resources. Nevertheless, all of the cities suffered from cramped living quarters, poor sanitation, inadequate water supplies, vermin infestation, and a host of similar problems. Poorly constructed apartment buildings six stories high frequently crumbled to the ground with a roar, snuffing out the lives of occupants. The half-mad Emperor Nero probably had urban renewal on his mind when he set fire to the city of Rome in 64 C.E. and then blamed the arson on Christians.

The empire was characterized also by enormous disparities in wealth. Although there was a middle class, most of the populace clustered at opposite poles. The wealthy lived in grand villas on the outskirts of the city. They enjoyed comforts and conveniences put at their disposal by slaves. The poor squeaked by with bare subsistence of food, clothing, and the necessities. Unable to maintain their families, they frequently left newborn children, especially girls, exposed to the elements to die. Christians adopted many of these unfortunates in the next several centuries, a custom that continued until the sixth century.

An increasing number of persons depended on state maintenance. Rome's conquests, of course, enabled emperors to draw supplies from elsewhere to curry favor with the masses. The dole became so burdensome, however, that Octavian was compelled to limit it to 150,000 and later to 100,000 persons.

Side by side with greater brutality were signs of growing sensitivity to human beings. The Roman army, challenged to conquer more and more new territories, conscripted all and sundry. Thoughtful persons such as the Stoic Seneca, however, composed treatises *On Clemency* in criticism of careless regard for human life.

Roman society was divided into several layers. At the lowest level, where Christianity made its first inroads, people waged a daily struggle for survival and worried about losing their property, heavy taxation, the draft, and other matters familiar today. Moral standards varied widely, ranging from the admirable thought of the Stoics—Seneca, Epictetus, Cicero—to the deplorable outlook of the masses. Illiteracy was common. The uneducated hired professional scribes to write letters for them and then signed them with an X. Families strained to survive. Children manipulated parents for money. People despaired in the face of sickness and death.

The Religions of Rome

Paul's compliment to the Athenians about their being "extremely religious . . . in every way" (Acts 17:22) would have suited the people of the

Roman Empire quite well, for the word he used, *deisdaimonia*, meant both "religious" and "superstitious." The religions of the Roman Empire fell into three categories: the state cultus revived by Octavian, the oriental religions that attracted the masses, and the philosophies that functioned increasingly as the religion of the better educated. The state cultus still retained much vitality among the masses. An amalgam of many sources, particularly the Greek pantheon, it suffered from impersonalism and formalism. What had made Rome great, the Romans believed, was not merely the gods but their devotion to the gods, manifested in precise rituals and observances. When Rome conquered other nations, it tried to incorporate the defeated countries' deities into the Roman pantheon so that none might be neglected. The addition of the cult of the emperor with the goddess Roma helped momentarily, but state religion proved too perfunctory to satisfy all. It lacked the warmth of personal appeal found in oriental cults.

Numerous oriental religions thrived in the West when Christianity put in its appearance. The Mysteries of Eleusis, originating several centuries before the Christian era, were patronized by emperors from Octavian on. They used the planting of seed as a symbol of the promise of life that lies beyond death. Mysteries of Dionysus, found also under the name of Orpheus, extended throughout the Greco-Roman world. They were noted for enthusiasm and ecstatic prophesying. The three stoutest competitors in the first several centuries, however, were Cybele, or the Great Mother, Isis and Osiris, and Mithra.

The cult of the Great Mother, a fertility goddess connected with agricultural rites, enjoyed wide currency in the ancient world as far west as the British Isles. Acknowledged in Rome as a legitimate foreign cult in 205 B.C.E., by the time of Augustus it had gained immense popularity. Originally a wild and enthusiastic cult, involving even human sacrifices, it was modified by combination with the cult of Attis. The mythology of a dying and rising god replaced earlier orgiastic rites. A colorful pageantry combined with the promise of immortality to attract many. In time Cybele adopted the *taurobolium*, a bath in bull's blood, popularized by Mithra. Symbolically "buried" in a pit covered by a lattice-work of boards, the devotee was said to be purified of sins and raised to new life.

Isis and Osiris, an ancient Egyptian cult, was introduced to the West by the Ptolemies. Soldiers, sailors, slaves, and popular writers disseminated it all over the empire. Its most attractive features were the myth of a dying and rising god and an appealing liturgy. The myth told how the young god Osiris, civilizer of Egypt, was hacked to pieces by the jealous Typhon and his remains scattered along the Nile River. Osiris's faithful wife, Isis, however, searched diligently until she found all parts save the male sexual organ and restored her husband to life. Periodically, Osiris would return to visit his wife and son. Daily rituals and two impressive annual ceremonies dramatized this myth. On March 5 a magnificent processional to the river celebrated the reopening of the seas at the end of winter. From October 26 to November 3 the cult dramatized the "Finding of Osiris." Here worshipers simulated funeral lamentations for the fallen god, then rejoiced as Horus, son of Osiris, overcame Typhon. An impressive initiation rite added to the appeal of this religion.

Mithra, a Persian sect that grew out of Zoroastrianism, advanced westward by way of the Roman army during the Flavian era (68–96). Remarkably similar to Christianity in many respects, it turned out to be the strongest competitor, though limited by the fact that the cult excluded women. Like Judaism and Christianity, Mithraism emphasized morality. It viewed life as a perpetual struggle between good and evil, light and darkness, the gods and demons. Mithra, one of the lesser deities in the Zoroastrian hierarchy, identified with human beings in their struggle. Mithraic altars depicted Mithra astride the back of a powerful bull, hurling his dagger into its side as a serpent twines around one of the bull's legs to lap up the blood spurting from the wound. To underline the importance of morality, Mithraism emphasized judgment. At death anyone stained with evil would be dragged by the emissaries of Ahriman to the depths of hell to suffer indescribable tortures, whereas the pure would ascend to the celestial realm, where the supreme god Ormuzd ruled. En route, Mithra himself would serve as the guide past the seven planetary spheres guarded over by angels. After a general resurrection, Mithra would judge all humanity once and for all and cause fire to consume all wicked spirits. Mithraism developed rites and organization similar to Christianity's, but, since they were of late origin, most were probably borrowed. The most important rite was the *taurobolium*, which promised immortality.

There has been much debate about the similarities between the mystery cults and Christianity. At one time the German history of religions school theorized that Christianity was an oriental mystery cult that Paul had given historical credence by attaching it to the person of Jesus. Some scholars doubted whether Jesus ever existed. Much subsequent research, in Jewish and Greek or Roman as well as Christian sources, however, has demolished this view. There remains, nevertheless, considerable question as to the extent of borrowing. The very nature of Christianity as an offspring of Judaism favors, at most, a cautious accommodation, but there is evidence of increasing borrowing of language and ideas as time passed.

The Philosophies

At the beginning, Christianity competed chiefly with the oriental religions in enlisting converts among non-Jews. From the first, however, persons of education and culture manifested an interest in this offspring of Judaism, just as they had in Judaism itself. By the mid-second century, apologists were presenting Christianity as "the true philosophy," a competitor of the philosophies that responded to the religious needs of the better educated and more sophisticated upper classes.

A multiplicity of philosophies vied with one another, but the one that attracted the largest following in this period and left the deepest mark on Christian thought was Stoicism. Originating about 300 B.C.E. with Zeno of Citium, this school entered its third major phase in the New Testament era with such representatives as Seneca, Epictetus, and, in the second century, Marcus Aurelius. Stoicism was based on the assumption that only matter is real. Yet, unlike Democritus, who ascribed the operation of the universe more or less to chance movement of the atom, the Stoics believed all things hold together in a coherent, indeed monistic, system. Zeus, destiny, providence, universal law, nature, or God penetrated and gave order to all things. The world operated according to divine law, which even God must obey. To live a happy life, human beings had to know and obey this law, which is equivalent to God's will. To discover the law of nature, they had to use their reason. Living according to nature was the same thing as living according to reason. The key lay in constant self-examination, probing of conscience. Conscience and duty were the cornerstones of Stoic ethics. Acting out of enlightened self-interest necessitated concern for all persons. The ideal, however, was to become self-sufficient, controlling actions by reason rather than by passion or desire.

By the second century, Platonism began to edge out Stoicism. Christianity encountered Platonism first in the latter's middle phase. While Platonism was a school of philosophical thought, Christians' earliest encounters with it were chiefly in the form of Gnosticism, a popular religious system that embodied many Platonist perspectives. There is considerable debate about the origins of Gnosticism. The older theory was that it represented the radical Hellenization of Christianity. Discovery of a Gnostic library at Chenoboskion in Egypt in 1947, however, has forced scholars to abandon this theory. Some have interpreted Gnosticism as a pre-Christian religion, others as the result of a failure of apocalyptic thought in Judaism and Christianity. The Nag Hammadi (Chenoboskion) documents indicate that Gnosticism took a variety of forms—some non-Christian, some Jewish, some Christian. Since Christian Gnosticism will receive specific attention later, it suffices here to mention general tenets that may have impressed themselves on early Christian thinking in the first century.

Gnosticism was characterized in its more extreme forms by a metaphysical dualism. Matter is evil; the spirit alone is good. Between these there should be no contact. Since matter is evil, the visible, physical world cannot have been created by God, who was by definition pure spirit. God entrusted

26

this work to a Demiurge, a secondary deity. To keep the material from intermingling with the spiritual, a series of concentric spheres, aeons, separated the world from God. Demons kept watch over these spheres, allowing no one to ascend without a password. As in Platonism, so in Gnosticism human beings were bipartite, consisting of body and soul. Since the body is material, it could not be saved. The soul, however, if enlightened by *Gnosis,* could be. Indeed, souls fell into three categories: the spiritual, who upon death would ascend like helium-filled balloons; the material, who had no prospect of salvation; and the psychic, who could be saved through *gnosis,* or knowledge. *Gnosis,* though, meant mystical rather than cognitive apprehension. Where did one obtain *gnosis?* From the Redeemer, who descended from the realm of the One (God), taught secret knowledge, and reascended. Not all Gnostic systems, as indicated above, were Christian, but those that attached themselves to Christianity identified Jesus as the Redeemer, a phantom rather than a human being.

The extent to which Gnostic thought shaped that of New Testament writers is debatable. Rudolf Bultmann believed Paul drew the basic framework for his theology from Gnosticism, but many other scholars have demonstrated its essentially Jewish structure. Some New Testament writings, particularly the Johannine, explicitly repudiated Gnostic dualism, docetism (belief that Jesus was a phantom), and moral indifferentism.

Other philosophical schools attracted fewer adherents and exerted more limited influence on early Christianity. Cynics, claiming origins in the fifth century B.C.E., still traveled around preaching that salvation lies in a return to nature. Their diatribes may have affected the form of some early Christian literature. Cynicism later merged with Stoicism. Neo-Pythagoreanism, a Greco-Alexandrian school, thrived during the first century. Its most famous representative was Apollonius of Tyana (ca. 1–98 C.E.), whom Philostratus celebrated in the third century as the miracle-working pagan answer to Jesus. Neo-Pythagoreanism combined Platonism and Pythagoreanism (sixth century B.C.E.), thus introducing a religious element into pagan philosophy. Dualistic like Gnosticism, the Neo-Pythagoreans encouraged asceticism as a path to liberation from the body. They shared many ideas with the oriental mystery cults.

The Common Person's Outlook

What has not been covered in connection with religions and philosophies can be adequately summed up under two headings: fate and demons. A profound fatalism gripped the minds of most persons in the ancient world. Thus the Romans took over the Greek deity Tyche, Chance or Fortune.

The philosophers commented often and at length on chance and necessity. The Stoics obviated the problem of chance with their doctrine of Providence, but it, too, amounted to a virtual determinism of nature's law. The average person had little sense of control over life. "Assuredly, if Fortune is against it," Apuleius said on behalf of many, "nothing good can come to mortal man."

Belief in occult powers resulted in a similar sense of the futility of life. The average person lived in a world teeming with demons, sprites, spirits of departed ancestors, "ghoulies and ghosties and long-leggety beasties/ And things that go bump in the night." Both good and bad, such beings controlled one's fate. If one drank a glass of water, one might swallow a demon and become deathly ill, go insane, or drop dead. Another person might invoke a curse through the agency of a demon. Having none of the testing instruments of modern science and technology, only the very skeptical denied and questioned this worldview. The average person searched frantically for ways to get the good demons and powers on their side and to placate the evil. They consulted soothsayers. They employed magicians to compose formulas to ward off evil. They probed the entrails of animals and birds. They carried amulets and magic charms. They entreated the gods with votive offerings. They erected temples and public buildings. They did anything to bring a proper balance to the fearful unknown.

We can see here the challenge to early Christianity if it was to attract and enlist converts in a world so unlike the one in which it began. Like the oriental cults flowing westward at the time, it had to respond to the cry for infallible revelation, for assurance as to the meaning of life, for victory over the malign forces that threatened to engulf human beings, for hope. Yet, like those same cults, it could have lost its own identity as it incorporated the diverse and syncretistic peoples of the empire and beyond. It needed a historical anchorage in its parent religion and, more specifically, its founder.

CHAPTER THREE

THE FOUNDER OF CHRISTIANITY

Since the late nineteenth century, scholars have debated whether Jesus should be regarded as the founder of Christianity or only as the "presupposition" for it. Was Christianity rooted in his life and thought and ministry? Or did it arise only out of the conviction of the first believers that Jesus, though crucified and buried, has been raised by God? Or, phrased in the words of the noted French Catholic Alfred Loisy, was not the church the (unintended) *result* of Jesus' preaching of the kingdom of God rather than something he himself founded?

Such questions cannot be answered easily. Few scholars today would defend the view held since ancient times that Jesus founded the church essentially as it now exists save for growth and development. Nevertheless, it does seem important to insist that Christianity has some connections not merely with the resurrection experience but with what antedated it. Paul, to be sure, accentuated the resurrection as the *sine qua non* for Christianity (1 Cor. 15:17-19), and he seemed to devalue the historical when he declared that "even though we once knew Christ from a human point of view, we know him no longer in that way" (2 Cor. 5:16). Yet he could make a word of Jesus about divorce assume the force of command contrasted with his own word of advice (1 Cor. 7:10, 12), and he counted traditions about Jesus essential to the very existence of Christianity (cf. 1 Cor. 14:3-8). Certainly important as he was to early Christian self-understanding, Paul cannot himself be regarded as the founder of Christianity as some scholars once contended.

The Life and Ministry of Jesus

If critical studies of the century and a half since David Friedrich Strauss published his *Life of Jesus* (1835) have reached any firm conclusion, it is that the sources at our disposal will not allow us to write a biography of Jesus. Jesus' existence, of course, is no longer open to question, as it was for a time, but some scholars do doubt the possibility of reconstructing a framework for Jesus' life and ministry. The first witnesses were not writing biography but giving testimony about the "good news" that they had heard and taken part in.

Some high points in Jesus' life and ministry, however, are evident. Since Herod the Great was still alive when Jesus was born, his birth must have occurred before 4 B.C.E., when Herod died, perhaps about 6 B.C.E. Although December 25 has been celebrated as Jesus' birth date since about 335 C.E., there is no evidence to indicate even the time of the year. Prior to 335, Christians in the East celebrated January 6 as the day of Jesus' birth.

Because Joseph and Mary were devout Jews, Jesus doubtless received an upbringing similar to that of other Jewish youth. Accordingly, he was circumcised on the eighth day and presented in the Temple, as prescribed by Numbers 6:10 (cf. Luke 2:22). "Presentation" had to do with dedication of a "firstborn" son (1 Kings 1:24-25). Although Catholic tradition has held that Mary had no more children, the Gospels name four brothers—James, Joses, Jude, and Simon (Mark 6:3; cf. Matt. 27:56). Joseph may have died early in Jesus' life, leaving him the responsibility for supporting the family, for Joseph is not mentioned anywhere during Jesus' ministry.

Jesus' ministry began in connection with John the Baptist. At first he may have contemplated following John, or he might actually have done so. Eventually, however, he gathered a following of his own. Subsequently a John the Baptist sect competed with early Christianity (cf. Acts 19:1-7). This sect claimed that, because John baptized Jesus, John was the superior one. Christians replied by noting that John himself claimed only to be a forerunner.

John's mission and message reflect close enough similarities to those of the Qumran or Essene sect that many scholars have theorized a direct connection, such as his adoption as an orphan on the death of his parents. Like the Essenes, John denounced Jewish society, especially priests; insisted on a baptism of repentance for all, Jews as well as Gentiles; and proclaimed a judgment of fire soon to come. Unlike them, however, he administered baptism rather than let people baptize themselves, and he carried his message to the main arteries of traffic rather than waiting for something to happen. If he was once an Essene, he broke with them, perhaps over the timing of the age of fulfillment.

Luke dated the beginning of John's ministry "in the fifteenth year of the reign of Emperor Tiberius" (Luke 3:1), which could mean either 28/29 or possibly 25/26, depending on whether it is dated from the death of Augustus (August 19, 14 C.E.) or from Tiberius's co-reign with him. John did not minister long, however, for his criticism of Herod Antipas soon led to his imprisonment (Luke 3:19-20) and beheading (Mark 6:17-29).

There can be no question that Jesus was baptized by John, for his baptism supplied support for the argument of the John the Baptist sect. Since John's baptism had to do with repentance of sins, however, it posed a serious problem for Christian theology. Why was Jesus baptized? According to the Synoptic accounts, his baptism had something to do with his self-understanding and mission. Through this acted-out parable, as it were, Jesus proclaimed his identification with his people as the Messiah of the Remnant, conceived in terms of the Servant of the Lord in Deutero-Isaiah. At the same time, God confirmed his perception. The voice from heaven conflated two passages of scripture: Psalm 2:7 and Isaiah 42:1, the first a messianic text, the other a servant text. The "temptation" experiences that followed depicted an interior struggle concerning these options. Would Jesus be a messiah like David, and gather an army and drive out the Romans? Or would he take the servant role, submitting his cause to God?

Jesus' ministry may have begun in Judaea and continued in Galilee. Not only is this made evident in John 1–3, but it is also implied by Mark's report that "after John was arrested, Jesus came to Galilee" (Mark 1:14). However that may be, the most extensive part of Jesus' ministry took place in his homeland, centering on the little town of Capernaum, nestling in a cove alongside the Sea of Galilee. It was a natural site for his ministry, for all Galilee converged on Capernaum, from which Jesus drew his most ardent supporters.

The sequence of events cannot be accurately reconstructed. Combining proclamation of the advent of the kingdom of God with a ministry of healing, Jesus impressed people in different ways. Some thought of him as a rabbi; others as John the Baptist restored to life; others as Elijah, popularly anticipated as the forerunner of the Messiah; others as Jeremiah or one of the prophets; and some, evidently very few, as the Messiah (cf. Matt. 16:14-16). Even his closest disciples, however, had difficulty comprehending the Servant/Messiah concept that the title "Son of Man" encompassed. Nationalistic concepts of the Messiah precluded the idea of suffering and death of the coming ideal king.

With whom did the concept originate? Jesus or the "early church"? Some scholars have argued the latter. According to some, Jesus may actually have led a revolt that the Romans ruthlessly put down (the cleansing of the Temple). Thence he was tried and sentenced to death as a revolutionary. Subsequently, some early Christian or Christians rewrote the story from the point of view of his crucifixion, superimposing the servant motif.

One cannot speak dogmatically here, but this interpretation ascribes a level of sophistication to the early disciples that the sources would seem to deny. It assumes a massive rewriting such as neither a committee nor an individual could pull off within the brief time span in which it would have had to occur. The apostle Paul, for instance, converted no more than two to five years after the death of Jesus, had no suspicions of this; he simply assumed the servant motif derived from Jesus himself, and he passed on early baptismal traditions that incorporated this motif (cf. Rom. 6:8-11). The evidence certainly favors Jesus as the originator of the idea.

Jesus gained enough of a following to generate considerable concern among authorities. In a land bubbling with resistance to authority, it is not hard to see why his purpose would be misunderstood.

Sometime in the Galilean period, Jesus selected a band of Twelve from the larger following. Although some scholars have ascribed this symbolic group to the early community rather than to Jesus himself, Paul's acquaintance with it as part of early tradition makes that unlikely (1 Cor. 15:5). It is more likely that Jesus, facing the prospect of death before God consummated his purpose in history, wanted to leave this remnant to continue his ministry. Whereas the twelve tribes and the twelve patriarchs provided the foundation of Israel under the old covenant, this Twelve would supply the foundation for Israel under the new. The Last Supper, one of many fellowship meals Jesus shared with his followers, confirms this interpretation. The "cup" of his death was to be the "new covenant" in which they would share (Mark 14:24).

Although Jesus had the reputation of a rabbi, his calling of disciples differed from that of other rabbis. In the latter case, the disciples sought the teacher; in Jesus' case, the teacher sought the disciple and issued an authoritative call not just to repentance and faith but to follow Jesus himself. His call left no room for equivocation. "Here! Behind me!" he exclaimed. Following meant renunciation of family (Matt. 19:29; Mark 10:29-30; Luke 18:19b-30), participation in Jesus' suffering and even in his death (Mark 8:34).

According to Matthew's account, Jesus withdrew from Galilee after sending the Twelve on a mission like his own. This trip to Syria, beyond the bounds of Israel, appears to have been a kind of watershed in his career, for thereafter he set out directly for Jerusalem, the heart of Israel but also the place where the prophets were stoned. Neither Jesus nor the disciples had gotten a kind reception in Galilee (Matt. 13:56; Mark 6:4; Luke 4:24; cf. John 1:11). Rejected in his hometown of Nazareth (Luke 4:28-30), he went to Capernaum. The Twelve extended his ministry. But neither Jesus' efforts nor their own produced the repentance among the people that Jesus expected to usher in the kingdom (Matt. 10:23). The Galileans went on playing like children in the marketplace. Jesus had to pull back and dig deeper into himself to sort things out. The servant image loomed larger and larger.

Jesus probably took the "pilgrim way" to Jerusalem, via Capernaum, Samaria, and Jericho. On the way he continued to proclaim the message of the kingdom and to try to explain his mission to the disciples, preparing them for his death. By this time the opposition of religious authorities was reaching a high pitch. The cleansing of the Temple came as the last straw in his criticisms of the twin pillars of Judaism—the Law and the Temple.

The Message of Jesus

What in Jesus' self-understanding led to this event? By what authority, religious leaders demanded, did he act? Was he a prophet? Or, as his actions indicated, was he more than a prophet?

In some respects Jesus did act like a prophet, and it is not difficult to understand why some identified him as one. The Temple cleansing fit the prophetic category. He acted like a rabbi as well. Nevertheless, he went beyond both prophet and rabbi in claiming to act in God's stead. He taught "as one having authority, and not as the scribes" (Mark 1:22; Matt. 7:29; cf. Luke 4:32). Although he employed the rabbinic formula, "You have heard that it was said . . . " he diverged from them with the authoritative, "But I say. . . . " He not only interpreted, but he also corrected Moses (Matt. 19:8). If this were not enough to bring an indictment for blasphemy, he had the audacity to offer forgiveness of sins, a prerogative that religious leaders reserved for God alone (Mark 2:7).

Behind both the rabbinic and the prophetic consciousness of Jesus must be seen a "filial" consciousness. He was "Son of God" in a unique sense, one that transcended or swerved from even Jewish expectations of a Messiah. Nothing is so revealing of Jesus' self-understanding as his address of God as *Abba,* an intimate Aramaic term. This was not merely *a* way Jesus addressed God; as Joachim Jeremias has demonstrated, it was *the* way, unique in itself. By contrast, God was seldom referred to as "Father" either in the Old Testament or in Judaism prior to the first century, and then usually in the corporate sense.

Jesus taught his followers to approach God as a loving parent. They did not need to badger God with their demands, piling up words and phrases, for "your Father knows what you need before you ask him" (Matt. 6:8). If earthly parents supply their children's needs, how much more should one expect that of a heavenly parent (Matt. 7:9-11).

A major inference from this understanding of God precipitated a vigorous debate over Jesus' embracing of sinners and outcasts. Is it fair, his critics wanted to know, that God accepts those who have scorned his demands and gone their own way? Maybe not, Jesus responded, but it belongs to his paternal nature. If a poor woman lost a coin, wouldn't she put other coins down and find the lost one? If a shepherd noticed that one sheep had strayed, wouldn't he leave the other ninety-nine to find that one? If a son took his inheritance and squandered it in a foreign country, wouldn't his father keep watching and welcome him home when he repented and returned (Luke 15)? God acts not on the basis of human merit but out of grace, like the owner of a vineyard who paid those who worked one hour the same wage he agreed to pay those who labored twelve. The latter had no complaint. They got what they agreed to work for (Matt. 20:1-16).

The heart of Jesus' message had to do with the kingdom of God. According to Mark, Jesus proclaimed, "The time is fulfilled, and the kingdom of God has come near; repent, and believe in the good news" (Mark 1:14). In what way was the kingdom "close at hand"? Scholars have disputed this question at length. Albert Schweitzer, in his famous *Quest of the Historical Jesus*, contended that Jesus expected the kingdom to come within his own lifetime, and disappointed that it did not, tried to force God's hand. Thus he, as it were, "hurled himself on the wheel of the world," which turned and crushed him, "the one immeasurably great man." C. H. Dodd, contrariwise, interpreted Mark 1:14 in terms of a present realization. In Jesus himself, in his life and work, the kingdom was already present. Accordingly, Jesus' response to critics of his healing ministry, which they attributed to Satan, was: "If it is by the Spirit of God that I cast out demons, then the kingdom of God has come to you" (Matt. 12:28; cf. Luke 11:20). Other scholars have spoken of an "inaugurated eschatology." The kingdom in its full expression is still future, but it has been inaugurated in and through Jesus' ministry.

A look at Jesus' understanding of the kingdom may help to resolve the problem. The kingdom or rule of God had to do, first of all, with a relationship that God and not human beings would establish, a rebuke evidently to Jewish nationalists. Like seed or like leaven, the kingdom grows by itself in a mysterious way (Matt. 13:33; Mark 4:26-30; Luke 13:20-21), a point that makes the question of present or future virtually irrelevant. In his deeds and words, Jesus announced the day of salvation. The kingdom was present in restoration of sight to the blind, in recovery of physical faculties by the lame, in cleansing of lepers, in deaf persons' hearing again, and in the poor receiving relief (Matt. 11:5; Luke 7:22).

The imminence of the kingdom in Jesus altered the situation of Jesus' disciples vis-à-vis Jewish observances. They did not have to fast, as the Pharisees or John's followers did, for wedding guests do not fast so long as the bridegroom is still with them (Mark 2:19).

Its imminence also sounded a warning about an imminent catastrophe, God's judgment, and called for repentance. The day of the Son of Man's coming as judge would occur suddenly, unexpectedly, and without warning, like the flood in Noah's day (Matt. 24:37-41; Luke 17:22-28). People ought to act with dispatch, like the debtor who sought to settle accounts before being taken to court (Matt. 5:25-26; Luke 12:57-59). They should also act wisely and not like the foolish maidens who did not bring extra oil for their lamps (Matt. 25:1-13).

34

What did the kingdom signify morally and ethically to Jesus? How did its demands differ from those of the scribes and Pharisees? How did a life based on grace differ from one based on adherence to the Jewish *halakah?*

In the Sermon on the Mount, which contains the essence of Jesus' teaching, those who enter the kingdom are instructed to exceed the scribes and Pharisees in their righteousness. Given the commendable ethic of these two groups, how could that be?

Jesus gave several examples. Whereas they said, "Don't kill," Jesus said, "Don't be angry or insult your brother. Instead, seek reconciliation" (see Matt. 5:21-26). Whereas they said, "Don't commit adultery," Jesus said, "Remove the source of infidelity, the inner desire which leads astray" (see 5:27-30). Whereas they would protect the wife's interest by giving a legal document, Jesus forbade divorce altogether on the grounds that it forced the wife into adultery (5:31-32). Whereas the Old Testament condoned oath taking, Jesus urged the disciples to make their word their bond (5:33-37). Whereas they encouraged exact retaliation, he promoted nonresistance, reconciliation, and giving without expectation of return (5:33-42).

How could anyone meet such high expectations? Some have insisted that Jesus did not mean for them to be met. They have spiritualized them, relegated them to the future ideal kingdom, or accommodated them to present exigencies in some way. Such explanations, however, seem to miss the point: grace alone suffices. Human beings have to be changed from within, become pure in heart, single of mind, downright good. Is this not the point of the parable of the judgment of the nations in Matthew 25:31-46? Those whom the "king" invited to enter his kingdom did good out of the goodness of their hearts without even knowing it. They had to ask, "Lord, when was it that we saw you hungry and gave you food, or thirsty and gave you something to drink?" Good trees bear edible fruit, bad trees inedible (Matt. 5:18; cf. Luke 6:43). Persons made righteous by God would not invoke the Corban rule to escape an obligation to parents. They would not play-act at religion. They would not let sabbath observance or rules and regulations concerning food and fasting get in the way of "weightier matters." That is how kingdom righteousness exceeds that of scribes and Pharisees.

One additional question should be asked about Jesus' teaching: Did he intend the church? Was his expectation of the consummation so intense, as Albert Schweitzer thought, that he left no room for the remnant of Israel? Hardly anyone would contend that Jesus envisioned the church as an institution, but several bits of evidence point to the direction of the remnant concept. First, some direct sayings—parables about fasting, passages in which Jesus called for allegiance to himself, and the title "Son of Man" with its corporate implications—point to Jesus' expectation that the disciples might carry on after his death. Second, challenges to faith, calling for allegiance not only to himself but also to the Father, imply a continuation of the people of God. Third, his calling of the Twelve offers direct evidence of the continuance of his ministry. Fourth, the meals he shared with the disciples suggest a continuing fellowship. Fifth, his ethical teaching would have no meaning unless he envisioned a time in which it would apply. As a prophet, he doubtless foreshortened the time of the consummation, but he did not presume to determine the schedule and forewarned his followers against doing that very thing.

Jesus' Death

The least debated and debatable aspect of the Jesus story is his death. No Christian, surely, would have invented the crucifixion story. Resurrection maybe; crucifixion no!

The sequence and details of the passion narrative, however, are open to question. Among the many disputed points, the most important is this: Why was Jesus put to death? According to all early accounts, the Romans did so because they feared Jesus was a revolutionary. Confronted by Rome's demand that he keep the peace no matter how volatile and explosive the situation, a weak governor like Pontius Pilate could have been expected to take decisive action. His one question of Jesus was "Are you the king of the Jews?" (Mark 15:2; Matt. 27:11; Luke 23:3). The fact that Jesus had Zealots in his entourage and replied somewhat evasively (Mark 15:3; John 18:34) did not help his case. If he had been a Zealot and the Temple cleansing an abortive coup, Pilate would not have equivocated at all. But this theory, as noted earlier, poses massive problems.

Behind the Roman action, according to the evangelists, lay a conspiracy among Jewish officials. Many contemporary scholars have questioned the "conspiracy" idea, particularly in the light of the flames of anti-Semitism that it has sometimes fanned. How should the evidence be evaluated? Admittedly, the Gospel writers may have sometimes overblown the case. John, for instance, virtually isolated Jesus from his heritage when he lumped Jesus' opponents together under one label, "the Jews." Such general opposition to Jesus can hardly have existed among the Jewish people, for he was popular among the masses. Thus we must handle the reports with care.

Strong opposition to Jesus originated chiefly with religious leaders: Herod Antipas, son of Herod the Great and Tetrarch of Galilea and Perea; the scribes and Pharisees; the Sadducees; and the Zealots. According to Mark, the Pharisees counseled with "Herodians" regarding Jesus' death (Matt. 12:4; Mark 3:6; cf. Mark 12:13). Herodian antipathy may have stemmed from Jesus' association with John the Baptist (Mark 6:14-16). Jesus himself had warned his followers against "the yeast of the Pharisees and the yeast of Herod" (Mark 8:15). Herod, too, was zealous about the observance of the Law.

The scribes and Pharisees smarted over the cavalier attitude of Jesus and his disciples toward the Law. Although Jesus never disputed the seriousness of their intention, he did question the effect of their call for punctilious observance. They generated "sons of the Gehenna" (Matt. 23:15) rather than children of God. In contrast, he sought to discover in the Law God's intentions for humankind, sometimes correcting the Law itself. To the scribes and Pharisees this was insufferable, for it could do nothing but undermine the whole Jewish legal system, and, in claiming to speak for God, Jesus asserted authority in a blasphemous way.

More directly responsible for the "plot" against Jesus were the Sadducees. Anxious to guard the Temple and to preserve the civil peace under Roman occupation, the Sanhedrin indicted Jesus for blasphemy on two charges: his statement regarding the destruction of the Temple and his claims to messiahship. Although some scholars hold that the charge of blasphemy was restricted in the first century to saying the divine name, YHWH, it may have been construed more broadly on many occasions, thus bringing these two charges under a broader umbrella. Whatever else it may have signified, Jesus' cleansing of the Temple represented a flagrant violation of the authority of the priestly aristocracy. The accusation laid against him was the boast "I will destroy this temple that is made with hands" (Mark 14:58; Matt. 26:61; cf. John 2:19). Further, his citation of the Son of Man saying from Daniel 7:13 came dangerously near to a direct claim of divinity. He was not claiming messiahship merely of the Davidic type but of the heavenly Son of Man type. All religious leaders needed to confirm their suspicions of blasphemy was this quotation from Daniel.

The Zealots may have attached considerable hopes to Jesus at one time, but, as it dawned on them that he was not the Messiah like David, their crushed hopes turned to opposition. Disappointment of this kind possibly figured prominently in Judas's betrayal of Jesus. Although other motives may have entered the picture (money, for example; cf. Matt. 26:15; John 12:13), Judas may have acted from a nobler concern. He might have been the first of the disciples to grasp what Jesus was trying to say and decided he would no longer be a party to a suicidal mission.

Another element in the narratives concerning the death of Jesus from which problems arise is the Last Supper, problems having to do with date, type of meal, words spoken, and meaning. From the first century on, there were two traditions concerning date, Nisan 14 (John) or Nisan 15 (the other three Gospels), which led to a second-century controversy over the celebration of Easter, to which we will return later. Although early tradition considered the supper a Passover meal, several elements of that meal conflict with what we know of Passover observances in the first century. Scholars have speculated that the meal may have been of another type: a *Haburah*, a fellowship meal celebrated on many occasions; a sabbath-*kiddush*, at which the head of a household said a prayer of sanctification over a cup of wine and drank it along with other members of a household; or a Qumran-type messianic banquet. Two major traditions (Mark/Matthew vs. Luke/Paul) exist concerning the words of Jesus. Interpretation of the words has, of course, divided Christians for centuries. Views range from the more literalist interpretation of the words "This is my body. . . . This is my blood" by Roman Catholics or Orthodox to the more metaphorical interpretation of many Protestants.

Certainty is no longer possible on the *place* of crucifixion and burial of Jesus. Since 336 C.E., when Constantine's mother, Helena, had a church erected there, the traditional site of crucifixion and burial has been the Church of the Holy Sepulchre. Another is the "Garden Tomb" located near a cliff weather marked or quarried to resemble a human skull. Scourging, a horrible form of beating meant to weaken the prisoner and hasten death, preceded the impalement at 9:00 A.M. In this cruel method of execution, reserved for runaway slaves and criminals of the worst sort, the victim was either tied or nailed to a crossbeam attached to an upright post. The whole apparatus was then hoisted and dropped into a deep hole. Wine mixed with myrrh was often given to deaden the pain (Mark 15:23). Jesus died at 3:00 P.M., suffocated perhaps, like most others, as the body sagged further and further.

The Resurrection

Although some would pronounce "the end" here, to stop with the death of Jesus will in no way explain the origins of Christianity. Neither a noble life nor, surely, an ignominious death can account for the movement that soon spread from Jerusalem throughout the ancient world. The only thing that can account for that is the conviction of some of his earlier followers that God had raised Jesus from the dead.

Now historians *qua* historians cannot "prove" Christian claims about resurrection for two reasons. One is that the resurrection is a singular event, one of a kind. Although there have been resuscitations, temporary restorations of life processes, there have been no other resurrections such as Christians ascribe to Jesus. The other is that resurrection, as attested in early Christian writings, is suprahistorical as well as historical. By its very nature it goes beyond the powers of the historian to examine by the empirical methods historians employ.

Does this leave the historian, then, with nothing to say about the resurrection of Jesus? Not at all. Historians can examine the *impact* of this belief (and Christians have always made this an article of belief) on the Christian movement and the ways in which Christians have understood it.

Two kinds of evidence substantiate the conviction of the first disciples that Jesus had been raised from the dead. One is the empty tomb accounts. Since the earliest written reports about the resurrection, the apostle Paul's (e.g., 1 Cor. 15:3-8), make no mention of an empty tomb, many scholars regard these as later and less reliable than evidence from experience. From the time of Cerinthus (about 90 C.E.), attempts have been made to explain this evidence away. Cerinthus, a Jewish Gnostic of Asia Minor, thought the "Christ" descended on "Jesus" at the baptism and forsook him at the cross. The body laid in the tomb, therefore, was Jesus' and not the Christ's.

The other kind of evidence is appearances of the risen Christ to his followers. Although reports of these appearances may have undergone editing in response to Gnostic threat, belief in them alone will explain the church and particularly the vigorous mission of early Christianity. For any other historical event, the witnesses listed by Paul in the tradition he had received would offer overwhelming confirmation: Peter; the Twelve; "more than five hundred brethren at one time, most of whom are still alive, though some have died"; James; "all the apostles"; and finally Peter himself. The fact that the resurrection was suprahistorical, however, takes it beyond the historian's realm of competence and puts it into the realm of faith.

CHAPTER FOUR

JERUSALEM AND BEYOND

The chief task in writing the history of early Christianity is to explain its remarkable success in thrusting beyond its Jewish homeland to the boundaries of the Roman Empire and beyond. Little in its origins would have assured success. It began in a "corner" of the empire among a people not at all popular with those who ruled them. Its founder suffered an ignominious death as a revolutionary. Its first adherents belonged chiefly to the lower levels of Jewish society, possessing limited education for the task of propagandizing for their faith. Indeed, the death of their leader left them shattered and disillusioned. How, then, can one account not merely for the survival of this sect of Judaism but for its phenomenal spread, outstripping not only numerous competitors but its own parent as well?

The complex answer is best brought forth by unfolding the story of Christianity step by step. A major factor was the bursting of the bonds that tied Christianity to Judaism. The key figure in that was the apostle Paul, self-designated "Apostle to the Gentiles." But Paul did not single-handedly precipitate this break. He simply gave further momentum to an impulse that this new/old religion had within and that was already impelling it away from its parent and its homeland.

The earliest part of the story is most accurately related in connection with certain centers of this messianic movement, for Christianity assumed a variety of forms in different places. In Palestine alone, for instance, Christian missionaries fanned out from Jerusalem to Samaria (Acts 8:4-25), the coastal strip stretching from Gaza to Caesarea (8:26-40), Damascus (9:25; Gal. 1:17), Galilee (Mark 16:7), and Antioch in Syria (Acts 11:18–13:3). Studies of Christianity in both Galilee and Samaria have further confirmed the thesis of Walter Bauer that, in its origins, Christianity exhibited great variety. Therefore, though it has been popular throughout Christian history to hang heterodox labels on Christianity in places like Samaria, today scholars proceed with greater caution.

In this chapter, Jerusalem and Antioch will receive the most attention chiefly because we possess the most detailed information about them and because both played exceptional roles in the spread of early Christianity. Neither Damascus nor Caesarea should be glossed over entirely, however, for both served as centers of Christianity from which the gospel would radiate outward to the surrounding region.

Jerusalem

Jerusalem is where Christianity began. There Jesus died. There his disillusioned and disheartened disciples came to the conviction that God had raised him from the dead. There, according to Luke, they organized for the mission that would carry them to the "ends of the earth."

The Jerusalem community exhibited already the diversity that would characterize Christianity everywhere for at least two centuries. At Pentecost, Jews and Jewish proselytes from Parthia, Medea, Elam, Mesopotamia, Judaea, Cappadocia, Pontus, Asia, Phrygia, Pamphylia, Egypt, Libya, Cyrene, Rome, Crete, and Arabia were present in Jerusalem. If, as Luke recorded, any substantial number of these adopted Christianity, they would have multiplied the diversity Palestinian Judaism already assured. Not surprisingly, tension arose quickly between "Hellenists," Greek-speaking Jews, and "Hebrews," Aramaic-speaking natives of Palestine (Acts 6:1). Since Judaism was highly diversified both inside and outside of Palestine, its offspring could have been expected to take on the same characteristic. Early on variety was visible in Christianity's theology, worship, and organization.

Although the beliefs of individual members of the community cannot be reconstructed with precision, it is possible to note points of difference. James, the brother of Jesus, was, according to early tradition, highly respected by the Pharisees. In Galatians 2:12, Paul indicates that James headed a conservative group zealous about continued observance of the Law (cf. Acts 15:13-21). Stephen, on the other hand, represented a position that challenged the place of both the Law and the Temple. Hailed before the Sanhedrin, he was accused of "never stops saying things against this holy place and the law." His accusers charged, "We have heard him say that this Jesus of Nazareth will destroy this place and will change the customs that Moses handed on to us" (Acts 6:13-14). His reply, as William Manson noted, corresponds in many ways with the argument of the so-called Epistle to the Hebrews: "You stubborn people, with your pagan hearts and pagan ears. You are always resisting the Holy Spirit, just as your ancestors used to do. Can you name a single prophet your ancestors never persecuted? In the past they killed those who foretold the coming of the Just One, and now you have become his betrayers, his murderers. You who had the Law brought to you by angels are the very ones who have not kept it" (Acts 7:51-53 JB). This radical position vis-à-vis Temple and Law has been associated with the Hellenists, but it should be noted that Jews from Cyrene, Alexandria, Cilicia, and Asia were Stephen's accusers (Acts 6:9).

Some scholars have noted parallels between Stephen's thought, especially his criticisms of the Temple, and that of the Essenes. Peter evidently tried to straddle the fence on this highly controverted issue of Christianity's relationship to Jewish institutions. The apostle Paul, at any rate, accused him of vacillating at Antioch. "His custom had been to eat with the pagans, but after certain friends of James arrived he stopped doing this and kept away from them altogether for fear of the group that insisted on circumcision" (Gal. 2:12 JB). This led other Jewish Christians, including Barnabas, astray on the same point. Peter's speech in Acts 2:14-36, if indicative of this thought, exhibits a much more moderate tone than Stephen's. The age of fulfillment has dawned through the death and resurrection of Jesus Christ. This is signified by the outpouring of the Holy Spirit upon all persons. Jesus is going to return to consummate what he has initiated. Repent and become a member of the community of the new covenant.

The Jerusalem disciples participated in at least two types of worship. As would be expected where the lines separating Christianity from Judaism had not yet formed, they continued to worship in the Temple and in the synagogues. According to Acts 2:46, "they went as a body to the Temple every day" (JB), obviously thinking themselves observant Jews. Until the persecution scattered them, the leaders evidently made the Temple area their base of operations, resisting warnings from the Sanhedrin to stop (Acts 4:20). There were no synagogues in Jerusalem where they would have gathered, but outside of the holy city Christians participated in them as they had before. The apostle Paul chose the synagogue as his point of entry for spreading the gospel in cities throughout the ancient world.

The distinctive beliefs of Christians about Jesus also necessitated special gatherings. From the very first these beliefs generated a sense of community distinct from the larger Jewish community or any of the other sects or parties. When persecuted or threatened, the community became still more close knit and well defined. According to the somewhat idealized picture presented in Acts, it was sufficiently close to allow the sharing of goods (Acts 4:32). It also provided the context for a more distinctively Christian type of worship. "They devoted themselves," Luke reported, "to the apostles' teaching and fellowship, to the breaking of bread and the prayers" (Acts 2:42). The heart of this worship was doubtless some kind of fellowship meal that believers participated in daily in various homes (Acts 2:46). From Luke's terminology, it is not possible to determine the degree to which this approximated the Lord's Supper described by Paul in 1 Corinthians 11:17-34, which consisted of both an actual and a symbolic meal. There can be little doubt, however, that "the breaking of bread" reminded them of the crucified and risen Christ who had called their community into existence.

Where Essene converts were present, it may have taken on features of the Qumran meal.

The organization of household meetings cannot be determined. Presumably the apostles, a much larger group than the Twelve, would have presided and taught. For the total community, however, the structure seems to have paralleled closely that at Qumran. James, by virtue of his relationship to Jesus, played a distinctive role like the Essene *Mebaqqer* (Superintendent or Overseer). Peter and others evidently deferred to him on important matters such as the admission of Gentiles, and James issued the so-called apostolic decree (Acts 15:19-21) on this matter. Peter, James (the brother of Jesus), and John were what Paul called "the three pillars" (2:9), meaning perhaps that they held positions of esteem by virtue of their association with Jesus. The Twelve had symbolic importance, for the community elected Matthias to replace Judas (Acts 1:15-26), but they seem not to have had a special function. The Twelve plus the three pillars sound remarkably like the Council of Twelve laymen plus or including three priests at Qumran. The larger group of apostles and elders apparently carried the burden of decision making just as the priests did at Qumran. They were the ones who, with the concurrence of the whole church, chose delegates to go to Antioch with Paul and Barnabas (Acts 15:22), and it was they whose names headed the official letter about the decision reached at Jerusalem regarding admission of Gentiles (Acts 15:23). Finally, "the many" participated in administration of discipline (Acts 15:22) just as they did at Qumran. Although the Essenes are never mentioned in Acts, the number of correspondences is too great to ascribe to coincidence. The Essenes, ardent apocalypticists that they were, would have made the likeliest prospects for the Christian message. They could have dominated the Jerusalem community's outlook at a number of points, including community of goods.

A number of factors encouraged adoption of this custom: anticipation of Christ's return; the poverty of many (especially of the Essenes); the interknittedness of the persecuted believers, strongly reliant on faith alone; and a famine that struck during the early phase of Christian history. Although Luke had a special predilection for communitarianism, he did paint a realistic picture. Alongside people like Barnabas (Acts 4:36-37), there were those like Ananias and Sapphira (5:1-11), who did not fully embody the ideal—from each according to ability, to each according to need (Acts 2:44-45; 4:32). The enterprise also broke down with reference to the Greek-speaking converts living in Jerusalem, requiring a new distribution of responsibility.

The appointment of the "seven" has traditionally been regarded as the beginning of the diaconate in early Christianity. According to the account in Acts, these persons were to "wait on tables" (Acts 6:4), which probably

43

meant that they took charge of the charities. It should be noted, however, that none of the seven, all of whom had Greek names, functioned solely in this way. The two mentioned subsequently in Acts, Stephen and Philip, had much to do with the inauguration of the mission to the Gentiles, which the apostle Paul continued with such elan. In Lukan thought the number seven probably symbolized the Gentile mission.

Dispersion and Expansion

Christianity might have sundered its bonds with Judaism more slowly had persecution not scattered the Jerusalem community far and wide (Acts 8:1). The leader of the onslaught was the Pharisee Saul of Tarsus (Acts 8:3; 9:1-2; 1 Cor. 15:9; Gal. 1:13; Phil. 3:6; 1 Tim. 1:13), zealous to conserve his ancestral faith now threatened by the growth of Christianity. There can be little doubt that the faith was taking hold rapidly in Jerusalem and beyond.

Indicative of the spread of Christianity in Palestine prior even to this persecution is its vitality in Damascus, capital of Syria. According to Luke, Paul sought authorization of the high priest to arrest and take to Jerusalem "any who belonged to the Way" he could find, whether men or women (Acts 9:2). The Damascus community subsequently furnished the converted persecutor a context within which to sort out his faith (Acts 9:23-30; Gal. 1:17). There perhaps he began to glimpse the missionary dream that absorbed the remaining years of his life. In future years, Damascus was destined to play an important role in the planting of Christianity in the East, for it was the logical route for the faith to have spread to Edessa, a major center for Eastern Christianity.

Why did the faith catch on in Damascus so early and so vigorously? Like other cities of Syria, Damascus boasted a strong Jewish population, including Essenes. One Essene document that laid down prescriptions for Essene "camp communities" is now known as *The Damascus Document*. Messianic ideas may have gotten a foothold long before Christian missionaries came with their message.

Following the persecution, the scattered community transported the gospel to numerous cities throughout Palestine. Samaria was evangelized by one of the Hellenists, Philip (Acts 8:4-8). This was fortuitous, for, as Raymond E. Brown has pointed out, the Samaritans accepted neither Jewish messianic beliefs nor the Temple, so that the more critical Hellenist theology would accord more readily with their desire to worship God "in spirit and truth" (John 4:23). The "beloved disciple" who wrote the Gospel was acquainted with a community consisting at one time of a considerable number of converts of Samaritan background, whose conversion the evangelist ascribed to Jesus' meeting with the Samaritan woman (John 4:39).

44

This community later broke up, with a substantial part of it becoming heterodox. Luke recounted how Simon Magus tried to obtain the disciples' "secret" for conferring the Holy Spirit (Acts 8:9-24), presumably to supplement his magical act. The early church fathers, however, regarded Simon as the first of the heretics. Another to come from this locale was the Gnostic teacher Basilides.

Among towns dotting the coastline to which missionaries carried the gospel, the port city of Caesarea would eventually play a stellar role in the history of Christianity in Palestine. The old Phoenician city was called Strato's Tower. The Romans, who had captured it from the Maccabees in 63 B.C.E., later gave it to Herod the Great. Herod lavishly rebuilt it and renamed it in honor of Caesar Augustus (Octavian). It became the official seat of the procurators and the capital of Palestine. Although predominantly pagan, it had a strong Jewish minority. Interestingly, a Roman, the centurion Cornelius, opened the door in Caesarea to Christianity. A "god-fearer"—that is, a devout monotheist not yet received into the Jewish community—and a generous contributor to Jewish causes (Acts 10:1-2), he may have been fairly typical of converts to Christianity in this city. The notable feature of the story of his conversion was the extreme reluctance of "middle-of-the-road" Peter to let Cornelius become a Christian until he first became a Jew. Yet Peter had to defend his actions in Jerusalem (Acts 11:1-18).

Caesarea subsequently figured prominently in the apostle Paul's missionary journeys and career. He passed through this port going to and returning from Cilicia (Acts 9:30; 18:22). On his fateful journey to Jerusalem, bearing the relief offering he hoped would gain Jewish Christian sanction for the Gentile mission, some of the disciples from Caesarea accompanied him and his party and took them to lodge in the house of a Cypriote named Mnason, one of the earliest disciples (see Acts 21:16). A Caesarean cohort spirited Paul away from Jerusalem. During his two-year imprisonment and trial in Caesarea before Felix, Festus, and Herod Agrippa, Paul doubtless experienced the solicitude of the community many times. After the destruction of Jerusalem in 70 C.E. and again in 135, Caesarea became the seat of Palestinian bishops and a center of learning under Origen (who came in 232), Pamphilius (240–309), and Eusebius (260–340).

Antioch

Next to Jerusalem, Antioch played the most crucial role in the expansion of Christianity beyond the bounds of Judaism. Whereas in other places cultural diversity was stretching the cords that still held Christianity fast, in Antioch, Luke observed, "the disciples were first called 'Christians' "

(Acts 11:26), a term indicating separate identity. If previously people could not tell the difference, now they could.

Located at the head of navigation on the Orontes River, Antioch was an important trading center connecting the Mediterranean world with the Syrian hinterlands and Eastern countries. Founded in 300 B.C.E. by Seleucus, it attained a political and cultural importance in the East rivaled only by Alexandria. When Roman armies occupied it in 64 B.C.E., they made it the capital and military headquarters of the new province of Syria. A large and ancient Jewish colony attracted numerous Gentiles, perhaps including Nicolaus of Antioch, who was chosen as one of the "seven" (Acts 6:5). More tolerant than Jews in Jerusalem as a consequence of their pluralistic surroundings, Antiochene Jews would have received Christianity with sympathetic interest.

According to Luke, Christianity came to Antioch by way of persons scattered by persecution (Acts 11:19). Although the latter usually confined their preaching to Jews, Hellenists from Cyprus and Cyrene started preaching to Gentiles, and "a great number became believers and turned to the Lord" (Acts 11:21). Hearing about this, the church in Jerusalem sent the Cypriote Barnabas to check on the report (Acts 11:21-23). Impressed with the success of the mission, Barnabas went to Tarsus and brought Paul back with him to Antioch, where the two spent a year instructing the converts (Acts 11:25-26).

When a famine struck Jerusalem in 46 C.E., the community at Antioch sent Paul and Barnabas with a relief offering (Acts 11:17-30). There they had to defend the incorporation of Gentiles without requiring circumcision and observance of the law. Some understanding was evidently reached, allowing Gentiles to become Christians without observing the law strictly (Acts 15:19-35; Gal. 2:1-10). Yet the issue remained in dispute. Peter visited Antioch and ate with Gentile Christians (Gal. 2:11-12), but, when James sent Judas Barsabbas and Silas as emissaries to win over the Jewish Christians to the view that Gentiles had to observe the law strictly (Acts 15:22-29; Gal. 2:12), Peter and Barnabas broke with Paul, pulling others away with them.

Antioch sponsored the missionary journeys of Barnabas and Paul, presumably supplying financial aid as they could (Acts 13:3-4). These two parted company, however, when Paul refused to let John Mark accompany them on a second tour; Paul took Silas instead (Acts 15:36-40). After his third journey, Paul returned not to Antioch but to Jerusalem (Acts 18:22–31:18), thus ending his connections with that community.

The letters of Ignatius, Bishop of Antioch, composed between 108 and 117, reveal a continuing division in Antioch over the question of Christian affiliation with Judaism. Ignatius himself, as will be shown later, tried to steer between two extremes—those who endangered Christianity by surrendering faith in the incarnation, on the one hand, and those who wanted

Christianity to return to observance of the Jewish law, on the other. Virginia Corwin has suggested that the latter were Essene converts to Christianity. To unite the fractured church, Ignatius emphasized adherence to the bishop, oneness of doctrine, and commonness of worship. Obviously, none of these prevailed in his day.

Antioch, however, did not stand alone in diversity and division. With strong Gentile influence it may have represented the extremes more than other churches. But Judaea, Samaria, and Galilee as well as Syria knew more variety than unity as Christianity tried to define its identity in relationship to its parent within the context of the multifaceted and variegated cultures of the ancient world. Some wanted to loosen all ties with the parent. Others wanted to surrender none of them. Others strove for a middle ground.

CHAPTER FIVE

THE PAULINE MISSION

The Christian story cannot be told without special attention to Paul, the "apostle to the Gentiles" (Rom. 11:13) or the "minister of Christ Jesus to the Gentiles" (Rom. 15:16). Although he did not originate the idea of incorporating Gentiles into the church without circumcision or fulfillment of other requirements of the Jewish law, he supplied a rationale for this practice, developed a strategy for the mission to the Gentiles, and gave momentum to the mission such as it had received from no other. Had there been no Paul, the erudite rabbi who once persecuted but then became a zealous convert, the Christian story would have turned out far differently from the way it did. While he cannot be credited with the founding of Christianity, he deserves at least the title of "refounder."

Paul's own story is difficult to reconstruct. References to his life and activities are fragmentary in the letters that bear his name. Additional evidence found in the book of Acts sometimes provides a different framework for his life than the letters suggest. Fortunately, his thought, though never presented systematically, is more readily ascertainable from the eight letters now usually considered his without question (Romans, 1 and 2 Corinthians, Galatians, Philippians, 1 and 2 Thessalonians, and Philemon) with additional help from writings that some scholars label post-Pauline (Colossians, Ephesians, 1 and 2 Timothy, and Titus). Hebrews, once ascribed to Paul and included in the canon on that basis, reflects a wholly different mind-set and outlook and cannot be used to frame his thought.

For the historian of Christianity, however, Paul is of interest not only for his own life and thought but also for the kind of Christianity that emerged from his labors. Born and reared in a Hellenistic setting, once converted he held a very different perspective on his new faith than did James and Peter and many other Palestinian converts and even many Hellenistic converts. Paul's outlook probably had its roots in the thought of Hellenists like Stephen and Christians from Cyprus, Cyrene, and Antioch who did not let cultural differences pose major barriers to the admission of Gentiles. Paul, however, was better equipped than any of these to sort out and define this position, and the churches he planted throughout Asia Minor and the Greek peninsula took on a character of their own.

The boldness of Paul in detaching Christianity from its parent, nevertheless, opened the door to massive problems on two sides. Externally, Judaists dogged his steps, mounting a campaign to stop him that led eventually to his imprisonment, trial, and death. Internally, communities he founded misconstrued his conviction that "Christ is the end of the law" (Rom. 10:4), some taking it as a license to do whatever they pleased, others reverting to the safer havens promised by Judaists. In the end, however, Paul's decision was to be "all things to all people" that he might win as many as possible (1 Cor. 9:22).

Paul

Born of Jewish parents and reared in Tarsus in the Roman province of Cilicia (Acts 9:11; 21:39; 22:3), Paul was educated at the feet of Gamaliel II, one of the leading rabbis in Jerusalem in the first century (Acts 22:3). Self-depicted as being "of the people of Israel, of the tribe of Benjamin, a Hebrew born of Hebrews," he belonged to the party of the Pharisees (Phil. 3:5). Zealous for the law, like most Pharisees, he carried his commitment to it to the extreme, and it is not difficult to see how this induced him to become a persecutor of the sect that threatened the institution he revered (Acts 23:6; 26:5; Phil. 3:6).

Somewhere in his savage effort to destroy the church (1 Cor. 15:9; Gal. 1:13; Phil. 3:6), whether, as Luke depicted it, on the road to Damascus (Acts 9:1-19; 22:6; 26:12) or elsewhere (Paul himself speaks only of Arabia in Gal. 1:17 as the place where he recuperated before returning to Damascus), Paul experienced a radical conversion. His conversion entailed a mystical encounter with the risen Christ that he counted the equivalent of the experiences of the other apostles, despite the fact that it occurred two or more years later, "as though I was born when no one expected it" (1 Cor. 15:8 JB). According to the third-person account of 2 Corinthians 12:1-4, he was caught up "to the third heaven" or "into Paradise," where he heard things human beings cannot put into words; he could not say whether this happened "in the body or out of the body."

The confrontation with the Christ whom he had persecuted changed things completely. On the one side, it smashed his loyalty to the law. Whatever advantages he had possessed by right of birth as a Jew now became disadvantageous. All that was refuse (Phil. 3:7-8). On the other side, it generated a different loyalty, zealous as the old one, but now directed to Jesus Christ (Phil. 3:8, 10). This new fealty carried with it a commission to be the Apostle to the Gentiles.

Paul's claims to apostleship provoked heated debate even in communities that he started. Others had credentials he lacked; they had been eyewitnesses and participants in Jesus' life. So Paul, suspect for a time because of his activities as a persecutor, had to base his case on his encounter with the risen Lord he now served. Although he insisted that he was not deserving of the name of apostle because he had persecuted the church (1 Cor. 15:19), he was, by God's grace, no less an apostle than the others (1 Cor. 9:1-3), especially so to those congregations he had founded. The Corinthians were "the seal" of his apostleship (1 Cor. 9:2). Yet Christ himself had given the certification Paul needed (Rom. 1:1; 1 Cor. 1:1; 2 Cor. 1:1; Gal. 1:1; also Eph. 1:1; Col. 1:1; 1 Tim. 1:1; Titus 1:1), not merely as an apostle but as his "minister to the Gentiles" (Rom. 15:16). Unable or unwilling to defend himself on grounds of competency, Paul rested his case on God's grace in Christ (2 Cor. 3:6). Paul was only a clay pot into which God had placed the treasure of the gospel, "to make it clear that such an overwhelming power comes from God and not from us" (2 Cor. 4:7 JB).

Subsequent to his conversion, Paul stayed for a brief time in Damascus (Acts 9:20-25) and then sequestered himself in Arabia, probably meaning the region near Damascus, for three years. He went to Jerusalem for the first time three years after his conversion (Gal. 1:18), where he spent fifteen days conferring with Peter and James, Jesus' brother (Gal. 1:19-20). From thence he proceeded via Caesarea to Tarsus (Acts 9:26-30). In his homeland, he evidently carried on mission work until Barnabas came from Antioch to bring him there to work with new converts (Acts 11:25-26), a period of at least eleven and perhaps as much as fourteen years (Gal. 2:1), at the end of which time Paul participated in the so-called Jerusalem Conference (Acts 15). Calculating backward from the latter, which took place in 49 C.E., Paul would have been converted about 32 C.E., perhaps two years after the crucifixion. Thus he would have returned to Damascus after three years in Arabia in 35 C.E. and would have gone to Antioch in 48 C.E., working a year before going with Barnabas to Jerusalem with the relief offering (Acts 11:27-30).

Scholars have usually divided Paul's missionary journeys into three phases, although the divisions are quite artificial. On the first, Barnabas and Paul, commissioned by the church of Antioch (Acts 13:3) and accompanied by John Mark, evangelized first Barnabas's (Cyprus) and then Paul's (Pamphilia, Pisidia, Lycaonia, and Cilicia) home territories. On the mission to Cyprus, Barnabas led (Acts 13:3), on that to Asia Minor, Paul led (Acts 13:13). If accurately depicted by Luke, the strategy differed at this early stage from that which Paul was later to employ. As would be the case throughout their ministry, the missionaries sought to win over Jewish synagogues. Yet they seem not to have intended lengthy residency, unlike Paul's later practice, in which extended stays allowed him to nurse the churches along until they became well-established. The entire journey lasted only a few months. Although Luke mentions the appointment of elders church by church, this would appear to view what happened in retrospect many years later (Acts 14:23).

By the *second* journey, on which Paul took Silas and parted company with Barnabas, who took John Mark again (Acts 15:39-40), Paul had worked out his strategy more fully. He would plant churches in major centers in each of the Roman provinces from which the gospel could radiate outward like spokes on a wheel, staying long enough, unless prohibited, to see the seed sprout and become strong. On this particular journey, he evidently hoped to reach Ephesus, largest of all the cities of Asia Minor and a center of culture. This plan, however, was deferred. From the provinces they had worked in during the first journey, they proceeded through Mysia to Troas and from there crossed over into Europe. They labored with considerable success in Philippi, a leading city of the province of Macedonia (Acts 16:11-40). After three weeks in Thessalonica, however, they came near to being mobbed (Acts 17:1-9). Trouble followed them from there to Beroea, where they nonetheless also enjoyed some success (Acts 17:10-15). After a brief encounter with sophisticated Athens, where they made few converts (Acts 17:34), they put down roots for a long stay of a year and a half in one of the most important cities on the Greek peninsula: Corinth (Acts 18:11). Although Luke has telescoped this important ministry into a brief paragraph, we can gain much insight into the struggle of these Pauline churches from Paul's correspondence with them.

Following his work at Corinth, which, like that in other cities, ended in controversy with Judaists, Paul finally achieved his diverted goals of establishing a base of operations in Ephesus. Interrupting this with a brief visit to Caesarea, Antioch, and the cities of Asia Minor he had worked in earlier, he remained in Ephesus possibly three years and wrote 1 Corinthians there.

A curious aspect of the planting of Christianity in Ephesus was its anticipation by a sect knowing only the baptism of John the Baptist, a member of which was the Alexandrian Jew Apollos (Acts 18:1–19:7). Prisca and Aquila, the refugees from Rome who had just come to Corinth (Acts 18:2), evidently converted Apollos (Acts 18:26) when he came there from Ephesus, but Paul converted twelve others when he arrived in Ephesus (Acts 19:1-6). Very likely, this John the Baptist sect drew recruits from the Essenes, whose "camp communities" dotted the empire. The eloquent Apollos became the focus for at least a part of the Corinthians' criticism and opposition to Paul (1 Cor. 1:12; 3:4-6; 4:6). Apart from this, Paul's work in Ephesus followed the now well-established pattern. For three months he presented his case in the synagogue until the congregation polarized over his teaching. Then he withdrew with converts to hold daily discussions in the lecture room of Tyrannus for two years. Both Jews and Gentiles thus had a chance to hear the message (Acts 19:8-10). Inevitably, however, a public disturbance broke out as Christianity began to have economic effects, notably on the manufacture and sale of idols. The confrontation between Christ and Artemis, goddess of the Ephesians, triggered Paul's plan to go to Jerusalem in hopes of gaining acceptance for the Gentile mission among conservative Christians there.

Meantime, Paul's relations with the Corinthian church had simmered. He wrote an early letter, which some scholars think may survive at least in part in 2 Corinthians 6:14–7:1, urging them to shun persons living immorally (1 Cor. 5:9). The Corinthians responded by sending a delegation to report on the Corinthian situation and writing a letter in which they raised several questions. To these, Paul replied in 1 Corinthians. Some at Corinth, however, remained recalcitrant. When they received 1 Corinthians borne by Timothy, they reacted in anger at Paul's interference and attacked his claims to speak as an apostle. A quick visit to Corinth only exacerbated the problem, and Paul returned to Ephesus to write a "harsh" letter (2 Cor. 2:1-4), which many scholars think is to be found in 2 Corinthians 10–13, sending it by Titus. Worried about the state of the situation as Titus delayed in returning to Ephesus, Paul then set out for Corinth via Troas. Meeting Titus, bearing good news, Paul dashed off the much happier and more optimistic 2 Corinthians 1–10.

From this point on, Paul fixed his attention on the Gentile mission. He sought zealously to collect relief funds for the church in Jerusalem in the hope that it would gain their approval for the inclusion of the Gentiles (2 Corinthians 8–9). He did not dare entrust either the collection or its delivery into anyone else's hands. He had to deliver it himself (Rom. 15:25-7). From Philippi (Acts 20:6) Paul and his entourage headed for Jerusalem via Troas (Acts 20:7-12) and Miletus (Acts 13:13-16), where Paul addressed the Ephesian elders (17-38). Dire warnings of prophets along the way were no deterrent to the determined apostle (Acts 21:10-14).

Events in Jerusalem dashed the apostle's dream. Charged with bringing uncircumcised Gentiles into the restricted area of the Temple, he was barely able to escape with his life. A Roman cohort, fearful of a riot, rescued him from a mob about to stone him (Acts 21:30-31). When the tribune ordered him flogged to find out why he had caused such a tumult, Paul appealed to his Roman citizenship (Acts 22:25). After a contentious encounter with the Sanhedrin and the threat of assassination, Paul was removed to Caesarea, spending two years in prison before finally being sent to Rome for trial.

Paul had wanted to go to Rome and be sent by the Romans still further to the West, to Spain (Rom. 15:24). He would have arrived in Rome about 62 C.E. and spent considerable time there awaiting trial. Whether he ever went to Spain is debated, but early Christian tradition reported that he was released after one trial, went to Spain as well as other areas he had worked in earlier, and then returned to Rome. There he went through a second trial, which ended in condemnation and beheading, probably about 66 C.E. By this time the Neronian persecution was in full swing.

Corinth

Thanks to the difficulties Paul encountered there, Corinth opens a window on the embodiment of Christianity in a predominantly Gentile setting. It reveals once more the immense diversity of early Christianity and the struggle Christians went through when detaching themselves from either Greek or Jewish moorings to establish their identity as Christians.

A large and diverse Jewish community existed there when the apostle Paul arrived about 50 C.E. A partial inscription reading "Synagogue of the Hebrews" found on a lintel in recent excavation may represent the successor of the synagogue in which Paul preached (Acts 8:4). The community would have been composed of Jews from Rome, Naples, Alexandria, or Antioch. Some proselytes and "godfearers" also belonged. Aquila and Prisca brought the Christian message when an edict of Claudius expelled them from Rome in 49 C.E. (Acts 18:27), where riots had resulted from debate over a certain "Chrestos," according to Suetonius. Paul arrived in 50 C.E.

The Corinthian Christian community soon came to consist predominantly of Gentiles, for, according to Paul, not many were well-educated, influential, or of noble background (1 Cor. 1:26). They also knew "many gods and many lords" (1 Cor. 8:5), a comment hardly applicable to Jews. And some had been people of immoral lives (1 Cor. 6:9-11), indicative surely of lower socioeconomic status among Gentiles. Jewish converts would likely have belonged to the middle or upper middle classes.

Typical of early Christian communities, the faithful may have congregated in several different homes, doubtless of the more wealthy, and here they may have split into parties: one for Paul, another for Peter (Cephas), another for Apollos, and even another for Christ (1 Cor. 1:12). The differences in views cannot be established, but, given the varied background of this church, one would expect much confusion. Questions that the Corinthians themselves raised with Paul had to do with marriage and virginity (1 Corinthians 7), eating food that had come from pagan temples (1 Corinthians 8–10), conduct during public worship, including spiritual gifts (1 Corinthians 11–14), and the resurrection (1 Corinthians 15). The larger agenda, however, was how the Corinthians should relate to their natural cultural backgrounds now that they were Christians.

Paul's stance had created a lot of difficulty on this issue. "Christ has set you free," he proclaimed. "He has brought an end to legalism. Believe and do what you will." For Paul, this translated into Jews' going on as Jews, Gentiles as Gentiles vis-à-vis their customs, save where these were blatantly immoral or kept others from knowing Christ (1 Cor. 9:19-23). Whatever one does, Paul insisted, it should redound to the praise of God (Col. 3:17). To some persons at Corinth, however, this message translated into "Anything goes!" Worse still, it gave rise to ridicule of those they regarded as "weak" because they could not live freely in the same way the "strong" could. With these the apostle could agree that "there are no forbidden things," but he had to add, "If my exercise of freedom causes others to stumble, then I should limit my freedom" (see 1 Cor. 10:23-33). Otherwise, God will not be glorified and the church will not be built up.

Some scholars have classified the Corinthian opponents of Paul as Gnostics, but this is too simple a solution to a complex problem. Although the Corinthian community doubtless had some persons in it who entertained views similar to those held by Gnostics in the second century and after, the evidence of the letters does not suggest well-defined and consistent views. Some individuals, for instance, denied the resurrection altogether (1 Cor. 15:12-19) while others expected a resurrection of a crassly literal sort (15:35-49). Some may have combined Jewish and Gentile ideas in hodgepodge fashion as they tried to sort out their new faith.

In response to this challenge, Paul struggled to define faith more precisely by citing tradition and patterned instruction. In his letters he left specimens of confessions of faith, catalogues of virtues and vices, household codes for new converts, and assorted instructional materials used to instruct the uninstructed. Contrary to what many have said in the past, Paul did not operate independently of tradition. Indeed, he commended the Corinthians for maintaining "the traditions just as I handed them on to you" (1 Cor. 11:2). Innovative as the apostle was, he anchored Christianity to the actual events out of which the Christian perception of God springs—that is, the life, death, and resurrection of Jesus of Nazareth.

Worship at Corinth differed substantially from that at Jerusalem. Although the church in Corinth began in the synagogue, it did not remain there long (Acts 18:16-17), and the Corinthian letters do not show much evidence of synagogue influence on worship. Two types of gatherings, rather, stand out. One was the "Lord's Supper" described in 1 Corinthians 11; the other a more charismatic type of worship. The former combined an actual meal concluded by the symbolic observance now called the Lord's Supper. The purpose of the meal seems to have been charitable. The "haves" were to supply food for the "have nots." In this community, however, good intentions went awry, for the "haves" ate what they brought before the poor arrived (1 Cor. 11:22-23). This, Paul remonstrated, contradicted the very essence of the symbolic meal.

The charismatic gathering included some elements similar to synagogue worship, but it evidently majored on prophetic preaching rather than interpretation of scriptures. Here is where speaking in tongues entered in and went out of control. Alongside these, however, the service also included chanting of psalms, singing of hymns, and some other items (1 Cor. 14:26-33).

The Corinthian community seems to have had much difficulty settling on a suitable structure. Paul himself may not have commended a particular one to them, emphasizing instead openness to the Spirit of Christ. Although some communities that he founded (the one at Philippi, for example) eventually adopted the twofold pattern of bishops or presbyters and deacons, the Corinthians resisted this development as late as the end of the first century, when Clement of Rome pleaded with them to restore the presbyters and deacons whom they had kicked out. Instead of drawing models from Judaism, they may have looked to their predominantly Gentile context, represented by competing religions, funerary societies, or guilds of craftsmen. Their main concern, however, was control by the Spirit, and, in response, the apostle had to underline boldly the importance of order within the body. Paul denied that the church was a "purely spiritual entity," insisting instead on the three concrete leadership roles of apostles, prophets, and teachers as a means of counterbalancing the "spiritual gifts," which he considered of lesser importance (1 Cor. 12:28). From the sequel to 1 Corinthians we can see that the Corinthians were not prepared to accord the apostle Paul the special status he claimed here.

Other Churches Founded by Paul

Other churches founded by Paul seem not to have caused him the grief the Corinthian community did. That impression, of course, may be due to the scantiness of the information available on these churches, to the briefer time he spent in these by comparison, or to the disappearance of many of them. Obviously none was without problems. The churches of Galatia experienced terrible turmoil vis-à-vis the reception of Gentiles without circumcision, but, so far as Paul's letters tell, not over worship or organization. The Philippian community was also disturbed by Judaists (Phil. 3:2-16), whom Paul called "the circumcision" party, but otherwise they pleased the apostle immensely by their good sense and personal support. A stronger Jewish constituency may have assisted in this, as their structure suggests. The church at Thessalonica engaged in much debate over Paul's eschatological teachings, some idly waiting for the Second Coming (2 Thess. 3:6-15); many misunderstood Paul's instructions about the resurrection and other matters (2 Thessalonians 2). Unless Romans 16 is a letter to the Ephesians, as personal references suggest, we do not have much information from Paul on the community of the church at Ephesus. By the second century, this church assumed a place of great prominence in the development of Christianity in Asia Minor. If it was the site of the Johannine community, as tradition has assumed, it led the way in the formation of Logos christology. If Paul wrote Colossians, we can see again the powerful struggle of communities he founded to determine the relationship of Christians to Jewish culture, on the one hand, and Gentile culture, on the other, for some of the Colossians found themselves pulled toward a hodgepodge of both. At the same time, Paul's letter to Philemon opens up a more personal scenario concerning the runaway slave Onesimus, whom Paul sent back with instructions to obey his master as he did the Lord Jesus.

By the end of his career, Paul had scattered quite a few seeds through Asia Minor and the Greek peninsula. Most of the communities he founded would have been small, struggling congregations barely able to survive. Nonetheless, they possessed a powerful sense of responsibility for extending the message beyond themselves. The apostle had also invested them with a strategy for mission. From these would come powerful competition for the other religions moving westward at the same time.

PART TWO

INTO ALL THE WORLD
70–180 C.E.

CHAPTER SIX

BROADCASTING THE SEED

Although the first Christians spoke of the world as their field, they were acquainted with only a fraction of the vast planet that subsequent generations would evangelize. In the main, this world consisted of the Roman Empire and its immediate environs, but here and there it reached some distance beyond, particularly eastward to what is now Iran and possibly to India. Riding the crest of a wave with the oriental religions sweeping westward, Christians struggled during this period to retain their identity as a monotheistic missionary people as they incorporated the syncretistic peoples of the Roman Empire who sought infallible revelation and assurance of salvation. By 180 C.E., they had succeeded in scattering the seed of their religion all over the Mediterranean world and were beginning to attract an educated and cultured constituency that had once despised this "alien" cult, convincing them that Christianity was "the true philosophy."

The Geographical Spread

The ancients' lack of concern for statistics prohibits one from tallying precisely the number of Christians or the many places in which they planted churches. It is possible, however, to discern some areas in which Christianity showed enough strength to evoke the attention of the upper echelons of Roman society and sometimes popular resentment and persecution. The fact that persecution remained local, spasmodic, and unofficial until the third century shows that Christianity exhibited greater impact on some areas than on others, but that it had a limited effect on the empire as a whole. Occasionally, more specific accounts of Christian activity come from reports such as the letter of Pliny, the governor of Bithynia, to the Emperor Trajan (112).

Christianity made little impact on Jesus' homeland and people after the first wave of conversions. During the Jewish revolt of 66–70 C.E., Palestinian Christians probably identified largely with the Jewish people and grieved with them in 70 C.E. over the destruction of the Temple. A succession of conservative leaders assured they would not depart far from their native faith. After the Bar Kochba Rebellion (132–135 C.E.), however, the Romans turned Jerusalem into a pagan city, Aelia Capitolina, expelling the Jewish population. Jewish Christians fled to Pella in Transjordan, where they continued under the name "Ebionites" ("the Poor"?). Caesarea, the Roman capital of Palestine, replaced Jerusalem as the center of Palestinian Christianity, whose constituency consisted largely of Gentiles by this time. When Origen migrated to Caesarea in 232, the Palestinian star began to rise again. Apart from these cities, there is little specific information on the state of Christianity in the holy land.

Churches existed in Tyre, Sidon, and other cities of Phoenicia during this period, but Antioch in Syria replaced Jerusalem as the chief Christian center along the Palestinian littoral. Composed predominantly of Gentile converts almost from the start, it continued the vigorous mission effort begun in apostolic times. Ignatius, its second bishop, who gained fame by virtue of his martyrdom in Rome, called himself "the Bishop of Antioch and Syria," implying some sense of responsibility for the evangelization of the entire province. Antioch probably played a part in the planting of churches in Edessa, itself a center of Eastern Christianity, and Mesopotamia as well as throughout Syria. Antioch's prestige in the East is manifest in the synods over which the bishops of Antioch presided from the mid-third century on. Besides Ignatius, the church boasted one other noted author among its early bishops: Theophilus, who composed an apology addressed to an official named Autolycus shortly after 180 as well as several other works now lost.

As both direct evidence and persecutions indicate, Asia Minor provided the most fertile field for Christian witness. Like some of the great cities of the empire, this region was dotted with Jewish communities that had accommodated themselves already to Hellenistic thought and life. Cults such as Zeus Sabazios, an amalgam of Jewish and pagan ideas, show the extremes to which this process was at work. It is not surprising that the person who bridged the gulf between Jewish and Gentile worlds, the apostle Paul, came from Tarsus in Cilicia, one of the provinces of Asia Minor.

Christianity evidently grew slowly and steadily in Paul's home state and in others that he evangelized during his travels through Asia Minor, notably Galatia and Asia. During the second century, Ephesus in the Roman province of Asia vied with Antioch and Rome as one of the most prominent Christian centers in the empire. The Revelation and the letters of Ignatius of Antioch, however, highlight other churches in Asia at Smyrna, Pergamum, Sardes, Philadelphia, Thyatira, Troas, Magnesia on the Maeander, and Tralles. The letter of Polycrates, Bishop of Ephesus, to Victor, Bishop of Rome, during the controversy over the date of observing Easter (about 190), points up the self-consciousness of the churches of Asia in the late second century. Speaking for the bishops of Asia, Polycrates reminded Victor that "in Asia also great lights have fallen asleep" (in Eusebius *H.E.* 6.24).

First Peter and Pliny's letter to Trajan in 112 furnish testimony of the wide diffusion of Christianity in Bithynia and Pontus during the late first and early second centuries. The governor spoke of "a great variety of cases" brought before him and "an anonymous pamphlet . . . containing many names." Using torture, he "found nothing but a depraved and extravagant superstition," but he consulted the emperor "on account of the number of those imperiled; for many persons of all ages and classes and of both sexes are being put in peril by accusation." He feared that the "contagion" had "spread not only in the cities, but in the villages and rural districts as well" but was confident it could be checked. The temples had been "almost deserted" but were again being frequented, and the sale of sacrificial victims was increasing.

Lucian confirmed the vitality of Christianity in Pontus around 170 when he wrote that "the whole country is full of atheists and Christians" (*Alex. Abon.* 25.38). Dionysius of Corinth addressed letters to churches there also during the reigns of Marcus Aurelius and Commodus. Amastris was the chief city.

Phrygia had a thriving Christian populace when the Montanist sect emerged between 156 and 172. Montanus gained a considerable following in Galatia and Ancyra as well as Phyrgia. Cappadocia probably did not become a strong Christian area until the third century, when Gregory of Neo-Caesarea, "the Miracle Worker," evangelized it, but 1 Peter 1:1 implies that Christians were already there in the first century. Tertullian reported persecution in Cappadocia between 180 and 196 perpetrated by Claudius Lucius Herminianus, who became enraged when his wife converted to Christianity (*Ad Scap.* 3).

Christianity established an early hold on the islands in the Mediterranean. There is not much evidence in this period concerning the growth of the churches planted by Barnabas and Paul, but the Gnostic leader Valentinus is reputed to have spent his last years on Cyprus. Churches founded there by Titus during the Pauline era thrived in the second century. Dionysius of Corinth wrote a letter about 170 "to the church of Gortyna and to the other churches of Crete" and a second to the church at Cnossus, whose bishop, Pinytus, replied (Eusebius *H.E.* 4.23). The smaller islands around Crete were probably also evangelized in this period, but we have limited evidence for that.

In the Balkans and the Greek peninsula there were vigorous churches in cities evangelized by Paul. Polycarp's letter to the Philippians, written around 115 (with a later section perhaps added about 135) demonstrates the continuation of the church started in Philippi by Paul. For Thessalonica and Athens, the Emperor Antoninus Pius left evidence of a noticeable

Christian constituency when he forbade a pagan uprising against them (Melito in Eusebius *H.E.* 4.26). Dionysius of Corinth accused them "almost of apostasy from the faith since the death of their martyred bishop Publius" but mentioned a revival under Quadratus (Eusebius *H.E.* 4.23). Athens was the home of the apologist Aristides and perhaps of Clement of Alexandria. The church at Corinth, which troubled Paul so much, was the most thriving of the churches in the Greek peninsula. Clement of Rome intervened in the expulsion of presbyters by the congregation in 96 C.E. Dionysius played a notable role in the affairs of churches in the region during the second half of the second century. Dionysius's letter to Lacedaemon urging peace and unity would attest that the Corinthians had done mission work throughout the Peloponnese area.

Christian communities dotted other cities and provinces in Europe. Antoninus Pius forbade an uprising against Christians in Larissa in Thessaly (Melito in Eusebius *H.E.* 4.20). There was a bishop at Debeltum and Anchialus in Thrace near the end of the second century (Eusebius *H.E.* 5.19).

In the West, Christianity took hold significantly in Italy, Gaul, and Spain. In Rome, it spread first among the Greek-speaking population. Victor (189–199), an African, was the first Roman bishop to write letters in Latin. Antedating Paul's advent there, the Roman Church acquired a reputation for faith (Rom. 1:8) and charity early on. Clement's letter to the Corinthians evinces a consciousness that the Roman church held a unique place among all the churches. Ignatius's letter to the Romans reveals that others shared the feeling as he extolled it as "the leading church in the region of the Romans" and "the leader of love." The fact that the Roman church had extensive means at its disposal in the second century is evidenced in the letter of Dionysius of Corinth to Soter, praising the Romans for sending contributions to "many churches in every city" to relieve the wants of the needy and to make provision for Christian prisoners (Eusebius *H.E.* 4.23). The church, as the *Shepherd of Hermas* substantiates, had not only large numbers but also certain quite wealthy members who could give liberally to "charity's chest." On joining a Roman congregation about 140 C.E. Marcion, a wealthy shipbuilder of Pontus who made shipwreck of his own faith, made a huge contribution of 200,000 sesterces. Apologists such as Justin (martyred in 165) founded evangelistic-apologetic schools for the purpose of enlisting the cultured and better educated who knocked on church doors from about the mid-second century on. Meantime, virtually all sects and heresies—Marcionites, Valentinians, Montanists—gravitated toward Rome, creating an immense problem for Christian unity and resulting in a heavy-handed effort by Victor to enforce uniformity of faith and practice.

Some evidence can be cited for Christian communities in the south of Italy, although little can be adduced for their presence in the north. In Gaul, however, the emergence of churches at Lyons and Vienne resulted in a violent outburst of persecution in 177. Although the number of victims was not large (no more than 49), the severity of the pogrom would indicate that pagans viewed Christianity as a major threat. Victims included the aged Pothinus, whose successor, Irenaeus, escaped by virtue of being sent to Rome beforehand. He returned to lead the church at Lyons in a vigorous mission effort not only in Gaul but also in Germania. About 185, Irenaeus claimed that the beliefs and traditions of the German churches did not differ from those in Gaul or elsewhere (*Adv. haer.* 1.10), but he did not name specific locations.

Critical scholarship raises serious doubt about Christianity in the British Isles before about 300, but churches emerged early in Spain. In addition to the early tradition that the apostle Paul had visited Spain, both Irenaeus and Tertullian (*Adv. Jud.* 7) reported churches there. A letter of Cyprian (about 250) listed Christian communities at Leon, Astorga, Merida, and Saragossa.

The Roman province of Africa competed with Asia Minor for rapidity of church growth during the late second and third centuries, aided again by Jewish antecedents. The extensive writings of Tertullian, converted to Christianity in 195, presupposes a large church at Carthage and a scattering of churches throughout the province. Contemporary evidence of Christianity in the neighboring province of Numidia may be found in the martyrdom of several persons from Madaura and Scilium. Africans began translating the Bible into Latin during the second century and, in Tertullian, produced the first great Latin theologian.

Historians draw an almost complete blank when searching for information about Christianity in Egypt before 180, when the Alexandrian church first appeared in daylight under Demetrius. The church that emerged, however, was a powerful one. Attached to it was the famous school founded by Pantaenus, the "Sicilian bee," which attracted Clement and later the brilliant Origen. Egypt drew Gnostic scholars, too, like Basilides and Valentinus. As was already mentioned, a Gnostic library was discovered at Chenoboskion, or Nag Hammadi, in 1947; many of its writings date from the second century.

The Method of the Mission

In this period as in the one before it, Christianity spread chiefly through the sustained effort of organized Christian communities, vying with Judaism and the mystery cults to win adherents. The typical convert probably heard about Christianity by chance—a word dropped by a friend or neighbor, witnessing a martyrdom, overhearing a conversation—for, in time of persecution, direct and open efforts to solicit members would have evoked popular or governmental reaction and endangered the lives of many persons.

Numerous features exerted an attraction to Christianity. Charity offered without expectation of return or consideration of merit; fellowship opened to all social levels—masters and slaves, men and women, young and old, rich and poor; Christian steadfastness in the face of persecution; high moral standards; Christian assurance of victory over demons; the Christian rejection of fate and belief in providence; sacraments conveying tangible assurances of salvation; these and other considerations contributed to the spread of the faith in this period.

Christians astounded the ancients with their charity. Although Romans were noted for their largess, they gave expecting return in kind, at least in honor and friendship. Stoic sages regularly cautioned them to single out the deserving. Social aid, therefore, seldom reached the most needy, those belonging to the very dregs of society. It was precisely these whom Christians sought to help, regularly exhorting their constituency to openhanded and openhearted giving. The *Didache* and the *Epistle of Barnabas*, for instance, urged complete community of "corruptible things" on analogy to the complete community of "incorruptible" (*Did.* 1; Barn. 19.8). The pagan Lucian knew that Christians "despise all things equally and count them common property" (*Pereg.* 13). Although most Christians did not divest themselves of all possessions, the rich heard plenty of pleas to liberal giving. In an elaborate appeal for stewardship, Hermas counseled the rich to "circumcise" their riches (*Vis.* 3.6.6). Riches, he said elsewhere, distract one from devotion. Yet in assisting a poor person, the rich person may become rich by attracting the poor one's intercession. The two thus become partners in righteousness.

The chief means of charity was alms collected in connection with the main worship service on "the Lord's day." As in Judaism, Christians ascribed immense religious potency to almsgiving. For many, charity supplied the ultimate test of true worship and faith. Matthew could speak of doing "righteousness," the ideal of religious service in Jewish thought, and almsgiving almost synonymously (Matt. 6:1-2). A virtual slogan of early writings is "equipped for every good deed."

Besides money, the faithful also brought "oblations" or offerings consisting of all kinds of foodstuffs—oil, grain, eggs, meat, cheese, olives, bread, and wine. According to Justin, when the needs of the liturgy were met, the remaining portions were distributed to the poor, to prisoners, and to other needy persons. Most of the alms and other gifts doubtless went to the Christian poor, for the resources were too limited to expect more. Nevertheless, the advice of the *Didache* to "let your alms sweat in your hands" is exceptional, obviously sensitive to abuses (*Did.* 1:5). Actually, the author of the *Didache* contradicted his own reserve in quoting the words of Jesus, "Give to everyone who asks" (Matt. 5:42; Luke 6:30). It was more characteristic to give without attaching strings (Hermas *Mand.* 2.4.6; cf. James 1:5; Barn. 19:11; *2 Clem.* 16:4).

The range of charity was broad: care of widows and orphans; care of the sick, poor and disabled; ransom and care of prisoners and captives; burial of the poor and other dead; redemption of slaves; furnishing work for the unemployed; and aid to victims of calamities. Like charity, the fellowship that communities of believers shared openly with all comers would have proved powerfully attractive to the masses. The oriental cults offered some of the same appeal in their intimate gatherings for communal meals, but, where they used only local organizations, Christianity developed an empire-wide network of churches open to travelers. Besides liturgical services stressing community, the churches also continued *agape* meals chiefly for charitable purposes. At first connected with the Lord's Supper, or eucharist, these gradually became separated. *The Letter of Pliny to Trajan*, usually dated around 112, reported a eucharist before dawn and "the taking of food" at a later assembly. In the East, however, Alexandria may have continued the joint services until the time of Clement in the late second or early third century (*Paed.* 2.10.96).

Christian steadfastness in the face of persecution evoked both criticism and admiration from pagans. The latter sometimes censured Christians for "obstinacy," but, more often than not, they expressed begrudging praise that common folk died "like philosophers." Epictetus (d. ca. 135), for instance, paid a backhanded compliment when he argued that, if the "Galileans" could face death with such courage when "conditioned by madness and custom," surely the intelligent person could "learn by reason and demonstration" that God is the universal Creator and arranger of all things (*Diatr.* 4.7.6). Emperor Marcus Aurelius (161–180) lauded the person ready for death "not out of sheer obstinacy like the Christians, but rationally and reverently and without theatrics, so as to persuade others" (*Medit.* 11.3). Lucian of Samosata (d. after 180) was amazed at both the gullibility of Christians and their courage, arising, he thought, from their belief in immortality, which would allow them to despise death or even to put themselves voluntarily into the hands of the authorities (*Pereg.* 13). Justin, a martyr himself, attributed to his viewing of a martyrdom a complete change of heart regarding Christianity (*2 Apol.* 12).

In the last analysis, Christianity had to back up its claims in its product— above all, in the lives of its members. Pagans scrutinized Christian moral behavior closely. In his letter to Trajan, Pliny reported a morally favorable impression based on direct investigation. Although he faulted Christians' "inflexible obstinacy," he found nothing socially harmful in their meetings. Likewise, the physician Galen (129–199), like many other intellectuals of his day, criticized Christianity for philosophical naïveté, but expressed appreciation for Christian courage in the face of death and self-restraint in regard to their passion. Demonstrated high moral standards doubtless had a major effect in the conversions of both Justin and Clement of Alexandria, for the writings of each clearly indicate the centrality of Christian ethical behavior.

Those who sought Christian conventicles for the same reason they turned to the mystery cults demanded tangible psychological assurances also. Living in abject fear of the demonic and of fate, they responded gladly to promises that believers could participate in the victory of Christ over demons and in his rule over the universe. Where cults such as Mithra or Cybele attached their assurances of eternal rebirth and life to expensive rites such as the taurobolium, however, Christianity used baptism and eucharist to do so. Through the action of the Holy Spirit or the risen and living Christ, Christians promised, the believer could experience the power of resurrection in sacramental rites. The actual incorporation of converts occurred through a process centered around a catechumenate and baptism. At the beginning, the process was relatively simple, but by the end of this period, Christians tightened it up out of concern for lapses from faith and betrayals. There is no evidence in this period, however, of the four- or possibly five-stage process outlined by Hippolytus in the *Apostolic Tradition* when he split from the Church of Rome in 217.

Although organized communities deserve the most credit for the spread of Christianity, contributions of individual Christians should not be forgotten. Soldiers, sailors, merchants, artisans, and travelers of all kinds scattered the word all over the ancient world. Wherever Christians traveled, they could expect hospitality from others. They preferred to have charlatans take advantage of them, as often happened, than deny "angels unawares" (Heb. 13:2) or Christ himself in the guise of a stranger. In time, the churches did feel compelled to search for safeguards. Second John 10–11 forbade entertaining and even greeting anyone who did not bear orthodox teaching. The *Didache* limited hospitality for traveling "prophets" to two days and a single day's bread supply and forbade giving money or allowing the prophet to eat during an ecstatic trance (11.5ff.). Christians preferred, however, to err on charity's side. Third John, for instance, commended Gaius for his hospitality to "the brothers and strangers at that" and condemned the usurper Diotrephes not only for a lack of hospitality but also for prohibiting those who wished to give it to do so. And Lucian chided them for caring for the charlatan Alexander of Abonoteichos, for whom they risked life and limb by going to feed and tend him in prison.

Philosophical-Evangelistic Schools

As Christianity spiraled upward socially during this period, traveling philosopher-evangelists and schools also played an important role in winning adherents. Although some schools originated in the catechumenate, many others were at least begun by individual initiative. Christian "philosophers" such as Valentinus, Justin, or Pantaenus attracted a following much as Stoic or Platonist philosophers did. Little is known of the activities of Pantaenus in founding the Alexandrian school, but he blazed a trail for Clement and Origen. In Rome, Justin assisted the transition of Christianity from Jewish to Gentile cultures and from competition with the religions alone to competition with both religions and philosophies.

Born in Flavia Neapolis (modern Nablus), Justin studied in succession with a Stoic, with an Aristotelian (Peripatetic), with a Neo-Pythagorean, and finally with a Platonist. The Stoic taught him little about God. The Aristotelian only wanted money. The Neo-Pythagorean rejected him on account of his "ignorance." The Platonist pleased him, but served chiefly as a guide to Christianity. Witnessing martyrdoms and an encounter with an aged Christian who directed him to the "prophets" resulted in his conversion. After a period in Ephesus, where he may have come in contact with Polycarp, the saintly Bishop of Smyrna, Justin made his way to Rome, where he founded an apologetic school. Here he attracted persons of education and culture who had formerly spurned Christianity. His pupils included Tatian, founder of the Encratite sect, and Irenaeus, Bishop of Lyons and antiheretical writer of some distinction.

The schools may have made few converts, but they rendered an incalculable service in helping Christianity to reach a constituency whose needs it might otherwise have neglected. Even the heretical schools aided the cause, for they pushed Christianity toward the outer limits of accommodation and forced the churches to define their faith with greater precision. Although their intense evangelistic fervor pushed them too far, they tried to make an essentially "alien" Jewish idiom intelligible to persons of Platonist mind-set. In pursuit of this goal, they fashioned the first commentaries on scripture and applied radical methods to solve problems of interpretation and application to different contexts. They also posed many of the great theological questions that later generations would have to answer.

A New Day Dawning

At the beginning of this period, Christian communities were shifting from a predominantly Jewish to a Gentile constituency. Although Irenaeus could still say in his day (about 185–189) that Jews were easier to reach than

Gentiles because they knew the Old Testament promises, most churches would have consisted of persons of non-Jewish culture and outlook. Among Gentiles, Christianity at first attracted predominantly persons of lower socioeconomic status, but that had changed noticeably by the last quarter of the second century. Even early on, Christian communities had claimed some persons of wealth and culture among their constituency. By 175, the number of such persons multiplied as the churches ascended the social ladder and presented their appeals in more sophisticated ways. A new day was dawning.

CHAPTER SEVEN

AS MASTER, SO DISCIPLES

Christianity's success within the Roman Empire proved threatening enough in some regions to evoke violent responses not only from officials but also from the Roman public. In some respects, this is strange, for the Romans were tolerant in religious matters. In their Pantheon, they made room for the gods of all nations they conquered and would gladly have done so for the God of the Jews and Christians had either of them permitted it. Romans could comprehend even Jewish tenacity in adhering to their ancestral divinity and did not feel threatened by the few who trickled into the Jewish synagogues. What boggled their minds in the case of Christianity was the fact that great numbers of *Romans* abandoned their ancestral gods to worship the God of Jews and Christians, separating themselves not only from the worship but also from the public life of Rome. Such a religion, demanding allegiance to a law and throne other than that of Rome, must have sinister and subversive implications.

Christ and Caesar

In this period, Christians were by no means uniform in their attitudes toward Roman society. At one end of the spectrum stood those who clung tightly to Christianity's Jewish roots and repudiated all things Greek and Roman. Tatian, for example, who founded an ascetic sect called the Encratites after the martyrdom of his teacher Justin around 165, attributed any fragment of truth found among Gentiles to borrowing from the Jews. He derided the philosophers, including Plato and Aristotle, for errors and vices and particularly for their varied opinions, which are nothing "but the crude fancies of the moment." Still worse, he claimed, was the fact that Greek mythology and the doctrine of Fate had been perpetrated by demons. Philosophy is "the art of getting money," its teaching "a labyrinth."

On the opposite end of the spectrum were Marcion and some who usually wore the label of "Gnostics" who undertook to detach Christianity completely from its Jewish moorings and radically to "Hellenize" it. (The views of both will receive further examination in chapter 9, "Struggle for Identity and Unity.")

Somewhere between these extremes, others saw good in both Jewish and Greco-Roman antecedents, insisting on adherence to central tenets of Judaism—such as monotheism, high moral standards, and historical teleology—but recognizing the importance of accommodating Christian faith to the Roman context. The *Epistle to Diognetus,* an anonymous apology of uncertain date (but probably originating during the second century), for instance, offered a critique of both pagan and Jewish worship. With that critique in mind, the author proceeded to spell out the true distinction Christians could claim. They differed, he said, "neither in country nor language nor customs" but in respect to the citizenship they held. For "while living in Greek and barbarian [Jewish] cities . . . and following local customs, both in clothing and food and in the rest of life, they show forth the wonderful and confessedly strange character of the constitution of their own citizenship" (5.3.-10).

Justin, guarding against both extremes, took a mediating position that both preserved Christianity's Jewish connections and freed Gentiles to appropriate the best of their own culture. Reminded by Trypho, a Jewish apologist, that Christians were not "separated in any particular" from Gentiles and did not distinguish themselves from Gentiles in mode of living by such observances as the sabbath or the rite of circumcision, Justin replied that, even though Christians worshiped the same God as the Jews, they trusted God through Christ rather than through Moses and the law. Scriptures pointed to Christ as the one through whom God would effect a new covenant for "the true spiritual Israel" (*Dial.* 10–11). Responding to pagan attacks on the other side, Justin accentuated the correspondences between Christian teaching and behavior and the best in Gentile as well as Jewish teaching. He explained the affinities in two different and conflicting ways—by pagans' borrowing from Moses and by inspiration of the divine Logos. The Logos instructed both the prophets of Israel and the Greek greats such as Heraclitus, Socrates, Plato, and others. Both borrowing and the Logos, therefore, prepared for the advent of Christ, and all who "lived reasonably" in previous centuries—the great philosophers and persons like them—are "Christians" (*1 Apol.* 46). In Jesus, the Logos became incarnate and taught explicitly the complete truth, which previous generations had grasped in a partial and fragmented way.

At the level of everyday life, Christians had to struggle to maintain their identity over against the absorptive culture of Rome. Conservative Christians sought security in a "clamshell" approach: They refused to attend parties in the homes of neighbors, thus earning scorn for being too aloof; they did not send their children to public school, where they would be exposed to pagan myths; they refused to witness athletic contests in the arenas; they would not hold public offices, most of which had some connection with pagan religion; nor would they do any number of other things that might result in compromises of faith. The first evidence for Christians' serving in the army, for example, comes from the end of this era in connection with the famous "thundering legion," reputed to have consisted chiefly of Christians. However, most Christians opposed military service, chiefly for two reasons: dominance of the military by the state religion and biblical injunctions against killing. Soldiers in the ranks could often avoid the obligation to offer sacrifices, but officers could not. None, however, could avoid killing. If soldiers decided to join a church, therefore, they would likely be asked to surrender their commissions in the army.

Persecution and Martyrdom

Roman absorptionism and Christian exclusivism made a clash between Christ and Caesar inevitable. Non-Christians—relying usually on hearsay, often about heretical sects, for their understanding—found a variety of Christian ideas and customs offensive. Christianity sundered families and discouraged marriage, they claimed. Some Christians espoused voluntary poverty and community of goods and sowed seeds for the decay of slavery. They held "secret" meetings at nighttime and spoke of "eating the body" and "drinking the blood" of Christ or exchanging "the kiss of peace," customs that invited pagan charges of cannibalism and incest. The very best of Christian intention turned against them in the dark imagination of pagan minds. Some supposed that Christians took unwanted infants, deposited along with human excrement to die, chopped them into pieces, and ate their bodies and drank their blood. Others claimed that in their nocturnal assemblies Christians gorged themselves with food, turned dogs loose to scramble across the tables and turn over the lamps, and then engaged in sexual orgies (Tertullian *Apol.* 7). Christian martyrdom was construed as a perverse "obstinacy"; their refusal to hold public office, serve in the army, or attend public games acts of disloyalty; their breaking away from customs of Jews or Romans impiety; and their abandonment of altars, images, and temples "a sure token of an obscure and secret society" (so Celsus).

Roman officials were intensely circumspect regarding new religions on two counts: immorality such as what occurred in the Baccanalian rites of the second century B.C.E. and danger to the state. For the period at hand, persecution arose much less from officials than from mobs, but some official charges were set forth for trial and punishment of Christians. Scholars have offered three theories about the specific nature of the charges. (1) Christians were punished under no specific charge but only by virtue of the power of coercion. (2) They were accused and tried for violation of Roman criminal law, particularly for the crime of treason and also for sacrilege, immorality, magic, incest, murder, and the like. (3) They were dealt with under a special law issued by Nero that proscribed Christianity as such—that is, made it illegal to be a Christian. Whether the third was in effect as early as Nero, however, is unlikely. The first definite evidence for punishment simply for "the name" appeared in the time of Trajan (98–117). It is more likely that Christians were punished for the general charges of "hatred of the human race, cannibalism, and incest" until, in the second century, Christianity itself became illegal.

There is only the scantiest evidence of Jewish harassment and persecution for the period under discussion, although synagogue and church continued their debate. "Dialogues" such as Justin's with "Trypho" may have occurred publicly on occasion, but pagan use of Jewish arguments against Christianity necessitated written replies. As the Christian mission to the Gentiles waxed strong, however, the Jewish mission relented and drew back, thus undercutting the debate. When Christianity chose the route of accommodation to Gentile culture, it left Judaism with the option either of accommodating still more radically or else withdrawing and emphasizing Jewishness. When Jewish leaders opted for the latter, they virtually took the synagogue out of the competition altogether.

For a study of persecution in this era, therefore, it suffices to focus on persecution that arose from popular resentment and misunderstanding or from official action. After some respite from the brief pogrom during the late years of Nero's reign (64–68 C.E.), intermittent persecution broke out in 91 C.E. under Domitian (d. 96 C.E.). Fiercest in Asia Minor, where Christianity was growing rapidly, it claimed the lives, among others, of Flavius Clemens, cousin of the emperor; his wife, Domitilla; and Achilius Glabrio, an ex-consul.

During the reign of Trajan (98–117 C.E.), popular hostility to Christianity threatened to run out of control. At the request of Pliny, the governor of Bithynia, where the number of believers had reached significant proportions, the emperor laid down the following guidelines: (1) Christians were not to be sought out, and anonymous accusations were to be ignored. (2) Those persons regularly accused and who admitted they were Christians were to be punished. (3) But those who denied they had ever been Christians or declared that they had ceased to be such and proved it by offering a sacrifice were to be pardoned. This rescript remained in force until Septimius Severus (195–211). The most celebrated martyr in this persecution was Ignatius, Bishop of Antioch, who pleaded in a letter that Roman Christians do nothing to prevent him from imitating "the example of the death of my God." He longed to be "crushed like wheat between the teeth of wild beasts" that he might "attain to Jesus Christ."

During Hadrian's reign (117–138), Christians enjoyed comparative peace. In a directive to Minucius Fundanus, governor of the province of Asia, Hadrian repeated the first two provisions of Trajan's rescript.

Antonius Pius (138–161) reiterated the same provisions in rescripts to cities of Macedonia, Thessaly, and Achaia. The most celebrated victim of persecution in this region was Polycarp, eighty-six-year-old Bishop of Smyrna. The twelfth martyr in Smyrna, his "birthdate into the eternal realm" on February 23, 155, was celebrated annually and became the subject of the first martyrology. The careful gathering up of his bones "to have fellowship with his holy flesh" (*Mar. Pol.*) initiated the cult of relics, which became so important in subsequent centuries.

Marcus Aurelius (161–180), Roman emperor and a Stoic philosopher of considerable distinction, intensified the persecution by reissuing the third provision of Trajan's rescript. Numerous martyrdoms occurred in the province of Africa and in Gaul as well as in Rome and Asia Minor. Popular suspicion of the now-thriving sect fanned the flames of official action. In Rome, Crescens, a philosopher whom Justin had bested in an argument, vented his anger on his opponent by having him brought to trial and put to death. In Scilli, a city in Africa whose location is unknown, numerous persons, both men and women, suffered martyrdom on July 17, 180. In Lyons and Vienne, in Gaul, Christians were first excluded from homes, public baths, and markets and then attacked with vehemence—being beaten, dragged through the streets, robbed, stoned, imprisoned, tortured in the most inhumane ways, and then killed. The martyrs included several persons of high social status, especially women, willing to expose themselves in defense of Christian friends.

The steadfastness of large numbers of Christians in persecution is in itself an interesting phenomenon that has received several explanations. Some scholars have pointed to analogous accounts of Greek and Roman heroes, but the analogies break down when motives are closely examined. Others have emphasized instead the conditioning process that converts went through in the catechumenate that prepared them for such opposition. Although this would offer a partial explanation, it too overlooks the deeper theological perspective out of which the martyrs themselves acted. The martyrs belonged to the lineage of Jewish martyrs and inherited from Judaism the idea of martyrdom as personal witness to the truth of their faith over against heathendom, the hope of personal resurrection and vengeance on apostates and persecutors in the hereafter, and the view that the true oppressors were not earthly powers but cosmic and demonic ones. It was not by chance that pictures of Daniel among the lions and the three "children" in the fiery furnace turned up frequently in the catacombs, for the stories of the Maccabean era fed the Christian faithful just as they had fed the Jewish people.

The Christian Apologia

Christian defense against attacks, whether Jewish or Gentile, did not reach the sophisticated level it would achieve in the subsequent phase of Christian history, but it gradually improved as Christianity attracted an increasing number of cultured constituents. The earliest apology (the so-called *Preaching of Peter*, appearing between 100 and 110 C.E. probably in Egypt) is known only from quotations in Clement and Origen. An Athenian named Quadratus addressed a formal appeal to the Emperor Hadrian on his visit to Athens in 125 or 129, but this work too exists only in citations by Eusebius. The *Apology of Aristides* addressed to Antoninus Pius (138–147), recovered in an almost complete Syriac text in 1889, argued the superiority of Christian to Chaldean, Greek, Egyptian, and Jewish worship. About 140, Aristo of Pella established a model for apologies addressed to Jews or replies to Jewish arguments with *The Christian Dialogue,* but his composition is known only from quotations in Origen's treatise *Against Celsus* (246). Justin defended Christianity on two fronts with his *Dialogue with Trypho* and two apologies (ca. 150). His pupil Tatian wrote his bitter invective against Greek arts and letters, *Address to the Greeks,* about 152–155. Only small fragments survive of Melito of Sardis's *Apology,* written about 169 to 176. Athenagoras, evidently writing from Rome to Marcus Aurelius and Commodus, joint emperors between 177 and 180, tried an upbeat approach with some success. Finally, about 180, Theophilus of Antioch addressed an influential treatise *To Autolycus* in favor of Christian doctrine and against paganism.

Many scholars dispute whether the "dialogues" represent actual encounters of the synagogue and the church after the first century, but a growing number seem to think that they do. Even if designed, as some think, to reply to Jewish arguments raised by pagans like Celsus in his *True Discourse,* they played an important role in Christian apologetics as a whole. According to Justin's *Dialogue with Trypho,* the Jewish people objected to the Christian use of the Greek Old Testament, known as the Septuagint (LXX); the claim that Jesus was the Messiah; the claim that Jesus was God; Christian contempt for the Law (that is, the ritual Law: fasting, sabbath observance, feast days); the concept of a crucified messiah; and the resurrection, both as a general idea and the specific conviction that Jesus had been raised.

In response to objections to the Septuagint, both Jews and Christians produced more literal versions. About 140, Aquila, a native of Sinope in Pontus who converted to Judaism, reproduced individual Hebrew words and phrases exactly. Later in the second century, Symmachus and Theodotion responded with freer and more readable translations, but Origen judged Symmachus's version more faithful to the Hebrew than the LXX. In answer to the further charge of quoting only passages supportive of the Christian argument, Justin contended that other passages were given on account of the nature of Israel. He met the other five objections by citing scriptures, sometimes literally and sometimes as types. Although his handling of scripture would not have convinced many Jews, modern scholarship has shown that he was familiar with rabbinic methods of interpretation. As a clinching argument, he cited the facts of history to prove that not the Jews but Christians were the chosen people: the dispersal of the Jews, the destruction of the Temple, the cessation of sacrifices, the disappearance of the princes of the house of Judah, and the reception of the good news by the Gentiles.

Pagan charges varied from time to time and place to place, but some of the main themes appeared consistently. As noted earlier, polemicists accused Christians of cannibalism and incest, treason, social aloofness, atheism, theological absurdity, and responsibility for the calamities befalling Rome and the decline of the state.

Christians responded to moral charges with outright denials. They then turned the charges around by pointing out that their own philosophers and poets had condemned non-Christians for the unspeakable things of which they had accused Christians.

The charge of treason was trickier. Christians had to admit that they did not and could not worship the emperor and fulfill perfunctory obligations in the state cultus. Yet, they went on to say, this did not mean disloyalty or bad citizenship. They prayed for the emperor. They paid taxes and discharged other duties. Justin cited the emperors themselves as writing about Christian innocence, clinching his remarks with a spurious account, supposedly written by Marcus Aurelius, of how the "thundering legion" had saved him and the rest of the Roman army at Carnuntum by prayer.

The apologists accepted the charge of social aloofness and turned it to their advantage. Christians differed in commendable ways from both Jews and Gentiles, they said, and thus deserved to be called "a third race," as pagans chidingly suggested.

Some apologists rejected the charge of atheism arbitrarily, but those better equipped in philosophy cited the arguments of Socrates, Plato, and others in favor of monotheism and against polytheism and idolatry (so Aristides and Theophilus). They made much of the immorality of Homeric gods and heroes.

Charges that Christian teachings were absurd could not be easily refuted because of vastly different ways in which Jews and Gentiles sometimes approached reality. Occasionally an apologist responded by citing parallels to beliefs such as resurrection (Theophilus), but at other times they emphasized the uniqueness of Christianity (Tatian) and its antiquity (Justin). To these arguments they added "proofs" from miracles, prophecy, the correspondence of the gospel to the moral nature of humankind, Christian life, and the spread of the gospel (Justin).

Christians rebutted the remaining charge—that they were responsible for the calamities and the decline of Rome—by framing a doctrine of providence based on the Old Testament and on Christian belief. Not Fate but God controls history, they argued. Those faithful to God—the Christians—are responsible for saving the world from more horrible events than were already happening. They are in the world, the author of the *Epistle to Diognetus* observed, what the soul is in the body.

As the number of Christians increased and their influence spread, Christian apologists attacked their highly vulnerable competitors more and spent less time in defense. They lambasted polytheism and immorality. They argued for Christianity as "the true philosophy" (Justin), superior to all others, and noted the positive contributions of Christianity to the peace and security not only of individuals but of the empire as well. A new day had indeed begun to dawn.

CHAPTER EIGHT

LIFE TOGETHER

The period under discussion is often referred to as a "tunnel period" from which Christianity emerged with its institutional life more or less fully elaborated but during which the process of formation remained hidden. Although this characterization holds some truth, it is somewhat misleading, for writings dated in this era do give glimpses of development and allow one to make some judgments about the reasons for it.

In the past, Protestants have often viewed the development of the church during this period in a negative way, as a kind of "fall" of the church analogous to the "fall" of humankind. According to the German jurist Rudolph Sohm, the church began as a "purely spiritual entity" and became, during the second century, a church of law far removed from the intention of Jesus. Sohm's opponents, from Adolph Harnack on, have correctly pointed out that Sohm imposed a modern (i.e., nineteenth century) concept of law on the early church, which created a false conflict between spirit and institution. Harnack himself, however, also defined *Catholicism* as "the church of apostolic tradition fixed as law" and ascribed this development, evident first around 200 C.E., to "Hellenization." The weakness of Harnack's analysis was that it focused on doctrine and neglected the church in its total corporate life. If one views the issue in that broad scope, one comes away with a more positive view of development and is more impressed with early Christianity's understanding of itself as a covenant missionary people as the major motive for the changes that occurred. Institutional development would not represent some kind of sinister power play by opportunistic bishops, although occasional instances of that can be cited, but a natural consequence of Christian effort to discharge what they perceived to be Christ's commission.

In its total corporate life, early Christianity confronted during this period the awesome challenge of conserving its identity as a covenant missionary people while attracting and incorporating the syncretistic peoples of the Roman Empire and beyond. The churches' institutional forms—catechumenate and baptism, the Eucharist as the central act of worship, discipline, scriptures and creed, and apostolic ministry—helped in two ways. On the one hand, they drilled into converts an exclusive identity as the People of God under a new covenant. On the other hand, accommodated to the Greco-Roman setting, they served as a basis of appeal for conversion. Accommodation, far from a lapse from genuine Christianity, dispelled its "alien" character and enabled the average Roman to feel at home in a subgroup that began as a sect of Judaism. Because of its security in its own identity, Christianity proved more capable of genuine assimilation to Roman culture than its syncretistic competitors, the oriental mystery religions.

The ideology under which Christians interpreted themselves and their mission in this period was that of the army of Christ doing battle with Satan and his hosts. Borrowed originally from the Essenes, in the Roman context it was elaborated with terminology and imagery taken from Roman military parlance. In some ways this is ironic, for Christians held strong reservations about military service, but it was a case of an inherited ideology fitting into the frame of a dominant cultural motif; the Romans employed a military structure even in administration of the provinces.

Baptism: The Soldier's Oath

The use of the catechumenate and baptism in the enlistment of converts was discussed in an earlier chapter and need not receive further attention here. It will be worthwhile, however, to spell out some developments in baptismal theology and practice during this crucial phase of early Christian history. The debate among Christians today between those who practice infant baptism and those who practice believer's baptism, unfortunately, has often diverted attention from broader considerations. For this particular period, it suffices to point out that there is no explicit evidence for baptism of infants. The chief support for the view that the early churches baptized infants derives from references to baptism of "households" (Acts 11:14; 16:15, 33; 18:8; 1 Cor. 1:16; Ignatius *Smyrn.* 13.1) and the assumption that Christian baptism followed on the track of Jewish proselyte baptism and circumcision. Apart from this, until Tertullian supplied the first explicit evidence about 206, all evidence is indirect; for example, Polycarp's boast to the Pro-Consul of Asia that he had served Christ eighty-six years (surely meaning from birth) and Irenaeus's statement that Christ had come to save all, "all these, I say, who through him are reborn into God, infants, young children, boys, the mature and older people" (*Adv. haer.* 2.22.4).

The major themes under which the Christians of this era interpreted baptism reflect their concern to provide hope to people who were groveling in fear of demons and ridden with anxiety about fate, sin, guilt, and death. The chief theme was that of participation through the Spirit in Christ's victory over demons. Exorcism during the catechumenate, of course, gave palpable expression to this theme. Baptism supplied the Christian's armament against the powers of evil (Ignatius, Justin, *Dial.* 116).

A second theme centered on forgiveness of sin. Derived from John the Baptist's urging of baptism on the basis of "repentance for forgiveness of sin," this concept was elaborated more by Western than by Eastern writers, but it had universal application in a culture where people sought remedies for their guilt. A major debate arose in Rome as to whether one should be allowed to repent a serious sin (murder, apostasy, adultery) after baptism. *The Shepherd of Hermas* permitted one such formal repentance, a view that gained wide currency for a century or more.

Closely connected with the application of baptism to the problem of sin and guilt was the theme of renewal or regeneration. Christianity's main competitors also promised rebirth through rites such as the *taurobolium*, in which devotees were proclaimed to be *renatus in aeternum* ("reborn forever"). The idea of rebirth received strong emphasis in the Johannine writings and 1 Peter, so it is not surprising to find it often in later writings such as the works of Justin and the *Epistle of Barnabas*. Irenaeus molded his recapitulation theory around the idea of regeneration; he liked to speak of baptism as "the laver of regeneration."

Finally, the theme of illumination appears often, particularly in Eastern writings. The epistle to the Hebrews almost certainly alludes to baptism when speaking of "those once enlightened" (6:4). Justin Martyr, however, was the first to call baptism *photismos* ("illumination"). This understanding appealed to those who, like Justin or Clement of Alexandria, sought "the true Philosophy," for it suggested a recovery of faculties by which one could grasp truth intuitively in the Platonist sense. Gnostics who did not reject baptism altogether also majored on this theme.

Already in this period, baptism clearly distinguished passage from the old to the new, the kingdom of Satan to the kingdom of Christ. The *Didache*, an early church manual, restricted the Eucharist to the baptized, indicating that instruction in "the two ways" preceded baptism. Whether instruction in "the mysteries" (baptism and Eucharist) was withheld until after baptism is unlikely, for Hippolytus seems to suggest that candidates for baptism received such information *before* baptism. There can be little question, however, that those who took the *sacramentum* ("oath") were expected to dispense with all other ties. The fashioning of an increasingly elaborate process for incorporation of new converts in the army of Christ was obviously designed to help effect exactly that goal.

The Eucharist and Worship: Covenant Renewal

Where baptism was a kind of acted-out parable of a convert's initial owning of the covenant, the Eucharist, or Lord's Supper, represented a repetition of this first pledge. As a special Christian rite par excellence, it was restricted to the baptized; perhaps as early as 112, the unbaptized or excommunicates were dismissed during observance (*Pliny's Letter to Trajan*).

Two themes—sacrifice and real presence—dominated eucharistic theology. Although New Testament writings did not construe the Lord's Supper as a sacrifice, the very nature of it made the connection natural as Christians developed an apology both to Judaism and to the Greco-Roman world, in which the concept played a signal role in both theory and practice. Clement of Rome, for instance, related Christian practices to Old Testament sacrificial concepts easily and naturally when he spoke of "those who offer their oblations at the appointed seasons" (*1 Clem.* 40.4). The medieval concept of the Eucharist as sacrifice was not in evidence, but the apologists did not hesitate to claim that this observance supplanted both Jewish and Gentile sacrifices. It represented "the true sacrifice" or "oblation," of course, "Christ's death."

The concept of real presence was deeply rooted in the earliest Christian tradition of the Lord's Supper. Even before Paul's time, Christians gathered on "the Lord's day" at "the Lord's table" to eat "the Lord's supper," a combined charitable (*agape*) and fellowship meal. Against docetists, those who denied Jesus' real humanity, John and Ignatius cited the Eucharist as significative of genuine incarnation. Ignatius charged that docetists abstained from the Eucharist "because they do not confess that the Eucharist is the flesh of our Savior Jesus Christ who suffered for our sins" (*Smyrn.* 7). For him the bread and wine were "the medicine of immortality, the antidote that we should not die, but live forever in Jesus Christ" (*Eph.* 20.2). Justin explained how the bread and wine were "changed." As the words "This is my body" and "This is my blood" are spoken, the divine Logos "transmutes" them, and thus the blood and flesh of the risen Christ "nourish" the recipient (*1 Apol.* 66). Later Church Fathers would advance this thinking further as they explained how the Eucharist fortified believers against demonic poisons and assaults.

Although information in this period is fragmented and difficult to find, Justin supplies the first outline of a Lord's day or Sunday liturgy (*1 Apol.* 68) used in Rome. That description indicates that some interesting changes had taken place in Christian worship during the eighty years since the primitive era.

First, Christians were now observing a Roman rather than a Jewish calendar, meeting on Sunday morning, a change already reported in Pliny's *Letter to Trajan*. Obviously, the constituencies of the congregations in Rome, and probably elsewhere, were no longer predominantly Jewish but Gentile.

Second, the Eucharist was no longer attached to an actual meal, the *agape*. Abuses attested at Corinth in Paul's day and after (cf. 2 Peter 2:13) undoubtedly exerted pressure toward the separation. According to Pliny's *Letter to*

Trajan, Christians "departed and reassembled to take food," perhaps in the evening.

Third, once the connection with the *agape* had been broken, the Eucharist had been attached to a preaching service, modeled after either synagogue worship or the charismatic type of service described by Paul in 1 Corinthians 14. Justin does not allude to a dismissal of catechumens following the "service of the Word," but the "Amen!" hints at the distinction between the "Mass of the catechumens" and the "Mass of the faithful," which was characteristic by the late second century.

Aids to a Common Life

A number of other developments that assisted Christians in their private and corporate lives accompanied those related to baptism and the Eucharist. One of these was a schedule of prayer and fasting for individuals and families. According to the *Didache,* which still reflects strongly the interaction of church and synagogue, the devout said the Lord's prayer three times daily—at the third, sixth, and ninth hours (9:00 A.M., noon, 3:00 P.M.)—and prayed extemporaneous prayers on arising and going to bed. They fasted twice a week—Wednesdays and Fridays (rather than Tuesdays and Thursdays, as in Jewish custom). Sects such as the Montanists, who believed the return of Christ was imminent, increased the number of prayer hours and fasts.

A second aid to the common life was a calendar, partly taken over and adapted from either the Jewish or the Gentile worlds, but partly framed with distinctively Christian concerns in mind. One of the earliest and most significant of calendar observances was the "Lord's day" or, as it was sometimes called, "the eighth day," the day of resurrection. Observing it first in line with the Jewish week, by the mid-second century Christians had shifted to Roman reckoning and were reluctantly using the Roman nomenclature "day of the sun." Hesitancy in using the term stemmed from the fact that the day honored the *Sol Invictus,* the supreme deity of the solar monotheism of cults such as Mithra.

A second observance was Easter. How early Christians began to set aside one day annually in commemoration of the resurrection cannot be established, but during the mid–second century controversy over the correct date of Easter, both sides claimed ancient precedents. Christians of Asia Minor ended their fast, thus marking the resurrection, on the fourteenth of Nisan, that is, according to the Jewish Passover. Christians in Rome, however, celebrated Easter on the first Sunday after the first full moon after the spring equinox. The difference posed no problem until Anicetus (bishop of Rome 155–166) tried to pressure a congregation of Asian Christians living in his city to observe the Roman custom. Direct intercession of the saintly Polycarp, however, caused him to relent, and the controversy died down. It heated up again in the time of Victor (189–199) and nearly, if not actually, resulted in the excommunication of all Christians of the province of Asia. This time, Irenaeus, a native of Asia who was by then a towering figure in the West, interceded with Victor to avert a more serious rupture. The issue surfaced again at the Council of Nicaea in 325, which decided in favor of the Roman custom.

A third important observance on the early Christian calendar was Pentecost. *Pentecost* is a Greek word meaning "fiftieth"; thus this day designated the fiftieth day after Passover in the Jewish calendar. Originally an agricultural festival, it took on a different nuance for Christians: a celebration of the gift of the Spirit and the beginning of the church. In the early third century, Tertullian noted that converts could receive baptism on Pentecost as well as on Easter Sunday.

"Birthdays" of martyrs—meaning the date of their execution—began to enter the calendars of some churches during the second century with the martyrdom of Polycarp (155). After persecution ceased, it took only a short step to include "saints" in the calendar. There is no reliable evidence concerning observances in honor of Christ's birth prior to the fourth century. Clement of Alexandria, however, speculated privately that Jesus was born on April 18 or 19 or even as late as May 29.

In addition to daily prayer and the Christian calendar, a third aid to worship was hymnody. Already prominent in churches founded by Paul (see Eph. 5:19; Col. 3:16), what are usually called prose hymns can be found in many other early Christian writings (1 Tim. 3:16; 1 Pet. 3:18-22). The Revelation of John contains numerous "songs" similar to the Psalms of the Old Testament and Qumran. Pliny's *Letter to Trajan* (112) reports that Christians were singing hymns antiphonally to Christ. Metrical Greek hymnody developed gradually toward the end of the second century. Some Gnostics wrote hymns. Clement of Alexandria composed hymns that are still sung today. The churches of Syria distinguished themselves early by the composition of psalms or hymns in the vernacular. The so-called *Odes of Solomon* is a collection of forty-two hymns now dated as early as the first or second century. Although scholars debate whether these hymns were composed originally in Greek or in Syriac, they reflect distinctive emphasis on Christ as the Wisdom of God. Hymns in Latin, Coptic, and other languages appeared gradually, although not as early as Syriac hymns.

A fourth aid to the common life of Christians was art. From Judaism, Christians inherited some ambivalence toward art. Although the second commandment forbade "graven images," Jewish burial places and synagogues both in Palestine and elsewhere were adorned with carvings and paintings of a symbolic character. When Christians took over Jewish catacombs, they also took over art traditions, which they expanded along Christian lines. The catacombs of Rome contain numerous paintings from the second century and after that depict God's saving ways from Adam and Eve to the age of the apostles and martyrs. No one can determine the extent to which such art may have adorned Christian homes and then churches, but it is likely that wealthy converts retained artwork in their homes and perhaps "christianized" it after conversion. Houses remodeled to serve as church buildings would have carried this process further.

No buildings specially designed to accommodate Christian worship have survived from the second century, but it is quite possible that many houses were refurbished like the house-church at Dura-Europos, a Roman frontier fortress on the Euphrates, which dates from about 232.

Rescuing the Fallen

Protestants have usually held the view that Christian discipline deteriorated in the post-apostolic age, progressing from "strict" to "lax" treatment of offenders. It is more accurate to say that early Christian churches differed from one another on this issue from the start and continued to do so, torn between concern for the purity of the church and for restoration of offenders. Now one and then another attitude dominated in different churches.

Some favored severe treatment of persons who committed serious sins, such as apostasy, adultery, or murder. Hermas, for instance, cited a group in Rome who refused to allow for any repentance save that which preceded baptism. They based their argument chiefly on the epistle to the Hebrews, which carried great weight in the Roman congregations. Around 171 C.E., Pinytus, Bishop of Cnossus on the island of Crete, remonstrated with Dionysius of Corinth, who had advocated milder treatment of those found guilty of adultery. The Montanist sect, which originated in Phrygia about this time, was characterized by a rigorous exclusion of a whole range of offenders, including persons who married a second time.

A more lenient approach, based on the parable of the wheat and tares in Matthew's Gospel, existed alongside this rigorous one. Against the rigorists of Rome, Hermas proposed one repentance for serious offenses committed after baptism, a view that gained wide acceptance in other places. *Second Clement*, composed perhaps in Rome around 140 C.E., urged almsgiving as a form of repentance that "covers a multitude of sins." The handbook called the *Didache*, representing Syrian practice, counseled public confession before prayer and worship, with the implication that the guilty could be absolved. The clearest proof of the prevalence of this outlook, however, is Tertullian's change of attitude after he became a Montanist. In a treatise *On Repentance*, composed before he converted to

Montanism, he urged one repentance after baptism as proposed by Hermas and excluded no sins from the churches' power of absolution. In a later work, entitled *On Purity*, however, he denounced Hermas as "the shepherd of adulterers" and distinguished between forgivable and unforgivable sins. The latter included the usual list of apostasy, murder, and adultery, but added several others as well.

Known instances of excommunication during this period show that all of the churches took discipline seriously, although some more seriously than others. Tertullian's treatise *On Repentance* describes the formal confession (*Exhomologesis*) required in his day in the church at Carthage. A contemporary account concerning the repentance of a Roman Christian named Natalius, who had become a bishop in a heretical sect, confirms that the Roman churches used a similar procedure (Eusebius *H.E.* 5.28.12). Persons excommunicated for serious offenses were required to put on sackcloth and ashes; fast (taking "simple things for meat and drink") and pray; lament their sins with groaning and weeping; prostrate themselves before the elders of the church; and kneel before the congregation, entreating them to intercede with the elders for their restoration to communion. Exactly when or how this procedure was fashioned cannot be determined. Still earlier writings urged public confession (James 5:16; *Didache* 4.14; 14.1f.; Barn. 6.2), but did not outline a process for it.

The reason for a more exacting and formal approach was given by Tertullian himself (*On Repentance* 9). All too many had probably done as Cerdo, Marcion's teacher in Rome, had done: When excommunicated for heretical teaching, he repented frequently, thus embarrassing the churches (Irenaeus *Adv. haer.* 3.4.3).

Structuring for Mission

During the period 70–180 C.E., churches of both East and West moved from a predominantly twofold to a predominantly threefold pattern of ministry. Several motives can be seen in this. One was the struggle of the churches to discover or maintain their identity as they incorporated people who had a radically different cultural background (a Hellenistic one) from the one with which Christianity began (a Jewish one). A single authoritative figure, the bishop, assured greater consistency of interpretation and instruction. This factor, however, has often received too much emphasis to the neglect of one that played a far more significant role: the demands of the Christian mission itself. As the churches reached outward and drew converts inward, they revised old structures and fashioned additional ones that worked best. In a context where the military motif was the prevailing social model, it was natural for the churches to construe what they were doing in terms of that motif.

According to Acts 11:30; 14:23; and Titus 1:5, the apostles "appointed" presbyters "church by church." Whether this happened universally, at the beginning of this period the twofold pattern of presbyter-bishops and deacons alluded to in Philippians 1:1 prevailed in most churches. The terms *presbyter* (Greek *presbuteros)* and *bishop* (Greek *episkopos)* were used interchangeably. *Episkopos* was a functional term meaning "overseer" or "superintendent"; while this described the work of the *presbuteros,* the term itself was inherited from the Jewish synagogue but signified no more than an older person in the Gentile world. "Church" (*ekklesia*) normally delineated all Christians living within a *polis* ("city"), however many house churches or congregations that may have involved. Each polis-church would have had a number of presbyter-bishops or deacons who cooperated in meeting the varied needs of the area.

Like the presbyters of Jewish synagogues, presbyter-bishops exercised general oversight, administered finances, presided over public worship, taught, and supervised the charitable ministries (cf. 1 Tim. 3:2-7). In the Palestinian context, the shepherd motif supplied an image for the manner in which they would go about their tasks (Acts 20:17ff.; 1 Pet. 5:1-4). Deacons discharged most of the same functions under supervision of the presbyter-bishops (cf. Acts 6:1-6; 1 Tim. 3:8-13). Unlike the latter office, however, the Christian diaconate probably had no direct antecedent in Judaism but arose directly from the interpretation of Jesus' role in terms of the Servant figure pictured in the book of Isaiah. In the early churches, women as well as men functioned as deacons from the time of Paul on (Rom. 16:1; 1 Tim. 3:11). The Greek word *diakonos* designated the single office until the late second or early third century, when women deacons came to be called "deaconesses."

The threefold office (bishop, presbyters, deacons) emerged gradually from the twofold office during the late first and early second centuries. Some scholars discern a threefold office in the Pastoral Epistles, but it seems fairly clear from Titus 1:5, 7 that the terms *presbyter* and *bishop* were still used interchangeably as they continued to be until the late second century in some places. Ignatius of Antioch (110–117) urged the churches of Asia Minor to "do nothing without the bishop," but the frequency with which he repeated that refrain proves that they had not yet adopted the threefold pattern. Indeed, many scholars have observed that Ignatius's obsession with the idea, as well as some direct statements in his letters, indicates that this form was not yet secure in Antioch either. The Roman Church definitely had not opted for it, for Ignatius addressed his letter to the Roman Church rather than to its bishop. Although lists of bishops subsequently cited names of bishops of Rome, those listed first functioned as chairpersons of a college of presbyter-bishops and not as monarchical bishops (i.e., individuals who held responsibility for an entire polis-church, and under whose leadership both presbyters and deacons served).

How did the transition from the twofold to the threefold pattern take place? Some scholars have cited the crisis of leadership that arose as a result of the fall of Jerusalem in 70 C.E. When the star fell there, it rose in Antioch, putting pressure on the church to elevate its leader to the position of monarchical bishop. It was this concept that Ignatius carried through Asia Minor on his way to martyrdom in Rome.

The difficulty with this theory is obvious in the light of Ignatius's nervous effort to make a case for a monarchical episcopate and the varied rates at which different churches adopted it. A more likely explanation is J. B. Lightfoot's hypothesis that one presbyter-bishop emerged naturally from the position of chairperson of the board of presbyter-bishops to become a monarchical bishop. When this happened, it was natural that the term *episkopos* would be reserved little by little for the persons whose powers were elevated. Threats to the welfare of the churches, such as schism or heresy, supplied some of the motive, but the normal processes of a vital corporate life of the churches required a level of coordination that the twofold pattern did not supply. Threats to identity added to the need for further coordination.

Still to be explained is how the churches, sprawled all over the vast Roman Empire, opted gradually for the monarchical episcopate. Rudolf Sohm and Walter Bauer attributed this to a gigantic power play by the Roman Church that eventuated in Roman dominance and the office of the papacy. The evidence outlined earlier makes their theories highly unlikely. Even powerful organizations could hardly have imposed their will on others, and the Roman Church was by no means powerful. Far from a single church imposing on others, the churches throughout the empire, especially those in the giant metropolis, mutually affected one another.

In this period, as Jerusalem faded, the (at least symbolic) importance of cities like Antioch, Ephesus, Corinth, Alexandria, and Rome increased. Due to the Pauline strategy of planting churches in major centers that could serve as channels to surrounding regions, these cities had already established themselves as parental figures for other churches in their own provinces and beyond. If Rome had an advantage, it was as the capital of the empire to which all roads led. Thus Clement felt free to send a fraternal letter to the Corinthians to exhort them to restore the leaders they had expelled. Ignatius flattered the Romans, too, by speaking of their preeminence in the country of the Romans. Early lists of bishops enhanced Rome's position still more. Other churches, however, moved ahead of Rome in adopting the threefold pattern of organization, leaving little room to think about the imposition of a Roman pattern on other churches. Far more crucial was the intimate interaction of the churches everywhere, which led eventually to a common organization.

Accompanying the structural changes described previously was a tendency to distinguish more sharply between clergy and laity. In the primitive period, such a distinction was not evident. The whole church was referred to as *laos*, "the people." Clement introduced the first sharp distinction. Alluding to the Old Testament priesthood, he distinguished an order of clergy and an order of the laity (*1 Clement* 40). He undergirded this with the germ of a doctrine of apostolic succession (44.2). Ignatius's emphasis on the exalted place of the bishop sharpened the distinction further. The bishop, he contended, stands in the place of Christ and even of God. Thence whatever happens in the church must have the bishop's supervision—the Eucharist, marriages, baptisms, everything. A list of bishops compiled near the end of this period by Hegesippus laid the foundation for the full-blown theory of apostolic succession found in Irenaeus.

CHAPTER NINE

STRUGGLE FOR IDENTITY AND UNITY

The unity of Christianity has been viewed in different ways. The early Church Fathers saw it as a given that heretics and schismatics threatened to destroy. According to Tertullian's classical formulation in *Prescriptions Against Heretics,* Christ laid down "one definite system of truth" for his disciples. The disciples preached the same doctrine everywhere and established churches that would transmit this to others. "These churches, then, numerous as they are, are identical with that one primitive apostolic church from which they all come." Heresy thus represents a departure from the apostolic tradition, an intrusion of an alien culture. Heretics have no real concern for differences in theology "as long as they are all agreed in attacking the truth." They lacked discipline of any kind and were far from unified.

Modern scholarship allows nothing so simple. In his classic treatise *Orthodoxy and Heresy in Earliest Christianity,* Walter Bauer reversed the traditional formulation. Whereas the Fathers would say first orthodoxy and then heresy, Bauer argued first "heresy" (i.e., diverse expressions of Christianity) and then orthodoxy, the latter imposed as a result of a power struggle. In this struggle, Bauer thought, the Church of Rome carried out a major coup. In Clement's intervention in the Corinthian squabble in 96 C.E., "Rome succeeded in imposing its will on Corinth" and "casting its spell" over that church from then on. Subsequently, the Roman Church intervened also in Antioch at the time of Ignatius and then, "in a more limited manner more than one hundred years later," in Alexandria, using various tactics but especially grants of money in time of desperate need to do so. After overpowering diverse groups in Rome itself, the church turned elsewhere.

Few scholars now would agree with Bauer's theory of a sinister Roman campaign to impose orthodoxy, but most would acknowledge the idea of the initial diversity of early Christianity, which generated problems for Christian unity. In reply to Bauer, H. E. W. Turner suggested an interlacing of "fixed" and "flexible" elements in Christian doctrine, which eventually helped to establish a *Pattern of Christian Truth.* Along similar lines, most contemporary explanations make room for some kind of unity in diversity, whether or not the common elements were known and articulated. The center around which Christian identity and unity revolved was, of course, Christ himself, but it was not long before Christians realized that they depended on tangible means such as baptismal confessions, scriptures, and authoritative teachers to guide them safely to Christ. By the end of the period discussed here, they were laying down more definite formulas that could assure them that they were on the right track.

The Roman Situation

Early Christianity's problems can be placed in relief by considering the situation of one church—that of Rome—on which information is fairly extensive. In the period under study here, the congregations were highly diverse in background and character. Judging by writings reliably ascribed to Rome (Mark, Hebrews, 1 Peter, *1 Clement, The Shepherd of Hermas,* Justin's works), many of these congregations had a substantial constituency of Jewish background and outlook. The Jewish constituency, too, was diverse, some from a synagogue, others from an Essene background. Both Hebrews and *The Shepherd of Hermas* reflect vivid Essene ideas. Hermas, a former slave, may well have been, as one scholar has hypothesized, a son of Essene parents brought to Rome as captives after the Jewish revolt of 66–70 C.E. At any rate, he reveals deep and explicit influence of Essene ideas. *First Clement,* moreover, argued for maintenance of proper church order in Corinth on analogy to the hierarchy found only in Essene camp communities—the high priest, priests, Levites, and laypersons (1 *Clem.* 40.5) and alluded to "captains of fifties," a designation found only in Exodus 18:15; 1 Maccabees 3:55; and in Essene writings.

A whole row of Gnostic teachers turned up in Rome during the late first and second centuries: Simon Magus and his consort Helena; Menander, Simon's successor; Marcellina, a disciple of Carpocrates, who came during the time of Anicetus (155–165); Cerdo, teacher of Marcion; Valentinus, who migrated from Alexandria about 140; Ptolemaeus, Valentinus's successor; Marcus, a Valentinian who seduced gullible women; and others. The more orthodox Justin opened his school in Rome about the middle of the second century. Marcion, excluded from his father's church in Pontus, moved to Rome about 139. Montanism appeared in Rome by 177 C.E.

Besides these groups, Rome attracted Christians from all over the empire. Christians from the province of Asia were numerous enough to form their own congregation. When Anicetus (155–165) and Victor (189–199) sought to effect greater unity in Rome by pressing for conformity, they created a crisis for the Asians, who observed Asian customs concerning Easter. Polycarp interceded with Anicetus and persuaded him to relent in his insistence that the Asians observe the Roman Easter—the first Sunday after the first full moon after the spring equinox—rather than the Asian custom of breaking their fast on Nisan 14, the Jewish Passover. Victor, however, exerted far greater pressure and may actually have excommunicated Christians in the Roman province of Asia despite the intercession of Irenaeus.

This depiction of their multifarious character should not mislead one into thinking that the Roman churches had no centrifugal forces pulling them toward one another. They were using confessions of some type in catechumenate and baptism. They relied on the Old Testament and certain Christian writings for public worship and instruction. They followed the lead of presbyters and deacons appointed by established procedures. What dissonant voices such as Marcion's did was to speed up a process of definition—a more precise confession, a canon or list of New Testament writings to supplement the Old (which Marcion and most Gnostics rejected), and a more centralized organization. The early confession of faith known as the Old Roman Symbol dates from the middle of the second century and may respond to Marcion at one or two points. The so-called Muratorian Canon, which lists New Testament writings, was composed about 175. Victor was the first highly authoritarian bishop of Rome. Pressures he exerted toward uniformity, however, were unwise; they certainly had a mixed effect on the unity of the churches as a whole.

Jewish Christianity

The struggle for Christian identity proceeded in two directions at the same time. One involved the continuing relationship of Jewish Christians to their parent religion, the other the accommodation of Christianity to its increasingly Hellenistic constituency and milieu. Christians of Jewish ancestry were understandably anxious about the severing of ties with Judaism and radical adaptation to another cultural setting. Some chose to throw in their lot with Gentile Christianity, others to return to Judaism, still others to go their own way, retaining something from both faiths.

Any depiction of Jewish Christianity during this period will be sketchy by virtue of fragmentary information about it. It continued alongside Gentile Christianity, however, in a variety of forms. In Palestine, a group known as Ebionites (from the Hebrew *ebyon,* "the poor") fled to Pella in Transjordan after the fall of Jerusalem in 70 C.E., where they survived until the fifth century. Successors of "believers who belonged to the party of the Pharisees" mentioned in Acts 15:5, and possibly the "false brethren secretly brought in," cited in Galatians 2:4, they espoused views surprisingly close to Essene as well as Christian teachings. They observed ritual baths daily.

They believed God has established two beings—Christ and the devil—one to rule the world to come, the other to rule this world. They rejected the virgin birth, but they believed the Spirit descended on Jesus at baptism in the form of a dove. Jesus came to teach righteousness and to destroy sacrifices. They observed the Law faithfully.

A second Jewish Christian sect, known as the Elkesaites, appeared in Alexandria and Rome. Originating during the third year of Trajan's reign (101 C.E.), they had several points of similarity with the Ebionites. Both remained faithful to Jewish customs, rejected certain portions of scriptures (Paul's writings), and looked on Christ as a human being inspired to discharge the role of a prophet. The Elkesaites, however, claimed special revelations concerning forgiveness of sins after baptism, a view reminiscent of the *Shepherd of Hermas*.

In Ephesus, Cerinthus combined Jewish practices with Christian millenarianism. He believed in creation of the world by angels, an establishment of the kingdom of Christ on earth, and restoration of the Temple of Jerusalem and of sacrifices. He also practiced circumcision and kept the sabbath. At the same time, he rejected the resurrection of Christ and performed baptisms for the dead.

Several Jewish-Christian sects leaned in the direction of Gnosticism, including those of Simon Magus, Satornilus, the Sethians, the Ophites, and the Naasenes. Gnostic influences on Jewish sects prior to the advent of Christianity are quite evident. It was natural that these would draw elements of Christianity into their hodgepodge of doctrine.

Marcion

No early Christian thinker, heterodox or orthodox, did more than Marcion to bring to a head the question of Christianity's relation to Judaism. Although often classified as a Gnostic, he is more accurately viewed as an ardent opponent of legalism and thus of Christianity's ties with Judaism. Behind this opposition lay a personal story.

Marcion was excommunicated for "defiling a virgin" by his own father, a bishop. Although this statement has often been construed as a reference to Marcion's heresy, it fits better his views if taken as an actual seduction. On joining the Roman Church, he gave a gift of 200,000 sestercii, but he soon got into trouble regarding his theology and was excommunicated a second time. He founded a separate church about 144 C.E., which thrived during Anicetus's reign. Although it declined during the third century in the West, it remained strong in the East.

Marcion entitled his major work *Antitheses*. Although this work has not survived, its chief tenets can be reconstructed from Tertullian's detailed reply. Marcion established a series of antitheses between the God of the Old Testament, whom he viewed as the Demiurge who created the world and humankind, and the Supreme God who has revealed himself in Jesus.

> (1) The God of the Old Testament caused fire to come down from heaven; Jesus forbade this.
> (2) Stealing was encouraged in the Old Testament, forbidden in the New Testament.
> (3) The God of creation is neither omnipotent nor omniscient; the Supreme God knows all and is all powerful.
> (4) The Old Testament, with its ceremonial law and low standard of morality, is fit only for that God, not for the God of Jesus.

To emphasize the crudity of the Old Testament, Marcion rejected allegorical or spiritual interpretation and insisted on a literal approach. Having thrown out the Old Testament, he elected for his canon ten letters of Paul (exclusive of the Pastorals) and the Gospel of Luke, both edited. His emphasis on Paul as the only true apostle led Adolf Harnack to characterize Marcion as a Paulinist rather than a Gnostic. Although he adopted the Gnostic idea of Demiurge and thought Christ only "appeared" to be human, his primary emphasis lay on the gospel of the free grace of God. Christ revealed the God of love and forgiveness. There will be no resurrection of the flesh, second coming, or judgment by Christ. Marcion vehemently repudiated the idea of judgment. According to him, the God of the Old Testament was to have sent a messiah to collect the chosen people into the kingdom to rule over the whole earth and then to exercise judgment over sinners. But at this point the good God appeared, showing mercy on sinners and freeing all from the bonds of the God of the Jews. Curiously, Marcion also preached strict asceticism, denied the right of marriage, and formulated stern regulations concerning fasting.

The Gnostics

Until 1945, when Egyptian peasants found an entire library consisting of fifty-two (mostly Gnostic) treatises, Gnosticism was known almost exclusively from the writings of its opponents, notably Irenaeus, Tertullian, Hippolytus, and other Church Fathers. This cache of writings, all written in Coptic but dependent on Greek originals and dating from the mid-third to the first half of the fourth century, confirms the Church Fathers' impression that Gnosticism was highly diverse. Some of the texts, such as *The Gospel of Thomas*, a collection of sayings of Jesus, and Valentinus's *Gospel of Truth*, claim to be explicitly Christian, although gnosticized. Others, such as *The Apocalypse of Adam*, reflect a Jewish type of gnosis based on allegorical interpretation of the Old Testament. Others, such as *Zostrianos and Allogenes* or *Trimorphic Protennoia*, are more philosophical and Neoplatonic than either Christian or Jewish.

The variegated character of this library has added weight to the view that Gnosticism was not merely an "acute Hellenization" of Christianity, as Adolf Harnack and F. C. Burkitt conjectured. Yet it would not seem to establish the theory of Richard Reitzenstein, Wilhelm Bousset, Hans Jonas, and Rudolf Bultmann that Gnosticism was a pre-Christian religion. It is more accurately characterized, as James M. Robinson has said, as "a radical trend of release from the dominion of evil or of inner transcendence that swept through antiquity and emerged within Christianity, Judaism, Neoplatonism, the mystery religions, and the like and subsequently became a religion in its own right" (*The Nag Hammadi Library*).

Gnostic sects appeared in various parts of the Christian world. Associated with Egypt were Naasenes, Sethians, Cainites, Ophites, Basilidians, and Valentinians; with Syria, Simonians (after Simon Magus), Dositheans, Menanderians, Basilidians, and Saturnilians; with Asia Minor, Cerinthians, Nicolaitans, and the Jewish syncretistic cults of Zeus Hypsistos and Zeus Sabazios; and with Rome, most of the above. Although it is impossible to catalogue all of these, their main tenets can be summarized.

All of the Gnostic sects were concerned about redemption by liberation from the material world and reintegration with the spiritual world, the One. A profound metaphysical dualism formed the base for their systems of thought. Matter is evil; the spirit alone is good. Consequently, these two must have no contact. Dualism necessitated a theory of creation by some being other than the Supreme God, who is pure spirit. The Valentinians, who leaned strongly toward Platonism, explained creation by way of a series of emanations from the One. Others ascribed creation to a lesser deity, usually called the *Demiurgos*. Gnostic cosmology pictured a three-storied universe with a series of concentric spheres, or aeons, rising above and around the earth to serve as filters between the spiritual and the material worlds. Some projected thirty spheres and others as many as 365 (for the days of the year). Ruling over these spheres were lesser deities, called *archai, daimones, exousiai*, and others (see Colossians 1–2).

Redemption, for the Gnostics, required first a release of the soul from the body, which, since it is material, is a "tomb." The soul is a "divine spark" separated from the One and trapped in a body. Gnostic groups differed sharply on the way a soul could obtain its freedom. Death, of course, would release it, but one could prepare for liberation before death. Many Gnostics encouraged ascetic practices and self-mortification, rites of purification, and regulation of life according to the dictates of the higher elements within. The Carpocratians, however, urged indulgence, seeking every human experience for the soul so that it would not be forced into another body, which they believed would happen if they did not exercise wanton freedom.

Release from the body is only the first stage in redemption. The second is a return through the heavenly spheres ruled over by demonic forces. Here the later Gnostics usually divided people into three categories: the *pneumatikoi*, or "spiritual," who would reascend like helium-filled balloons; the *hylic*, or "material," who had no prospect of salvation; and the *psychikoi*, or "semi-spiritual," who could be saved if they followed the right prescription. The key lay, they thought, in *gnosis*, a special knowledge of the names of the ruling powers and "passwords" to obtain their permission to ascend through the aeons. The goal of most Gnostics was a mystical vision and enlightenment that would bring deification.

Where would one obtain *gnosis*? From the Redeemer sent from above to lead the soul on its journey. Here Gnostics could make use of Christ, although most viewed him as a kind of loose addendum to their systems. In some systems, he could be seen as the Redeemer whose purpose was to reveal the secret *gnosis* to selected teachers. Accordingly, the Gnostics produced gospels and apostolic writings of their own. *The Gospel of Truth* is a treatise on the Valentinian system with scant reference to Jesus, but *The Gospel of Thomas* combines sayings parallel to those in the canonical Gospels with otherwise unknown sayings of Jesus, some of which have a gnostic flavor. When challenged to authenticate their teachings, Gnostics either allegorized canonical writings or rejected them on the grounds that they had received Jesus' secret teachings by way of apostles other than those who composed the canonical writings.

Valentinian Gnostics made a significant contribution to the interpretation of the Bible in that those who did not reject the Old Testament out of hand faced seriously the problems it posed for Christian use. In his famous *Letter to Flora*, Ptolemaeus, Valentinus's successor, pointed to subtle distinctions that should be made among various parts of the Old Testament. One part must be attributed to God, a second part to Moses, and a third to the elders of the people. Yet even the first part must be subdivided further. It contains "the pure legislation not mixed with evil," that "interwoven with inferiority and injustice," and that "which is exemplary and symbolic." As examples of the first class, Ptolemaeus cited the Decalogue; of the second, the eye for eye, tooth for tooth legislation; of the third, such things as offerings, circumcision, sabbath, fasting, Passover, unleavened bread, and the like. His examples of what could be "spiritualized" are not unlike those given by orthodox writers such as Irenaeus and Tertullian.

94

Montanism

Montanism does not belong in the same category as Gnosticism and Marcionism, but it, too, mottled the early Christian picture and heightened the struggle for unity. This charismatic sect originated in Phyrgia in Asia Minor either in 156 or 172, the conflicting dates given by different sources, when a converted priest of Cybele named Montanus began to prophesy and speak in tongues. Montanus's first disciples included two women, Priscilla and Maximilla, who also claimed prophetic inspiration. The movement spread quickly throughout Asia Minor and to Rome and Carthage. In Carthage, it produced a number of martyrs and, in 206, the brilliant apologist and theologian Tertullian. Tertullian, however, separated from the Montanists about 222 and formed a sect of his own. As its first prophets disappeared from the scene, the influence of the movement waned, but it continued as late as the sixth century.

Unlike the Gnostics or Marcion, the Montanists espoused no views that would have been judged heretical by contemporary or even later standards. Later orthodox writers accused Montanus of claiming to be Christ or the Holy Spirit, but Tertullian, whose orthodoxy was never questioned, could hardly have joined a sect whose theology would have deviated so far from the center.

Montanists designated their sect "the prophecy" or "the new prophecy." They divided history into three stages: (1) Old Testament prophecy, (2) the "instruction of the Lord," and (3) the Paraclete. The last, promised by Jesus (John 14), opened the way for new revelations. Montanus was quoted as saying: "Lo, man is as a lyre and I play on it as a plectron. Man sleeps and I awaken (him). Lo, it is the Lord who sets human hearts in ecstasy and who in it gives men hearts" (Ephiphanius, *Heresies*, 84.4D). For the Montanists, glossolalia (speaking in tongues) was a form of prophecy.

In accordance with their view of history, the Montanists expected Christ to return soon and set up the millennial kingdom with headquarters at Pepuza, Montanus's hometown. Living on the eve of the parousia, they demanded a higher level of discipline than did other churches, extending the church's fasts accordingly. According to Jerome, they kept three lents a year (*Commentary on Matthew* 9.15; *Epistle to Marcella* 41) and observed two weeks of what Tertullian called *Xerophagia* or *Raphanophagia*, during which they abstained from meats, wine-flavored drinks, and baths (*On Fasting* 1). Moreover, where other churches encouraged voluntary fasting, Montanists required it. They also forbade second marriages even in instances where a spouse had died. Tertullian denounced remarriage as "nothing but a type of fornication" (*Exhortation to Chastity* 9). Along similar lines, Montanists elevated virginity. Tertullian listed three levels of purity: virginity from birth, virginity from the new birth, and faithfulness in marriage. He did, however, defend marriage against Gnostic teaching that it is evil.

In line with their eschatology, Montanists held rigorous views about exclusion and restoration of offenders. Nothing makes this clearer than Tertullian's hardening of his views after conversion. In his treatise *On Chastity,* he repudiated his own earlier statements that grace is free and unlimited, divided offenses into remissible and irremissible, and refused readmission of persons in the latter category only. Montanists gloried in martyrdom and forbade flight to avoid persecution. Opponents charged that they provoked and counseled others to provoke persecution and preferred apostasy under torture to flight.

Montanists emphasized the Spirit in their concept of the church. They liked to label themselves "pneumatics" and other Christians as "psychics," although they did not deny that the latter were Christian. Pneumatics have the advantage of possessing the Spirit, and it is the Spirit that guarantees discipline and order and whatever else the church requires. The Spirit, not ordination, determines leadership; thus women, such as the prophetesses Priscilla and Maximilla, could assume dominant roles. If there were grades or degrees, they would depend on prophetic inspiration and not official classifications. "Are not even we lay persons priests?" asked Tertullian.

CHAPTER TEN

CONFESSING FAITH

Adolf Harnack viewed canon, creed, and episcopate as the three bulwarks that early Christianity erected against heresy. Although each of these did serve this purpose in some way, recognition of the diversity of early Christian life and thought necessitates a more complex depiction of Christian efforts to discern and retain their identity as the churches incorporated the peoples of the Roman Empire and beyond. Side by side with the three traditional "pillars of authority" in the early church—the process of defining a New Testament canon, the framing of confessional statements for baptism that could serve as summaries of faith and guides to interpretation, and location of the teaching function increasingly in the hands of bishops—went a process of theological reflection in response to questions posed both within and outside of the churches. The apologists in particular sought to meet this challenge and merit recognition as the early church's first theologians.

Presenting Christ

For early Christians, theology was christology. The major question was always, why do we ascribe to Jesus the honor that belongs to God, whom we believe to be One?

Early Christians stood between two worlds as they wrestled with this question. One was the monotheistic world of Judaism; the other was the polytheistic world of Greece and Rome. Early on, Jewish perspectives dominated, but as the Jewish constituency of the churches diminished, they faded into the background and Hellenistic perspectives overshadowed them. The transition was risky and led in many instances to theological shipwreck. Some, however, managed to steer the ship safely between reefs on either side, relying heavily on baptismal confessions as their pilots in interpreting scripture.

Two christologies vied for acceptance during this period. One, known as pneumatic christology, reflected continuing Jewish influences; the other, known as logos christology, addressed itself more sharply to the Gentile setting.

Pneumatic christology probably originated in Jewish Christianity, but it continued to have strong play in Rome and other centers where there was a basic Jewish constituency. It tended toward adoptionism but differed from it in emphasizing Christ's pre-existence. Clement of Rome accentuated the monotheism of the Old Testament. He conceived of Christ as the pre-existent Servant of Isaiah 53 and expected the Second Coming and bodily resurrection. Similarly, Hermas was strongly monotheistic. He viewed the incarnation as a union of "the holy, pre-existent Spirit that created every creature" with human flesh (*Similitudes* 5.6; 9.1). Some scholars have charged him with adoptionism, but he differed from adoptionists in his theory of pre-existence.

Near the end of the second century, a divergent form of pneumatic christology known as monarchianism developed in Rome and elsewhere. Monarchianism emphasized the single rule (*monarche*) of God. One form of it was known as dynamistic or adoptionistic monarchianism. According to this view, Christ was a man endowed at birth or baptism with divine power (*dynamis*) and thus able to perform miracles. Because he fulfilled the divine will perfectly, he was raised from the dead, given divine authority, and appointed judge and savior of humankind. In this sense, he can be recognized as Lord and worshiped as such. The first exponent of this view was Theodotus the Tanner, who migrated to Rome from Smyrna about 190. He was succeeded by his student, Theodotus the Money-changer, as well as by Asclepiodotus and Artemas. The most influential representative of this perspective, however, was Paul of Samosata, Bishop of Antioch and a civil official under Zenobia, Queen of Palmyra, who was condemned at the Synod of Antioch in 268.

The other form of monarchianism was known as Modalism or Sabellianism (after Sabellius, its leading exponent) or Patripassionism. Beginning with the basic premise that there is only one God, the Father, Modalists proceeded to equate Father and Son. If Christ is God, he is surely the Father. If he suffered, then the Father suffered (thus Patripassionism). To avoid charges of Patripassionism, some Modalists distinguished between the flesh (the Son) and the spirit (the Father). But the cardinal tenet of Modalists was that Father, Son, and Spirit are identical. These are merely names or modes (thus Modalism). God is at one time in the mode or role (*prosopon*) of Father, at another time in the mode or role of Son, at another time in the mode or role of the Spirit. The chief representatives of this view were Praxeas, Sabellius, and Noetus (d. ca. 250). Modalism also gained adherents in Asia Minor and Africa.

The christology that eventually triumphed was logos christology. The early Christian proclamation had posed the question, *Who* was with God— became human—and reascended? Jewish thought supplied several possible answers. Torah, the revealed will of God, was thought of by the rabbis in near-anthropomorphic terms. Wisdom was feted in a highly personal way in Proverbs 8, Ben Sirach, and the Wisdom of Solomon. The Word of God (*dabar*) figured prominently in Old Testament understanding of creation (Gen. 1:1), revelation, and redemption. Translated *Logos* in Greek, the concept of the Word had some affinities in the Stoic and Platonic ideas of the universal Reason, which gives order and illumines understanding. Philo of Alexandria, moreover, had already blended elements of both traditions in his apology for Judaism.

Logos christology caught on in Asia Minor. The prologue to the Gospel according to John, which tradition associates with Ephesus, combines both Old Testament and Greek motifs concerning the Logos, but it adds also the profound assertion "And the [Logos] became flesh and dwelt among us" (1:14). Not long afterward, Ignatius of Antioch spoke in like manner of Christ as the Logos, contesting some of the same errors of doctrine John argued against. The Logos is the revealer of God, "the mind," "the unerring mouth of the Father" who "proceeds from silence" (*Magnesians* 9). He was not a phantom, merely appearing to be human, but rather he "was truly born . . . truly persecuted under Pontius Pilate . . . truly crucified and died . . . truly raised from the dead" (*Trallians* 9). Ignatius subordinated the Son or Logos to the Father, but he ascribed divine attributes to him (*Ephesians* 1.7; *Romans* 1). Christianity thus supersedes Judaism. "It is monstrous to talk of Jesus Christ and to practice Judaism," he asserted, standing history on its head. "For Christianity did not base its faith on Judaism, but Judaism on Christianity" (*Magnesians* 10).

In the mid-second century, Justin brought the Logos concept to Rome, where he fashioned an apologetic based on it. The Logos was for him the key to morality. Human beings have free will, which sets them apart from all other creatures. However, they do not exercise this because they have been misled by demons and custom or example. To be saved, they must become convinced that God demands virtue and will reward and punish them according to their deserts. Yet they will not repent unless they have knowledge of what is demanded—that is, God's purpose of rewarding the good and punishing the wicked. This knowledge is to be found in Christianity, in its high moral standards and in Christ, the divine messenger sent to reveal God's will and truth. He is the Logos, who became human in order to teach truth and thus to reveal God. Justin viewed the Logos more as the universal Reason of Stoic-Platonic thought than as the Word of the Old Testament. But he could refer to him as the "second God" of the Old Testament theophanies. This Logos inspired the prophets and illuminated the minds of great philosophers, such as Heraclitus and Socrates. In Christ, however, he became incarnate. Thus, although he spoke to and through the others, in Christ, humankind came to possess complete truth.

Tatian (ca. 175), Athenagoras (ca. 177), Theophilus of Antioch (ca. 180), and other apologists echoed Justin's basic thought. Theophilus, however, advanced the logos concept further than any of his predecessors by distinguishing the "internal Logos" (*logos endiathetos*) and the "uttered Logos" (*logos prophorikos*) through whom creation occurred (*To Autolycus* 2.10, 22). Theophilus was also the first to apply the word *Trias* ("threefold") to the Godhead.

The Charters of the Church

As a sect of Judaism, early Christianity inherited at least one means for conserving its identity: the Old Testament law and prophets. Christian attitudes toward the ritual law, however, made these writings highly problematic. If some instructions were to be disregarded, why not all?

Early Christian thinkers were eventually to frame a response to that question, but one (Jewish) Christian touched instinctively on the right answer when he said, "If I don't find it in the charters, I do not believe in the gospel" (in Ignatius *Philadelphians* 8.2). However many elements Christians chose to ignore, they nevertheless rooted their faith in the Old Testament. Thus when Marcion decided to scrap the Old Testament and emphasize the newness of Christianity, he precipitated a massive identity crisis. That he himself recognized the problem is evident in the fact that he created a canon to replace the one he discarded. The arbitrary way in which he went about putting together this canon forced the churches to delineate a canon or list of writings of their own, which they used in public worship alongside the Old Testament. A canon of some kind already existed and was in use, but it was Marcion who narrowed the list of writings to be included and forced a process of reflection regarding the nature of the canon upon the churches.

Apart from the one put together by Marcion, the earliest known canon of scriptures is one discovered by L. A. Muratori in an eighth-century manuscript. Most scholars date it between 170 and 200 C.E. on the basis of the author's allusions to Pius I, Hermas, Marcion, Basilides, and Montanus as his contemporaries. Although the first part of the manuscript is missing, the list includes the four Gospels and all other writings now found in the Western New Testament except Hebrews, James, and 1 and 2 Peter. It mentions also the *Revelation of Peter* and the Wisdom of Solomon and rejects some other writings, including *The Shepherd of Hermas*. It is quite clear that the core of a New Testament canon was solidly formed by this time. Did such a core precede Marcion?

Probably. Barnabas, the *Didache*, Ignatius, Papias, and Marcion himself all noted one or more of the Gospels. About 170, Tatian produced his

Diatessaron, a harmony of the four Gospels. The letters that bear Paul's name were circulating as a collection when 2 Peter was written (ca. 130). They may have been gathered in small collections by exchange of letters between churches Paul visited or, as E. J. Goodspeed theorized, they may have been collected suddenly after the appearance of Luke-Acts about 90 C.E. The Apostolic Fathers cited most of Paul's letters. Writing to the Ephesians, Ignatius cited Paul, "who in every letter mentions you in Christ Jesus" (*Ephesians* 12:2). Marcion himself used a ten-letter collection, but later Marcionites used all thirteen letters. The book of Acts probably circulated with the Gospel according to Luke. First John and 1 Peter were also widely used.

What authority did the New Testament writings have? At first, for obvious reasons, not as much as the ancient scriptures of Judaism. Clement of Rome (96 C.E.) quoted only the Old Testament or words of Jesus as scripture; otherwise, he invoked Peter and Paul as examples. Ignatius, however, seldom cited the Old Testament. For him "the charters are Jesus Christ, the inviolable charter is his cross, and death, and resurrection, and the faith which is through him" (*Philadelphians* 8.2). This would mean not Christ as known through New Testament writings but through the bishop was the sure and safe guide to the gospel. Like Ignatius, Polycarp put apostolic writings a rung higher than the Old Testament. He echoed the thoughts and sometimes quoted many New Testament writings, especially Paul's. Justin, on the other hand, based his argument for Christianity principally on the Old Testament, viewed in its entirety as prophetic—something equally true of Justin's writings whether he was debating Jews or Gentiles. The divine Logos spoke through the prophets about Christ. Justin's *Dialogue with Trypho* is essentially a collection of proof texts from the Old Testament. Trypho and his companions would not "have tolerated your [Justin's] conversation," they declared, "had you not referred everything to the scriptures" (*Dialogue* 56).

Not all theories of inspiration of scriptures were as subtle as Justin's. Other apologists, such as Athenagoras, employed a theory of mantic inspiration, according to which the Spirit was believed to move the lips of the prophets "as if they were musical instruments" (Athenagoras *Embassy* 7), "their own reasoning falling into abeyance and the Spirit making use of them as a flutist might play upon his flute" (9). This near-mechanical theory opened the way for an immensely difficult problem of interpretation, for it necessitated the spiritualizing or allegorizing of obscure or difficult passages and the discovery of meaning in every jot and tittle.

The Gnostics led the way in this process of spiritualizing, but they were not alone. The *Epistle of Barnabas*, composed in the early second century—perhaps in Alexandria—was written as a dissuasive against Jewish literalistic interpretation of the ritual law and an application of the same to morality. Justin tried to steer a course between Jewish literalism and Gnostic allegorism. In some instances, he came close enough to the latter to evoke warnings from his opponent Trypho. In the main, however, he ventured no further than typology. Unlike allegorism, which often discards the historical sense of scripture in favor of the figurative, typology was predicated on the assumption that there are real historical correspondences between Israel under the Old Covenant and Israel under the new one. Nevertheless, it was only a short step from typology to allegory. Both could be defended on the basis of claims of special gifts for interpretation. As Christianity distanced itself further and further from Judaism, Christians felt less and less pressure to adhere to the historical sense with ominous consequences for their reading of the Bible and application to life.

The Living Voice

The most significant locus for the handing on of Christian tradition and thus for the safeguarding of the faith would have been the catechumenate. Here inquirers and converts got their first taste of Christian doctrine and guidance in interpreting the scriptures. Some New Testament writings, such as Matthew's Gospel, were assembled in such a context for instruction of new converts. So also were confessions of faith, such early manuals as the *Didache*, and apologies, such as Justin's. Confessions drew together the whole instructional process and served as beacons for their Christian lives from then on. When the churches disciplined errant members, they alluded back to the catechumenate and baptism, particularly to the confessions learned there. Christians had made their pledge in that process, and they had to answer for it.

Although confessions took shape in the catechumenate and baptismal process, they were invoked in numerous contexts: exorcism of demons, reply to persecutors, worship, and doctrinal disputes. Exorcists made the sign of the cross and invoked the name of Christ or the Trinity, symbolizing a believer's participation in Christ's victory. In situations of persecution, Christian martyrs responded to their persecutors with simple confessions. Because they were often punished simply for being Christians, they replied as Polycarp did in Smyrna: "I am a Christian." Sometimes, however, they took advantage of the occasion to deliver a full confession of their faith in God the Father and in Jesus Christ, the Son of God, as Justin did when brought before the prefect Rusticus in 165. Confessions did not become a regular part of the Christian liturgy until the fifth or sixth century, but they were used on occasion prior to that time. The *Letter of Pliny to Trajan* reports the recitation of hymns to Christ and the taking of oaths in services, which authorities investigated.

Scholars debate the extent to which theological controversy shaped confessions of faith. There can be little doubt that confessions antedated controversy, for some type of confession existed from the beginning. The earliest New Testament writings contain affirmations that are both one-part (statements of faith in Christ) and two-part (statements of faith in Christ and God, or in the Father and Son), and also formulas that paved the way for three-part confessions. It is not necessary to assume from this that confessions were first christological, then bipartite, and then trinitarian. The experience of God to which early Christians bore witness demanded trinitarian expression. What doctrinal debate did was to spur forward a process of refinement and elaboration.

The so-called Old Roman Symbol, a catechetical-baptismal statement employed in the Roman Church in the mid-second century that eventually evolved into what came to be called the Apostles' Creed, reflects the predominantly traditional or biblical character of such confessions. Only three or four clauses can be construed as addressing Gnostic or Marcionite challenges to faith. This confession contains no word or phrase that is not found also in scriptures, but some of its phrases may be viewed as darts thrown at Marcion or the Gnostics, and possibly even the Montanists. "Father Almighty" could be a repudiation of the idea that a lesser deity, the Demiurge, created the world. Emphasis on judgment could respond to Marcion's obstinate hostility to any idea of judgment on the part of the God and Father of Jesus Christ. "Forgiveness of sins" could oppose the Montanist unwillingness to restore communion to persons excommunicated for serious offenses. "Resurrection of the flesh" could throw up a bulwark against Gnostic docetism. Except for the last statement, however, none of these phrases was specific enough to require opposition to heresy as an explanation. They certainly lacked the precision of later creeds such as the Nicene, and it is wise to conclude that the normal process of instructing converts supplied the chief motive for framing the Old Roman Symbol. Catechists would have interacted with contemporary currents as they taught the uninstructed, but that would not have forced a constant revision of the confession itself.

Who Teaches?

The crucial issue in the definition of identity by early Christians lay, as Ignatius perceived, not in what was taught to whom but in who taught what. Both scriptures and tradition, even confessions of faith, required interpretation. The question was, *Who* should teach authoritatively?

One group that laid claim to that role was the teachers, both those who taught in catechetical schools and those who taught in schools founded on private initiative, such as Justin's in Rome, Pantaenus's in Alexandria, or Valentinus's in both cities. Jesus was a teacher, and a teaching office existed in early Christianity at least as early as the apostle Paul (1 Cor. 12:28). Teachers such as John Mark traveled with apostles and continued the instruction of converts. A teaching tradition developed out of a strongly felt sense of responsibility for Christianity's evangelistic and missionary enterprise.

For a time the separateness of the teaching office posed no serious threat to Christian identity, but that was no longer true by the late first or early second century. The incorporation of more and more people of highly diversified backgrounds complicated matters immensely. Gradually bishops emerged as the successors of the apostles and thus the authoritative teachers and interpreters of Christian identity.

Acts, the Pastoral Epistles, and *1 Clement* delineate the basic scheme, which would come to be known as apostolic succession: Jesus taught the apostles, and the apostles preached city by city, appointing selected converts to be their successors as presbyter-bishops and deacons (Acts 14:23; Titus 1:5; *1 Clem.* 42ff.). According to Clement, they did so because they knew "there would be strife for the title of bishop" (*1 Clem.* 44.1). Ignatius of Antioch did not develop the succession idea, claiming for himself direct inspiration of the Spirit, but rather seems to have thought of the apostles as in some way subordinate to the bishop. The bishop presided in God's place, the presbyters in that of the apostles (*Magnesians* 6.1). Nothing was to be done without the bishop. Contrariwise, Ignatius disparaged the role of teachers, claiming that Christ is the only Teacher (*Ephesians* 15:1f.).

A full-blown theory of episcopal succession appeared about 180 C.E. in Hegesippus's *Memoirs*. According to Eusebius, on a journey to Rome, Hegesippus, a converted Jew, received the same doctrine from all the bishops he met and concluded that "in every succession and in every city [the doctrine] that is preached as the law and the prophets of the Lord" (Eusebius *H.E.* 4.22.1, 3). He proceeded to draw up a list of episcopal succession for the Church of Rome. His list, and the theory that lay behind it, was elaborated by Irenaeus a few years later in his treatise *Against Heresies*.

Teachers continued to have an important function in early Christianity until the time of Origen (185–254/5). Yet by the end of this period, bishops were gradually supplanting them as the chief interpreters of Christian doctrine.

PART THREE

NEW STATUS 175–313 C.E.

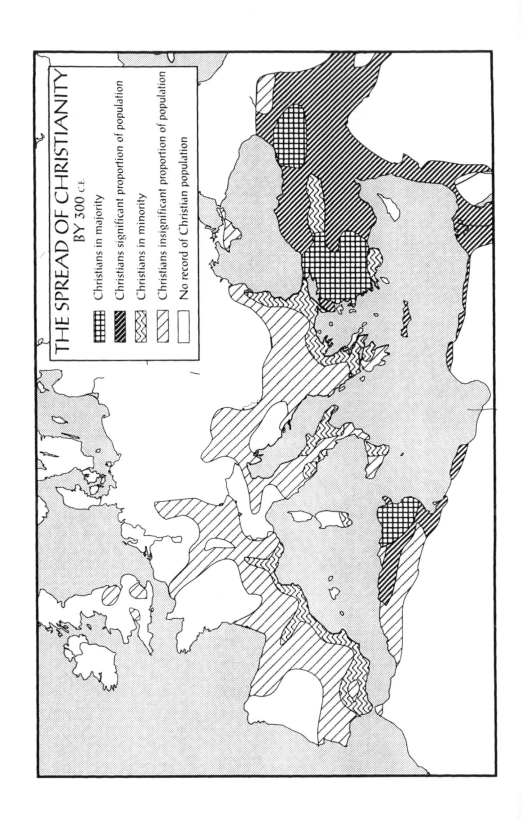

THE SPREAD OF CHRISTIANITY
BY 300 C.E.

Christians in majority

Christians significant proportion of population

Christians in minority

Christians insignificant proportion of population

No record of Christian population

CHAPTER ELEVEN

VICTORIOUS VICTIMS

Christianity experienced a dramatic change of status within the Roman Empire after about 175–180. Largely unnoticed or ignored by people of wealth and status up to that point, it began to attract sufficient numbers from the middle to upper echelons to invite comment and attack from pagans. Celsus, Autolycus, Marcus Aurelius, and the satirist Lucian have been mentioned. Before 217, Philostratus put forth a first-century pagan miracle worker named Apollonius of Tyana as the pagan answer to Jesus. The distinguished Neoplatonist Porphyry (ca. 232–ca. 303) composed a bitter invective *Against the Christians* for their lack of patriotism and unwillingness to support the religious revivals fostered by the emperors Decius (248–253) and Aurelian (253–260). Persecution, once local and spasmodic and unofficial, became universal, systematic, and official as Decius perceived Christianity to be "an empire within the Empire" and a serious threat to his control. When persecution abated, as it did from 203 until 250 and again from 260 until 303, the churches mushroomed. Slowly gaining confidence of toleration, they witnessed with growing boldness and even built buildings specially designed for their assemblies. A new era was dawning.

Why Christianity Succeeded

What accounts for this substantive change in pagan perceptions and fears of Christianity? One factor was the deterioration in the situation of the empire itself. The prosperous years of the Antonines (96–180 C.E.) were followed by a period of continuous internal struggle and threats from new enemies on the frontier—the Alamanni, the Franks (236), the Goths (247–251), and the Sassanids or Neo-Persians (260–268). As in other perilous periods, the fear-ridden responded with suspicion. Emperors increased their control; Diocletian finally consolidated complete power in 284 as he took the title of Dominus. They, like Augustus, sought to undergird centralization by reviving the state cultus. Yet the masses looked for reassurance not to the formalized and ritualized cult of Rome but to oriental cults such as Mithra, Isis and Osiris, Cybele, Judaism, and Christianity—all of which addressed their anxiety and fear.

The anxiety of the masses, already visible in earlier centuries, heightened. A cursory survey of "magical" papyri from the period reveals an increase in resort to the occult to control fate, overcome the demonic, ward off illnesses, gain power over enemies, escape death, and otherwise cope with the fearful unknown. Men and women consulted prophetesses and prophets, augurs, pebbles, horoscopes, sages, and spirits of the departed to gain insight into reality. They sought healing through cults such as that of Aesclepius, which came to new prominence with the publication of *The Life of Apollonius* by Philostratus, or Isis and Osiris, which Lucian propagated in his *Metamorphoses* or *Golden Ass*. Philostratus claimed healings of all kinds—demoniacs, the blind, paralytics, the lame—power to predict plagues and earthquakes or other natural disasters, and even resuscitations of the dead by his hero.

Christianity benefited also from a shift of consciousness that occurred during this era. Platonism eclipsed Stoicism as the dominant philosophy in the latter half of the second century, blended into the mystery cults to pull off a coup for solar monotheism. Neoplatonism was created during the mid-third century by Plotinus (ca. 205–270) and, some scholars argue, Origen, both of whom had studied under Ammonius Saccas (ca. 175–242). It emphasized return of the rational soul to unity with the One as the path of salvation. Philosopher preachers itinerated everywhere urging repentance and moral reform with a view to purging the soul for its reascent to unity. The *Corpus Hermeticum*, popular Platonist writings dating from the second to the fourth centuries, pled with the masses to be "born again" in order to overcome "destiny" (*heimarmene*) or "fate." Some Platonists repeated Plutarch's hierarchical scheme: the sun god; planetary gods; demons or Olympian gods; and spirits of the departed.

Nearly every popular religion aligned itself in some way with solar monotheism. The sun cult of Mithraism, attuned in so many ways with this trend, however, captured the interest of the emperors. The initiation of Emperor Commodus (182–192), spurred on by his wife, Julia Domna, inaugurated the first great period of growth for the sun cult. Septimius Severus (193–211) had erected an elaborate three-story facade called the Septizodium or Septizonium, which had zodiacal implications. On coins he portrayed the sun god wearing the emperor's beard and carrying the imperial title *Invictus* ("unconquerable"). Caracalla (211–218) boasted that when driving his chariot he was imitating the sun. Elagabalus (218–222), whose name is a variant of *heliogabalus* ("devotee of the sun"), adopted it when he entered the hereditary priesthood of the sun god at Emesa and made an elaborate point of installing this deity in Rome when he ascended the imperial throne. Although he failed to convince the Roman populace of the supremacy of his cult, he did not destroy it by his excesses. His successor, Severus Alexander (222–235), featured the sun god on his coins. It remained, however, for Aurelian (270–275) to establish the sun as the supreme god of Rome. Emperors from Aurelian to Constantine pledged their allegiance to the "unconquered sun," and Constantine himself had to choose between this faith and the monotheism of Christianity when he was "converted." After he opted for the latter, he worked diligently to translate images of the sun into Christian symbols.

In assessing the rising fortunes of Christianity during this period—a period that culminated in Constantine's embrace of the church—a question comes to mind: Why Christianity and not Mithraism? The two obviously had much in common: a form of monotheism, strong moral teachings, promise of life after death, rites of initiation and passage that brought tangible assurance. Yet Christianity differed from Mithraism both in inclusiveness and in exclusiveness. Mithraism evidently restricted its membership to men, although it may have sponsored some affiliate societies for women; Christianity included all persons. Contrariwise, Mithraism tolerated crossing lines to join other cults; Christianity did not. Yet what may have attracted an emperor looking for a religion to hold a shattering empire together was the structural cohesiveness of Christianity. Mithraism could not match Christianity's empire-wide network of churches, charities, mission effort, and the like. Nor could it point to a personality and teaching like Jesus', which accounted for the uniqueness of Christianity. Renan was far from accurate when he remarked that if Christianity had not triumphed, Mithra would have. None of the other religions possessed the intense motive for mission that was inspired by the Christian conviction that in Jesus of Nazareth the "last days" had begun.

The Expansion of Christianity

Christianity continued its geographical expansion in most parts of the empire and beyond its fringes during this era. After the establishment of Aelia Capitolina on the site of ancient Jerusalem, the focus shifted to other cities, particularly Caesarea, which became the metropolitanate of Palestine when that system came into existence about 190. A list of bishops can be traced from 190 on. Eusebius, the first church historian, became bishop about 315 and spent much of his career (d. ca. 340) trumpeting the advent of the "millennium" with Constantine. Caesarea's star rose, however, when Origen took up permanent residence there in 232 and established it as "a second Alexandria" in terms of learning and influence. Pamphilus (ca. 240–309), Origen's pupil and successor in Caesarea, collected a great library that survived until the Arab invasions of the seventh century.

In Palestine at large, Christianity survived chiefly in cities and towns with predominantly Gentile populations. The Council of Nicaea in 325 was attended by bishops of fifteen Palestinian cities. Evidence of Christian presence in other cities exists, but information is skimpy. Jewish Christians continued, too, in Pella, but Christianity did not survive in Jewish centers such as Tiberias, Diocaesarea, Nazareth, or Capernaum, where rabbinic influence prevailed.

Although Jerusalem, as Aelia Capitolina, lost most of its Christian as well as Jewish populace, it recouped much of its significance during the third and later centuries by virtue of Christian pilgrimages there. Alexander, Bishop of Jerusalem, established a library in Aelia in the early third century. By the time Constantine was converted, Jerusalem was drawing pilgrims from everywhere. By erecting churches on holy sites, Constantine and his mother, Helena, encouraged a revival whose outcome was the restoration of Jerusalem to a select status alongside Rome, Constantinople, Antioch, and Alexandria at the Council of Constantinople in 381.

Christianity gained a stronger hold in Phoenicia, particularly in coastal cities with largely Greek populaces. Eleven bishops from Phoenicia attended the Council of Nicaea. The center was, of course, Tyre, the leading manufacturing and trading city in the East. The bishop of Tyre played a major role in a Palestinian synod convened to deal with the date of observing Easter. During the persecution under Diocletian, Tyre suffered numerous martyrdoms. Tyre was to Phoenicia what Caesarea was to Palestine.

In Coele-Syria, Antioch remained the chief Christian city. Most bishops had Greek names, indicating a predominantly Gentile constituency in the church. Antioch rivaled Alexandria as a center of Christian learning under the presbyters Malchion, Dorotheus, and Lucian, who was the teacher of Arius. Antioch took part in numerous theological controversies—Montanist, Origenist, Novatianist, as well as Arian. When Rome could not decide between Cornelius and Novatian, the Roman leaders sought the counsel of Fabius of Antioch, Dionysius of Alexandria, and Cyprian of Carthage. Antioch also mediated between the Greek and Latin West and Syriac East. And it hosted numerous synods during the late third and fourth centuries. The synod that tried Paul of Samosata, Bishop of Antioch, in 268 drew no less than seventy or eighty bishops from all provinces stretching from Pontus to Egypt. In the late fourth century, Chrysostom estimated that half of the 200,000 citizens of Antioch (excluding slaves and children) belonged to the chief church. It would be safe to guess that by 313 anywhere between one-fourth and one-half of the populace had become Christian.

Little is known of Christianity in Syria outside of Antioch. By 313, numerous other cities had churches of some size, and bishops came to Nicaea from twenty-one of these. Two country bishops (*chorepiskopoi*) also attended, attesting that the spread covered most of the province.

To the East, Edessa was the center of Syriac-speaking Christianity. Although the legendary correspondence between King Abgar of Edessa and Jesus and the *Doctrine of Addai* (Thaddaeus) conjectured apostolic foundations of the church in Edessa, solid evidence for Christianity is lacking until the third century. Yet by 300 Christianity had established itself strongly in Edessa. A reliable martyrology records the deaths of simple village folk in the great persecution under Diocletian. Bishop Qona began to construct the cathedral of Edessa, probably in 313, and initiated a line of bishops extending into the Middle Ages. Edessa was represented at Nicaea and at all important councils thereafter. One interesting peculiarity of the church in Edessa was the use of Tatian's *Diatessaron* until the time of Rabbula (ca. 420).

Outside of Edessa, Christianity did not have strong representation in Mesopotamia and the East. Bishops of Nisibis, Resaina, Macedonopolis, and Persa, all in the vicinity of Edessa, attended the Council of Nicaea. The *Chronicle of Arbela*, a sixth-century work, recorded the founding of churches in numerous cities in Mesopotamia and Persia during the third century, a fact confirmed by the martyrdoms during the Persian persecution of the fourth century. Constantine's conversion aroused suspicion among the Sassanids that Christians were subversives. According to Origen, the apostle Thomas evangelized Parthia; the third-century *Acts of Thomas* ascribed the evangelization of northwest India to Thomas as well. Traditionally, Andrew evangelized Scythia. Although these traditions have little credibility, they would indicate that Christians were in all three areas in the third century.

Christian churches also existed in Arabia, the region south of the Dead Sea, during this period. Hippolytus alluded to a Christian heretic whom he called "the Arabian Monoimus," and Origen referred to bishoprics there as being grouped together in a single synod. According to Eusebius, "a large number of bishops" disputed with Beryllus of Bostra about 240 when he questioned the concept of Christ's pre-existence. Origen participated in two synods at Bostra, one of which was attended by fourteen bishops. At the latter, bishops debated whether the soul expired and was resurrected with the body. These disputes indicate a continuing Semitic influence on the theology of the area that countered Hellenistic perspectives. About the mid-third century, Arabian Christians, according to Dionysius of Alexandria, sought assistance from Rome. Bishops from Philadelphia, Esbus, Sodom, Bostra, and Beritana (whose location is unknown) participated in the Council of Nicaea.

As in the preceding era, so too in this one Asia Minor supplied Christianity with its most fertile field. Maximinus Daza's edicts against Christians declared that "almost all persons" had gone over to Christianity in Asia Minor (Eusebius *H.E.* 9.9). Lucian of Antioch cited "whole cities" that had become Christian by the time of this persecution, a statement that can be corroborated from other sources.

Paul's home province of Cilicia sent three bishops to the synod of Ancyra in 314 and nine, along with one "country bishop," to the Council of Nicaea in 325. Many Christians from other areas were deported to the mines of Cilicia during the persecution under Diocletian.

Cappadocia was deeply permeated by Christianity in the third century. Tertullian reported a persecution in the province between 180 and 196. In 258, Gothic invaders dragged off many Christian captives, including some clergy and the parents of Ulfilas, the apostle to the Goths. Caesarea, the metropolis of Cappadocia, gained esteem through Alexander, a bishop who later became bishop of Jerusalem, and Firmilian, bishop from ca. 230 until ca. 268. Alexander hosted Clement after he fled Alexandria during the persecution of Septimius Severus. Both Alexander and Firmilian were admirers and supporters of Origen and transmitted Origen's influence to their native province. Cappadocia sent seven bishops and five "country bishops" to Nicaea, testimony surely of its vitality. Through Ulfilas, moreover, Cappadocia was home base for evangelization of the Goths.

In Armenia, Christianity existed at least as early as Marcus Aurelius (161–180), for the Thundering Legion, which was composed largely of Christians, was quartered in Armenia Minor. Dionysius of Alexandria (d. ca. 264) wrote to "the brethren in Armenia, whose bishop is Meruzanes" (Eusebius H.E. 6.46). The persecution of Licinius claimed the lives of forty martyrs in Sebaste, confirmation of the wide dissemination of the gospel throughout Armenia Minor. In 300 C.E., Armenia Major became the first country officially to adopt Christianity. Curiously, the evangelization came from two sources—the Greek Christianity of Caesarea in Cappadocia and the Syriac Christianity of Edessa. The "apostle to Armenia" par excellence was Gregory the Illuminator, who fled to Caesarea due to a Persian persecution and returned to win over King Tiridates (261–317), who evidently adopted Christianity as a bulwark against the Persians. After the conversion of the king, Gregory proceeded systematically to overthrow the Zoroastrian priesthood and to install Christian bishops.

In Pontus, Christianity had a firm grip by 170. Lucian of Samosata charged that "the whole country is full of atheists and Christians" (Alexander Abonuteichos 25.38). Hippolytus reported that a millenarian caused numerous farmers to desert their fields and sell their property in expectation of the return of Jesus a year hence (Commentary on Daniel). Bishops from six cities attended the Council of Nicaea. Amasia was recognized as an episcopal see and metropolis as early as Greogry Thaumaturgus.

In Bithynia, Christianity existed from apostolic times with Nicomedia as the capital. Origen spent time there about 240 C.E. When Diocletian's persecution began, the imperial court itself was full of Christians. The

112

rescript of Maximinus Daza attests the large number of Christians in Nicomedia and throughout the province. Both Hierocles and the other unnamed attacker of Christians lived in Bithynia. Bishops from nine cities and two "country bishops" from Bithynia attended the Council of Nicaea. Novatianists had numerous churches both in Pontus and in Bithynia.

Christianity was also strong in Phrygia when "the New Prophecy" broke out in the late second century, for it met stern resistance. This movement quickly spilled over into Galatia and Asia. Large synods attended by bishops from Phrygia, Galatia, Cilicia, and Cappadocia were held at Iconium and Synnada between 230 and 235 to discuss the validity of heretical baptisms.

The province of Asia continued to be the focal point of Christianity in Asia Minor. Polycrates, Bishop of Ephesus, took the lead against Victor of Rome during the Easter controversy. Although this controversy resulted in a decline of Asian influence, the number of Christians there remained large. Lucian reported that people came "from several towns of Asia" to tend to Christian prisoners. Irenaeus, himself a native of Smyrna, gives evidence of the close ties between Christians of this province and of Rome and Lyons. When the terrible pogrom claimed many lives in Lyons and Vienne in 177, they communicated with the churches of Asia. Asia and Caria sent sixteen bishops to Nicaea.

Little specific information is available on Christianity in the three southernmost provinces of Asia Minor (Lycia, Pamphylia, and Isauria), but they sent no less than twenty-five bishops to Nicaea. One notable figure in Lycia was Methodius, Bishop of Olympus, martyred during the persecution under Diocletian.

There is no information about the state of Christianity on the island of Crete after the second century, and no Cretan bishop attended Nicaea. Bishops from Rhodes, Cos, Lemnos, and Corcyra, however—the other islands—attended. Three bishops of Cyprus came to the Council.

The Greek peninsula, unlike Asia Minor, did not provide a uniformly good field for Christianity. The hold was strong in Thrace and in cities like Athens, Corinth, and Thessalonica, but most of the peninsula had a sparse Christian population before Constantine's conversion. Thracian Christianity was tied closely to Bithynia. Origen mentioned the Athenian church in his treatise *Against Celsus* (248) as "a peaceable and orderly body" not deserving comparison with the refractory civic assembly. He spoke of Corinth in a similar vein. Several bishops from the peninsula were present at Nicaea.

Christianity was beginning to gain a strong foothold in the Balkans in the provinces of Moesia, Dacia, Pannonia, and Dalmatia by the end of this period, for the acts of martyrs record numerous martyrdoms during the persecution under Diocletian. Few bishops from Moesia and Pannonia attended the Council of Nicaea, signifying probably that there were few to attend. Pannonia could claim at least one notable writer in Victorinus of Pettau.

Christianity was thriving in Rome, middle and lower Italy, Sicily, and Sardinia by 325. Even though only four Western bishops attended the Council of Nicaea, the evidence of Western synods at Carthage, Elvira in Spain, Rome, and Arles in Gaul leave little doubt of the strength of Rome. By the time of Fabian (236–250) the Roman church had increased sufficiently to necessitate two major organizational changes: creation of a lower clergy with five ranks and division of the Roman Church into seven districts corresponding to the ancient quarters, each under a deacon. Cornelius (251–253) reported that the Roman rolls included 46 presbyters; 7 deacons; 7 subdeacons; 42 acolytes; 52 exorcists, readers, and doorkeepers; and 1,500 widows or otherwise indigent persons. Forty-six presbyters may indicate the number of congregations in the city, and the total Christian constituency must have been over 30,000. A synod convened in connection with the Novatianist schism was attended by sixty bishops and a still greater number of presbyters and deacons. Dionysius of Rome (259–268) established a system of dioceses under the bishop of Rome and possibly began the division of Rome into something like parishes. Even before Constantine, emperors began to show some deference to the church because of its obvious influence. Gallienus (260–268) inaugurated a long reign of peace, perhaps yielding to pleas from his own household. Even the usurper Maxentius feigned friendliness to Christianity "in order to cajole the people of Rome" (Eusebius *H.E.* 8.14), although he soon took off the mask and became a persecutor.

Under Roman influence, middle and lower Italy had at least a hundred bishoprics by about 250. Upper Italy, however, was less hospitable to the Christian faith. By about 300 C.E., the only known bishoprics were located in Milan, Aquileia, Brescia, Verona, Bologna, and Imola. During the last half of the fourth century, Ambrose of Milan still looked on the province of Aemilia and Liguria as pioneer mission fields.

Missionary efforts of bishops like Irenaeus of Lyons were effective in Gaul and provinces bordering on it. From lists of bishops at synods in Rome (313) and Arles (314) and martyrologies, it is possible to determine that there were bishops in at least twenty towns or cities. Nevertheless, like northern Italy, much of Gaul remained unevangelized until the late fourth century, when Martin of Tours (ca. 375–ca. 397) carried out his remarkable work.

Christian communities existed in Germany as early as 185 C.E., when Irenaeus remarked that the churches planted there adhered to the same kind of tradition as those in Gaul (*Adv. haer.* 1.10). A bishop of Cologne attended the synod of Rome in 313, a deacon the synod of Arles in 314; yet the Roman historian Ammianus Marcellinus called the church in Cologne a "little gathering" still in 355. Evidence for other churches is post-Constantinian. There is, however, evidence for congregations in Augsburg and Regensburg in what was then the Roman province of Rhaetia, which separated Germany and Italy.

It is impossible to determine when Christianity first penetrated the British Isles. Pious legend ascribes the conversion of the first Britons to Joseph of Arimathea and another to missionaries sent in 167 by Pope Eleutherus at the request of Lucius, King of the Britons, but such accounts cannot be given credence. The first of the Church Fathers to include Britons among peoples who had accepted Christ was Tertullian, about 200 C.E. Fifty years later, Origen referred numerous times to Christians in Britain. By the time of Constantine, Britain had numerous churches. Three British bishops (of London, York, and Lincoln) attended the Synod of Arles in 314, but none seems to have been present at Nicaea.

Christianity was thriving in Spain by the time Constantine issued the Edict of Milan in 313. Both Irenaeus (185) and Tertullian (ca. 210) mentioned the existence of churches in Spain. By the mid-third century, Cyprian's reply to a letter from Spanish bishops alluded to Christian communities in Leon, Astorga, Merida, and Sargossa—all cities having large Latin communities. No fewer than thirty-seven Spanish bishops signed the canons of the Synod of Elvira (modern Granada) in 305. The range of issues touched on by the canons suggests that rapidly expanding membership in the churches was generating huge problems in sorting out the demands of Christian faith. A canon disallowing martyrdom for those who attacked images would point to a build up of a violent campaign against paganism, only possible if Christians constituted the majority of the populace in some areas.

Christianity blossomed in North Africa during this period. While Proconsular Africa was reaching its peak of prosperity during the third century, the churches there rivaled those in Asia Minor for growth. Tertullian's writings presupposed a large and strong Christian populace in Carthage, the capital city, and its environs. The deaths of several Christians in Scilli, a town probably located in Numidia, indicate a strong Christian presence there by 180. Tertullian also mentions persecution of Christians in Mauretania. As one might expect, Christianity made its greatest gains among the Latin population at first, but it also won converts among the Punic (Phoenician) settlers who preceded the Roman colonists and even among the Berbers. The Donatist schism that would so trouble the North African Church represented in part a native protest against the Latins.

Carthage, of course, remained the center of African Christianity. Between the time of Tertullian and the time of Cyprian (converted in 248), the church grew rapidly in the capital city of Africa. Seventy African and

115

Numidian bishops attended a synod convened by Agrippinus (no later than 218) to discuss the issue of heretical baptisms; ninety attended a synod convened by Cyprian's predecessor, Donatus (no later than 240); and eighty-seven attended a synod convened by Cyprian himself in 256 or 257. Cyprian's treatise concerning *The Lapsed* shows that Christianity had penetrated all classes of society and obtained a kind of legal status. The church included enough persons of wealth to contribute 100,000 sesterces to the ransoming of Numidian Christians captured by brigands. The Decian persecution understandably took a heavy toll on the church of North Africa, as large numbers of persons apostatized during persecution.

The African churches enjoyed a second period of rapid growth between 260 and 303. Once again, the persecution of Diocletian, although lasting only a couple of years, took a heavy toll in both casualties and apostates, for, by this time, Christianity stood on the verge of converting most of the populace. The number of bishoprics nearly doubled between the death of Cyprian in 258 and the outbreak of persecution. No less than 270 Donatist bishops assembled in Carthage in 330. Like Asia Minor, North Africa had a profusion of bishops, whereas Italy and Egypt had few.

In Egypt, Christianity evidently had an earlier start, but the church there did not emerge into the clear light of day until 180 (Demetrius). The famous school of Alexandria began to thrive about the time Clement arrived. During the persecution under Septimius Severus in 202, Christians were rounded up in Alexandria and were dragged there "from Egypt and all of Thebes" (Eusebius *H.E.* 6.1). When Origen wrote his reply to Celsus in 248, however, he still had to admit that the number of Christians was "extremely scanty" by comparison with the total population; yet he was witnessing sufficient success to contemplate the triumph of Christianity even among the affluent. Although Christianity began among Greek-speaking Christians, it soon spread among those who spoke Coptic, necessitating translation of scriptures into that language, probably as early as the third century. Significant of the growth in the late third and early fourth centuries, Alexander reported the assembling of almost a hundred bishops for a synod around 320, despite the fact that the Egyptian churches opted for fewer bishops.

Missionaries and Their Methods

Missionary methods did not undergo significant alteration during this period. Church planting and churches assembling and worshiping and pursuing the many facets of corporate life remained the lynchpin for the mission. Two long periods when persecution virtually ceased (203–250 and 260–303) permitted the churches to operate more openly and to engage in evangelization with increased effect. The sudden flurry of persecution that burst forth under Diocletian resulted in the destruction of numerous buildings erected during the preceding peaceful interlude.

Itinerants still spread the word. Origen, for instance, knew of persons "who make it their business to itinerate not only through cities, but even villages and country houses that they might make converts to God" (*Against Celsus* 3.9). Soldiers, sailors, merchants, and travelers of all kinds carried the word wherever they went.

Evangelistic schools also continued their efforts. In Alexandria, Clement adapted his appeals and instruction to the wealthy and well-educated who increasingly inquired concerning Christianity. In *Protrepticus*, or *Exhortation to the Greeks*, he urged pagan hearers to forsake their worship of vain and lifeless idols and to worship the Truth, the Logos, who became human for the salvation of humankind. He derided pagan religions for immorality and unreasonableness in worshiping idols. Idol statues, he insisted, are only blocks of wood and stone. Even philosophers failed to adhere to the Truth, though some moved in the right direction. Plato, for instance, argued for one God. More reliable were the Old Testament prophets. Ultimately, however, it is to the Word that one must come because the Word has brought all truth. He is the one human beings must imitate. In *Paedagogos*, or *The Instructor*, Clement offered converts guidance for Christian living. Above all, he enjoined, Christians must follow the Word, who is *the* Instructor, as the unerring Guide. They must come as little children to the Paedagogue, the model of the true life, both human and divine. Looking at specific items, he argued like a good Stoic for the golden mean—in the use of foods, drink, household furnishings, conduct at parties, speech, adornments, sleep, sexual indulgence, clothing, jewelry, and everything else. Christianity in Alexandria had obviously moved up the social ladder, enough so that Clement addressed himself also to an explanation as to how a rich person could be saved even though Jesus' words (Mark 10:17-31) seemed to leave little hope. Jesus' words, spiritually or allegorically interpreted, urged good works rather than literal dispensing of wealth. In *Stromateis*, Clement carried his hearers beyond the level of "faith" to the realm of "gnosis," mystical knowledge, perfection in love. The "gnostic" alone is truly pious.

When Clement fled Alexandria during the persecution under Septimius Severus, Origen, then only seventeen, continued his educational, evangelistic, and apologetic efforts. In 232, however, Origen moved permanently to Caesarea, where he carried on a dialogue with both Jews and Gentiles and trained a cadre of missionary personnel. A major feature of his apology to Judaism was the *Hexapla*, a six-column Old Testament indicating points at which the Greek versions differed from the Hebrew. After supplying the Hebrew and a Greek transliteration in columns 1 and 2, Origen published current Greek versions proceeding from the most literal ones by the Jew Aquila and the Jewish Christian Symmachus to the less literal ones of the Septuagint and Theodotion. At the request of a wealthy sponsor named Ambrose, he replied point by point to the attack on Christianity made by Celsus. Although seventy years old by Origen's day, Celsus's *True Discourse* continued to unsettle conscientious Christians enough that Ambrose thought it should have a reply. More important still from the point of view of the Christian mission, Origen won over and inspired persons like Gregory of Neocaesarea and his brother Athenodorus to return to their native lands as missionaries. Gregory turned out to be one of early Christianity's most innovative missionaries.

Born of pagan parents in Neocaesarea in Pontus around 213, he was trained in law. Brought (as Gregory thought) "providentially" in 233 to Berytus (Beirut) as companions for their sister, whose husband had already been employed there as a lawyer by the governor of Palestine, to engage in further legal studies, Athenodorus and Gregory proceeded on to Caesarea, where they fell into Origen's net. Although they intended to extract themselves and return either to Berytus or to Pontus, they could not escape Origen's personal attentions and persuasive arguments from Greek philosophy.

After five years under Origen's tutelage, Gregory returned to his native city, where he was reluctantly appointed bishop of the church. According to popular legends, he overwhelmed the pagan population by performing miracles (thus the surname Thaumaturgus, "Miracle Worker") such as the moving of a mountain and the drying up of a swamp. In reality, he performed his evangelistic feats in much more ordinary ways. When Christian discipline disintegrated during the invasion of Pontus by the Goths in 253–254, he established grades or degrees of repentance that could restore order. An early biographer claimed that whereas there were but seventeen Christians in Pontus when Gregory returned, when he died in about 270, there were but seventeen pagans.

At the end of this period, new approaches to evangelization emerged with the conversion of nations or peoples to the Christian faith through the conversion of their rulers. The first example was Armenia, supposedly won over through the work of Gregory the Illuminator (ca. 240–332).

Emphasis on the miraculous in accounts of Christian missionary endeavors was not uncommon from apostolic times on and seems to have increased as Christians came more and more into contact with the barbarians. Claims of healing, prophecy, and other phenomena associated with the effort to win the heathen probably inspired anti-Christian treatises such as Philostratus's *Life of Apollonius of Tyana*, composed about 220. Hierocles, governor of Bithynia, wrote a second life about 303, which evoked a refutation by Eusebius of Caesarea. Pagans, too, could play the power game.

CHAPTER TWELVE

THE SEED OF THE CHURCH

The success of Christianity in attracting not only persons of lower socioeconomic status but also those of the upper classes brought it increasingly into public view and precipitated a more serious danger. Whereas prior to this period harassment and persecution arose largely from popular hostility, now they came increasingly from official sources and took on a more systematic and organized form. The more Christianity succeeded, the more it threatened a deteriorating and unstable government. The emperors, however, were by no means consistent, and the churches took advantage of every respite to enlist converts and to solidify their own constituency. Four severe spates of persecution came as heavy blows, but they did not destroy the growing movement. The blood of martyrs only served, as Tertullian insisted, as "seed."

Septimius Severus's Severity

Christianity survived four major imperial efforts to suppress it and nullify its influence within the empire. The first occurred under Septimius Severus (193–211). At the beginning of his reign, judging from Tertullian's writings, Christians stood in danger still of punishment for the name alone. They were summarily condemned if they admitted to being Christians. If they did not admit their faith, they might be tortured or even executed. No punishment was too cruel—beheading, piercing with a red hot tong, crucifixion, being fed to wild beasts (Tertullian *Apol.* 12). Some judges loved to dishonor Christian women rather than put them to death (*Apol.* 50). Although Septimius Severus, like his predecessor, Commodus, showed some sympathy for Christianity early in his reign, he issued a severe edict against it in 202 during a sojourn in Palestine, prohibiting conversions either to Judaism or Christianity under threat of severe penalties (Spartian *Severus* 17). For the first time an emperor, evidently alarmed by rapid expansion, sought to put a stop to the growth of the church by punishing converts and their converters.

Severus's edict struck hard at centers of Christian growth. It was implemented first in Alexandria, which Severus entered via Arabia in 202, where

119

the famous school begun by Pantaenus flourished under the leadership of Clement. Citing Jesus' instruction to flee from one city to another, Clement took flight. Many other devout Christians, including Leonides, father of Origen, lost their lives. Origen would have followed his father into martyrdom save for the quick thinking of his mother, who hid his clothes. At age eighteen, he succeeded Clement as head of the school. Many of his students, evidently adhering to his strictures against flight to avoid persecution, went bravely to their deaths (Eusebius *H.E.* 6.1-3).

Severus's persecution also dealt a blow to Christianity in the Roman province of Africa, especially Carthage, a thriving center of growth. According to Tertullian, not only individuals but also congregations paid to escape persecution and martyrdom (*On Flight in Persecution* 13). Tertullian, soon to join the Montanists, took a dim view of flight to avoid persecution. The names of many African martyrs are known. Most were ordinary saints like the catechumens Perpetua and Felicitas, whose unflinching faithfulness in the face of torture and death bears witness to the excellence of Christian formation in this period.

In the province of Asia, the edict of Severus also claimed numerous victims. Although not as well documented as the African persecution, it coincided with the Montanist heyday and claimed many in that sect. Less is known of Severus's persecution in Rome and Gaul, but we do have evidence of martyrdom among the disciples of Irenaeus of Lyons, if not of Irenaeus himself.

Thirty-seven Years of Peace

Severus's son and successor, Caracalla, continued his father's effort to suppress Christianity for only a few years. Persecution was especially bitter in Africa under Scapula Tertullus, the proconsul to whom Tertullian addressed his brief but strong letter. After 212, the churches enjoyed thirty-seven years of relative peace; neither Elagabalus nor Alexander Severus wished to disturb Christians. Elagabalus viewed anything oriental, including Judaism and Christianity, as useful in fostering his solar monotheism. Alexander Severus (222–235) not only tolerated but also proved to be a benefactor of Christianity. His mother, Mamme, had studied Christianity and, during a stay at Antioch, received Origen with great honors (Eusebius *H.E.* 6.21). From her or from Christians who filled his palace, Alexander gained respect for Christian discipline and the maxims of the gospel, inscribing the Golden Rule on the facade of his palace and ordering it heralded during execution of criminals (Lampridius *Alexander Severus* 51). He practiced syncretism, including in his pantheon statues of Alexander the Great, the more noble Caesars, Apollonius of Tyana, Orpheus, Abraham, and Jesus (*Lampridius* 29)! According to his biographer, Lampridius (43), Alexander wanted to build a temple to Christ and elevate him to the rank of the gods. More important for the churches, Alexander permitted churches to hold title to property. Unfortunately, the emperor's relative impotence as a ruler still permitted much violence against Christians.

A brief flurry of localized persecution under Alexander's successor, Maximin (235–238), interrupted the calm. Maximin, alarmed by the number of Christians in the imperial household, directed his repression at church leaders as those responsible for teaching. In Rome, authorities exiled to Sardinia Pontianus, Bishop of Rome, and Hippolytus, a presbyter who separated from the Roman Church in 217. Pontianus died as a result of tortures a year later. His successor, Anteros, may also have suffered martyrdom, dying after just over a month in office. In Caesarea, Maximin summoned Ambrose, Origen's benefactor who had followed him from Alexandria, a scholarly priest named Prototectus, and several others to Germany to appear before him. It was in these circumstances that Origen composed his *Exhortation to Martyrdom*, addressed to Ambrose. If he answered the summons at all, Ambrose lived to tell about it, for he was still living in 247 or 249 during the reign of Philip (242–249), who was, according to Jerome (*On Illustrious Men* 54), "the first Christian emperor."

Philip, a native of Trachonitis in Transjordan, may have been born into a Christian family. His ruthless seizure of power from Gordian, however, caused Christians to look askance at him. When he sought to participate in the paschal vigil at Antioch, the bishop required him to do penance "on account of many charges made concerning him" (Eusebius *H.E.* 6.34). Although Philip sought to improve public morality, he continued traditional religious observances, and we can see little of the effects of Christianity, save perhaps in the omission of gladiatorial combats. However, he did issue a rescript declaring "a general amnesty which permits the return of exiles and deportees" (*Codex Just.* IX 51.7). Even more than Alexander Severus, Philip allowed Christians to be Christians. The Empress Otacilia Severa made no mystery of her faith. She corresponded with Origen, and according to Eusebius (*H.E.* 6.36), Origen wrote to both emperor and empress. Fabian, Bishop of Rome, was permitted to retrieve the body of Pontianus and return it for burial in the cemetery of Callistus in Rome, an act dependent entirely on imperial permission. Origen's wide travels during the period bear witness to the favorable situation for Christianity's expansion. Success, however, resulted in a dampening of discipline that left the churches poorly prepared for the reversal of imperial favor under Decius (249–253) and Valerian (253–260).

Decius's Devastation

Partiality shown to Christianity by Philip evidently enraged pagans throughout the empire and precipitated a savage rebellion that led to his overthrow and death and replacement by Decius, a Pannonian serving as a commander of legions in Mysia and Pannonia. Dionysius, Bishop of Alexandria, described how, a year before Philip's defeat at the hands of Decius, pagan mobs unleashed their fury against hapless Christians. Christians could not pass through any street or alley without risking life and limb. Only the intervention of imperial troops restored order during the remainder of Philip's reign (Eusebius *H.E.* 6.41.1-11). Such outbursts doubtless took place throughout the empire and prepared the way for Decius's vicious edict against Christianity.

Like his ancient predecessors, Decius could not distinguish loyalty to the ancestral gods from loyalty to the state. Reacting, Christians thought, against Philip, he saw in this fast-growing religion a little empire within the empire. Faced with severe threats from barbarians on the frontier, he sought to consolidate his control within, viewing Christianity as the major obstacle to that goal. There were a great number of Christian soldiers in the army, as even Tertullian conceded, despite objections to Christians' serving there (*Apol.* 37, 42; *On the Crown of the Soldier*). Yet Christians did act circumspectly regarding those aspects of military or public service that bore so heavily the imprint of the state cultus. Some groups, such as Montanists, took a still stronger and often belligerent stand against either.

For the first time, persecution arose not from religious fanaticism or popular hatred but from cold and calculated administrative logic designed to destroy Christianity as a fearful threat to the empire. To kill all of them was impossible, given their numbers. The aim was to terrify by examples and thus frighten away any who would join them—using long prison terms, torture, temptations, seizure of children to be raised as pagans. Where Septimius Severus concentrated on converts and converters and Maximin on bishops and teachers, Decius ordered all citizens, not just Christians, to obtain a *libellus* stating that they had poured a libation, offered a sacrifice, and eaten meat offered in sacrifice. Three types of punishment were prescribed: banishment, confiscation of property, and capital punishment. Judging by actual cases, local authorities could exercise considerable discretion in how they applied each. The number of deaths was relatively small since Decius sought to induce conformity and commitment and destroy Christianity's infrastructure rather than kill.

The Decian persecution had a far more devastating effect than earlier ones, partly because of its systematic, organized, and universal character, but more particularly because Christians converted during the long era of peace were unprepared for it. Having grown accustomed to tolerance and, in some places, even favor, they would not have understood fully what constituted Christian commitment. Throughout the empire, therefore, a considerable portion of the flock stepped forward voluntarily to offer sacrifices. Others obtained the required certificates by secret means to avoid outright apostasy. Leading bishops such as Cyprian in Carthage, himself a recent convert, and Dionysius of Alexandria went into hiding at the urging of fellow clergy and people, a decision that caused serious problems later on. Some other bishops and clergy shamelessly hastened to deny their faith, thus giving the authorities exactly what they sought—apostasy rather than martyrdom. At Saturnum, Bishop Repostus led a group of people to offer the sacrifice. Fortunatus, Jovinus, and Maximus, three other bishops, also gave in. According to Cyprian, Spanish bishops Basilides of Sargossa and Martial of Merida complied with some eagerness. Subsequently, Basilides repented, sought restoration as a layman, and then tried to regain his office by appealing to Stephen, Bishop of Rome, without telling him of his apostasy (Cyprian *Ep.* 67.6).

Not all Christians acted unfaithfully. There were notable martyrs. Although the Decian persecution did not single out bishops and other leaders, it turned in that direction as a way to force them to set an example of unfaithfulness. Since Decius left considerable leeway for local enforcement, however, persecution varied from place to place and so, too, did steadfastness. At Rome, Fabian was martyred on January 20, 250, scarcely three months after Decius ascended the throne. Other Roman clergy and some laypersons received lengthy prison sentences designed to break their spirits. In Africa, about which we have the most extensive information, thanks to Cyprian's letters, persecution was particularly severe. Although Cyprian escaped for a time by taking advantage of connections in the upper echelons of society, others did not. Alongside a huge number of apostates were many others among both clergy and laity who offered faithful witness in prison as "confessors."

Presbyters, deacons, and laypersons alike risked imprisonment themselves to tend the physical and spiritual needs of the confessors. Despite such solicitude, a number perished of hunger or of other causes. At Alexandria, where the revolt took place against Philip, Christians also suffered harsh treatment, especially at the hands of irate mobs anxious to see the edict of Decius enforced. Although Decius's edict achieved its aim here, too, among large numbers, it met resistance. Dionysius related the story of an old man named Julian who, enfeebled by gout, had to be carried by two other men before the authorities. One of his helpers immediately capitulated, but the aged Julian and the other man, Eunus Cronion, refused to yield despite being carried on camels throughout the city and beaten. The mob finally burned them in quick lime. A soldier named Besas, standing by as these men were led away, opposed their attackers and, after a vain battle, was beheaded (Eusebius *H.E.* 6.41.14-16). Many Egyptian Christians fled, like Dionysius, to regions almost as dangerous as Alexandria, wandering in deserts and mountains and dying of hunger, thirst, cold, disease, robbers, or wild beasts (Eusebius *H.E.* 6.42). Dionysius survived in a wild section of Libya until the persecution ended. In his absence, four presbyters and three deacons carried on in Alexandria. Martyrdoms also occurred in other places—Italy, Gaul, Greece, Asia Minor—but evidence is scanty and unreliable. In Antioch, Babylas, who had refused permission for Emperor Philip to celebrate Easter before doing penance, died in prison (Eusebius *H.E.* 6.39.4) or, as Chrysostom reported (*Saint Babylas* 11), was beheaded. At Caesarea in Palestine, Alexander, an intimate friend of Origen, also died in prison (Eusebius *H.E.* 6.39.2). Origen, then in his sixties, survived severe treatment. Obviously hoping so eminent a figure would renounce the faith, the authorities stretched his feet four notches apart in the stocks "for many days," threatened him with fire, and inflicted numerous other cruelties. The great "Adamantius" (Flint) did not flinch, but such tortures hastened his death in 254 or 255.

Fortunately, Decius's devastation did not last long. By mid-251, most prisoners had been freed and persecution had ceased. Decius had evidently concluded by this time that the empire had worse enemies than Christians. Although he did not revoke his edict, he ceased to incite magistrates and governors to enforce it. Meantime, his attention turned again to the Gothic threat on the Danube. The Goths had already sacked Thrace and were threatening Macedonia. Departing from Rome in the spring of 251, Decius perished soon afterward along with his sons in a battle against the Goths.

Although Decius's successor, Gallus, revived the persecution, Christians proved better equipped to face it. In addition to the experience of persecution, an empire-wide plague, during which Christians distinguished themselves by caring for the dying, toughened them. Unfortunately, most pagans blamed Christians for this calamity as they had done for others. In Carthage the cry went up, "Cyprian to the lion!"

Gallus, frightened by the progress of the epidemic, wanted to revitalize worship of the gods and thus commanded celebration of solemn sacrifices in all cities. Like his mentor, Decius, he attacked first the Bishop of Rome, Cornelius, shipping him off into exile in Centumcelles, where he died in June 253. He also dispatched Cornelius's successor, Lucius, elected in July. Contrary to their behavior under Decius, Roman Christians surprised pagans by imitating their leader in seeking exile, prison, or martyrdom. Some of the lapsed of the Decian persecution proved boldest, many shedding their blood as martyrs. Cyprian repudiated Demetrian's charge that Christians provoked the gods and thence caused all kinds of maladies to befall people. Dionysius of Alexandria, likewise, reproved the emperor for persecuting persons who had sustained the empire with their prayers.

Gallus did not have long to pursue his policy of persecution. He and his son Volusian were killed by the legate of Pannonia, Emilian, who had halted a Gothic invasion. When Volusian's own forces revolted and killed him, Valerian, dispatched earlier by Gallus to stop Volusian, was acclaimed emperor by his troops. Wanting widespread popular support, he immediately halted the persecution of Christians.

Valerian's Vindictiveness

After four years of peace, Christians did not anticipate the severe persecution initiated by Valerian in 257. Dionysius of Alexandria remarked that the emperor's household "was full of devout believers and a church of God" (Eusebius *H.E.* 7.10.3). A ruler who tended to rely on the advice of intimates, early on he not only tolerated but also showed partiality to Christianity. What, then, changed his mind? Several controversies rocked the churches—the Novatianist schism; efforts of Spanish bishops of Leon and Merida to dethrone Stephen, the bishop of Rome, and retain their sees; the rebaptismal controversy—and these could have caused a shift of opinion. More likely, however, the key issue was financial. In documents relative to his persecution, Christianity was denounced for its powerful hierarchy, extensive properties, and wealth. At the time of Cornelius, the Roman Church cared for 1,500 indigents. In Carthage, Cyprian raised 100,000 sesterces to redeem captives taken by nomadic tribes in Numidia. Such charities astounded pagans and aroused suspicions of sinister hoards of money that weakened the already flagging economy. The question of money figured heavily in Valerian's attack on the churches. Before his edict he interrogated and put to death a wealthy family of Christians noted for their charities. His counselors apparently convinced him that the material prosperity of the churches, if tolerated too long, posed a real danger to the empire.

Valerian's edict, unlike Decius's, did not demand a denial of faith but sought rather to secure a recommitment to the national religion by sacrificing to the gods of the empire. Christians could continue to worship Christ so long as they also took part in official ceremonies and burned incense at the feet of the gods—kind of a pledge of allegiance. In addition, the edict sought to dissolve Christian control over cemeteries, the legal base for Christian assemblies. Instead of making general application, it named only bishops, presbyters, and deacons for submission. Valerian sought to make neither numerous victims nor apostates. He wanted, rather, to obtain an official adherence to the gods of the state by way of the submission of the chief leaders in the churches. The laity would run into trouble only if they tried to frequent the cemeteries or hold assemblies. Refusal to swear allegiance to the gods was punishable by exile, visiting cemeteries or holding assemblies punishable by death. In the latter, Valerian surpassed the intolerance of Decius and Gallus.

Valerian's first edict resulted in the exile of some of Christianity's most cultured and well-educated leaders. Cyprian, the transcript of whose hearing before the Proconsul Paternus has been preserved, was exiled for a time and then put to death. When the proconsul asked why he hadn't followed the emperor's directive, Cyprian replied, "I am a Christian and a bishop. I don't know any gods except the one true God who has made heaven and earth, the sea and all that they contain. It is this God that we Christians serve." When he refused to budge from this decision, Paternus sentenced him to exile at Curubis. Cyprian, trained in law, readily accepted this order, but he refused to divulge the names of his presbyters on the grounds that Roman law forbade *delatio.* The proconsul declared that he would find them and noted that the rest of the edict prohibited holding assemblies and entering cemeteries on penalty of death (*Acts of Saint Cyprian*). The exile was not harsh. The authorities, however, arrested other bishops, presbyters, and deacons as well as laypersons and sentenced most to the mines— evidently because they continued to meet or use cemeteries in contravention of the edict—and some to death. Cyprian corresponded with confessors from exile, encouraging and counseling them in their frightful situation. Judging by letters exchanged, the prisoners were whipped, branded on the forehead, chained to avoid escape, and forced to labor long hours extracting gold and silver without adequate food or bodily care.

Dionysius of Alexandria received more lenient treatment at the hands of Aemilian, the prefect of Egypt. Accompanied by a presbyter, three deacons, and a visiting "brother" from Rome, Dionysius rejected the prefect's demand that they hold no more assemblies, saying, "We must obey God rather than human beings" (Acts 5:29). Aemilian sentenced him to exile in a little village called Cephro in Libya, threatening due punishment either for assembling or frequenting cemeteries. When Dionysius gathered a flock in Cephro, Aemilian transferred him to "rougher and more Libyan-like places," but these turned out to be still more favorable for gathering with other Christians. In his letter (in Eusebius *H.E.* 7.12), Dionysius proceeded to name a whole list of indignities heaped on the faithful—imprisonment, confiscation, proscription, plundering of goods, loss of dignities, and the like. Those persons brought to trial for violation of the edict usually were tortured and put to death.

Valerian toughened his edict in 258. In a rescript sent to the Roman senate, he ordered that "bishops and priests and deacons should be put to death immediately; senators and outstanding men and Roman knights should lose their rank and also be deprived of their goods and, if, after this, they still persevered as Christians, they should be decapitated; matrons should have their goods confiscated and be sent into exile; members of the imperial household who had confessed either before or now, should have their goods confiscated and be sent as prisoners to the emperor's estates" (Cyprian *Ep.* 80). The emperor aimed to bring down Christianity from the top.

The new edict resulted almost immediately, on August 6, 258, in the death of Sixtus, Bishop of Rome, and four deacons. The schismatic Bishop Hippolytus, a confessor during the persecution of Maximin, also suffered martyrdom. In Africa, Galerius Maximus, succeeding Paternus as proconsul, recalled Cyprian from exile in Curubus and confined him to a residence in Carthage. On August 24, 258, the proconsul surprised a great number of believers of every age at worship and summarily had them decapitated or, according to Prudentius, buried alive in a lime pit (*On the Crown* 3.76-87). A short time afterward he summoned Cyprian and, when the bishop refused to repudiate his faith, sentenced him to beheading.

In this persecution, unlike the Decian, the faithful did not apostatize *en masse*. To the contrary, in this instance, as Cyprian thanked God for the sentence, a multitude cried out, "We, too, we want to be beheaded with him." Cyprian's martyrdom flashed a signal for persecution throughout Africa. This time most remained firm in their commitment. Indeed, in Africa hysteria may have impelled some deliberately to seek martyrdom in imitation of Cyprian's example. The persecution was more violent still in the neighboring province of Numidia, where nomadic tribes threatened and heightened Roman fears of Christianity. The authorities enforced the letter of the second edict, recalling many exiles to put them to death. In Caesarea, according to Eusebius (*H.E.* 7.12), three persons presented themselves to the imperial legate and were fed to wild beasts. Here and there, some did lapse, but we find few references of this type in the Valerian era.

In the summer of 258, Valerian headed east to head the campaign against the Neo-Persian or Sassanid armies threatening to overrun Asia Minor, leaving Gallienus in charge of the West. A disorganized and weakened army left the northern frontier exposed to barbarians. In North Africa, Berbers continued to wreak havoc. While both emperors were engaged in wars on different fronts, the Boradi and then the Goths invaded Asia Minor. Valerian succeeded in preventing a union of Gothic and Persian forces but could do little more. Leading an army half-decimated by famine and disease, he suffered a humiliating defeat at the hands of Shapur and was taken captive to spend the rest of his years in chains as a personal slave of the Persian king. Christians looked on this as a just retribution for the vicious persecution he had inflicted on them.

Forty Years of Peace

Very soon after receiving news of his father's capture, Gallienus rescinded his edicts against the churches and, according to Eusebius, "directed the bishops to perform in freedom their customary duties" (*H.E.* 7.13). For the first time since Nero, Christianity became a *religio licita*, permitted to reclaim churches and cemeteries, the former having been sold and the latter merely closed by authorities. The Edict of Milan in 313 granted no more than this. What Gallienus's motives were cannot be definitely established. Some point to his Neoplatonism, others to the influence of his wife, Salonina, believed to have been a Christian; but evidence is scanty.

Christianity fared well under the so-called Thirty Tyrants who shared Gallienus's rule in different parts of the empire. Where persecution occurred, it was due to local hostility or confusion about Christian legal status. In Alexandria, Aemilian, the prefect who had sent Dionysius into exile, delayed the application of Gallienus's edict during a brief coup attempt, but his revolt was quickly squelched. Christians once again gained popular support through heroic deeds during a plague that struck the city at the time.

For more than forty years (260–304) Christians enjoyed only relative and not unqualified peace. Under Claudius (268–270), Gallienus's edict remained in effect, but the Senate may have expressed its hatred of Gallienus by making Christians expiatory victims for a war against the Goths (in 269), although Rome and Italy were the only areas from which came reports of martyrdom during this period. Aurelian (270–275), however, intending to restore both religious and imperial unity by way of Mithraic solar monotheism, found Christianity standing in his path. In the late fourth century, Mithraism, a cult in which Aurelian's mother was a priestess, was the most widespread form of solar monotheism, especially in the camps along the Danube. Aurelian erected a temple of the sun on the Quirinal in 274 that surpassed all others in magnificence and proclaimed the Sol Invictus "lord and master of the Empire." Despite Christian unwillingness to be merged into his syncretistic religion, Aurelian did not begin persecuting Christians until his later years. In 272, he forced Paul of Samosata, denounced for heresy by a council of bishops in 268, to relinquish church properties to "those in communion with the bishops of Italy and the bishop of Rome" (Eusebius *H.E.* 7.30.19), an indication of Christianity's standing at the time. Aurelian evidently initiated some persecution in 274, but accounts are not reliable. If he issued a general edict, it has not survived; in any event, Aurelian was assassinated in March 275 before his edict could have had widespread effect. In the seven-month interregnum following his death, however, the still predominantly pagan senate continued to persecute

Christians in Rome and its environs on the charge that they abandoned and led others to abandon Rome's ancestral gods. A delayed effect of Valerian's order may also have caused some deaths in other provinces after his demise.

Assumption of imperial office by Tacitus, an old senator descended from the famous historian, on September 25, 275, signaled a new period of peace, but Tacitus died after holding office only six months. His successor, Probus, a highly competent army captain who had achieved many victories over barbarians, showed little interest in religion. Here and there, however, popular fear and hostility resulted in Christian martyrdom during this period, especially in instances where Christians let their zeal get out of hand.

The Great Persecution

Nothing definite can be said about persecution of Christians during the brief joint reigns of Carus and his two sons, Carinus, who ruled the West, and Numerian, who ruled the East. Christianity's worst hour, however, occurred under Carinus's competitor for rule of the West: Diocletian, who ruled longer than any other emperor (284–304). Scattered instances of persecution occurred during the joint reign of Diocletian and Maximian (286–292), a bitter opponent of Christianity. Early on, however, Diocletian himself seemed to favor Christianity. His wife, Prisca, and daughter Valeria were either Christians or catechumens (Lactantius *On the Deaths of Persecutors* 15). Many Christians held positions in the imperial household, and, according to Eusebius, Diocletian "treated them like his own children" (*H.E.* 8.6.1). He also extended favors to Christians who wanted to hold public office, dispensing them from the duty of offering sacrifices, as he did his wife and daughter. One small town in Phrygia had only Christian officials (Eusebius *H.E.* 8.11). Many cities extended Christians, who represented a sizable part of the populace of Asia Minor, considerable freedom vis-à-vis public religious observances. Governors and magistrates accorded bishops of churches genuine respect (Eusebius *H.E.* 8.1). The churches built houses of worship comparable to public buildings. In Rome, Christians enlarged and adorned the catacombs and erected new buildings in the very center of the city. Many congregations, believing themselves secure, forgot the still-present dangers.

At Milan in 292, Diocletian and Maximian, who both held the title of Augusti, decided further to partition imperial administration by appointing Galerius and Constantius Chlorus as Caesars to serve under them. Diocletian, as chief emperor, retained the East with Egypt, Libya, the islands in the Mediterranean, and Thrace. Galerius, Diocletian's Caesar, took charge of the Danubian provinces, Illyria, Macedonia, Greece, and Crete. Maximian kept Italy, Africa, and Spain. Constantinus Chlorus ruled in Gaul and Britain. Galerius hated Christianity passionately; Constantius Chlorus, though a pagan, was at least tolerant.

During this period of the tetrarchy (292–302), Diocletian issued a rigorous edict against the Manichaeans as a Persian sect dangerous to the empire (*Gregorian Code* 14.4.4). As for Christians, however, he seems first to have undertaken to purge them from the army, where by this time they served under all four rulers in substantial numbers. Only in Africa did Christians still manifest much reserve about military service, perhaps under influence of Tertullian, and it may have been an incident there in 295 that touched the rulers' alarm button. Maximilian, the twenty-one-year-old son of a soldier, refused conscription on the grounds that a Christian could not serve in the army. The repeated pleas of Dion Cassius, proconsul of Africa, citing Christian service in all of the rulers' armies, failed to persuade him otherwise, and he was beheaded. According to Eusebius, the persecution that followed this incident was first initiated by Galerius, who now gave vent to a long-restrained hatred of Christianity (*H.E.* 8.1.7-8). Galerius proceeded cautiously at first, stripping officers of their titles and mustering out the rank and file, but he gradually ordered more and more put to death (Eusebius *H.E.* 8.4.4-5). Many Christians hastened to leave the army, but numerous others remained and died as martyrs. Diocletian and Constantius Chlorus evidently were not directly involved in this military purge, though it occurred in the East under Galerius and in the West under Maximian. Yet Diocletian apparently changed his mind in 302 during a visit to Antioch when a Christian disrupted a sacrifice by making the sign of the cross (the offender was not put to death but was expelled from the palace guard [Lactantius *On the Deaths of Persecutors* 10]).

Diocletian issued his first general edict in February 303, commanding that churches be leveled to the ground, scriptures burned, persons holding places of honor degraded, and household servants (perhaps commoners) who refused to submit deprived of freedom (Eusebius *H.E.* 8.2.4). Galerius wanted the emperor to require all Christians to sacrifice, but Diocletian did not include this requirement in the first edict. The edict went into immediate effect in Nicomedia, where city authorities tore down the doors of the main church, burned scriptures, and took whatever booty they could lay hands on (Lactantius *Deaths of Persecutors* 12). Watching from a window of the imperial palace, Diocletian vetoed Galerius's suggestion that they burn the building for fear of a city-wide conflagration. According to Lactantius (who was no friend of Galerius), the caesar, not content with the destruction of the building, had secret agents set fire to the palace and blamed Christians for it. Diocletian had his domestics tortured to uncover the truth. When he failed to obtain confessions from them, Galerius set fire to the palace again and fled. The whole affair threw Diocletian into a mad rage of persecution, compelling all in the city of Nicomedia to offer sacrifices and sending an order to Maximian and Constantius Chlorus to require the same (Lactantius *Deaths of Persecutors* 14-15). Magistrates in Nicomedia and in surrounding cities proceeded to carry out this order. The edict, however, made its way slowly to other parts of the empire, requiring at least two or three months, for instance, to reach Palestine. In the West, Maximian enforced the edict vigorously in Italy, Africa, and Spain. Constantius Chlorus, however, seems to have enforced only the provision calling for destruction of churches. During this phase of persecution, authorities forced many to surrender copies of scripture, precipitating in 311 a bitter debate concerning apostasy that resulted in the Donatist schism.

Some kind of an uprising in Cappadocia and Syria became the pretext for two new edicts against Christianity. The second edict ordered all ecclesiastical leaders arrested and imprisoned. A third arranged for all prisoners to be set free on the condition that they offer sacrifices to the gods but stipulated that those who refused be punished (Eusebius *H.E.* 8.6.8-10). The issuance of these new edicts may have had something to do with Christians' refusal to accept military conscription in some areas. From 303 on, Diocletian sought to build up his army in order to fortify the frontiers. When Christians in Cappadocia refused conscription, troops stationed there proceeded either to demolish or to set fire to churches.

Illness struck the emperor late in the year 303. At first he resisted Galerius's demand that he and Maximian step aside, but they finally relinquished their titles to Galerius and Constantius Chlorus, appointing Severus as Caesar in the West and Maximin Daia, Galerius's nephew, as Caesar in the East. At this point, Galerius intensified the persecution. This tetrarchy did not last long, however, for Constantius Chlorus, in ill health, recalled from Britain his son Constantine, whom Galerius reluctantly appointed Caesar, elevating Severus to Augustus. On the death of Constantius in 306, Maximin's nephew Maxentius sought to usurp the title Maximian had abdicated, but Constantine's soldiers proclaimed Constantine emperor instead, and Galerius declared Severus Augustus. Maximian, however, defeated Severus and had him imprisoned and executed. In his place, Galerius appointed Licinius. From 308 to 310, therefore, Galerius and Maximin Daia ruled the East, while Licinius, Constantine, and Maxentius ruled the West after the removal of Maximian.

From 304 to 311, Christians suffered severely in the eastern and part of the western portions of the empire. Many, unaccustomed after years of relative security to such severity, defected from Christianity. Some authorities, squeamish about applying the edict, encouraged confessors to fulfill the requirement for all persons to sacrifice to the gods in minimal ways, perhaps creating confusion in the process. Yet many Christians remained steadfast and unyielding when confronted with the order to sacrifice to the gods. They continued to gather for worship, sometimes secretly but often openly, until authorities seized them and dragged them away.

In 304, with Diocletian sick and discouraged, Galerius issued a fourth edict requiring "that all citizens in every country in each city offer sacrifices publicly and libations to the idols" (Eusebius *Martyrs of Palestine* 3). Here was a declaration of war not only on churches, scriptures, and members of the clergy but also on all the faithful without regard to status, age, or sex. Galerius probably applied the edict first in Macedonia and Pannonia. From there persecution spread elsewhere—Cilicia, Thrace, Galatia, Cappadocia, Syria, Phoenicia, Palestine, Egypt, Rome, Italy, Sicily, Africa, and Spain. Everywhere authorities did their best to force apostasies. Acts of martyrs recount the process repeated with dull regularity:

"Why didn't you sacrifice to the gods as the emperors ordered?"

"Because I am a Christian."

"Don't you realize the penalties for disobedience?"

"Yes, but I am happy to suffer for Christ."

Beatings, torture, other indignities ensued, often accompanied by sentencing to prison or death. What is remarkable is that so many persons remained faithful in the face of such sufferings, witnessing perhaps to the effectiveness of the preparation and support they received.

By the end of 305, the persecution appears to have diminished somewhat even in the East, becoming less frequent and less widespread. In the first half of 306, however, a "second war" of extermination renewed the old fervency in all provinces governed by Maximin and Galerius (Eusebius *Martyrs of Palestine* 4.8). Fortunately, this edict did not change the situation of Christians in the areas ruled by Constantius and then by Constantine, Licinius, and to some extent under the pretender Maxentius.

In 310, Galerius contracted a cancer that claimed his life within a year. Finding no remedy in medicine or the pagan cults of Apollo and Asclepius, according to Eusebius and Lactantius, Galerius turned in desperation to Christians, halting the persecution and permitting them to exist and to reestablish their assemblies with the proviso that they pray for his healing, for the welfare of the state, and for their own welfare. Although probably written in 310, this edict ending persecution was not promulgated until April 30, 311. The names of Constantine and Licinius also headed it. Since Maximin Daia's name was not attached, it did not apply in Cilicia, Syria, or Egypt, but it had some effect there anyway. Sabinus, prefect of the Praetorium, circulated an order to provincial governors that, in effect, recognized the rescript of Galerius without preserving his apology for earlier policies and recognizing the right of Christians to exist.

Maximin Daia continued insidious attacks on Christianity during the following year. Licinius challenged his rule in the East, however, and took control of the European part of Galerius's territory. As soon as Constantine and Licinius consolidated power in the West by defeating Maxentius at the Milvian bridge in Rome in 312, they put pressure on Maximin. In 313, they jointly issued the Edict of Milan, which firmly established freedom of religion in the Roman Empire, specifically addressing the situation of Christians.

In the edict, the emperors "resolved to make such decrees as should secure respect and reverence for the Deity, namely, to grant both to Christians and to all the free choice of following whatever form of worship they pleased, to the intent that all the divine and heavenly powers that be might be favorable to us and all those living under our authority." The document went on to direct care that Christians have "free and unrestricted authority to observe their own form of worship" and that places of worship destroyed earlier be restored along with other properties (Eusebius *H.E.* 10.5.2-17). Not surprisingly, some Christians viewed this as the beginning of the Millennium.

CHAPTER THIRTEEN

ALIENS IN THEIR OWN HOMELAND

Advancement not only numerically but also socially and culturally brought Christianity to the attention of literate Romans such as Emperor Marcus Aurelius, the physician Galen, and the Platonist philosopher Celsus and generated commentary from them. The larger Christianity loomed in the consciousness of educated Romans, the more seriously they tried to respond to its claims and the harder Christians had to work to frame an adequate case for their religion. On the whole, the Roman elite treated the Christian religion somewhat more graciously than Christians treated Roman religions. So long as Christians remained a clear minority, of course, pagans could speak diffidently and confidently; as Christians grew strong enough to pose a threat to an empire in which devotion to the gods was viewed as the source of health and prosperity, pagan polemicists took the "offenders" more seriously.

Christians Through Roman Eyes

Cultured Romans grudgingly admired Christians for living and dying like philosophers but faulted them for their "inflexible obstinacy" and mystifying motives. The Stoic philosopher-emperor Marcus Aurelius (161–180) lauded readiness for the soul to leave the body "not from mere obstinacy, as with the Christians, but considerately and with dignity and in a way to persuade another without tragic show" (*Meditations* 11.3). The famous physician Galen (129–199) evidently considered adopting the Christian "philosophy" at one point, but decided against it on account of Christian gullibility. Both Jews and Christians accepted the irrational and illogical "on faith." Yet Galen had to admit, even if reluctantly, that Christians sometimes did as philosophers should on the basis not of reason but of "parables," promising future rewards and punishments. What especially evoked his admiration and interest was the fact that "their contempt of death and of its sequel is patent to us everyday, and likewise their constraint in cohabitation" (Walzer, p. 65).

Not all of those who took an interest in Christianity were as objectively curious and appreciative as Galen. Celsus, about 175–178, and Porphyry, at the beginning of persecution under Diocletian, put together much harsher and more thoroughgoing critiques. In his *True Discourse,* about 70 percent of which can be reconstructed from Origen's reply, Celsus sought not only to point up the weaknesses of Christianity but also to make a case for Roman ancestral religion. A Platonist, he knew Christianity intimately and could highlight its weak points. Like Galen, Celsus criticized Christians for lack of concern for reason and reliance on faith alone. He depicted Christians as "wool-workers, cobblers, laundry-workers, and the most illiterate and bucolic yokels, who could not dare to say anything at all in front of their elders and more intelligent masters" (Origen *Against Celsus* 3.55). He was the first to label Jesus a magician and to charge Christians with practicing magic. By magic, he claimed, Jesus performed miracles; by magic, his followers perform feats using spells and incantations (1.6). Claims that Jesus is the Son of God were based on his sorcery and not due to divine endowment (1.68). Replying perhaps to Justin's arguments for Christianity as "the true philosophy," he insisted that Christianity taught little that was new, actually deriving most of its doctrines from the ancient Greeks. What it teaches, he went on to say, it distorts. Celsus criticized especially the Christian doctrines of incarnation, resurrection, and the divinity of Jesus. Incarnation would require a change of God's nature, which is impossible if God is omnipotent and omniscient (4.14). Resurrection, Celsus maintained, is contrary to reason; God would never desire to preserve the flesh (5.14). If there is only one God, Christians err in worshiping a man whose life had ended on a cross; better to worship Jonah with his gourd or Daniel delivered from lions (7.53). Jesus was no more than a low-grade magician. By making Jesus equal with the Father, moreover, Christians violate their monotheism, thus robbing the highest God of his due.

Celsus went to a lot of trouble to discredit Jesus. He was not born of a virgin—which he considered a fabricated story (1.28)—but of a peasant who earned her living by spinning and a Roman soldier named Panthera (1.32). Growing up in Egypt, Jesus learned sorcery from the Egyptians (1.28). Stories recorded in the Gospels about him—for example, his baptism or his resurrection—have no basis in fact. They are concoctions of his followers designed to make him a hero. The resurrection tale is a fabrication of a "hysterical woman" deluded by sorcery or perhaps given to hallucinations (2.55). Christianity, Celsus went on to argue, abandoned its parent, Judaism, and thus disqualified itself by no longer adhering to Jewish teachings set forth in scriptures—circumcision, sabbath observance, festivals, food laws.

Christians also showed poor citizenship. If they were good citizens, they would have served in the army and fought for the emperor (8.73), accepted public office (8.75), and worshiped the gods (8.2). Worshiping the hierarchy of gods would not offend but rather honor the Supreme God, whose intermediaries they are (8.63). If Christians became too numerous, they would disrupt the stability of the empire because they would undermine the law that assures order.

Christianity encountered numerous critics during the third century. The most learned was Porphyry, biographer of Plotinus, founder of Neoplatonism and editor of the *Enneads*. Whereas the *True Discourse* of Celsus drew a reply only from Origen, and that seventy years or more after he wrote it, Porphyry's polemic merited responses from Eusebius, Methodius, Apollinarius, Jerome, and Augustine. Unfortunately, Porphyry's treatise *Against the Christians* has not survived, and the ideas it contains must be reconstructed from replies, always a tricky business. Writing as Diocletian inaugurated a new persecution, Porphyry may have undertaken the task at the emperor's request. From extant fragments, scholars have established that much of Porphyry's argument centered on the Old Testament, refuting, among other things, Christian interpretation of Daniel as future prophecy and arguing that it was a writing of the Maccabean era. Eusebius, Methodius, Apollinarius, and Jerome all replied at length to this contention. The issue was crucial, for Porphyry struck at the very foundations of Christian claims—namely, proof from prophecy. Porphyry also refuted Christian arguments about the antiquity of Moses and made fun of the story of Jonah being swallowed by a whale and God's command that Hosea marry a whore and have children by her.

Porphyry evidently critiqued the New Testament as well. In doing so, he must have raised some of the same objections Celsus voiced about Christian worship of Christ as God, which (he claimed) dishonored the Supreme God. If Augustine alluded to Porphyry when he spoke of pagan critics in his *Harmony of the Gospels* (1.11), the distinguished Neoplatonist thought Christians should honor Christ "as the wisest of men" but not worship him as God. The substantive part of his argument, however, was not philosophical but biblical. He proceeded through the Gospels chapter by chapter, pointing out their differences, inconsistencies, and contradictions. He may have done the same for the rest of the New Testament.

In a second work, *Philosophy from Oracles*, Porphyry assembled a defense of the traditional religions of the Greco-Roman world and sought to locate Christianity within his scheme. Unlike other writings where he used philosophical arguments, in this one he argued from authoritative texts for a hierarchical system of deities: one high God, the Olympian deities, stars and heavenly beings, demons, heroes, and divine human beings. He placed Jesus among the heroes. Christians, on the contrary, have led people into error by worshiping him rather than the gods. The number of responses Christians penned indicates the danger they saw in this approach. Eusebius, citing Porphyry almost a hundred times, wrote his *Preparation for the*

Gospel chiefly to prove that Christianity was not unreasonable to depart from Roman traditional religion. The concerns of Eusebius and others notwithstanding, however, Christianity faced a graver threat to its identity from absorption into the Roman sponge than it did from persecution.

Romans Through Christian Eyes

In this era, as in the preceding one, Christians varied widely in their attitudes toward their fellow Romans, their culture, and their religious competitors. As Christianity incorporated more and more persons of wealth and culture, however, they moderated extreme views and increased their efforts to give more adequate replies to polemicists like Celsus and Porphyry as well as to the illiterate masses. In the East, Clement of Alexandria, Theophilus of Antioch, and Athenagoras of Athens, all writing in the last quarter of the second century, represented the "new breed" of apologists. In the West, Tertullian and Minucius Felix marked this transition in the early third century. Subsequently, Christianity could list among its supporters such distinguished advocates as Origen of Alexandria and Caesarea, Arnobius of Sicca, Lactantius, and Eusebius of Caesarea, foreshadowing a day when Christianity would dominate the Roman religious scene and play a major part in shaping its outlook.

On one end of this spectrum of leaders stood Tertullian (especially during his Montanist phase), insisting that although Christians had to live with pagans, they did not have to "sin" with them by participating in pagan culture. Behind this rejection of culture lay a strong sense of a "fall" from its original purpose. Since God created the universe and the soul, they are both good, but "there is a vast difference between the corrupted state and that of primal purity" (*Spectacles* 2). Within the society he lived in, Tertullian judged the religions to be more corrupt than anything else, but Christians should deliberately set themselves over against their society and shun other activities as well because pagan religion pervades them all. They ought to avoid attendance at games, public service, military service, and teaching in pagan schools. "What has Athens to do with Jerusalem?" Tertullian wanted to know. "What in common have the disciples of Greece and the disciples of heaven?" Idolatry, he claimed, had crept into even the best of pagan culture (*Idolatry* 10).

To assume that Tertullian was consistent in his "Christ against culture" stance would be to ignore his own learning and culture, but he did represent an extreme that Montanism only intensified. Toward the opposite end of the spectrum stood Christian Gnostics, such as Clement of Alexandria, who earnestly yearned to win the flocks of affluent and better educated Romans who inquired of the churches and schools how they might attain salvation. Like Tertullian and virtually all of the other early Christian apologists, Clement spoke harshly about other religions. He ridiculed fables about the gods and the sacrifices, worship of images, and immoral behavior connected with them, citing the philosophers' criticism of them. In reply to persons like Celsus who insisted that Romans should not have abandoned the customs of their ancestors, Clement argued that the divine gift of truth in Jesus Christ made this the only sensible alternative. Quite different, however, was his attitude toward philosophy. He rejected some elements of Greek thought and blamed some philosophers for leading Christian sects astray. He had no patience, however, for those who said "faith alone" was sufficient for the Christian or who considered all philosophy a product of a malign influence. For him philosophy was "in a sense a work of Divine Providence" (*Stromateis* 1.19). Clement discerned no real conflict between Greek philosophy in its best expressions and the Judeo-Christian tradition. Both are pedagogues leading to Christ, in whom the divine Logos became incarnate. In *The Instructor*, Clement fashioned a Christian Stoicism, a kind of "liberal Puritanism" (so Henry Chadwick), wherein the rule of moderation would guide Christians as it had the Stoics. Although he undergirded his counsels with the words of Jesus—*the* Teacher—where he could, Clement was not keenly aware of highly visible differences between Christian and genteel pagan behavior. The distinction would be an interior and invisible one, for the Word, Christ, would instruct and guide them just as he had illumined sages for centuries, whether Jewish or Gentile.

Clement's student and successor Origen took a much more critical stance on pagan culture, even philosophy, despite the fact that Platonism influenced him far more deeply than it did Clement. In a letter to his disciple Gregory (Thaumaturgus) of Neocaesarea, Origen advised the missionary-to-be to focus his efforts on what benefited Christianity and "to extract from the philosophy of the Greeks what may serve as a course of study or a preparation for Christianity, and from geometry and astronomy what will serve to explain the sacred scriptures." Christians should imitate the Jews departing from Egypt in the exodus. They should "steal" only the valuable items and reject the rest. In theory, he operated along these lines, but in practice he could not avoid crossing over them. Above everything else, of course, he aspired to explain the truth found in scriptures, every jot and tittle of which is inspired. Finding three senses in them—literal, moral, and spiritual or symbolic—opened a wide avenue for engaging his culture. The prevailing Platonism of his day consequently exerted far greater impact on what he said and wrote than it did the words and writings of Clement. Yet Origen could differentiate Christian thought from philosophy with much greater precision than could Clement. By temperament, moreover, Origen would never have felt comfortable in the polite circles Clement frequented.

On issues such as flight to avoid persecution or public service, he took positions nearer the rigorist Tertullian's than to the urbane Clement's.

Lactantius, invited by Diocletian to be a teacher of Latin rhetoric in his new capital of Nicomedia, was forced to resign his office when persecution broke out in 304; subsequently he became a Christian. A master of Ciceronian style, he wrote the *Divine Institutes* between the years 304 and 313. Lactantius first derided Roman gods and Roman worship of the gods, citing Cicero and a few other philosophers in support of monotheism. Christians had used the same strategy, inherited from Judaism, many times before. The gods are only deified human beings who behave indecently, unwisely, and unjustly. The crass and materialistic way Romans try to worship them does them no honor. What good does it do, for instance, to carve statues in which the gods supposedly reside when they are impotent to prevent birds from nesting there or leaving droppings on their heads? Far from Christians' acting unreasonably in departing from the folly of their ancestors, the only sensible thing to do is to abandon the images and direct our gaze to the one true God.

Lactantius found fault not only with Roman gods and worship but also with the philosophies, even the Stoicism of his rhetorical model, Cicero. Cicero erred in assuming the eternal existence of matter. To posit that would be to posit two eternal principles: God and matter. If matter were eternal, it would not change. If it changes, it must owe its existence to God's creative work. God alone is impassible, immutable, and incorruptible (2.8). "Philosophy" per se received harsher treatment. It should entail a search for wisdom, but it fails to do so, ending up only in speculations, something Zeno and the Stoics repudiated. The vast number of philosophical sects proves the unreliability of philosophy in a search for truth. Academicians (Platonists) lapsed into skepticism, physicists into positivism. Different schools fail to agree about what leads to a happy life; whom can we believe? None makes God the highest good, not even Zeno, who sees living according to nature as the highest good, or Cicero, who opts for virtue as the highest good. Philosophers erred especially in seeking the highest good in the lowest—the earth—rather than in the highest—heaven. As a result, philosophy teaches neither virtue nor justice. If you are a philosopher, you will not live rightly or well, for you will not seek heavenly wisdom. All philosophies err on immortality. Epicureans make light of death. Stoics and Pythagoreans believe in immortality but do not base their belief on knowledge. Cicero and Plato thought it best never to have been born. Socrates "was a little more prudent than others," but many things about him are "not only not worthy of praise, but even most worthy of censure" (3.20). He, too, made light of heavenly things and taught sharing of wives. Simple observation proves how much more God's commands accomplish in human hearts. "Give an unjust, foolish sinner, and immediately he will be just and prudent and innocent, for with one washing all malice will be wiped out" (3:20). What philosophers can claim this? The whole of human wisdom lies, rather, in knowing and worshiping God.

Daily Life of Christians

As both the anonymous author of the *Epistle to Diognetus* and Tertullian made clear, Christians of the second or third centuries could not separate themselves from their neighbors and live in ghettos. They lived in the same cities and observed most of the same local customs regarding food, clothing, and the like (*Diognetus* 5.1-4; Tertullian *Apology* 42). They did, however, try to distinguish themselves in substantive moral matters not only from pagans but also from quasi-Christian sects such as Gnostics who, believing the flesh is evil, sought to commit every sin as a way of showing contempt for the flesh (Irenaeus *Against Heresies* 1.25.4; 1.31.2). Early on, they relied on a Jewish ethic based on the Old Testament. Theophilus, Bishop of Antioch, summed up the goal: Christians lived according to divine law taught by the prophets, which prohibits idolatry, adultery, murder, fornication, theft, love of money, perjury, anger, and all licentiousness and uncleanness and teaches that "whatever a person does not want done to him/her, that person should not do to another . . . thus a person who acts righteously may escape the eternal punishments and be judged worthy of receiving eternal life from God" (*To Autolycus* 2.34). Practice doubtless fell far short of theory, but Theophilus proceeded to refute charges of sharing wives, incest, and cannibalism (3.4). Citing the Ten Commandments, he argued that Christians consistently taught justice, chastity, love, and good citizenship. They were forbidden to witness gladiatorial combats or other shows. Far from committing sexual crimes, they practiced continence, observed monogamy, and guarded purity (3:15).

As more and more Gentiles entered Christian churches, Christians adapted their ethic to Stoic and Platonist modes of thought. The character of this adaptation depended to a considerable degree on social, educational, and cultural levels, just as it does today. Clement of Alexandria, for instance, opened the way for the wealthy to work out their salvation alongside the masses who possessed little. The rich, rather than despairing, need to realize that they have hope "if they obey the commandments" (*How the Rich Can Be Saved* 3). They should put themselves under the Teacher, Christ, and make his New Testament their food and drink and the commandments their exercises. Jesus' words to the rich young man (Mark 10:17-31) must be understood "mystically" rather than literally. What Jesus commanded was stripping ourselves of the desires of the soul so that we can use money wisely in the care of others. Salvation does not depend on external things but on the virtue of the soul. The call is "Abandon the alien possessions that are in your soul so that, becoming pure in heart, you may see God" (19). If the rich can free themselves from the power of wealth and exercise self-control, seeking God alone, they will become "poor." They can fulfill the righteousness expected by Jesus' parable in Matthew 25:31-46. Love of God and of neighbor is the goal.

In *The Instructor*, Clement laid out particulars of his Christian-Stoic ethic for the genteel more than for the *hoi polloi*. Those who have come to know the Teacher should "eat to live"—that is, in moderation—and not "live to eat." They should eat plain and unpretentious meals that give health and strength. If they eat in moderation, something will be left over to share with the needy (2.1). Christians should drink wine also in moderate amounts and perhaps abstain altogether. There is no need to import exquisite wines, for this merely indicates self-indulgence. Wine ought to be drunk with proper decorum, sipped and not slurped like barbarians. Although he would not forbid drinking from alabaster cups altogether, Clement would forbid drinking from them alone as "overostentatious" (2.2). Drinking from gold, silver, or gem-studded cups would have no purpose but "fraudulent display." Christians should not own ostentatious glassware, couches made of silver, gold or silver dishes and utensils, ivory inlaid couches, or other luxurious items, for these exceed the limits of moderation. Christians' possessions should be "in keeping with a Christian way of life" (2.3). Christians should avoid drunken parties, lewd songs, and gatherings that violate "the law" of Christ (2.4). They should observe propriety in speech, avoiding off-color jokes and unrestrained laughter (2.5), indecent talk, evil companions, sexual license (2.6), insults to others, immodest dress, rudeness in eating, brash speech or actions, whistling or spitting or violent coughing while eating (2.7). Christians do not need to use perfumes, but neither should they fear to use some in moderation; so also garlands and oils (2.8). They should exercise temperance also in bedroom furnishings and in sleep, sleeping "half-awake" and not too long (2.9). Sexual intercourse is for the purpose of procreation; thus Christians must avoid unnatural sexual practices, such as sodomy and bestiality. They must not seek sex apart from marriage, and they must exercise moderation and propriety within marriage. Christians ought to avoid expensive apparel, ornamentation, cosmetics, and the like. Wives must dress in such a way as to enhance their purity (2.10). Footwear should also be modest (2.11). Christians have no need of gems, pearls, or other ornaments (2.12). Rather than acquiring and bedecking themselves in outward things, Christian women should seek inward beautification and ornamentation (3.2). Men, too, should avoid frippery in hair styles, dyes, plucking beards, shameful public exposure, and debauchery (3.3).

Christians should not possess too many slaves or servants in order to escape work or to aid immoral behavior (3.4). Women should not frequent the baths or cavort around naked (3.5). Christians should share their wealth generously, thus "laying up treasure in heaven" (3.6; cf. Matt. 6:20), setting an example of frugality (3.7), and developing discipline (3.8). They should not engage in baths for warmth or pleasure but only for cleanliness or health (3.9). Physical exercise is necessary and healthy, but it could be as easily obtained as a part of daily labor (3.10). Christians may wear gold and use soft garments in modest ways if they avoid indulgence. Clothes should be in keeping with a person's age, personality, place, character, and occupation. Posture, look, gait, and speech all need attention (3.11). In the end, Clement sums up, we must rely on the Teacher. He has laid out his "rule" in the law, the prophets, and the Gospels so as "to eliminate fear and free the will for its act of faith" (3.12).

If Clement deserves the title of a "liberal puritan," his contemporary in the West, Tertullian, might be described as an "illiberal" one. Although he admitted in an early writing that Christians differed little from their contemporaries as regards occupation and general condition (*Apology* 42), he sought more zealously than Clement to put distance between Christians and Romans as regards moral behavior and outlook. Vows taken at baptism, Tertullian insisted, absolutely prohibit Christians from attending the spectacles, for they entailed renunciation of idolatry, the very essence of these activities with all of their religious trappings. Nonattendance is the Christian's chief badge among pagans, and those who remove this "openly deny their faith" (*Spectacles* 24). In the treatise *The Apparel of Women*, Tertullian emphasized modesty of dress that would set Christians apart from pagans. Since Eve brought sin into the world, a penitential garment is the suitable one for women. External beauty only incites lust, something Christians must avoid lest they cause others to sin. Wives should take care only to please their husbands, who ask that they be chaste. This is not to call for a lack of cleanliness or untidiness but only for what is natural and neat. What is natural is God's work; what goes beyond that is the devil's work. To paint the face is to commit adultery in appearance. To dye the hair is foolish and shameful. To spend a lot of time arranging the hair is wasteful. Men as well as women must choose modesty over fashion regarding beards, dyeing hair, ointments, powders, and the like. The dress of women should not detract from their natural beauty. If wealthy and prominent women need to dress more elaborately for public functions, they should "temper the evil" of it. Although God provides wood to manufacture elaborate garments and gold to fit jewels, God placed them in the world to test the restraint of persons devoted to God. There is no reason for Christian women to appear in public in fancy dress. They appear publicly for serious purposes, such as visiting the sick, attending worship, or hearing the Word of God. If anyone must visit a pagan friend, let her go "dressed in your own armor" (2.11). Fancy apparel is related to prostitution, and Christians must never cause others to sin.

The fact that Tertullian strains to find scriptural support for his views indicates that many women resisted his rigorism. As a Montanist, he would have found still stronger opposition. As more and more converts flooded the churches in the two long eras of peace (212–249; 260–304), the question of Christian lifestyle grew increasingly vexing. The large number of apostates during the persecutions under Decius and under Diocletian illuminates the fact that many had not thought through their commitments. Fleshing out this point are canons of the Synod of Elvira in Spain held in 305 or 306. If the canons represent actual cases, as is likely, they point up the grave difficulties many converts, including clergy, had in sorting out what distinguished Christian from pagan even in elementary ways. Some upper-class converts could not decide whether they could continue to function as *flamines*, offering sacrifices to the gods or preparing for public games. Divorce, adultery, fornication, and sodomy were common. Parents sold their children into prostitution. Some intermarried with pagans, Jews, and heretics. Both clergy and laity exacted interest from borrowers. Some failed to attend church regularly. Others still kept idols in their homes. An adulterous catechumen conceived a child and had it killed. Some served as informers during the persecution under Diocletian. Such problems mounted higher and higher after Constantine as the constituency of the churches multiplied many times.

CHAPTER FOURTEEN

THE STRUGGLE FOR UNITY IN AN AGE OF PERSECUTION

Persecution sometimes knit Christians together more tightly as they offered one another mutual support, assurance, and comfort. Bands of the faithful rallied around the martyrs as they bore testimony to the God they worshiped and tried to obey. Christian leaders encouraged and exhorted martyrs and confessors through treatises and letters. Tertullian, Cyprian, Origen, and others composed exhortations to martyrdom. As one of his earlier (pre-Montanist) treatises, Tertullian's *To the Martyrs* reflects real sensitivity to the sufferings of the victims of Severus's persecution. Although the flesh is in prison, he said, the spirit is free. If ancient Romans could suffer for earthly things, how much more could Christians suffer for heavenly ones? Cyprian's *Exhortation to Martyrdom*, a treatise prepared in response to the request of a person named Fortunatus, perhaps Bishop of Tucca, collected scripture texts under a series of propositions designed to encourage faithfulness, the essence of which is that God will punish the unfaithful but protect and reward the faithful. Origen addressed his *Exhortation* to his friend and sponsor Ambrose when Emperor Gallus summoned Ambrose to Gaul to answer for his Christian faith. Cyprian dispatched numerous letters of encouragement to confessors and martyrs not only of Carthage but also of Rome when that church had no bishop during the Decian persecution. Letters from confessors to Cyprian acknowledged the solace and help those letters added to personal ministrations of minor clergy he had sent.

Some letters indicate the strain persecution placed on the most ardent Christians. Confessors themselves sometimes broke down as a result of their depressing circumstances, not only yielding to torture but also behaving in reprehensible ways. Yet such incidents paled alongside the controversy and division that attended the persecution, and that wracked the churches everywhere: the question of readmitting the lapsed to communion.

144

Hippolytus's Schism

The first noteworthy schism of this period involved a Roman presbyter and learned theologian named Hippolytus. When Victor, Bishop of Rome, died in 198, Hippolytus evidently expected to succeed him. However, Zephyrinus was elected instead. Although he spoke warmly of Victor, Hippolytus had little good to say about Zephyrinus. He called him "an ignorant and illiterate individual" who was "accessible to bribes and covetous" (*Refutation of All Heresies* 9.6), hinting that he was really a dupe of his successor, Callistus, of whom Hippolytus spoke still more harshly. Callistus, "cunning in wickedness and subtle in deceit," obtained the episcopate through fraud, Hippolytus charged, by catering to Sabellians as well as to orthodox Christians. Whether Callistus was guilty of all of the connivances Hippolytus accused him of, the latter did make a strong case against him on both doctrinal and disciplinary grounds. Hippolytus sincerely believed that Zephyrinus (perhaps unwittingly) and Callistus (knowingly) favored a modalist or Sabellian doctrine of the relation between the Father and the Son. In response, Callistus charged Hippolytus with ditheism. Hippolytus also raised strenuous objections to changes of discipline that Callistus introduced: forgiving all sins, letting clergy who married two or three times retain office, allowing clergy to marry after being ordained, permitting wealthy women to marry their slaves, and sanctioning second baptisms. In defense of greater leniency, Callistus cited the parable of the wheat and the tares (Matt. 13:30). The election of Callistus in 217 was the last straw for Hippolytus, who was elected as a bishop of Rome by a small but influential minority, drafting *The Apostolic Tradition* as a guide for his followers. According to early tradition, he was reconciled when Pontianus (Bishop of Rome from 230 to 235), exiled with Hippolytus to Sardinia, resigned the office. The Roman community then elected Anteros (235–236).

The Novatianist Schism

During the persecution under Decius, as noted earlier, large numbers of Christians lapsed. Individual offenses varied, however. Some hastened to obtain the certificates (*sacrificati*) by doing everything the decree required. Others, called *libellatici*, acted more circumspectly, getting certificates without actually offering incense, sacrificing, or eating the meat offered in the sacrifices. Still others, called *thurificati*, only offered incense. At the center of the controversy was the issue of whether all cases should be lumped together and treated as apostasy or whether they differed enough to require individual examination. Figuring prominently in the schism, however, were personal offenses and jealousies among the clergy in Carthage and in Rome.

When the lapsed in Carthage started to apply for restoration of communion as the persecution under Decius abated in 250, Cyprian, himself in hiding, refused to readmit any until a council of bishops could convene and decide how to handle the situation. In this he was standing fast on the traditional rigorous policy of the churches in Africa. The lapsed, however, eager to return, obtained some help from a disaffected group of clergy and from the confessors, who issued letters of commendation appealing for their readmission (*Ep.* 15). A faction headed by the deacon Felicissimus, and including Novatus and five other presbyters, had opposed Cyprian's ordination as bishop and sustained an attack on him when he went into hiding during the persecution (*Ep.* 43). Cyprian evidently further alienated some of his clergy by appointing a commission, composed of three neighboring bishops and two presbyters of Carthage, to administer his diocese in his absence, contrary to the customary rights of presbyters (*Epp.* 41-43). Novatus took a lenient view about readmission of the lapsed. Cyprian had his commissioners excommunicate Felicissimus and other members of this faction, but not all of the presbyters, until a council could meet and decide formally how to deal with them. When the council convened in 251, it excommunicated Felicissimus and all five presbyters (*Epp.* 45, 59).

Meanwhile, another faction was developing in Rome. After Fabian, Bishop of Rome, was martyred on January 20, 250, the see remained vacant for a considerable time because it was unsafe to elect a successor. In the interim, presbyters, among whom Novatian was the most prominent, took the lead. Although the Roman clergy criticized Cyprian for going into hiding (*Ep.* 8), other letters penned by Novatian agreed with his policy concerning the lapsed (*Epp.* 30, 36). When the election of Fabian's successor finally was held, the Roman people split their vote between Novatian and another presbyter named Cornelius. They then appealed to the bishops of three other sees—Fabius of Antioch, Dionysius of Alexandria, and Cyprian—to help them decide. Responding promptly, Fabius voted for Novatian, and Dionysius voted for Cornelius. Cyprian, evidently trying to see who the presbyter Novatus might rally to his faction during a trip to Rome, delayed about three months. When he cast his vote, he did so in favor *not* of Novatian, who had supported his reinstatement as Bishop of Carthage, but Cornelius. Novatus and Novatian thus proceeded to unite their factions to begin the Novatianist schism in 251, a surprising development considering the fact that they held opposing views on readmission of the lapsed until this time and one that illustrates the force of personal factors in the schism.

Novatian and his followers differed from the Catholic Church, represented by Cornelius and Cyprian, only on the matter of discipline, and not on any basic doctrinal issues. Novatian was, in point of fact, one of the West's better theologians, writing among other things a widely used treatise on the Trinity that theologians would later cite in opposition to the Arians. In the two letters he wrote to Cyprian on behalf of the Roman presbyters, Novatian hinted at his rigorism, not only in supporting Cyprian's opposition to readmission of the lapsed until a council could decide, but also in the praise he lavished on vigorous discipline (*Ep.* 36). Indeed, according to Cornelius, Novatian had cultivated some partisans for this view among some of the confessors two or three months before the split (in Eusebius *H.E.* 6.43). When Cyprian cast his vote for Cornelius, Novatian locked the door on his position.

When the council met in Carthage in May of 251, the bishops adopted what most persons today would consider a stringent policy. Although they feared that too great severity might cause many to give up hope altogether and fall back into paganism, they decided to impose lengthy penances and punish offenders proportionally according to their offenses. They differentiated, for instance, between those who sacrificed voluntarily in some haste and those who did so involuntarily under torture or threat of it. *Libellatici* were also distinguished from *sacrificati*, the former to be reconciled immediately and the latter only after long penances (Cyprian *Ep.* 52). In the autumn, Cornelius assembled a synod composed of sixty bishops in Rome that confirmed the decrees of the Council of Carthage and excommunicated Novatian and his party. In May 252, spurred on by the resumption of Decius's edict under Gallus, Cyprian convened a second synod at Carthage. This council decided immediately to restore to communion all who manifested genuine signs of repentance as a means of fortifying them for the new onslaught of persecution (Cyprian *Ep.* 54).

Novatianists never gained a strong constituency, but they survived until the sixth century or later. Their support was welcomed by Nicaeans in the Arian controversy. In 410, however, Emperor Honorius I included them in his effort to repress dissidents.

The Rebaptismal Controversy

The strong stand Cyprian took vis-à-vis Novatianists nearly precipitated a schism between Rome and Carthage over the question of readmitting or admitting Novatianists. Cyprian held that Novatianists would need to be rebaptized in order to enter the Catholic Church, since they did not possess the Spirit. The Spirit can be conferred only in the Catholic Church which, by definition, is the church in communion with the bishop. Thus no bishop, no baptism! For Cyprian, it did not matter whether Novatianists had received baptism in the Catholic Church before they separated. If they left the church, they cut themselves off from the Spirit, and they could not again receive the Spirit without baptism in the Catholic Church. Councils convened in Carthage, Iconium, and Synnada seem to have sustained this view by declaring baptism conferred by heretics invalid.

In Rome, Stephen took the position that baptism administered with the trinitarian formula, whether by heretics or by schismatics, was valid. Toward the end of 253, he informed Helenus, Bishop of Tarsus, and Firmilian, Bishop of Caesarea in Cappadocia, that he would not commune with them in the future because they rebaptized heretics (Dionysius of Alexandria in Eusebius *H.E.* 7.5). In 255, a second council of Carthage, presided over by Cyprian, responded to an inquiry by eighteen Numidian bishops by decreeing that schismatics and heretics should be rebaptized, "since no one can be baptized outside the Church" (Cyprian *Ep.* 70.1). They sent a copy of this decision to Stephen with a letter from Cyprian that reinforced it, expressing a hope that Stephen would agree. Stephen, angered by it, refused to allow emissaries sent by Cyprian to appear before him or to communicate with them, forbade all Christians in Rome to give them hospitality, and called Cyprian "a false Christian, a false apostle, and a deceitful workman" (Firmilian to Cyprian *Ep.* 75.25). He then informed the Africans, in a letter now lost, that they held an untenable position in opposition to his own. In September 256, the Africans responded with a third council devoted to the subject, with eighty-seven bishops in attendance. Cyprian polled each bishop, assuring them that none would be excommunicated for differences of opinion. They unanimously agreed on the necessity of rebaptizing schismatics and heretics.

Firmilian's letter to Cyprian upon receiving the report of this gathering reflects much greater bitterness and anger than Cyprian himself displayed. It is possible, however, that the rigidity of both Stephen and Cyprian would have pushed them toward a rupture of communion had not the Valerian persecution interrupted their rancorous debate in 257. Stephen died in August 257, while Cyprian was exiled to Curubis at about the same time. Evidently Stephen's successor, Xystus, smoothed over the ruffled feelings of Cyprian and other bishops, for Cyprian's biographer labeled him "a good and peaceable presbyter" (Pontius *Life of Cyprian* 14). On September 14, 258, Cyprian fell to the sword. His views about baptism lived on in Africa, however, among the members of the Donatist sect, who regularly cited him in defense of the rebaptism of Catholics.

The Donatist Schism

Time wise, the Donatist sect belongs to the next phase of church history. Since the schism began in connection with the persecution under Diocletian, however, it would appear appropriate to discuss it at this juncture. Like the Novatianist schism, Donatism too grew out of the contorted situation created by persecution. Once again, vast numbers of believers, wholly unprepared for the new onslaught, either fled or hastened to surrender copies of scriptures, as the first edict demanded, or to offer sacrifices. According to Optatus (*Against the Donatists* 3.8), the temples of Numidia would not hold the crowds of apostates. In Milevis, Bishop Paul, summoned before the curator of the city, gave up one copy of scriptures and said that the readers had the rest. Brought before the authorities, the latter tried to cover for one another but finally yielded and brought not only copies of scriptures but also chalices, lamps, clothes kept for relief of the poor, and other objects.

One of the persons who took part in this, Silvanus, later became a Donatist bishop. When twelve bishops met after the death of Bishop Paul to elect a successor, four admitted to having surrendered copies of scripture, one actually throwing the Gospels in the fire, and a fifth having escaped by feigning blindness (Augustine *Against Cresconius* 3.27, 30). On the other side of the picture, numerous Christians did remain faithful, some with fanatical zeal, especially in Numidia, where persecution was so intense. In Carthage, some presented themselves to the authorities voluntarily, claiming to possess copies of scriptures, which they refused to give up. Great crowds rallied outside the prisons where confessors were kept. As the persecution let up in March of 305, many fanatics fanned popular resentment of the *traditores* ("surrenderers" of the sacred books).

Before Mensurius, bishop of Carthage, left for Rome to appear before Maxentius in defense of one of his deacons, he entrusted the valuables of the church to the *seniores*, or presbyters, who were to preside in his absence. When he died before returning, the presbyters hastened to elect a successor, but they could not agree between two of their own, Botrus and Celestius, and the choice fell to the archdeacon Caecilian. Although publicly acclaimed by the citizens of Carthage, Caecilian was unpopular in the church. He had alienated many as a result of his opposition to the cult of martyrs, so popular in Africa at the time. In addition, the clergy did not like him because he forced them to turn over the gold and silver treasures they had hidden away. In addition, one of the three bishops who had consecrated him—Felix of Aptunga—was suspected of being a *traditor*.

Although Caecilian obtained the approval of other important sees, Numidian bishops led by Secundus of Tigisis and Donatus of Casae Nigrae contested the election on the grounds that Caecilian was personally unworthy and was consecrated by only three bishops rather than the twelve customarily required, one of the three being a *traditor*. In Carthage, they readily enlisted the support of opponents of Caecilian. Secundus, convinced that Caecilian's installation was invalid, appointed an interim administrator, who was subsequently murdered. He then convened a council and invited Caecilian to attend, but Caecilian declined and instead asked Secundus to come to the cathedral to state his complaint. To have done so would have acknowledged the legitimacy of Caecilian's appointment, so Secundus proceeded to have Caecilian condemned in the council on the grounds that his consecration was invalid and that, as a deacon, he had denied food to the martyrs of Abitina. The council then elected Majorinus, a lector in the church, as bishop and sent ambassadors to Rome, Spain, and Gaul and letters to the African provinces to report the action. The Numidians then returned home. Caecilian, as one would expect, refused to step down, so the schism began. Majorinus died soon afterward, and Donatus, whose name the schism bears, was consecrated almost immediately (perhaps as early as the summer of 313). Donatus ruled for forty years.

News of the schism upset Emperor Constantine when it reached Milan. Without waiting to hear the opposition's side, he decided in favor of Caecilian, ordering the financial officer in charge of the imperial estates in Africa to put money at Caecilian's disposal and to restore to the church lands seized in the persecution. He also ordered that any who made vile and base accusations against the church be brought before the magistrates (Eusebius *H.E.* 10.6). In March or April 313, he exempted clergy supportive of Caecilian from municipal taxes.

The Donatists then appealed directly to the emperor. They asked for judges from Gaul to investigate the case (Augustine *Ep.* 88.2), taking the first step toward an alliance between church and empire. Although angered by the petition, Constantine required the proconsul Anulinus to send Caecilian with ten supporting bishops and an equal number of Donatists to Rome, where Bishop Miltiades of Rome, an African, and a certain Marcus, plus three bishops from Gaul, were to serve as judges. The commission cleared Caecilian of the charges against him and affirmed the validity of his consecration (Optatus *Against the Donatists* 1.24). The Donatists, however, were not content to let the matter rest. They appealed again to Constantine, this time for a council. Although this request also distressed the emperor, he convened the Council of Arles on August 1, 314, installing Marinus, Bishop of Arles, as president, with the understanding that the council's decision would be final. Despite their efforts to press the question of Felix of Aptunga's guilt, the Donatists lost again at Arles.

Like the Novatianist controversy, the Donatist schism entailed much more than personal jealousies. As W. H. C. Frend ably demonstrated in *The Donatist Church*, this dispute, more than any other, was fired by African nationalism and socioeconomic hostility to a Roman presence in Africa. Donatist support resided in the countryside among the Berber and Phoenician peoples who had controlled northern Africa before the Romans won the Punic wars. Donatist leaders came chiefly from the provinces of Numidia and Mauretania. Not surprisingly, the native populace never understood or accepted the decisions of Constantine's commission or the Council of Arles. The more fanatical of them, known as *Circumcellions* ("hut haunters"), carried on a guerrilla war.

Theologically, the Donatists differed from the Catholic Church in much more basic ways than did the Novatianists. They conceived of themselves as a church of the "pure" (*katharoi*). Whereas Catholics construed "holy" (as in the ancient formula of "one holy, catholic, and apostolic church") in terms of Christ's presence within a mixed body (*corpus permixtum*) of saints and sinners, the Donatists interpreted it in terms of individual members. Because the Catholic Church tolerated *traditores* in its constituency, even among the clergy, the Donatists argued, it has ceased to be holy and the Spirit has fled from it. All of its ministrations—baptism, eucharists, ordinations—are invalid, for they depend on the worthiness of the minister. The Donatists, as Catholics constantly reminded them, could not back up their claim of purity in all constituents, but they pressed the point nonetheless.

Until the time of Augustine, Donatists competed with Catholics for control of North Africa. In Numidia and small towns they held a clear numerical edge. A Donatist theologian named Tyconius (d. ca. 390), driven out of the sect by Parmenian, Donatist Bishop of Carthage, rivaled Augustine for eminence, and Augustine relied heavily on his *Rules* of interpretation. Donatist influence dwindled, however, after the Council of Carthage in 411, where Augustine bested their ablest leaders in a debate. Where Donatists stressed that the holiness of the church depends on the holiness of individual members, Augustine emphasized Christ. He distinguished between the validity and the efficacy or effectiveness of sacraments. Validity depends on Christ and not on the administrator. The fact is that no human administrator will be perfect. If baptism, Eucharist, or ordination confers grace, therefore, it will do so as one of Christ's sacraments. Whether they are effective for salvation depends on the faith of the recipient and not on the administrator. Infants, for instance, are baptized "in hope." When they reach an accountable age, they must believe if they want to appropriate the benefits of the baptism conferred by the Spirit. The Donatists could be admired for their concern about the worthiness of ministers, but they nullified much of that by the way they acted toward Catholics.

One of the tragic by-products of the Donatist controversy was Augustine's rationale for the use of force to reconcile dissidents. Until 406 he opposed coercion against the Donatists. The violent way in which the Circumcellions pursued the Donatist cause, however, induced him to change his mind. In a letter to Festus, an official charged with implementing imperial decrees against the Donatists, Augustine urged the use of force, like that which parents use on children because they love them (*Ep.* 98). In

417, he reinforced his position in a letter addressed to Boniface, Governor of Africa under Honorius. By this time he had discovered that force worked and laid aside an earlier hesitancy, seeing that "many through the imperial decrees have been and are daily being converted, who now give thanks both for their conversion and for their deliverance from that raging destruction" (*Ep.* 185.7). Like patients cured by their physicians' harsh measures, they discovered what great blessings they had received while complaining of being persecuted. They persecute Catholics unjustly; Catholics persecute them justly (11). The argument supplied the rationale for the inquisitions and crusades of the Middle Ages.

Although weakened, Donatists survived. They suffered along with Catholics as a result of the Vandal conquest and efforts to impose Arianism. In Proconsular Africa, and also in Mauretania, they seem to have lost ground, but they remained relatively strong in the villages of Numidia. The Byzantine reconquest of northern Africa returned Catholics to a position of ascendancy, as Donatists were proscribed alongside Arians and Jews. Donatism evidently revived in the late sixth century, however, for Gregory I wrote a series of letters to bishops and Byzantine officials in Africa expressing grave concern that Donatism and Manichaeism had reared their heads again and that Catholics in Numidia needed help. In 593, the pope made a vigorous effort to crush the movement, urging the Praetorian Prefect Pantaleo to enforce antiheretical laws against them (*Ep.* 3.32) and goading Catholics to act. There is some evidence for their survival to the very end as Moslems drew the shades on Christianity in North Africa.

The Meletian Schism in Egypt

During the persecution under Diocletian, Peter, Bishop of Alexandria, went into hiding. While he was absent, Meletius, Bishop of Lycopolis in Upper Egypt, visited the city and ordained two persons, Isidore and Arrius, as presbyters. He tried also through them to win over the presbyters to whom Peter had entrusted administration of his flock. When Peter learned of this, he instructed his people not to communicate with Meletius until he could investigate what was happening. Meletius may have acted out of genuine concern, but he violated established rules in invading another bishop's diocese and, worse still, ordaining presbyters in it. Peter, therefore, retaliated by deposing Meletius in a synod of bishops "for many lawless deeds and for sacrifice" (Athanasius *Apology Against the Arians* 59). The evidence is confusing, but it would appear that Meletius disagreed with Peter regarding readmission of the lapsed. Where Peter showed considerable leniency, Meletius adopted a rigorous stance. Soon after his deposition, he was sent by civil authorities to work in the quarries of the Thebaid and later to the mines in Palestine, thus bestowing on him credentials as a confessor. In Palestine and also upon his return to Egypt in 311 he ordained bishops, in effect initiating a Meletian Church fostering a rigorist image. In 325, the Meletians claimed twenty-eight bishops. Although the Council of Nicaea set guidelines for the readmission of Meletian clergy into the mainstream church, the sect persisted and linked up with Arians in opposition to Athanasius.

Marginal Christianity

The groups discussed thus far in this chapter did not involve deviations from the Catholic Church on basic doctrines, even if many Church Fathers refused to distinguish them from those that did. Although the Gnostic, Marcionite, and Montanist crises of the preceding era had already pushed the churches down the road to more precise self-definition, there remained still much room for critical reflection and debate. Neither Christianity's relationship with Judaism nor its relationship with the Greco-Roman world was settled. In the process of debating what constituted the essentials, some groups found themselves on the margin, unable to identify sufficiently with these sects to retain affiliation with the mainstream. Most marginal groups in this period tended to pull Christianity back to its Jewish roots rather than to its Hellenistic ones.

This was true of the Encratites, a conservative sect whom Irenaeus (*Against Heresies* 1.28.1) attributed to Tatian. According to Hippolytus (*Refutation of All Heresies* 8.13), the Encratites agreed with the Catholic Church about God and Christ. Beyond that, however, they fostered an extreme asceticism involving rejection of meat, intoxicating beverages, and sexual intercourse (Irenaeus *Adv. haer.* 1.28.1). Although the Church Fathers ascribed the latter to Gnostic or Marcionite influences, they would appear to have been much closer to Essene customs, admired by persons like Tatian and Hippolytus. After studying under Justin and teaching for a time in Rome, Tatian made his way to Syria where he assembled his *Diatessaron*, a synthesis of the four Gospels. His ascetic tendencies would have fitted into the Syrian context quite well.

Inclination toward Judaism was also characteristic of different forms of what is known as Monarchianism. The name comes from the strong emphasis these groups placed on the single rule (Greek, *monarche*) of God. Logos christology was seen by Monarchian Christians as a threat to Jewish monotheism. Some proponents of Logos christology—Justin and Origen, for instance—did not hesitate to call Jesus a "Second God." To avoid a charge of bi-theism (of which Callistus accused Hippolytus), the proponents of Logos christology framed a structure of belief that appeared illogical and contradictory:

1. God is One.
2. Jesus is God, that is, a worshipful Being.
3. Yet Jesus is other than the Father.

The Monarchians responded, in effect, by saying, "It can't be both ways. If God is One, either Jesus is God, or He is other than the Father." In time, the controversy tilted in favor of proponents of Logos christology, thanks especially to Tertullian and Hippolytus. In the late second and early third centuries, however, several marginal sects emerged and continued the tradition of pneumatic christology. Unfortunately, their writings have not survived and opponents often distorted the data about them.

Adoptionistic or dynamistic Monarchians sought to get rid of the contradiction in Logos christology by saying that God is one and Jesus is other than the Father, but denying that He is God. Several sects formed to advocate this viewpoint. One emerged in Asia Minor between 170 and 180 with the name *Alogoi*. They vigorously opposed the Montanists and their prophetic claims, rejected the Gospel of John and the Logos concept it propounds, as well as the Revelation of John, and objected to the term *Logos* as a Gnostic idea. Both Irenaeus and Hippolytus considered them schismatics rather than heretics, but nothing more definite is known of their christology. How long they existed or when, how, and why the churches of Asia Minor excluded them is not known.

About 190, Theodotus the Tanner, a well-educated Christian of Byzantium, founded a party of dynamistic or adoptionistic Monarchians. Although Hippolytus acknowledged at least partial orthodoxy in Theodotus's theology and cosmology, Bishop Victor excommunicated him because of christological errors. Influenced perhaps by the Alogoi, Theodotus taught a pneumatic christolology. Jesus, he said, was born of a virgin through the agency of the Holy Spirit, according to divine plan. After he had lived "promiscuously" and had become "preeminently religious," the Spirit descended on him at baptism and acclaimed him as the Christ. From the Spirit, Jesus received power (*dynamis*) to fulfill his mission and to live a righteous life. Some Dynamists believed that Jesus became God by virtue of the resurrection, but others thought he never did (Hippolytus *Refutation of All Heresies* 7.23). Other notable features of this circle, which included Theodotus the Banker and a certain Asclepiodotus, were their admiration of Galen, use of textual criticism, and grammatical rather than allegorical interpretation of scriptures. After being excommunicated by Zephyrinus (Bishop of Rome 199–217), this group made an abortive attempt to found a church at Rome, hiring Natalius, a confessor who soon deserted them, to serve as their bishop, (Eusebius *H.E.* 5.28).

Later writers ascribed to Theodotus the Banker the founding of a sect called Melchizedekians, who based their christology on Hebrews 5–7. There appears to be distortion of their thought, however. Rather than elevating Melchizedek above Jesus, as Epiphanius charged (*Against Heresies* 55), they regarded the Holy Spirit as the sole divine essence besides the Father and considered the Spirit identical with the Son. The Spirit, they claimed, appeared to Abraham. As in *The Shepherd of Hermas*, Theodotus viewed Jesus as a man anointed with the power of the Spirit but inferior to the Holy Spirit, who was the true Son.

A similar christology was propounded by followers of Artemas, or Artemon. They also denied to Jesus the ascription "God," as some Theodotians did. The sect still existed in 268, for a synod of bishops at Antioch condemned Paul of Samosata for scorning the mystery of faith and strutting about "in the abominable heresy of Artemas" (Eusebius *H.E.* 7.30.16).

The linking up of Artemas and Paul shifted the center of adoptionistic or dynamistic Monarchianism from Rome to the East, where, as Origen's references make clear, many opposed Logos christology. Beryllus, Bishop of Bostra in Arabia, apparently espoused the adoptionist christology until convinced of his error by Origen about 244 (Eusebius *H.E.* 6.33). About 260, Paul of Samosata, bishop of the prestigious see of Antioch, began openly to oppose Logos christology and to propound a much more subtle form of the dynamistic Monarchianism than had earlier exponents. In explicit opposition to Johannine christology, he denied the descent of the Son "from above" and instead asserted, "Jesus Christ is from below" (Eusebius *H.E.* 7.30.11). The bishops, however, criticized him not just for his christology but for his haughtiness as well. He preferred the title *Proconsular Ducenarius* of Queen Zenobia to that of bishop, they charged, and he acted more like a high public official than a servant of Christ. He behaved "like the rulers of the world" in church assemblies, rebuking people when they didn't applaud him sufficiently and assailing deceased preachers. He forbade singing psalms to Christ as "the modern productions of modern men" and trained women to sing psalms to him. With the support of Queen Zenobia of Palmyra, however, Paul proved a tough foe. It took three synods in Antioch before he was deposed and replaced by Domnus as Bishop of Antioch. Even then, Paul retained office under Zenobia for four more years. When he refused to relinquish control of the church building, his opponents petitioned Emperor Aurelian, who ordered the building given "to those to whom the bishops of Italy and of the city of Rome should adjudge it" (Eusebius *H.E.* 7.30.19).

Modalistic Monarchians took the other route to elimination of the contradiction posed by Logos christology, affirming that God is one and Jesus is God, but denying that Jesus is other than the Father. In the West, they were usually called *Patripassians* ("Father sufferings"); in the East, Sabellians. Modalism had considerable vogue in Western thinking generally from an early date, but it resulted first in a separate sect late in the second century. A major figure in the development of Modalism was Noetus, a teacher in Smyrna or Ephesus who was excommunicated for his views around 230. Epigonus (d. 200), a disciple of Noetus, came to Rome at the beginning of Zephyrinus's episcopate (199–217) and founded a separate Patripassian party based on Noetus's views. The party was first headed by Epigonus and then, after 215, by Sabellius. According to Hippolytus, who opposed them vigorously, the Patripassians rallied strong support in Rome, enlisting as allies both the gullible Zephyrinus and the wily Callistus (217–222). Callistus, however, trying to find a way out of an increasingly intense fight between two parties, excommunicated both Sabellius and Hippolytus and proposed a compromise formula that moved Roman doctrine in the direction of Logos christology. Sabellians, or Patripassians, survived for years in Rome. Their teachings reached Africa by way of Praxeas, who ran into a wall of resistance from Tertullian, who silenced him and forced him to write a retraction.

In the East, Sabellians stirred up a bitter battle lasting from about 220 until 270. Sabellius apparently developed far-reaching relations with the East after his excommunication by Callistus. The key tenet of the Sabellians was that Father, Son, and Holy Spirit are really different names for the same Being. Zealous to preserve monotheism, Sabellius called the one God the "Son-Father." God appears *successively* in the "modes" (thence modalism) of Father, Son, and Spirit and not simultaneously. From creation to incarnation, God is manifested as Father, the Creator and Legislator; from incarnation to assumption as Son; and from the assumption on as Spirit. The Arian controversy in the East was, in many respects, a continuation of the debate between Sabellians and proponents of Logos christology. Indeed, Arius accused Alexander, Bishop of Alexandria, of Sabellianism.

Whereas the preceding sects belong on the margin of Christianity, at least one known to the early Fathers, the Elkesaites, stepped beyond that point. This syncretistic Jewish Christian sect derived its central tenets from a mysterious book brought to Rome about 220 by Alcibiades of Apamea in Syria. Reputedly revealed by an angel who was the Son of God to Elkai in the third year of Trajan (101 C.E.), its contents were disclosed to no one except under oath of absolute secrecy. Among the distinguishing practices of the Elkesaites that show pagan influence were repeated ablutions in the name of the Father and the Son, not only to obtain forgiveness of sins but also to heal the sick. Elkesaites aligned baptismal days with the Zodiac. In line with their Jewish emphasis, on the other hand, they required circumcision and adherence to the Torah. They rejected sacrifices and parts of the

Old Testament, however, as well as Paul's letters in the New Testament. They viewed Christ as an angel and taught repeated incarnations, although they believed in the virgin birth. They used bread and salt in celebration of the Lord's Supper and forbade eating of meat. They also valued marriage and allowed renunciation of faith in time of persecution.

In this era, as in the preceding one, the churches struggled to define who they were in an often bitterly hostile environment. In some ways, persecution helped by forcing Christians to give serious attention to who they were and to whether the price they were paying was worth it. In other ways, however, it added to the problem, to the extent that some viewed Christianity entirely through lenses ground by persecution. Dispute about what Christianity required led, as we have seen, to several grievous schisms and left the larger family always wondering whether it really remained faithful enough.

CHAPTER FIFTEEN

CHRISTIAN SPIRITUALITY

The age of the martyrs, costly and painful as it was, laid the foundations for Christian spirituality. Living under threat forced the faithful to strengthen and deepen their commitments to God. Critical in this was the formation they received through the catechumenate and baptism. Exhortations to faithfulness constantly harked back to the renunciation of Satan and the oath (*sacramentum*) uttered there. Given the ominous conditions under which Christians lived, it is not surprising that the catechumenate lasted up to three or more years and, when it was compromised, lapses of discipline increased. Even in less fearsome circumstances, however, lapses occurred, necessitating a shaping of more formal procedures to rescue the fallen and restore them to their commitment. Nevertheless, Christian spirituality depended then as now on a regimen of regular worship, frequent and fervent prayer, fasting, and other disciplines exercised both individually and corporately.

However much Christians might aspire to a high level of obedience to God on the part of all, they have had to reckon with the reality that some will honor their commitments more fully than others. In this era, the martyrs set the standard, an artificially high one by virtue of the irregular demands exacted by persecution. When Gallienus opened the way to a long era of peace, the ideal of the martyrs inspired a few to seek solitary places like those to which martyrs fled or had been exiled to during the persecutions. Anthony was not the first hermit, but his flight to the desert in 271 marks the beginning of a stream of pilgrims that, a century or so later, turned into a wide river. In this same confluence of circumstances lived those present in every era and realm of human existence who sought more immediate and direct experience with God. This, quite clearly, was the goal of those now categorized under the Gnostic label. Although many of the Gnostic schools had fallen under the censure of the churches because of their dualism, there remained no small number of Christians, especially those of culture and education, who aspired to something more than "faith," defined as upright conduct and commendable demeanor. They, too, wanted direct and intuitive knowledge (*gnosis*) of the living God. To such persons, Clement of Alexandria and Origen rendered a priceless service. So also did the desert monks, some of whom could report success in their most earnest endeavor to "see" God.

Christian Formation

Because both Hippolytus and Tertullian fall into the rigorist category, it is unlikely that their demands would have been implemented in all of the churches during the early third century. Something similar to the formation process they describe, however, must have occurred everywhere Christians lived under the shadow of persecution. According to the *Apostolic Tradition* of Hippolytus, inquirers went through serious scrutiny before they were admitted to the catechumenate. They had to have the confirmation of those who brought them "that they are competent to hear the word." If they obtained sufficient approval, they underwent an inquiry into their personal lives. The demon-possessed could not be admitted until they had been cleansed. Persons in various occupations had to relinquish them or be rejected: panderers, sculptors or painters of idols, actors or pantomimists, teachers of children in pagan schools, charioteers, gladiators or their trainers or other persons connected with the combats, priests of other cults, military commanders or public magistrates, astrologers, diviners, soothsayers, users of magic formulas, jugglers, clowns, amulet makers, keepers of concubines. Harlots, licentious men, eunuchs, and magicians were rejected outright.

Candidates normally spent three years as catechumens, but Hippolytus granted some concession to the zealous. After the instruction period, catechumens had to withdraw and stay apart from baptized believers. After catechumens prayed, the instructor laid hands on them and prayed, then dismissed them. Before baptism, catechumens underwent a further examination to see "whether they have lived soberly, whether they have honored the widows, whether they have visited the sick, whether they have been active in well doing" (2.20). If they received a favorable report from sponsors, they were separated from other catechumens for a final phase of preparation for baptism. In this period, they underwent daily exorcisms. As they approached baptism, normally on Easter Sunday, the bishop laid hands on them to exorcise demons and to determine whether he was personally assured of their purity. Those designated for baptism were instructed to wash themselves on Thursday for baptism on Sunday. All candidates fasted on Friday. On Saturday, the bishop laid hands on them and exorcised them a final time; breathed in their faces; sealed their foreheads, ears, and nose with the sign of the cross; and then raised them up. That night, they kept vigil, "listening to reading and instruction."

Baptism established a clear dividing line between the old life, dominated by demons, and the new life, surrendered to God in Jesus Christ. At dawn, prayer was said over the water to invoke the Holy Spirit to purify and empower it. Those to be baptized stripped off all clothing and other apparel for nude baptism (in private, of course). No one was to enter the water wearing "any alien object" such as rings, bracelets, hair combs, or jewelry. According to Hippolytus (*A.T.* 2.21), baptisms took place in the order of children, grown men, and then women. Those receiving baptism faced west, the realm of darkness, and renounced Satan and "all his service and works" and were anointed with an "oil of exorcism" by a presbyter, who, on applying the oil, declared: "Let all evil spirits depart from you." Turning around to face east, they took a trinitarian oath (*sacramentum*), pledging absolute loyalty: "I believe and bow to Thee and all Thy service, O Father, Son, and Holy Spirit." Then they entered the water. The bishop, presbyter, or deacon performing the baptism interrogated them and baptized them after each response.

Their baptism completed, the newly baptized received a second anointing, this time with an "oil of thanksgiving." They then dried, reclothed themselves, and joined the assembly of believers to receive the bishop's confirmation and to partake of the Eucharist for the first time, both acts dramatically reinforcing their decision.

The bishop laid hands on the newly baptized, prayed for an infilling of the Holy Spirit "so that they may serve thee according to thy will" (Hippolytus *A.T.* 2.22), "sealed" their foreheads with the sign of the cross using an unguent, and gave the kiss of peace. In churches such as the one at Rome, the new Christians partook not only of the bread and wine of the Eucharist but also of a mixture of milk and honey, symbolizing their entry into the promised land. At Rome, according to Hippolytus (*A.T.* 2.23), they sipped three times from three cups—one of water, one of milk and honey, and one of wine—to emphasize their commitment to the trinitarian God. Already at this early date, the bishop imparted secret instructions following baptism, anticipating instruction in the "mysteries" that became common by the fourth century.

Sustaining Commitment

The degree of commitment Christianity demanded of those who wished to enter it distinguished it markedly from its competitors, with the possible exception of the state itself. Sustaining such a level of commitment, however, was no easy matter, particularly as the churches incorporated large numbers of members in times of peace, as lapses during persecutions under Decius and Diocletion demonstrate. Here, day-to-day discipline had to undergird and reinforce what transpired in the catechumenal/baptismal process. Exclusion and restoration of the "fallen" represented last-resort efforts and not the normal means for sustaining commitment. Other measures were both more common and more crucial for the vast majority.

In addition to worship on Sundays, which will be discussed later, the churches relied on several practices. One of these was a regular regimen of prayer. Hippolytus directed believers to pray as prescribed by the *Didache*, but also on arising in the morning, on retiring at bedtime, and at midnight. Treatises on prayer by Tertullian, Cyprian, and Origen reveal the central role they ascribed to prayer in sustaining religious fervor. They viewed the Lord's prayer not only as a model for prayer but also as "a compendium of the entire Gospel" (Tertullian *Prayer* 1.6). Cyprian argued strongly against private prayer and in favor of corporate prayer, doubtless due to the problem of schism in his day, but all three treatises contain instruction regarding how to pray.

In this era, persecution notwithstanding, Christians gathered early, as circumstances permitted, to receive instruction on other days besides Sunday. Hippolytus and Cyprian viewed corporate assemblies as the preferable practice, conscious probably of the supportive effect of the group. Catechists receive help from the Holy Spirit, so it would be best "to go to the assembly to the place where the Holy Spirit abounds." On days when no assemblies met, however, the faithful were expected to "take a holy book and read in it sufficiently what seems profitable" (Hippolytus *A.T.* 3.35.3). Gatherings such as these became increasingly common during the two long eras of peace before Decius and Diocletian, for both emperors aimed their repression at public meetings of Christians.

Fasting also contributed significantly to Christian discipline in this period. Besides the customary two-day fast prior to baptism and Wednesday and Friday fasts, Christians observed partial fasts during Holy Week in some areas, limiting their diet to bread, salt, and water. Lenten fasting, however, probably did not begin until about 325. The Montanists, who distinguished themselves from Catholics by their frequent fasts, observed two weeks of partial fasts (*xerophagies*) during the year. In his Montanist period, Tertullian accused Catholics of hating to fast, whereas they faulted Montanists for teaching people to fast more often than to marry (*Fasting* 1.3).

The most important factor in sustaining commitment was the little bands of Christians themselves exhorting, encouraging, and inspiring one another.

The Martyrs: Ideal Christians

Had there been no persecutions, Christian history would probably have turned out quite differently. Christian spirituality would certainly have been different, for some group other than the martyrs would have established the ideal, and the monks who emulated the martyrs would have looked elsewhere for their model. As the art of the catacombs shows at a glance, the martyrs continued the noble and heroic line of Daniel, the three children in the fiery furnace, and Jesus himself, crucified on behalf of others. Ninety-year-old Pothinus, Bishop of Lyons, although weakened by age and disease, gave a noble testimony "as if he were Christ himself." Blandina, hanged before beasts in the shape of a cross, appeared to other martyrs of Lyons to be the crucified Christ himself exhorting them. Perpetua and the other catechumens experienced visions, as Stephen had, of the victorious Christ urging them on in their confessions. When Felicitas cried out in pain brought on by advance of pregnancy, one of the guards asked, "What will you do when you come into the amphitheater if you cry out from such pains as this?" She replied, "Here I am being crucified; but there the Lord will suffer for me" (*Acts of Saint Perpetua* 8.2). Eusebius, commenting on the martyrdoms in the persecution under Diocletian, observed in the confessors "the divine power of our Savior who has borne witness, Jesus Christ Himself, as it became present and manifested itself distinctly to the martyrs" (*H.E.* 8.7).

Reverence for the martyrs immediately left its mark on Christian thought. One notable effect was the cult of martyrs and relics, visible already in the account of Polycarp's death in the second century. Not only the martyrs themselves but also any object they touched was considered holy and spiritually potent to ward off diseases or to bring good fortune. To have a martyr touch one's handkerchiefs or scarves would assure one certain power over the demonic. The remains of the martyrs themselves, then, would possess such power multiplied many times over and were thus interred in places, such as the catacombs, where the faithful could come and tap into it.

The influence martyrs wielded became clearly visible in letters of indulgence the lapsed or their families sought from confessors in order to secure restoration of communion. Cyprian had to plead with confessors during the Decian persecution to weigh carefully and cautiously all requests for the certificates that read "Let so and so be received into communion with his own people," possession of which would guarantee readmission (*Ep.* 15.3-4). He likewise had to caution his clergy regarding the "impudent manner" in which some confessors handed out commendations (*Ep.* 27). Paul, martyred in Carthage in 250, instructed the confessor Lucian to issue such certificates in his name to anyone who requested them after his death

(*Ep.* 22.2), and Lucian persuaded all the confessors in prison with him to support the same policy.

Martyrdom was regarded as a second baptism. Where the first baptism washed away sins of the past, martyrdom wiped out all sins. "Only the baptism of blood makes us purer than the baptism of water," said Origen. Those who receive baptism in water may sin again, but those who suffer martyrdom can never do so. In baptism, sins are removed; in martyrdom they are destroyed (*Sermons on Judges* 7.2).

Restoring the Fallen

Before proceeding to a discussion of the successors of the martyrs, it will be useful to see how the churches attempted to deal with persons who had lapsed and subsequently repented. During the persecutions of Decius and Diocletian, the "fallen" included a vast constituency, thus forcing the churches to reflect on the question of discipline more deeply than ever before.

The churches, of course, carried over from the preceding era a variety of attitudes toward the three most serious breaches of Christian discipline: apostasy, adultery, and murder. On the rigorist end of the spectrum stood the Montanists (with Tertullian, in his Montanist period, supplying the information on their views), Hippolytus, Novatian and his followers, and, at the end of the period, the Donatists. As a Montanist, Tertullian assumed an extreme position in opposition to what he characterized as an "edict" of the "Pontifex Maximus," now thought by some to be a bishop of Carthage rather than Callistus of Rome. Whereas in his Catholic days Tertullian affirmed restoration of all offenders one time as specified by Hermas, in his treatise *On Purity* he denounced restoration of adulterers or fornicators as well as murderers and idolaters and labeled Hermas "the shepherd of adulterers" (10). God may forgive such sins, and offenders should do penance for that reason, but the church cannot (11.21). Not even the martyrs can attain forgiveness for such sins as adultery, save for themselves (22). Hippolytus took a similar stand against the leniency of Callistus, claiming to forgive all sins on the basis of the parable of the tares (*Refutation of All Heresies* 8.12).

When the Decian persecution decimated the ranks of the faithful, the Catholic churches showed that they had not resolved polarities on the issue. Some leaders, such as the deacon Novatus of Carthage, favored ready restoration of all who applied, whereas Novatian and his followers pursued a line closer to that drawn by Tertullian and Hippolytus. Even the confessors disagreed on the matter. Cyprian and the African bishops allied with him steered a middle course between these extremes, wanting to evaluate individual cases on their own merits but forced by the new onslaught of persecution under Gallus to adopt a more lenient position. By the time the smoke settled over the Novatianist schism, the Catholic churches found themselves distinguishing degrees of penance according to the severity of the offense. Apostasy, adultery, and murder obviously required longer displays of remorse than did drunkenness, brawling, or lesser offenses.

The barbarian invasions occasioned a further step in this direction. During an invasion of Cappadocia by the Boradi and Goths in 256–258, discipline among Christians broke down dreadfully. In the confusion created by the invasions, some persons plundered hapless neighbors' property, claiming to have "found" it; others captured for their own use slaves who had escaped; and still others joined the barbarians in murdering, informing on neighbors, and pillaging. In a canonical letter, Gregory Thaumaturgus, Bishop of Neocaesarea, distinguished degrees of penance for various offenses. By about 300, the churches of the East had fashioned a full-blown system of penance. According to a spurious article added to the canonical letter of Gregory, penitents were separated into five categories: "weepers," who remained completely outside the church grounds; "hearers," who listened to the sermon from the portico only and left at the same time the catechumens were dismissed; "fallers," who prostrated themselves inside the building proper during the sermon and left with the catechumens; "bystanders," who remained even during the Eucharist but could not partake; and "restored penitents," who could again share the Communion. After 300, church councils such as that at Elvira levied various penalties for infractions. The churches obviously strained to maintain commitment at an acceptable level as converts flooded the churches during this period.

Latter-day Martyrs

Several factors, some external and some internal, combined during the reign of peace initiated by Gallienus to foster a powerful movement of Christian asceticism. Externally, of course, Christianity inherited some ascetic tendencies from Jewish sects such as the Essenes, who carried their rigorism into the churches. A widespread dualism encouraged these tendencies further. In addition, some persons were naturally inclined to a life of solitude, prayer, and self-discipline and found in it a counterweight to the dominance of the state. When persecution ceased, moreover, it left a vacuum for those who measured sanctity by the devotion of the martyrs. Men and women responded to Jesus' demand for self-denial and his appeal to the rich young man to sell his possessions and give the proceeds to the poor. They heard as well Paul's exhortations to bodily as well as spiritual discipline and self-control, and his preference for celibacy in view of the expected return of Christ (1 Corinthians 7). Many tried to emulate the example of the Jerusalem community in sharing goods and responded to the high moral standards set by the first generation of Christians.

Two different types of monasticism emerged during the late third and early fourth centuries: hermitic and coenobitic. Coenobitic, or "common life," monasticism originated shortly after Constantine and Licinius issued the Edict of Milan and, therefore, will receive treatment in the next section. Although Anthony of Egypt is often cited as the first hermit, he was not, for he himself sought guidance from other hermits. His popularity during a long career (270–356), however, gave impetus to the movement to the desert. Athanasius's biography of Anthony, written just after Anthony died, further fueled the burgeoning movement. Born in Egypt of Christian parents, Anthony did poorly in school, avoided other children, and "desired only to lead a simple life at home" (*Life of Anthony* 1). When he was about eighteen or twenty years old, his parents died, leaving a younger sister for him to care for. Shortly after their deaths, he was reflecting one day on the way the apostles had forsaken everything to follow Jesus and how the early Christians of Jerusalem laid all their possessions at the feet of the apostles. As he entered the church, Anthony heard Jesus' words to the rich young man being read; he took them to be directly spoken to him, and, leaving the church, proceeded to give away all of his property to the poor except for a little he reserved for his sister.

Entrusting his sister to the care of nuns (virgins), he visited hermits and learned from each some of the secrets of the solitary life. Although he did some manual labor, he set himself to the difficult task of "praying without ceasing" (1 Thess. 5:17). Nearly illiterate, he memorized scripture as he heard it read in the churches. In the desert, Anthony did battle with demons, which sought constantly to entice him away from his vocation, and he came out a victor. After living several years on the outskirts of a village, at age thirty-five he crossed the Nile and set out for Pispir, where he lived in an abandoned fort. His fame spread and great crowds came to see him. Spurred on by his example, many youth chose the monastic life.

As presented by Athanasius, Anthony viewed asceticism as a contest through which one may attain the prize of heaven. He was God's athlete overcoming the demonic. By prayer and fasting, one could be made a better person day by day. For those who opened themselves to God's working, the Spirit would drive out vices such as avarice, malice, covetousness, and lechery and instill virtues such as wisdom, justice, temperance, courage (the Greek cardinal virtues), love, faith, meekness, and hospitality. The devil and his hosts will do everything possible to subvert the faithful ascetic, but God's power in Christ is sufficient to overcome them.

Like most monks, Anthony yearned for martyrdom and narrowly missed it during the persecution of Maximin Daia in 311, when he ministered to confessors in mines and prisons and encouraged others before the judges. When the persecution ceased, he returned to the "daily martyrdom" of the hermit—fasting, wearing a hair shirt, and never bathing or even washing his feet. Again, so many besieged him that he had to flee to the Inner Mountains overlooking the Red Sea. There he guided other monks, performed miracles, saw visions, and did other things characteristic of a person utterly dedicated to God. He died at age 105.

The way of the desert monk, whether hermitic or coenobitic, was a way of holy obedience. The monks sought, first of all, to deny themselves, take up a cross, and follow Jesus (Luke 9:23). They wanted, above everything, to imitate Christ and the martyrs who had done so. Many were willing literally to meet Jesus' challenge to the rich youth to sell all possessions and give the proceeds to the poor so as to follow him (Luke 18:22). A decision so radical as this made theirs, in the second place, a movement of protest against both Roman culture and churches that allowed discipline to deteriorate. The more the churches accommodated the world, the louder these monks' protest sounded. Like the martyrs, the monks lifted loud voices against alliance with a state whose very fabric was woven from the thread of pagan religion. These latter-day martyrs still carried with them the early Christian suspicion of lives settled comfortably into customs shaped by superstition and idolatry. The earliest monks were rugged individualists, sometimes disdaining even the institutions of the church in their quest for complete obedience to God alone.

The means for achieving such complete obedience were solitude, self-discipline, and prayer. The Greek term *monachos* ("monk") derives from the word *monos* ("alone"). The object of the "solitary" was to confront the full mystery of the invisible God in silence. Even among coenobites, association with others was viewed as a barrier to this encounter. To be among other persons was to risk distractions. Solitude alone, however, will not assure centeredness on God. That requires discipline, especially the discipline of fasting. Here, to be sure, many monks fell under the spell of dualism, the idea that matter is evil and the spirit alone is good. Some literally attempted to destroy their bodies by starving themselves, wearing chains, disregarding personal hygiene, and otherwise displaying contempt for the physical. In time, such extremism gave way to more moderate disciplines designed to enhance the life of prayer.

The calling of the monk was, above all else, a calling to prayer. A monk's ultimate goal, of course, was the vision of God, like that experienced by Moses. Seeing God requires "purity of heart." Purity of heart is a product of God's transforming love at work in the lives of those who open themselves to God in prayer. Thus, in the words of Abba Isaac, a disciple of

Anthony, every monk's aim was "continual and unbroken perseverance in prayer" with a view to attaining "an immovable tranquillity of mind and a perpetual purity" (Cassian *Conferences* 9.2). Some prayed in simple ways, imagining God in human form, while others prayed in more complex style. They recited the Lord's prayer as "the method and form of prayer proposed to us by the Judge himself" (6.24). They chanted the psalms, some attempting to recite all 150 psalms every day. They repeated the petition taken from Psalm 69:1 ("O God, make speed to save me; O LORD, make haste to help me") as a kind of mantra designed to collect the mind in time of temptation. They developed "the prayer of the heart" or "Jesus prayer," which entailed reciting over and over: "Lord, Jesus Christ, Son of God, have mercy on me a sinner." The desert monks learned a lot about the psychology of prayer and how to induce moods that could facilitate intuitive experience of the divine.

Christian Mysticism

The Christian mysticism that blossomed during this era had some of its roots in monastic soil, others in the Old Testament Psalms and prophets, others in the Pauline and Johannine writings of the New Testament, and still others in the experience of the martyrs. However, Platonism supplied the sunshine and rain to produce a luxuriant plant.

Platonism circulated in a variety of forms, some more or less closely affiliated with Christianity and some independent of it. Platonist preachers traveled around proclaiming the message of salvation found in the *Corpus Hermeticum*, a collection of materials dating from the second to the fourth centuries. In the main, such popular promoters fell far below the level of Plotinus, but they aspired to the same basic goals: a return ultimately to unity with the One and, in the interim, "a flight of the alone to the Alone."

The Gnostics, who drew many ingredients for their hodgepodge from Platonism, coveted immediate, intuitive experience of God. *Gnosis* meant for them not intellectual but spiritual "knowledge." According to *The Gospel of Truth*, a work sometimes ascribed to Valentinus himself, the Word, the thought and the mind of the Father, came forth from the *Pleroma* ("Fullness") in order to bring the gift of the knowledge of God. God enlightened the "perfect," that is, Gnostics, with true knowledge. Those who have received such knowledge are "from above" and do the will of the Father. By knowledge, they purify themselves from multiplicity and enter into unity with God.

Clement of Alexandria and Origen both walked the Gnostic path, distinguishing themselves from heterodox Gnostics by repudiating their dualism. This direction was quite likely worked out by Pantaenus, the

"Sicilian bee" who founded the "school" of Alexandria. Clement, however, deserves credit for wedding biblical and Hellenistic traditions to give birth to a Christian contemplative tradition. According to Clement, *gnosis* should combine three features: contemplation, fulfilling the precepts of Jesus (as the Word), and instruction of good persons (*Stromateis* 2.10.46). For Clement, *gnosis* is a gift of the Teacher, Christ. In his *Address to the Greeks*, Clement has the Logos cry out, "Freely I give you the Word, the knowledge of God, I give you this freely, in perfection, in myself" (120.3). How? By reading and explaining the scriptures to us. Philosophy may serve as a guide if we will use it wisely, but the starting point for *gnosis* must be the scriptures. Heterodox Gnostics erred by starting with philosophy. The ultimate goal of the Gnostic is to "know" or "to see" or "to possess" God. The way to that goal is prayer or contemplation. We can ascertain whether we have reached the ultimate goal when we love as God loves. "God is love and is knowable to those who love God." Clement was the first Christian theologian to characterize this as "deification." "The Logos of God became human so that you might learn how human beings can become divine" (*Address* 11). Like the Stoics, from whom he drew many ethical insights, Clement urged gnostics to strive for *apatheia,* a lack of desire by which disorders of fallen human nature are overcome and stability is attained. Love is the supreme motive.

Scholars debate today whether Origen should be credited as a co-creator of Neoplatonism with Plotinus. Both, it is now recognized, studied under Ammonius Saccas, who, like Origen, was born of Christian parents and evidently remained faithful to his upbringing. From early on Origen practiced what Eusebius called "the most philosophic life possible" (*H.E.* 6.3.7-10), an extreme asceticism that induced him to take literally Jesus' observation that some should become eunuchs for the kingdom's sake. From Clement, Origen learned to put scriptures at the center of his quest for truth in a way that distinguished him from Plotinus, yet he went beyond his teacher in contemplation of Christ in the scriptures. Origen has received much criticism for his handling of scripture. He was obviously capable of commenting on it in the historical sense, but the higher, "spiritual" or allegorical sense fascinated him far more, precisely because it catered to his quest for *gnosis*. Since no item of scripture had gotten there by chance, Origen had to find its spiritual nuances even when he did not dare do a literal interpretation. Unlike Clement, however, Origen manifested only a passing interest in the moral sense of scriptures.

Origen laid foundations for both asceticism and mysticism, which, in his mind, were closely connected. The soul must increasingly detach itself from the egoistic desires that enslave it in the world. This detachment takes place by following Christ and participating in his life. To follow him, however, brings the Christian into a fierce battle against demons, for they resist the indwelling Word with all their power. At the heart of Origen's mystical theology was the action of the divine Logos, who grows in the soul and to whom the soul is wed. Origen was the first to interpret the Song of Songs spiritually, either in terms of Christ speaking to the church or of Christ speaking to the individual soul. Like Clement, Origen distinguished the "gnostic" from the ordinary Christian, yet with concern for humility and awareness of human limitations. Origen's mysticism of the Logos extends into a mysticism of God, who is "beyond knowing."

CHAPTER SIXTEEN

LIFE TOGETHER

Early Christianity distinguished itself from its competitors in a variety of ways, but no distinction stands out more clearly than its corporate consciousness and cohesiveness. Pagans as well as Christians discerned the difference. Whereas Mithra could claim conventicles scattered all over the empire, Christianity possessed an empire-wide network bound together by a complex array of charities, worship, ministry, and doctrine. Not surprisingly, competitors often suspected something sinister in this. Some of the emperors, as noted earlier, envisioned Christianity as "an empire within the empire" that threatened the latter's control. When Constantine made his decision in favor of Christianity, its structured unity apparently tipped the balances in its favor; this was the religion, he concluded, that could hold a tottering colossus together.

Charities and Social Aid

One of the strong links in the Christian chain was its charities and social aid, offered with little discrimination. Although the Romans practiced largess, they sought something in return, if not *quid pro quo* in the gift, then at least honor or friendship. Christians, however, gave with expectation of "treasures in heaven."

Charities and social aid originated in local communities with giving of alms and foodstuffs for the clergy, the poor, and widows and orphans. As Tertullian described the procedures about 200 C.E., each person made a monthly deposit as he or she could. Churches spent the money for burial of the poor, for orphans, for the aging, for shipwrecked sailors, or for prisoners in the mines, on islands, or in prisons (*Apology* 39.56). Cyprian's treatise on *Work and Almsgiving* indicates the accent churches increasingly placed on giving as a means of grace. After baptism, those who slipped could "safeguard salvation" through works of justice and mercy. Prayers and fastings have less potency when they are unaccompanied by almsgiving. Those who fear losing their patrimony should fear more the loss of their salvation on account of covetousness and avarice. Besides alms contributed weekly or monthly, the wealthy sometimes gave huge sums of money.

Direction of charities and social aid in this period was entrusted to the bishops. The actual distribution, however, was done by deacons. Because of the vastness of the charities in the city of Rome, Bishop Fabian appointed seven regionary deacons to oversee the work by districts. His successor, Cornelius, reported in 250 that, in addition to about a hundred clergy, the Roman Church supported 1,500 widows and indigents (Eusebius *H.E.* 6.43). As the touching story of Deacon Lawrence—who gathered the poor when commanded to assemble the church's treasures—would demonstrate, this church distinguished itself by the extent of its care. Yet it was not alone. Churches everywhere took care of widows and orphans; tended the sick, the infirm, and the disabled; buried the dead, including indigents; cared for slaves; and furnished work for those who needed it.

Three types of social aid attest to the broad scope of Christian interknittedness. One involved care for prisoners incarcerated or forced to work in mines and for exiles during periods of persecution. The apologist Aristides reported that when Christians heard of anyone imprisoned, "they all render aid in that person's necessity, and if the person can be redeemed, they set him [or her] free" (*Apology* 15). Eusebius claimed that the youthful Origen not only stood by the side of martyrs during their imprisonment until their final condemnation but accompanied them to their execution as well (*H.E.* 6.3). To visit prisoners was a special charge of deacons, but many others joined them. So notorious were Christians in their care that Licinius, before the Edict of Milan, passed a law to the effect that no one was to supply food to prisoners on pain of imprisonment themselves (Eusebius *H.E.* 5.8). Charity by no means remained at home. Cyprian related how in 253 Carthaginian churches quickly raised 100,000 sesterces to ransom Numidians captured by barbarian marauders, noting that "the captivity of our brothers [and sisters] must be thought of as our captivity" (*Ep.* 62.1).

A second type of social aid entailed care for people in time of calamity. When a plague ravaged Carthage in about 250 and Alexandria about 259, Christians in those cities risked their own lives to care for the sick and dying. During a widespread plague in the reign of Maximin Daia, they not only tended the sick but also gathered all the hungry of the city to distribute bread to them (Eusebius *H.E.* 9.8).

A third type had to do with hospitality to strangers and aid to churches in poverty or peril. The Roman Church owed much of its early influence to these two factors. About 170, Dionysius of Corinth commended Bishop Soter not merely for conserving the custom of hospitality but for extending it as well "by aiding the saints with rich supplies, which he sends from time to time" (Eusebius *H.E.* 4.23.10). He went on to note that Rome had made a habit of aiding churches everywhere. Dionysius of Alexandria remarked in a letter to Stephen of Rome that the Romans had sent help "regularly" to the churches of Syria and Arabia (Eusebius *H.E.* 7.5.2). With aid went letters encouraging and uplifting other churches and tying more tightly the cord that united them.

Fellowship Meals

Underlying the interknittedness of Christianity, which helped it to withstand assaults, was a fellowship preserved by tangible experiences of *koinonia* in *agape* meals. During the second century, as mentioned earlier, these meals were detached from the observance of the Eucharist, yet they continued to be observed. In the Catholic Tertullian's day (ca. 200) *agape* meals played a prominent role in Christian communal life in Carthage, not only as fellowship, but also as worship.

To pagans who construed such gatherings in the worst possible light, Tertullian retorted: "Our meal, by its very name, indicates its purpose. It is called by a name which to the Greeks means 'love' " (*Apology* 39.16). Clement of Alexandria spoke with similar feeling about the intended objectives of the meal to fix their gaze "on the holy assembly of love, the heavenly *ekklesia*" (*Instructor* 2.1.4).

By the mid-third century, the *Agape* meal had slipped from this high pedestal, for Origen scarcely took pains to defend it against Celsus. Sects like the Carpocratians abused it in the way pagans imagined (Clement *Stromateis* 3.2.10). As a Montanist, Tertullian derided Catholics for their continued observance (*Fasting* 17). Origen hinted at improprieties in the meals when he urged that the believers' kisses be chaste (*Commentary on Romans* 16:16). Cyprian, too, sounded cautious in urging "temperate festivity" with psalms or something "spiritual" (*To Donatus* 16). He denounced unfaithful bishops who "brought no aid to starving brothers and sisters" and others who neglected the offering for the poor (*The Lapsed* 6). Although the meals continued until the sixth century, they obviously looked more and more like pagan banquets and less and less like the charitable meals their name connoted.

Worship

The center of early Christian unity, in this era as in every other, was its worship of one God who was self-disclosed through the centuries to Israel and in a definitive way in Jesus of Nazareth. By the early third century, the worship service was beginning to separate into two parts, the first for catechumens and the second for the faithful. The second part, according to

Hippolytus, was observed in connection with baptisms or ordinations as well as on Sundays in regular worship.

The service for catechumens was designed primarily to instruct new converts, but persons already baptized were exhorted to attend both the daily and the weekly instruction. The catechist, usually a presbyter, read scriptures and explained them. At the end of the sermon, catechumens were dismissed. The formula *Ite! Missa est* ("Go! You are dismissed or sent!") may have been the source of the title "Mass" for the services.

The service for the faithful consisted still of the essential elements listed by Justin with some added details. Like the prayers of the *Didache*, these services too emphasize thanksgiving (*eucharistia*). They hint, however, at the sacrificial terminology and thought that would be more evident by the mid-third century. "Remembering his death and resurrection, therefore, we offer you the bread and cup" contains the imagery of sacrifice. Cyprian did not hesitate to speak of "offering the eucharist," "offering sacrifice," "partaking of the sacrifice," or "altar" and "priest." In this he moved well beyond Hippolytus and Tertullian.

Wherever Christians traveled throughout the empire, they would have found a two-part liturgy like this—the sermon featured in the first part, the Eucharist in the second. Existence of these basic elements, however, did not preclude diversity in different areas—North Africa, Rome, Syria, Egypt. Elaboration of this simple pattern and standardization, however, awaited the advent of Constantine and the entrance into the churches of more affluent and better-educated persons, who could appreciate elaborate and subtle ritual.

The Christian Calendar and Saints' Days

This period witnessed also the elaboration of the Christian calendar, but it did not change significantly enough to merit more than a few comments. Christians still observed Sunday as a day of worship and not as a day of rest, which it became in 321 by decree of Emperor Constantine. In the mid-third century, the Syrian manual entitled *Didascalia Apostolorum* (*Teaching of the Apostles*) revealed the importance of the day. Christians saw observance of Sunday as a law. This day established a rhythm for the rest of the week. On Wednesdays and Fridays, Christians fasted, as in the first two centuries.

Easter was also well established in the Christian calendar by the beginning of this era. The festival consisted of three major observances. It began with a strict fast of one, two, or more days. On Saturday night, the faithful held an all-night prayer watch consisting, in addition to prayers, of readings from the prophets, the Gospels, and the Psalms "until the third hour in the night after the Sabbath" (9:00 P.M.). At that hour they could break their fast and celebrate the Lord's Supper (*Didascalia Apostolorum* 21). As earlier, the churches baptized new converts on Easter Sunday.

The churches observed Pentecost as a single feast day during which fasting was forbidden. According to Tertullian (*Baptism* 19.2), baptisms were performed at this time just as they were at Easter. Near the end of this period, the Council of Elvira (305) prescribed special observance of the day of Pentecost, and, shortly after 332, Eusebius of Caesarea (*The Pascal Observance* 3) connected it with the ascension of Jesus. In the fourth century, Christians added another nuance when they noted that the period consisted of eight Sundays, thus connoting resurrection in a special way.

Whether Lent, the forty-day fast prior to Easter, began to be celebrated during the third century is debated. The *Didascalia Apostolorum* attests that the churches of Syria held a less strict fast from Monday through Thursday before the strict fast started on Friday. The diet consisted of bread, salt, and water only. A forty-day fast independent of the Easter fast appeared in Egypt either in the late third or early fourth century. This fast extended the two days per week (Wednesday and Friday) when Christians fasted regularly. Lent observance did not begin elsewhere until later in the fourth century.

Christmas observances on December 25 cannot be dated earlier than the fourth century, perhaps about 330 in Rome. In the East, however, where January 6 was the day for feasts of the winter solstice, some Christians attempted to connect this date with Christ's life. According to Clement of Alexandria (*Stromateis* 1.21.146), the Basilidians celebrated January 6 as the date of Jesus' baptism by spending the preceding night reading. No clear evidence exists for observance of Epiphany ("Manifestation") before the fourth century.

Art and Architecture

Christians met in the homes of members at the outset. The growth of their communities, however, necessitated adaptation of houses for use as church buildings. Fortunately, one specimen of this type of architecture survived the destruction of the Roman fortress at Dura-Europos on the Euphrates River in Mesopotamia in 256. As was done in the case of the synagogue discovered there, a private house of medium size was reconstructed for use by a Christian community soon after 232. Externally it retained its previous appearance to allay suspicion among authorities. On the interior, however, walls were removed to make three rooms—a large oblong room with a seat for the presiding presbyter or bishop at the northern end, a second large room perhaps employed for *Agape* meals or instruction of catechumens, and a small room turned into a baptistery.

The baptistery alone was adorned with paintings of a highly symbolic character. On the back wall of the baptistery were a painting of the good shepherd standing near his flock on an upper panel and, on a smaller scale, a painting of Adam and Eve, the tree of life, and the serpent on a lower panel—indicating that Christ has overturned the effects of the fall. On the western side wall an artist has depicted on the upper panel two of Jesus' miracles—the healing of the paralytic and the stilling of the storm—and on the lower panel a symbolic representation of the resurrection—the three Marys moving toward a tomb, holding torches and vases filled with myrrh in their hands. On the short north wall opposite the baptistery, the five wise maidens march in procession toward the left to meet the bridegroom. On the eastern wall between two doors the lower panel depicts David and Goliath and the Samaritan woman at the well as symbols of faith and hope. The objective was obviously to remind those who received baptism that they were participating in the power of the risen Christ to overcome evil and death.

A larger and more elaborate *titulus,* or church center, has been uncovered in Rome. Under a fifth-century edifice of saints John and Paul are the remains of at least four private houses, three of which date from the mid-second century, the other from the third. From the outside the three-storied house looked like an apartment building. On the first floor was a row of shops behind an arcade. On the upper floors, however, existed a room at least 50 feet by 40-60 feet, possibly two stories high. By the beginning of the fourth century, this building was owned by Christians, as frescoes with Christian symbols confirm. By that date, it contained a room for storing relics and an altar. Evidently the long periods of relative peace permitted Christians to obtain title to property and to utilize it more or less openly. When persecutions broke out, of course, they risked confiscation or destruction of it until the time of Constantine, but the risk did not deter them.

Like their Jewish forebears, the first generations of Christians were somewhat reserved in their employment of art, even as late as the Synod of Elvira in 305. Where they did use it, they followed in the same footsteps in depicting symbolically themes drawn from the scriptures, first of the Old Testament and then of the New. In the Greco-Roman world of the third century, this led to some rather curious specimens, for Christians often had to employ pagan artists who would not understand what they were depicting and would incorporate a vast array of pagan symbolism alongside the Christian. At the same time, in periods of persecution, Christians had to use Christian symbols such as the cross sparingly not only for fear of detection but also because of popular distortion and misunderstanding.

What happened, therefore, was that Christians attached their own interpretations to pagan symbols. The peacock represented immortality, the dove the Holy Spirit, and the palm of victory the triumph of martyrs. In one of their boldest reinterpretations, Christians depicted Christ as the Unconquered Sun driving his chariot across the sky. They construed the vine of the burial cult of Dionysius in terms of Jesus' words about the vine and the branches (John 15:1-3). They depicted Jesus the Good Shepherd as a Greek Hermes, the Ram-carrier (*Criophorus*).

In time, however, more distinctively Christian symbolism began to prevail. On an early tombstone, a Christian artist scratched an anchor, the shaft of which is a cross, with fish hooked to each end of the anchor. From Tertullian we know that Christians were using the Greek word for fish, ICHTHYS, as a cryptogram to denote the phrase "Jesus Christ, Son of God, Savior." In the catacombs, underground cemeteries cut into the soft tufa beds outside of Rome, Christian painters expressed their faith in imagery drawn from the scriptures in a manner similar to the scenes at Dura-Europos. Christian art emphasized deliverance from and victory over evil.

It is important to recognize the symbolic nature of early Christian art. Christian artists did not attempt to depict biblical or other scenes literally. Although they depended on both oriental and Roman art forms and techniques, they sought nothing less than to use symbolism to bring the mystery of Christ's redemptive work and his church in its transcendent character nearer to the earthly realm.

Holy Orders

In this critical period of Christian history, the churches relied heavily on authorized leadership to coordinate, educate, inspire, and guide a growing and increasingly diverse constituency. Although the main lines of Christian organization and understanding of ministry were in place by 180, significant new developments occurred in the period that followed as a consequence of rapid expansion, challenges posed by persecution, and the upward mobility of both the leaders and the constituency.

At the local level, the threefold office of bishop, presbyters, and deacons existed nearly everywhere. The roles that each played, however, varied considerably. In Asia Minor and North Africa, where there were large numbers of bishops, these bishops obviously played less significant roles than in Rome and Italy or Alexandria and Egypt, where there were few. On the other hand, where bishops had extensive responsibilities, as in Italy and Egypt, presbyters and deacons assumed greater importance; where bishops had smaller charges, as in Asia Minor or North Africa, presbyters and deacons figured less prominently. The fact is that presbyters of Rome and Alexandria and their surrounding territories had responsibilities equivalent to bishops of small towns in Asia Minor or North Africa. Indeed, according to the *Didascalia Apostolorum*, composed in Syria about 250, deacons had considerably more importance than presbyters. Presbyters held more or less honorific places, whereas deacons discharged extensive ministries under the direction of the bishop. Roman regional deacons appointed by Fabian to supervise the extensive charities of the city had no counterpart elsewhere.

Local offices were also extended, in part to bear the growing weight of ministry and in part to provide support for the needy. About 215, Hippolytus listed among the unordained confessors, widows, readers, virgins, subdeacons, and exorcists. The *Didascalia* deleted virgins and exorcists but added deaconesses. Cyrian referred to acolytes. The confessor, Hippolytus directed, was to be permitted to minister as a deacon or presbyter without ordination, "for he has by his confession attained to the dignity of the presbyterate" (*A.T.* 10). Readers, selected by the bishop, read scriptures during the worship service. Subdeacons assisted deacons. Exorcists did not require laying on of hands, Hippolytus said, "because the fact is evident" (15). Acolytes assisted in the Eucharist.

The role of women requires special comment. Widows were classified as an "order," although an unordained one, a fact that Tertullian explicitly indicated. Church orders regularly listed widows after the three ordained orders, and Clement and Origen listed widows several times in a quadrumvirate of clergy. Some widows seem to have performed a highly regarded function. Although Hippolytus excluded them from performing a liturgical role, he noted that they had a special duty to pray. The *Didascalia* directed, likewise, that widows do nothing but pray, both for those who gave alms and for the whole church. Hippolytus did not mention women deacons, or deaconesses, but the *Didascalia* listed their role separate from that of widows. Deaconesses were to perform the same ministry to women that deacons did to men—visiting the sick and tending to their bodily needs, anointing persons being baptized with the oil of exorcism and the oil of thanksgiving, and teaching the newly baptized how to keep "the seal" of baptism pure and unbroken (16). Like Tertullian, the *Didascalia* forbade women to baptize, but Tertullian himself went beyond others in constricting the role of women. He was scandalized that in some of the sects women taught, debated, exorcised, and "maybe even baptized" (*Prescription Against Heretics* 41.5). Even after joining the Montanist sect, which the prophetesses Priscilla and Maximilla had led alongside Montanus, Tertullian still refused women the right to teach, baptize, or offer the Eucharist, for such duties belong to males (*The Veiling of Virgins* 9.1). Women prophetesses could speak, but not during the regular worship.

At the regional level, the churches gradually accommodated their structures to conform to Roman dioceses and provinces. Although the Council of Nicea formalized this arrangement in 325, the trials of the second and third centuries accelerated the need for joint decision making by bishops. The first synods addressed the Montanist crisis in the late second century and the debate regarding the observance of Easter about 196. Apart from these, the custom of convening synods of bishops and other clergy to resolve debated issues seems to have caught on in the first half of the third century. Unfortunately, little data about the earlier conventions have survived. A synod held in Carthage between 218 and 222, for instance, dealt with the question of rebaptism of heretics. Two synods at Alexandria in 228 and 231 censured and excommunicated Origen because of his ordination in the diocese of Caesarea and perhaps because of his theology. A synod that convened in Iconium in Asia Minor under Firmilian of Caesarea in Cappadocia about 230–235 declared baptisms by heretics invalid. Ninety bishops of Numidia gathered to condemn Privatus, Bishop of Lambese, as a heretic. In 244, a synod convened at Bostra in Arabia to watch Origen overwhelm Beryll, the Bishop of Bostra, but no record of the actual debate has survived. Much deeper insight into the function of synods comes from those that dealt with the problem of the "lapsed" during the Decian persecution, where the interaction of bishops on these complex matters illustrates the growth of episcopal collegiality.

As can be seen in the action of these councils, the bishops of churches in metropolitan centers, such as Carthage, Rome, Alexandria, or Caesarea in Cappadocia, possessed respect and influence based on the size and preeminence of their churches. In the synods dealing with affairs in the Roman province of Africa, for instance, Cyprian presided as *primes inter pares* ("first among equals"). Dealing with the sticky issue of rebaptism in 255, Cyprian took pains to poll each bishop in attendance with assurance that none would be penalized for dissenting from the majority and Cyprian's own opinion. He then reported the action not only to Stephen, Bishop of Rome (*Ep.* 72), but also to the bishops of Numidia (*Ep.* 70). He also corresponded with Firmilian, Bishop of Neocaesarea in Cappadocia, and obtained his affirmation. Firmilian's opening greeting supplies an interesting confirmation of the sense of a universal bonding the bishops experienced. The fact that such "unanimity" did not include Stephen demonstrates the sense of equality among bishops of major sees.

Having said that, we must also recognize that, in the West, the Bishop of Rome as well as the Church of Rome held a position of prestige and perhaps authority not accorded to any other see. Irenaeus pointed to this standing in his often quoted, but much debated, statement that "every church must agree [*convenire*] with this Church [of Rome] on account of its more powerful origin [*propter potentiorem principalitatem*]," that is, as "founded and constituted by the two most eminent Apostles Peter and Paul" (*Adv. haer.* 3.3.1). Such a respectful attitude, however, did not preclude the Bishop of Lyons from remonstrating Victor when the latter threatened to excommunicate or did excommunicate the Christians of Asia for their retention of the Jewish date for breaking the fast at Easter. In the initial edition of his treatise on *The Unity of the Catholic Church,* Cyprian almost certainly acknowledged Roman primacy, as Tertullian did, based on succession from Peter. In a revision made during the rebaptism controversy, however, he modified his statement to demonstrate that all bishops equally hold a succession from Peter.

In the battle against heresies of one kind or another, succession lists of certain churches undoubtedly enhanced their standing. Churches such as Rome, Antioch, or Ephesus that could trace succession from apostles occupied enviable positions. When Irenaeus, although claiming to be able to cite numerous other succession lists, used the Roman list above in illustrations, he elevated the Roman claim above all others and assured it a permanency no other see could match, despite the unreliability of some of his information.

Another landmark change occurred in this crucial era, in this case in the understanding of the role of the ordained clergy. The clergy had already begun to be sharply distinguished from the laity as early as the time of Clement of Rome. Although the process of differentiation moved steadily forward during the second century, some sense of the oneness of the whole people of God persisted. Tertullian, for instance, insisted that laymen could baptize, dispensing what they had received (*Baptism* 17). Origen pointed out that baptism was the layperson's ordination. On preference for virginity, moreover, Tertullian thought laypersons should abide by the same rule as the clergy, asking, "Are not even we lay persons priests?" (*Exhortation to Chastity* 13.4).

What pushed the distinction forward was the gradually increasing tendency to interpret the Lord's Supper, or Eucharist, as a sacrifice. The process, however, advanced more slowly in some areas than in others. Whereas Irenaeus still identified bishops as presbyters, Hippolytus thought of them as "high priests" (*A.T.* 3.5-6). Both presbyters and deacons fell far below this level. Likewise, the *Didascalia* acclaimed bishops as "high priests" and "kings," whereas presbyters and deacons are "priests" and "Levites" (9), both chosen by bishops. Cyprian did not distinguish so sharply between bishops and presbyters, but he sounded a far more priestly note in the way he construed the offices. Since they are dedicated to the service of the altar, they must avoid all uncleanness (*Ep.* 67.1). They must receive honor due the priestly estate, for Jesus taught due respect for all true priests (*Ep.* 3.2). In a letter to a fellow bishop, moreover, he argued that water must be mixed with wine in the Communion cup on the grounds that "the priest who imitates what Christ did and then offers the true and full sacrifice in the Church of God the Father, if he thus begins to offer according to what he sees Christ himself offered, performs truly in the place of Christ" (*Ep.* 63.14).

The Alexandrians, deeply rooted in a teaching tradition, did not distinguish clerical grades as sharply as did Hippolytus and Cyprian. For them, the "gnostic" is the true presbyter. Clement decisively distinguished his "gnostics" from heretical ones in "maintaining the apostolic and ecclesiastical correctness of doctrine" (7.16), but he saw the improvement of persons through study of scriptures as their vocation. Origen distinguished the order of bishops, presbyters, and deacons more clearly than Clement did and could say that bishops offer to God the sacrifices of propitiation just as the high priest of ancient times did (*Homily 5 on Leviticus* 4). Because of his painful experience with Demetrius, however, he directed some harsh words at abuses of power by bishops, surpassing the worst secular rulers. Like Clement, he insisted that presbyters live worthily of their vocations. In Alexandria, presbyters elected bishops and installed them until the fourth century.

Throughout this critical era, the power and importance of bishops increased steadily. At the beginning of the period, Irenaeus, Tertullian, and Clement of Alexandria still thought of bishops as presbyters, albeit presbyters in a class by themselves. As the chief witnesses and guardians of apostolic tradition, bishops were those men most eminently qualified to hold the title of presbyter. By the middle of the century, bishops had supplanted teachers such as Clement and Origen as the trustworthy conservers of the faith. The action taken by Demetrius, Bishop of Alexandria, against Origen in 228 and 231 doubtless signified the triumph of the episcopal office over the teaching office. Not surprisingly, as a presbyter in Caesarea, Origen stressed that the bishop is a servant and not a ruler of the church (*Homily 6 on Isaiah* 1). At this point, he might have saved his breath. Church councils, once including others besides bishops, were becoming episcopal councils. Bishops resolved in them not only doctrinal but also moral issues of importance in their dioceses. Cyprian put it quite plainly: Whoever is not in communion with the bishop in a diocese is not in the church (*Ep.* 66.8). As head of the clergy, the bishop exercises a real primacy over the church and is the locus of its unity. That is why there can be only *one* bishop. Just as there is one God, one Christ, and one Holy Spirit, so also must there be only one bishop (*Ep.* 49.2). The bishop is the rock on which the church is founded. In cases where false claimants arise a bishop will receive confirmation from other bishops of the universal church.

In circumstances so contorted as those of this era, ordination also assumed increased importance. Election of bishops involved the laity, but ordination by laying on of hands was restricted to the clergy. Bishops alone, convened normally from churches in the same province, laid hands on bishops. The bishop of a particular diocese evidently appointed and laid hands on presbyters as a sign of ordination, but other presbyters also laid hands on those being ordained; presbyters could dispense what they had received. The bishops alone appointed and ordained deacons. By the mid-third century, Cyprian was speaking of ordination as a "promotion" from one "degree" (*gradus*) to another. He defended the election of Cornelius, for instance, on the basis of his "having been promoted through all of the ecclesiastical offices" (*Ep.* 55.8). Ordination obviously favored the episcopate.

CHAPTER SEVENTEEN

FIRST PRINCIPLES

Christianity confronted its most serious challenges during the period extending from Clement of Alexandria to Constantine. Nowhere does the challenge stand out more clearly than in the efforts of Christians to express their faith in a context radically different from the one in which they began. For some still, deviations from an essentially Jewish understanding posed a severe threat. For others, Christianity served more to legitimate what they had already absorbed from the Greco-Roman milieu. Church leaders of this period had to wind their way between these extremes, on the one hand remaining faithful to Christianity's inheritance from Judaism, but at the same time, on the other hand, accommodating to the culture and thought patterns of the Roman world sufficiently to make Christianity intelligible and appealing.

Against such a background as this it would be too much to expect anything like a systematic theology. The closest anyone came to such a work was Origen's *First Principles*, composed about 220, in which the brilliant Alexandrian set forth the items he counted essential to the church's faith and beyond which theologians could speculate with considerable freedom. Others, too, struggled to establish a pattern of truth that could guide the churches through a veritable jungle of ideas without getting lost completely. At the center of their efforts, they framed what most called "the rule of faith," a summary related to but not exactly equivalent to the baptismal confessions, and sought further to define the canon. It will be useful here to examine these two developments and then look at some of the leading writers and their ideas in order to discern how the churches established some guiding principles.

The Rules of Faith

During the late second and third centuries, theologians regularly invoked what they called "the rule of faith" or "the rule of truth" in response to the claims of heretical teachers. What they seem to have cited in a rather general way were the baptismal confessions employed in local churches, which they adapted and filled out according to specific circumstances. It is obvious from the use that Irenaeus, Tertullian, and Hippolytus made of these statements that they did not feel bound to exact formulations, indicating that these creeds had not yet attained a fixed form. Sometimes, for instance, they cited them as two-part (Father and Son), at other times as three-part (Father, Son, and Spirit) confessions, yet consistently highlighting christology. Taken together, the evidence shows that Tertullian could not have known a fixed creed, even a local one, yet he did know some kind of formularies. Not long afterward, Tertullian's contemporary Hippolytus attests the use of a formal and fixed baptismal confession in Rome.

When he composed the *First Principles* about 220, Origen still thought in terms of a summary of faith drawn from scriptures as his basic guides. His "summary" of what "has been transmitted in a clear manner by the apostolic preaching" went far beyond the normal trinitarian confession of baptism—the soul, free will, the devil and his angels, creation and destruction of the universe, inspiration of scriptures, and the angels of God. Interspersed with these items are notations about points of disagreement or divergence. He obviously felt free to explore beyond the parameters established by the "rule of faith." On some issues, this resulted in real danger. By the time he had moved to Caesarea, he hinted at what appears to have been a formal creed whose articles "in being believed, save the person who believes them" (*The Gospel of John* 13:16). Here he underlined that the Christian must achieve all of the articles and not pick and choose among them. Contemporary study had demonstrated, too, that Origen attached great importance to the ecclesiastical tradition.

By the mid third century, the baptismal questions had acquired official recognition in a settled form. In a letter to Cyprian, Firmilian of Neocaesarea spoke of an "ecclesiastical rule" of baptism, of an "established and ecclesiastical interrogation," and of "the customary and established words of the interrogation" (Cyprian *Ep.* 75.10-11). Several factors undoubtedly pushed this process forward—the needs of the instruction of converts for baptism, the battle to define faith in the midst of threats of heresy and schism, use of confessions for liturgical purposes, and recitation by confessors in time of persecution. The churches, nevertheless, did not at this point reach the level of precision mandated by ecumenical councils in the fourth century and later.

The Canon of the New Testament

Although the basic nucleus for the New Testament formed in the preceding era, important facets of the formation process occurred in this one. The four Gospels, of course, had a firmly established place by the end of the second century. Irenaeus and the Muratorian Canon, a list now usually dated about 175 or 180, confirm this for the West, although a lacuna at the beginning of the latter caused the omission of Matthew. Countering Gnostic claims of inspiration for other Gospels, the Bishop of Lyons declared it "impossible that the Gospels be either more or fewer in number than they are." Christ "has given us the Gospel under four aspects, but bound together by one spirit." Invoking Revelation 4:7, Irenaeus depicted Matthew as a lion, symbolizing Christ's "effective working, leadership, and royal power"; Mark as a calf, depicting Christ's "sacrificial and priestly order"; Luke as a human face, describing Christ's advent as a human being; and John as an eagle, pointing to the gift of the Spirit hovering over the church. Four Gospels replicate "the four catholic covenants" given humankind: under Adam, under Noah, under Moses, and under Christ (*Adv. haer.* 3.11.8). Tatian's *Diatessaron,* a collation of the four Gospels, demonstrates their fixed place in Syria and the East at this time. Like Irenaeus, Clement of Alexandria appealed to tradition to confirm the four Gospels.

The Pauline corpus of thirteen letters also had attained universal recognition. Although Irenaeus did not list them as he did the Gospels, he cited all thirteen. It was evidently customary to view the apostle's letters in two blocks—to churches and to individuals—a fact that accounts for the current arrangement. In opposition to Marcion, Tertullian listed all of Paul's letters. He also noted that Catholic Christians "generally ascribe Luke's narrative to Paul" in order to sustain a claim to apostolic authorship (*Against Marcion* 4.5). In the East, Clement cited all except Philemon.

Acts (in connection with the Gospel of Luke), 1 John, and 1 Peter had attained general acceptance as well. Irenaeus, Clement, and Tertullian cited all three writings liberally. At this period, the Revelation was also employed in public worship in many churches, but the Montanist crisis soon made such usage controversial. According to the Muratorian Canon, the Roman Church received "both the Revelation of John and the Revelation of Peter, though some of us don't want them to be read in the church." Irenaeus, Clement, and Tertullian, however, cited Revelation favorably. Nonetheless, it remained in the disputed category for two centuries more.

The other writings that are now a part of the modern canon vied with several other works for universal acceptance. Clement of Alexandria, for instance, included *Barnabas* and the *Revelation of Peter* with the books now recognized (Eusebius *H.E.* 6.14). Others cited *1 Clement* and *The Shepherd of Hermas.* Although of disputed authorship, Hebrews had strong support among the Alexandrine scholars if not in the West. Clement ascribed the writing to Paul but theorized that Luke translated into Greek a Hebrew original composed by the apostle. Origen, although acknowledging that Hebrews was "not inferior" to Paul's other writings, knew the apostle could not have written it. While some speculated about authorship by Luke or Clement of Rome, Origen concluded that God alone knows (Eusebius

H.E. 6.25). In North Africa, Tertullian quoted Hebrews only once as the work of Barnabas and evidently placed it below apostolic writings, though above Hermas, despite its support for his rigorous views on discipline (*Modesty* 20). Cyprian explicitly rejected Pauline authorship of Hebrews and never quoted from it. In line with this, no Western writer before Hilary (d. 368) quoted it as an epistle of Paul.

Both Clement and Origen were aware of differing attitudes to James, Jude, 2 Peter, 2 and 3 John, and the Revelation. In a sermon, Origen referred, among other things, to the "twofold trumpet" of Peter's epistles, James, Jude, and John "in his epistles and Revelation" (*Homily on Joshua* 7.1). Elsewhere, however, he labeled 2 Peter "doubtful" and reported that not all considered 2 and 3 John authentic, though he did not question common authorship of the Gospel, the Revelation, and 1 John (Eusebius *H.E.* 6.25.7-10). In the West, Tertullian revealed no acquaintance with James, 2 Peter, or 2 and 3 John, but he quoted from Jude as an authoritative writing. Cyprian evidently did not refer to any of these disputed writings. Tertullian frequently quoted the Revelation as the work of the same author as the Gospel of John. Every other Latin writer after Tertullian—including Cyprian, Commodian, and Lactantius—also quoted it as authoritative, perhaps especially so in times of persecution. Irenaeus, too, constantly cited the Revelation as the work of the apostle John. Although he quoted from 2 John, he never cited James, Jude, or 3 John. Hippolytus, who quoted from all universally acknowledged books except Philemon and 1 John, also made much use of Revelation, writing a commentary on it, but he evidently did not cite other disputed writings.

Interpreting the Scriptures

The early Christians obviously sought to do theology on the basis of the revelation found in scripture, initially the Old Testament but by this period increasingly the New Testament. Although they differed somewhat in their theories of inspiration, they all subscribed to some kind of verbal theory. The real author of the scriptures is the Holy Spirit. Every jot and tittle, therefore, must have meaning because God would not go to the trouble of speaking idle thoughts. Herein rested the crux of the problem of interpretation: How do we wrest from the scriptures the message God has placed within them?

By the late second century, allegorical exegesis was beginning to prevail throughout the Christian world, not only among Gnostics but among orthodox writers as well. Now that the New Testament had achieved a firmly established place alongside the Old Testament, the allegorical method was beginning to be applied to it too. The heterodox Gnostics

185

evidently initiated this process. The Valentinians, for instance, cited the parable of the vineyard laborers to sustain their theory of thirty aeons. Others confirmed the five senses from the parable of the foolish virgins. Valentinians had a special interest in allegorizing the Gospel of John. Catholic writers countered with allegorical interpretations of their own. Irenaeus allegorized the parable of the good Samaritan as the fall of the human race among evil demons and their rescue by the Holy Spirit (*Adv. haer.* 3.18.2). Origen gave a similar exposition (*Homily on Luke* 34). Tertullian tried hard to avoid allegory, but even he lapsed into it occasionally. Origen, of course, sometimes outdid the Gnostics in his creative interpretations.

The Gnostics contributed one other important item to early Christianity: the commentary. The earliest commentary known was a *Commentary on the Gospel of John*, by the Valentinian scholar Heracleon, which Origen cited frequently in his commentary. Hippolytus wrote soon after a *Commentary on Daniel*, perhaps more expository sermons than commentary. Origen expanded the commentary effort immensely.

The Western fathers used allegory cautiously, clinging still to the typological approach they inherited from Judaism. Irenaeus, conservative here as in most matters, often lapsed into allegory, but tried hard to find the simple and obvious meaning of texts or, where that proved difficult, types. Tertullian exhibited still greater restraint. Wary of Gnostic abuses, he preferred the literal sense of Jesus' words and did not allegorize even Old Testament dietary laws. He formulated the rule that it is better to find less meaning than more meaning in the text. Hippolytus continued along the line of caution in preferring typology to allegory, owing much to Justin and Irenaeus. Cyprian, likewise, manifested real restraint, usually prooftexting or finding "types" to sustain certain views.

The Eastern fathers, inspired by Philo, showed far less caution. Clement of Alexandria, to be sure, acted with greater restraint than Origen did by virtue of a special interest in the moral sense of scripture, often prooftexting ethical views by quoting Jesus' words. Origen, however, felt deterred only by his own scholarly gifts. He had no peer in exposition of the texts in the literal sense. But no one was more conscious than he that, taken literally, many texts, especially of the Old Testament, caused extreme perplexity and offense. Some problems could be solved by typology, but many others could not if one assumes that every iota of scripture is equally as inspired as every other. So Origen raced from literal to spiritual or mystical interpretation. Every detail had meaning because it had a counterpart in the invisible world. Origen's influence prevailed everywhere in the East until the Antiochene school began to challenge it during the fourth and fifth centuries.

The most accurate way to depict theological thought in this somewhat fluid period will be to look at individual contributors.

Irenaeus, Bishop of Lyon

Born around 130, Irenaeus (ca. 130–202) grew up in Smyrna, where he sat at the feet of the saintly Polycarp (martyred ca. 155), drawing from him his penchant for biblical theology. Present in Rome during Polycarp's debate with Anicetus, Irenaeus studied in the school of Justin, from whom he gained much in apologetic methods but diverged in preference for biblical theology over Platonism. Moving to Lyons sometime after 164, he was ordained a presbyter. He narrowly missed martyrdom in 177 when Pothinus, the ninety-year-old bishop, sent him to Rome with a letter for Eleutherius (175–189). On his return to Lyons after the pogrom there, he succeeded Pothinus as bishop. We know little of his activity as bishop apart from his theological writing. He interceded with Victor (189–199) when the latter rashly excommunicated Christians of Asia because they refused to observe the Roman custom concerning Easter. According to Gregory of Tours, Irenaeus died a martyr in 202, but the late date of Gregory's writing (576) makes this tradition suspect.

Two major works of Irenaeus—*Refutation and Overthrow of Knowledge Falsely So-Called* (usually entitled *Against Heresies*) and *Proof of the Apostolic Preaching*—have survived. Unlike Justin, Irenaeus had few kind words for nonbiblical writers. He placed his confidence, rather, in the Old Testament and in writings beginning to be collected as a New Testament. Against Marcion and some of the Gnostics, he argued that the same God inspired both testaments. He considered the Septuagint inspired in its entirety. What he included in the New Testament beyond the four Gospels and thirteen letters of Paul is uncertain. Although Irenaeus criticized the Gnostics for allegorical exegesis, he employed it freely himself even in his interpretation of the New Testament, the first orthodox leader to do so. To solve problems posed by the Old Testament, he proposed a theory of progressive education of humankind. In the last analysis, he relied for his authority on the tradition committed to the churches by the apostles.

Against Gnostic and Marcionite dualism, Irenaeus affirmed Jewish monotheism. One God created the world *ex nihilo* and not by emanations. Through the Son and the Holy Spirit, God acted directly in creation and not through intermediaries, and God continues to act in inspiration or revelation. Where his teacher Justin thought of Logos as the hypostatized Divine Person, Irenaeus viewed the Logos as the Word of John 1:1-14, not a "second God" but the one God self-disclosed. Biblical and Pauline also in his concept of redemption, he developed what is known as the theory of recapitulation, in which Christ reversed the effects of Adam's fall. Whereas Adam disobeyed, Christ obeyed and thus overcame the powers that hold humankind captive—sin, death, and the devil. To establish fully his theory that Jesus did this in every stage of human life—infancy, childhood, youth, adulthood—he argued that Jesus lived to age fifty on the basis of John 8:57. Alongside the recapitulation theory, Irenaeus also developed the Greek concept of divinization in a modest way. "He became man," Irenaeus said, "in order that we might become divine."

Much debate has occurred about Irenaeus's doctrine of free will. In opposition to the gnostic division of persons into material, spiritual, and psychic, the Bishop of Lyons insisted on survival of free will even after the fall. Although the fall affected the "likeness" of God, it did not mar the "image." Despite the fact that every person is born in sin, therefore, human beings still can and must choose between good and evil; they do not inherit guilt.

Although Irenaeus drew much of his thinking about the church from Paul, he did not develop the apostle's principal imagery of the Body of Christ. He thought instead of the church as the People of God under a new covenant. He presupposed adult baptism, though one passage related to his recapitulation theory has been used to support infant baptism. He said little about the Eucharist, which evidently played a limited role in his thinking. It was "the antidote of life" and "no longer common bread." He preferred the phrase "new oblation of the new covenant." His view of ecclesiastical authority has been hotly debated among Protestants and Catholics. His statement that "every church must agree or come together with [*convenire*] this Church [of Rome] on account of its more powerful authority or greater antiquity [*propter potentiorem principalitatem*]" remains very uncertain because the Greek original has been lost. On eschatology, Irenaeus was millenarian.

Tertullian

Little is known of the life of Tertullian (160?–225?), the first theologian to write extensively in Latin. Probably born and reared in Carthage, he received an excellent education. He was converted to Christianity around 193 to 195 and immediately assumed a position of leadership in the church of Carthage. A rigorist on matters of discipline, he joined the Montanist sect around 206, yet continued his leadership in the defense of Christianity against Gnostics and Marcionites. After several years he separated from the Montanists and formed a sect named Tertullianists after himself. Throughout his career he belonged to the literary circles of Carthage. The exact date of his death is uncertain.

Thirty-one of Tertullian's writings have survived. They cover a variety of issues but may be grouped into three categories: apologies for Christianity, treatises on the Christian life, and works composed in opposition to heresies. Shortly after conversion, Tertullian addressed apologetic treatises

To the Nations and *Against the Jews*. Subsequently, he revised the former and published it as the carefully argued and finely crafted *Apology*, his best-known work. Later he elaborated a purely psychological argument developed in one chapter of the *Apology* under the title *The Testimony of the Soul*. In 212, he summarized his apology for Christianity in a treatise directed *To Scapula*, the proconsul of Africa.

Tertullian's treatises on the Christian life reflect a rigoristic mentality that conversion to Montanism reinforced. In his treatises *On the Shows* (196 or 197), *On Idolatry*, *On the Dress of Women*, and *To the Martyrs*, he left little room for accommodation to customs of contemporaries. Christians should be different; so, too, in treatises or sermons *On Baptism*, *On Prayer*, *On Repentance*, *On Patience*, and *To His Wife*. Those who came for baptism should already have "*ceased* sinning." Some stiffening of these views is evident in treatises he wrote as a Montantist, particularly in the work *On Modesty*, in which Tertullian condemned second marriages as fornication, and in a treatise absolutely forbidding *Flight in Persecution*.

In antiheretical writings, too, Tertullian displayed a separatist mentality. Like Irenaeus, he argued that heresy represented a departure from the truth that Christ delivered to the apostles and they to the churches they founded. Tertullian regularly condemned heresy as a consequence of the influence of philosophy, despite the fact that he owed much to Stoicism. In the treatise *On the Soul*, he characterized philosophers as "patriarchs of the heretics." Although he could admit begrudgingly at times that some philosophers stumbled onto the truth, he insisted on obtaining truth from revelation, including visions granted Montanist seers.

Defending Christianity from the culture of his day, Tertullian accentuated the authority of "the rule of truth" and of the Bible interpreted more or less literally but with reference to context and his own situation. He also invented ecclesiastical Latin. No match for Irenaeus in his grasp of biblical theology, Tertullian drew many of his basic presuppositions from Stoicism and thus laid a foundation for a distinctive Latin theology. Stoicism influenced his concept of the corporeality of both God and the soul. From this assumption, he deduced that sin is transmitted by seminal generation so that every human soul inherits characteristics of Adam's soul. He did not, however, take the step Augustine took in connecting guilt with the transmission of sin.

Tertullian secured the victory of the Logos christology of the apologists and Irenaeus over modalism. Whereas Praxeas held that one God is successively Father, Son, and Spirit, Tertullian insisted that the one God, for whom he coined the word *Trinitas*, is simultaneously Father, Son, and Spirit. His formula for this was "one substance in three persons." Anticipating later debate, he also insisted that the divine and human natures were not mixed or confused during the incarnation so as to produce a *tertium quid*.

Montanism influenced Tertullian's eschatology as it did his disciplinary views. According to this view, the dawning of the age of the Paraclete promised in John 14:16 signaled a time of new revelations and of more rigorous Christian discipline—increased fasting, absolute prohibition of second marriages, and willingness to suffer martyrdom. In some ways, given the influence of Montanism, it is remarkable that Tertullian had such a great impact on later theology, testimony perhaps of his basic orthodoxy and ability to coin apt theological phrases.

Clement of Alexandria

For this period, the most creative and daring efforts at relating Christian faith to contemporary culture took place in Alexandria and, thanks to Origen's removal there, Caesarea in Palestine. Born of non-Christian parents, probably in Athens, as a Christian, Clement (ca. 160–211/216) visited lower Italy, Syria, and Palestine before settling in Alexandria. It is uncertain whether he was ever ordained. The first Christian to attain some distinction as a scholar, he fled Alexandria in 202 or 203 during the persecution under Septimius Severus. He died between 211 and 216.

Three of Clement's major writings have survived: *Protrepticus pros Hellenas*, or *Address to the Greeks*, an apology for Christianity; *Paidogogos*, or *The Instructor*, how new converts should conduct themselves; and *Stromateis*, how more advanced Christians can grow still more. In addition, Clement left behind a sermon discussing how a rich person can be saved, a collection of gnostic texts, some exegetical notes, and fragments of several other works.

Unlike Tertullian, Clement held Greek philosophy in high esteem. Both the Hebrew prophets and the outstanding philosophers, especially Plato and the Stoics, served as pedagogues leading to Christ. Apparently unaware of the contradiction, Clement held both that the divine Logos inspired Greeks who attained truth and that the Greek greats plagiarized from Moses. The truth became incarnate in Jesus of Nazareth. Like Justin, Clement argued that Christianity was a species of philosophy far superior to Greek mystery religions. In support of this, he cited hundreds of classical texts, perhaps taken from popular manuals. Walking a careful line between those who insisted on "faith alone" and the Gnostics, he concurred with the latter on the need for *gnosis*, spiritual knowledge, but rejected both their negative view of creation and their ethical attitudes, which led at times to libertinism and at other times to extreme asceticism. He also endorsed marriage and strongly advocated free will in opposition to gnostic dualism.

In typically Alexandrian fashion, Clement employed allegorical exegesis. Scriptures, he thought, have three senses: literal, moral, and spiritual. In practice, Clement showed greater interest in the moral than in the other two senses. *The Instructor* is primarily a guide to the Christian moral life centered around the Stoic ideal of temperance. He aspired, however, to guide Christians beyond mere ethical rightness to self-control and *apatheia* and ultimately to *gnosis*, a term he was not prepared to relinquish to the Valentinians or other Gnostics.

Origen

The most eminent theologian prior to the conversion of Constantine, Origen (ca. 185–ca. 254) was born in Alexandria of Christian parents. His father, Leonides, taught him Greek literature and the Bible. Following his father's martyrdom in 202 during the persecution under Septimius Severus, Origen became a teacher and then the headmaster of the school of Alexandria. As the school grew, he assigned introductory lessons to his pupil Heraclas and confined himself to the teaching of more advanced students. Between 215 and 220, he began writing, publishing his famous work *On First Principles*. He traveled widely—to Rome, to Arabia (modern Jordan), and, at the invitation of the governor, to Antioch. In 231, he passed through Palestine on a trip to Athens and was ordained at Caesarea by Theoctistus and Alexander. Angered by this, Demetrius, Bishop of Alexandria, gathered a synod of Egyptian bishops, which ordered Origen out of Egypt and a second that defrocked him, an act rejected by Palestinian bishops. In Caesarea, Origen attracted many bright and earnest seekers, such as Gregory of Neocaesarea in Cappadocia and his brother, Athenodorus. Acquiring a high reputation as a theologian, Origen received frequent invitations to defend the faith. During the Decian persecution, he was imprisoned and tortured severely, but he remained resolute. His health impaired by this, he died in 254 or 255.

Origen desired, above all else, to be an orthodox Christian and interpreter of the Bible. His writings, many of which have perished, consist chiefly of commentaries, sermons, and brief notes on texts of scriptures. While still in Alexandria, Origen began, but did not complete, the *Hexapla*. Only fragments have survived. During his Caesarean years, Origen wrote several important works in addition to homilies and commentaries: a treatise on *Prayer*, an *Exhortation to Martyrdom*, his *Dialogue with Heraclides*, and, most significant of all, his reply to the *True Discourse* of Celsus.

Origen surpassed all contemporaries as exegete, spiritual writer, and theologian—elements he mingled in all of his works. Like Clement, he ascribed three senses to scriptures—corporeal or literal, psychic or moral, and spiritual or mystical. Unlike Clement, however, he rarely dwelt long on moral application. Rather, he used his unsurpassable gifts for explaining the literal sense to open the way for his real love—the spiritual sense. Convinced that every jot and tittle of scripture was inspired, he hastened to find everywhere the manifestation of Christ in them. All scriptures prophesy of Christ both as a whole and in detail.

As a spiritual writer, Origen sought to ground his spirituality in scripture. Although Platonism clearly furnished him with the basic framework for his thought, he would not have considered himself a Platonist but a Christian and a Bible expositor. One of the chief architects of the language and themes of Christian spirituality, Origen interpreted the bride of the Song of Songs as either the church or the individual soul. Origen also laid the groundwork for Christian asceticism, soon to burgeon in the Eastern church.

As a theologian, Origen anticipated and, some would say, precipitated much of the debate that took place after the conversion of Constantine. His early treatise *On First Principles* (220) notwithstanding, Origen was not a systematic theologian but a Christian who earnestly sought to answer questions raised by persons like his friend and patron Ambrose. This philosophical foundation of his thought was the Middle Platonism of his teacher Ammonius Saccas—a combination of Platonism, Stoicism, and a little Aristotelianism. Speculative ideas for which later generations condemned Origen included his doctrine of the pre-existence of souls; *apokatastasis*, or final restoration of all things; and subordination of the Logos. Christian teaching on these matters, however, had not reached a definitive form. All of the outstanding theologians of the fourth century owed him a massive debt: Athanasius, Basil, Gregory of Nazianzus, Gregory of Nyssa, and Didymus the Blind in the East; Hilary of Poitiers, Ambrose, Jerome, and Rufinus in the West. Not until the turn of the fifth century did attacks on him begin. His thought was condemned at Constantinople in 553, rendering it suspect in the East. Yet Westerners continued to study Origen until the thirteenth century. Today he and Augustine are the most studied of the Church Fathers.

Hippolytus

Born before 170, perhaps in the Greek East, Hippolytus (d. 235) was ordained a presbyter under Victor (189–198). Strongly influenced by Irenaeus, under whom he may have studied, he was a vigorous proponent of Logos theology and opponent of the modalism of Noetus, Sabellius, and Cleomenes. As noted earlier, his efforts brought him into conflict with Zephryinus (198–217). The accession of Callistus, whom he accused of both

Sabellianism and lax discipline, led him to separate from the Church of Rome. In 235, both Hippolytus and Pontian were exiled to Sardinia. Resignation of the office by the latter opened the way for Hippolytus's reconciliation and the ending of the schism. His remains were returned to Rome in the third century, and Hippolytus was revered as a martyr.

Several of Hippolytus's writings have survived: the *Philosophumena*, or *Refutation of All Heresies*; *The Chronicle*; *The Apostolic Tradition*; a number of exegetical and homiletical works; and fragments of others. Like Tertullian, Hippolytus attributed heresies to the influence of pagan ideas. In opposition to modalism, he subordinated the Logos to the Father and distinguished, with Theophilus of Antioch, between the Unspoken (*endiathetos*) and Spoken (*prophorikos*) Logos. Indeed, he believed that, if God wished, God could make a man God (*Refutation* 10:33). Callistus, accordingly, charged him with ditheism. Hippolytus also represented a rigorist stance on matters of discipline.

Novatian

Although Novatian withdrew from the Catholic Church and formed a separate sect in 251, he deserves mention as the next important theologian after Tertullian to write in Latin. Four of his writings survived under the name Tertullian or Cyprian: treatises on *The Trinity, Jewish Foods, The Shows*, and *The Good of Modesty*. In *The Trinity*, Novatian repudiated Marcion, the docetists, the adoptionists, and the modalists, arguing for the unity of the Creator God and the Son as true God and true man, who is, nevertheless, distinct from the Father. On discipline, of course, he assumed a rigorous stand similar to Tertullian's. In *The Shows*, he also forbade attendance. In *The Good of Modesty*, he listed three stages: virginity, continence in marriage, and faithfulness in marriage.

Cyprian

As a theologian, Cyprian (d. 258) cannot be ranked alongside his mentor Tertullian or his Eastern contemporary Origen, but he merits comment for his ecclesiastical leadership and views about the unity of the church. Born at Carthage about 200 to 210 of affluent parents, he became a rhetorician (lawyer). Converted to Christianity by Caecilian, a Carthaginian presbyter, in 248 or 249 Cyprian was installed as Bishop of Carthage. During the persecution that erupted soon after this, he went into hiding, an act that complicated his leadership in the Novatianist controversy. When a fearful plague struck Carthage in 252 or 254, Cyprian organized a heroic ministry to the sick and dying that favorably impressed fellow citizens. He and

Stephen of Rome nearly precipitated another schism as a result of their controversy over rebaptism, but the Valerian persecution interrupted the debate, claiming the lives of both. Cyprian was beheaded outside of Carthage on September 14, 258.

Although a fine Latin stylist, Cyprian lacked the depth and creativity of Tertullian, whom he called "the master." His views on the church, however, exerted an immense influence on later Christian thinking, especially among the Donatists. The church is both one and universal. It is one because its founder is one. In order for it to retain its unity while spread throughout the world, said Cyprian in the first edition of his treatise *The Unity of the Church*, he gave the primacy to Peter. All of the apostles shared in the same power, but unity derived from Peter. In a later edition of this writing, Cyprian deleted this point and insisted that the rock of Peter is faith. The unity of the church depends on agreement among the bishops in synods. On a local level, Cyprian believed unity would be achieved through the common bond of all the people, both clergy and laity, with the bishop. Like Ignatius of Antioch, Cyprian insisted that anyone who was not with the bishop was not in the church. Yet he never acted without consulting the community on important matters.

For Cyprian, salvation depended on the church, which is the bride of Christ. Therefore, "no one can have God as a Father who does not have the Church as a mother" (*The Unity of the Church* 6). The Holy Spirit is active only within the church and not in conventicles of heretics or schismatics, between whom Cyprian recognized no real distinction. Consequently, "outside the Church there is no salvation" (*Ep.* 73.21). The church alone is the ark in which one can safely travel. Sacraments—baptism, Eucharist, ordination—are validly administered only in the church. When schismatics or heretics enter the church, therefore, they must receive baptism, a major element of Donatist doctrine.

PART FOUR

CHRISTIANIZING AN EMPIRE
313–400 C.E.

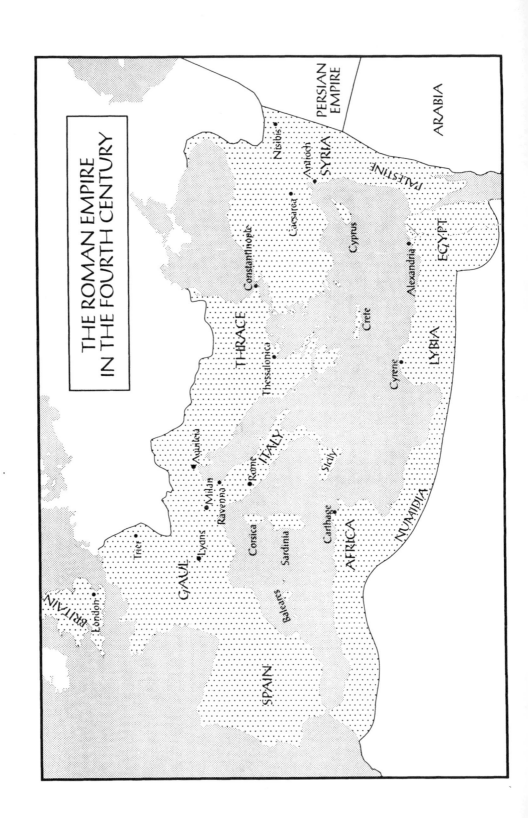

THE ROMAN EMPIRE
IN THE FOURTH CENTURY

BRITAIN

London

Trier

GAUL

Lyons

Milan

Aquileia

Ravenna

Rome

ITALY

Corsica

Sardinia

Baleares

SPAIN

Sicily

Carthage

AFRICA

NUMIDIA

THRACE

Constantinople

Thessalonica

Caesarea

Nisibis

Antioch

SYRIA

PERSIAN
EMPIRE

ARABIA

PALESTINE

Cyprus

Crete

Alexandria

EGYPT

Cyrene

LYBIA

CHAPTER EIGHTEEN

CONSTANTINE

Christians can scarcely be faulted for the enthusiasm with which they celebrated the conversion of Constantine and the beneficent era of peace he inaugurated. From the perspective of later history, they might have viewed more circumspectly some of the aid he gave the churches, but for most it must have appeared like the arrival of the Millennium. To the eyes of Eusebius, Constantine had redrawn the scheme of the history of salvation; once Abraham to Moses to Christ, now it was Abraham to Christ to Constantine. Christians could truly sing the "new song" of the psalmist (Ps. 98:1-3) and exult in the things martyrs longed to but did not see. Constantine had vanquished a "whole race of God-haters" and signaled a bright and glorious new day for Christianity. He had freed all humankind from the tyranny of oppressors and led all in confessing faith in the one true God. Not only so, but he was also raising up magnificent new edifices to restore those razed by the tyrants, sending bishops letters and gifts and honors, and, in other ways, showering the churches with favors. Eusebius, Christianity's first church historian, could not find phrases adequate to depict the first Christian emperor—"almost another Christ," "the only true philosopher," "vessel of the divine Logos."

Constantine envisioned his own role in much the same way before he died in 337. In 330, when he moved the capital of the empire from Rome to Byzantium out of disappointment that he could not convert its pagan aristocracy, he erected a church in honor of the twelve apostles. Between twelve coffins he had set up to serve as pillars, he placed a thirteenth for himself; thus he saw himself as the thirteenth apostle (Eusebius *Life of Constantine* 4.60). He called himself a "bishop ordained by God to oversee whatever is outside the Church" and, as Eusebius noted, took his charge seriously (4.24). In reality, he did not hesitate to act as a "bishop," directing affairs inside the church, especially in the Arian controversy. In front of his imperial palace in Constantinople, he had a large placard erected depicting a huge serpent into whose back Constantine and his sons triumphantly thrust daggers. Satan had at last been cast down.

Some modern historians would concur with Eusebius and Constantine in the importance they ascribe to the latter in the christianization of the empire. How one defines *Christian* here obviously will interject some qualifications into this conclusion. Others, including the author, would emphasize more strongly than this the effectiveness of Christianity at the grass roots. Yet there can be little question that Constantine radically improved the situation of the churches vis-à-vis competitors in the evangelization of the empire. From his conversion until about 324, when he took up the fight against Licinius, Constantine extended tolerance to other religions and displayed limited favoritism to Christianity. From 324 to 330, he adopted a harsher attitude toward paganism and leaned ever more heavily on the churches. After 330, he dropped all pretense of toleration and did all he could to eliminate paganism as well as divergent forms of Christianity.

Constantine's Conversion

Constantine's "conversion" has been the subject of immense debate for more than two centuries. According to Eusebius's *Life of Constantine*, as the emperor prepared his army for the deliverance of Rome from the usurper Maxentius, he prayed fervently for a sign. About noon he saw a cross of light in the sky above the sun bearing the inscription "By this conquer." His whole army witnessed the miracle. That night, Christ appeared to him with the same sign and commanded him to make an image of it as a safeguard in all engagements with his enemies (*Life* 1.28-29). Eusebius himself, much more rationalistic than the superstitious Constantine, reported this as an account declared "long afterwards" by the emperor himself. It should be noted that Eusebius did not include it in his earlier account, in which he presented Constantine as favorably disposed to Christianity from the beginning. If any doctoring occurred, it was done by the emperor himself and not by the Bishop of Caesarea.

On the basis of somewhat mixed evidence, some historians have contended that Constantine adopted Christianity only for political reasons and never became a genuine Christian. Jacob Burckhardt believed Eusebius intentionally concealed the real Constantine in his *Life of Constantine* and based his account of the vision on an earlier encounter Constantine had with Apollo in the Gallic sanctuary in 310. Other scholars contend that Constantine integrated the Christian God into the Roman pantheon in support of his claims to a universal monarchy. Still others consider his conversion, and thus his efforts on behalf of Christianity, authentic. Much depends, of course, on the weight placed on this single experience. If the whole of Constantine's efforts on behalf of Christianity is taken into account, one can hardly deny that he thought he was a Christian, but the experience at the Milvian bridge cannot have done more than start a process of conversion consummated in a deathbed baptism.

Constantine's Favors, 313–324

On his full accession to power—long before his defeat of Maxentius—Constantine favored Christians with toleration, though no ancient author labeled him a Christian at the time. Directly after the capture of Rome, he proceeded beyond mere toleration. In a letter written to Caecilian of Carthage in the winter of 312 to 313, he promised provision for expenses for a stated number of "the servants of the lawful and most holy Catholic Church" in Africa, Numidia, and Mauretania. He instructed Caecilian to request more if needed. He also arranged for Anullinus, the proconsul of Africa, to prevent "persons of turbulent character" (the Donatists) from distracting the Catholic Church. In one letter to Anullinus, he commanded him to restore property seized from the Catholic Church and given to private persons. In another, he directed that Anullinus and his staff "provide personal service to this holy worship in the Catholic Church over which Caecilian presides" and keep them "immune from all public burdens of any kind whatever," since "their conduct of the greatest worship towards the Divinity will in my opinion bring immeasurable benefit to the commonwealth." In this latter letter, a new attitude has emerged wherein worship of the Christian God is considered vital to the well-being of the empire.

Following Licinius's defeat of Maximin on April 30, 313, Constantine and Licinius issued the Edict of Milan on June 15. As the entire document makes clear, the main object was freedom for the Christian religion. To repeated assertions of "free and absolute liberty" for Christians to practice their religion, the emperors appended orders for restoration of places of worship and other property and compensation where these had been sold so as to assure that "the Divine favor toward us, which we have experienced in such great events, will prosperously continue for all time, to our success and the public happiness." Evidently, it was Licinius who insisted on impartiality here. In his battle with Maximian, he evidently adopted Constantine's advice to rely on the Supreme God of Christians with some reservation and dragged his feet when his co-Augustus pressed for recognition of Christianity alone. Early conclusions of both Eusebius and Lactantius that Licinius was also a convert to Christianity proved ill-founded. On the other hand, both pagans and Christians evidently believed Constantine had opted for Christianity. The Roman Senate, for instance, omitted any reference to the gods in the inscription they placed on Constantine's triumphal arch. The only negative evidence is the coins Constantine minted

199

during the years after Milan from which he failed to remove images and inscriptions referring to the gods.

Until 323, then, Constantine displayed his Christianity with reserve. He evidently sought to integrate in some way the leading religious competitors—the religion of the Unconquered Sun and the religion of Jesus Christ. In 321, he declared Sunday a legal holiday, construing it in Christian terms. Christ was, for Constantine, a manifestation of the Unconquered Sun. For his Labarum (official standard), he did not feature a cross but the Chi Rho. Yet he did not hesitate to show partiality to the church. In 318, he permitted bishops to rule in civil suits. In 321, he legalized bequests to the church and gave full legal recognition to many missions performed by bishops. He probably built the Basilica Constantiniana with its baptistery in the Lateran and endowed them. He endowed other churches in Italy, Sicily, Africa, and, to a lesser extent, in Gaul and Greece. In 316, he forbade the branding of prisoners on the face. In 320, he repealed Augustus's laws against celibates and childless married couples. He sided heavily with Catholics in North Africa against the Donatist Church.

Constantine set this earlier caution aside after defeating Licinius, Augustus in the East, in a series of battles between 314 and 323. Although married to Constantine's half-sister Constantia, Licinius viewed his rival with suspicion from the start. The final conflict was precipitated by Constantine's appointment of his sons, Crispus and Constantine II, as consuls without Licinius's consent. When Constantine trespassed on the latter's dominions in a campaign against the Goths, Licinius protested and, when Constantine refused satisfaction, went to war. Behind the conflict lay more than ambition. The two emperors diverged increasingly on religious matters. The more Constantine favored Christians, the more Licinius looked upon them with suspicion and hostility. Eventually, he initiated a series of retaliatory measures against the churches in his territory. He forbade councils and prohibited bishops from visiting one another's cities, an act designed to prevent ordination of new bishops. He enjoined worship of men and women in the interest of morality and ordered meetings to take place outside rather than inside the city gates on pretense of concern for public health. He purged his court and later the whole civil service by requiring public sacrifices as a test for office. Christian reaction led to arrests of a number of bishops and some executions and demolition of church buildings in some cities. This new outburst of persecution gave Constantine the pretext for undertaking a crusade against Licinius under the auspices of the Christian God. Until the outbreak of this war in 324, Constantine's coins still bore the legend "To the Unconquered Sun" or "To the Sun, the Companion of our Augustus." Thereafter, even this token of religious ambivalence ceased.

Constantine called on Christian bishops to assist him in his preparations for war. He picked fifty troops noted for their piety to guard the Labarum. He gave Christian soldiers leave to attend church on Sundays and marched pagan soldiers off to a parade where they had to recite a prayer to the Highest Divinity, acknowledging God as the only God. Licinius was thus cast in the role of defender of the ancestral gods. Although Licinius commanded a larger army and fleet, Constantine dealt his opponent a devastating blow at Hadrianople on July 3, obliging him to retreat with heavy losses to Byzantium. Crispus, whom Constantine put in charge of his fleet, bottled up Licinius's fleet in the Hellespont and inflicted a crushing defeat, sinking 130 ships. Licinius, at first holding fast at Byzantium, had to flee across the Bosphorus to Chrysopolis. There, on September 18, Constantine administered the second and decisive blow, ending the war. Although he spared his enemy momentarily on the pleas of his half-sister, Constantine soon had Licinius executed for fear of insurrection. Thus, Eusebius exulted, did Constantine unite again the Roman Empire into a single, united whole under a peaceful rule.

More Favoritism, 324–330

Following his triumph over Licinius, Constantine issued a decree directing that all injuries and losses inflicted upon individual Christians or churches during the persecution be remunerated. He proceeded to place the blame for the wars, famines, and other calamities on those who had formerly blamed Christians for them. He depicted himself as the instrument chosen and empowered by God to see "that the human race might be recalled to the worship of the august law, schooled by my agency, and that the blessed faith might be increased under the hand of the Almighty God" (Eusebius *Life of Constantine* 2.28). He went on to enumerate measures he enacted to redress injuries to Christians: release of exiles; return of confiscated property; freeing of Christians deported to the islands and those forced into servitude; granting of property of martyrs to their next of kin or, if there were none, to the churches. The edict closed with an exhortation to all to worship the Almighty God, who had effected so signal a victory over Licinius and his evil cohorts. Soon afterward, Constantine promulgated two new laws prohibiting the erecting of images, the practice of divination, and the offering of private sacrifices and providing for the erection or restoration of churches at public expense under direction of the clergy.

Few of Constantine's actions display his increased determination to advance the cause of Christianity more clearly than patronage of church edifices and the construction of a new capital at Byzantium. In a letter written to Eusebius after his victory over Licinius, Constantine lamented the ruinous state of church edifices and determined to change it. He empowered the Bishop of Caesarea to demand whatever he needed from provincial governors and the praetorian prefect. The same letter went to other bishops (Eusebius *Life of Constantine* 2.46). The emperor and his mother, Helena, sponsored erection of new church buildings to commemorate Jesus' burial and resurrection in Jerusalem, his birth in Bethlehem, and his ascension from the Mount of Olives. Later, Constantine himself commissioned another church to be erected near the Oaks of Mamre. In a letter to Macarius, Bishop of Jerusalem, he interpreted discovery of the tomb of Jesus as an act of divine providence, connected integrally with his victory over Licinius that called for the erection of an edifice surpassing all others in beauty (Eusebius *Life of Constantine* 3.29-32). Outside of Palestine, he ordered churches constructed in Nicomedia, where he had compelled Licinius to surrender; Antioch; Heliopolis in Phoenicia; and other cities. In Rome, he added basilicas dedicated to the apostle Peter and to the apostle Paul, endowing them with extensive Eastern estates. He completed erection of a church also in Cirta, capital of Numidia, in 329. When Donatists seized it, he promptly commissioned a replacement.

Dismayed that he could not convert ancient Rome, in 326 Constantine turned his gaze toward Byzantium as a "new Rome." It was to be a fully Christian city. There he commissioned the building of a church on a grand scale in honor of the martyrs and purged the city's pagan temples of sacrifices. He ordered the erection of a second church in honor of the apostles and the installation of a cross on the ceiling of his personal apartment in the imperial palace. The "new Rome," however, differed from the old one in that it had no sacral significance as *dea Roma*. In his capital, Constantine supervised the construction himself, turning nothing over to the bishops.

The bright hopes Constantine attached to Christianity were diminishing somewhat even as he announced these grand plans. Strife had been fracturing the churches of Alexandria and Egypt for several years in the form of the Meletian controversy. On top of this came the Arian conflict, which spread like wildfire from Egypt to other parts of the empire. Not one to stand idly by as a divided church threatened to disrupt his efforts at uniting his empire, Constantine immediately dispatched a letter to Alexandria by a specially chosen emissary: Hosius, Bishop of Cordova. As might be expected, however, neither the letter nor the Bishop of Cordova halted the bitter dispute.

Religious Intolerance, 330–337

Constantine ordered the building of his new capital immediately after his victory over Licinius at Chrysopolis on September 18, 324. His predecessor, Diocletian, had already begun to shift his administrative headquarters from Rome to Nicomedia, for the ever-growing demands on the monarchs necessitated an Eastern center. According to Lactantius (*Deaths of Persecutors* 7.8.10), Diocletian "aimed to make Nicomedia as great as Rome" and accelerated the building process. Constantine knew well the plans of his predecessors and carried his own designs in his head for a long time, frequently changing them—first thinking of Sardica (modern Sophia in Bulgaria), then Thessalonica, before deciding on Byzantium. After his victory at Chrysopolis, realizing he no longer had to rely on Western forces, he made his decision quickly. Tied to this was recognition that Old Rome remained pagan to the core. Although he celebrated his *vicennalia* (twenty-year festival) in Rome in 326 with dazzling games, he was not prepared to settle with the Senate for anything less than complete submission to the christianization of the city. But the Senate and people of Rome repulsed his efforts.

Constantinople first appeared on coins as the rival to Rome in 330, the year the Empress-mother Helena died. From this point, Constantine's policy changed to one of intolerance. He now loudly proclaimed his support of Christianity, rewarded pagans for conversion, and undertook the suppression of paganism, stopping short only at the uprooting of the imperial cult that might erode popular loyalty. So many religious practices intersected with devotion to the state that even Constantine could not abolish all of them and had to be content with stripping them of their most objectionable features.

Constantine's most severe attacks on paganism were restricted to the East. Even there, modern research into inscriptions has shown that the effect was far less devastating than some Christians or embittered pagans reported. Actually, the old religions had been hearing a death knell for a long time; Constantine merely hastened the process. Other emperors had laid hands on temples before, though none intended to destroy them as Constantine did. Between 330 and 337 began the destruction of the chief centers of the pagan cult. In its first phase, it involved robbery of treasures—gold, silver, bronze, and art masterpieces—to enrich Christian churches or the new capital. Next followed the actual demolition of buildings, such as the temple of Asclepius at Aegae in Cilicia and others at Apheca and Heliopolis in Phoenicia, that offended Christians by their rites of sacred prostitution. In the West, however, Constantine failed to bring paganism down despite the fact that his laws applied equally to both spheres. He may have framed a general prohibition of sacrifice, but death prevented him from enforcing it.

On May 17, 330, Constantine dedicated his new capital, thus giving his Christian Empire one center free from any touch of paganism. Although some scholars have questioned how "Christian" the new capital was, coins struck at the time show the globe set on the cross of Christ on the scepter of Tyche, the goddess of fortune, who personified the city. A solemn mass accompanied the dedication. However, Constantine could not escape the dominance of mythology connected with ancient Rome, interpreting Constantinople accordingly. The city of Constantine was, as it were, anti-Rome. The emperor had to create there even a Senate, like the one that had given him so much trouble in old Rome. He lured some aristocrats from old Rome by erecting grand houses for noble families, evidently mostly Christian, and began to celebrate the presence of Romans by placing the ancient inscription *populus Romanus* on coins in 335. He freed citizens of Constantinople from the burden of taxation. Calling it "the second Rome," he subordinated the city to the ancient capital. Rome itself continued down the road it had always traveled. When Constantine died, his sons had to agree to allow the Senate to apotheosize him in the old manner (Eutropius *Compendium of Roman History* 10.8.2). After his death, the pagan aristocracy in the old city still fought for their rights.

Shortly after the Council of Nicaea, the emperor issued a severe edict against heresies and schisms in the East—Valentinians, Marcionites, Montanists (Cataphrygians), and Paulianists (followers of Paul of Samosata)—depriving them of all meeting places. Later he retracted the decree against Novatianists. He did not mention Arianism, for the council had supposedly killed it. When he discovered three months later that Eusebius, Bishop of Nicomedia, and Theognis, Bishop of Nicaea, still clung stubbornly to Arius's views, he exiled them and ordered an election of bishops. When the Nicomedians demurred, Constantine personally replied, denouncing Eusebius and warning that they were approaching high treason. The Nicomedians and Nicaeans finally bowed and elected Amphion and Chrestus as successors. Meanwhile, the emperor kept up efforts to get Arius to retract, inviting him to come to the imperial court. Arius and his followers submitted a confession that satisfied the emperor but not Alexander, Bishop of Alexandria, who resisted his efforts to force a reconciliation. In 327, Constantine reassembled the Council of Nicaea to readmit Arius to communion. Eusebius of Nicomedia and Theognis petitioned for readmission also on the basis of complete submission to the original decision, including *homoousios*. The bishops accepted their pleas and restored them to their sees.

Although the apparent reconciliation elated the emperor, the controversy did not abate. Anti-Arians refused to recognize Arius and pressed their case against bishops who leaned toward Arian theology. When Marcellus, Bishop of Ancyra, and Eustathius, Bishop of Antioch, made accusations against Eusebius of Nicomedia, Eusebius of Caesarea, and Narcissus of Neronias, all Origenists, they themselves ended up being condemned in a council at Constantinople and sent off into exile. Constantine was now obviously shifting his support from the rigid Nicaeans, led by Athanasius, newly elected Bishop of Alexandria, toward Arians or semi-Arians. Athanasius proved to be a thorn in Constantine's side for the rest of his life, for he would not yield an inch to any position but his own, whereas the emperor's efforts mandated compromise, something in which Arians proved more to his liking. In 332, Athanasius responded to an imperial summons to the Palace of Psammathia to answer charges made against him the preceding year by four Meletian bishops, where the court acquitted him of the charges. Not content to let the matter drop, the Meletians accused him of the murder of a Meletian bishop named Arsenius, producing a severed hand as all that remained of the victim. Athanasius disproved the accusation promptly by producing the supposed victim. Constantine, furious at the way the Meletians had made a fool of him, wrote Athanasius a letter denouncing them. At this time, Arius, still barred from Alexandria by Athanasius, entreated the emperor, demanding "to be received back" and claiming that all the people of Libya were on his side. This petition only infuriated Constantine, however, and caused him to write a denunciation of Arius and his views in violent terms.

Growing more and more anxious to effect a reunion of divided Christians, in 334 Constantine ordered the convening of a Council at Caesarea under the presidency of Eusebius "for the purification of the holy Christian people." Although summoned by the emperor, Athanasius refused to attend because he saw it as a tool of the two Eusebiuses to get Arius reinstated. A year later, Constantine ordered the convocation of another council to meet at Tyre and issued a threat of deposition against any who refused to attend. This time, Athanasius yielded with reluctance, expecting condemnation on formidable charges. Clearly outvoted, Athanasius and the Egyptian delegation withdrew, leaving the council free to condemn Athanasius in absentia and to examine and accept an orthodox confession of faith sent by Arius. Before this decision reached Egypt, however, Athanasius hastened to Constantinople to intercede with Constantine. The emperor wavered in his presence, but finally decided, after a visit from the two Eusebiuses, to exile Athanasius to Treves in Gaul. The latter departed Constantinople on November 7, 334, to spend the first of five periods in exile. What probably tipped the balances was Athanasius's threat to prevent shipment of grain from Alexandria, which Constantine interpreted as confirmation of intransigence. He now viewed Athanasius as the chief obstacle to Christian unity, although he refused to allow election of another bishop to take his place. Egyptian bishops still declined to restore communion to Arius, so that the emperor ended up recalling him to Constantinople, where he had to order Bishop Alexander to give Arius communion. The day before that momentous event was to take place, however, Arius suddenly dropped dead. Hopes for restoration were thwarted again.

Although Constantine concentrated much of his help within the churches, he tried also to fulfill his promise to be a thirteenth apostle and a bishop for those outside the church. In 331, after his oldest surviving son, Constantine, defeated the Goths on the Danube, the Sarmatians begged for admission into the empire. Not long afterward, the Goths themselves were converted by the great Arian missionary Ulfilas. In the East, Iberia (Georgia) officially adopted the Christian faith during Constantine's reign. After the conversion of the queen, the king sent an emissary to Constantine to ask for instructors to teach his subjects. The kingdom of Axum (Abyssinia or Ethiopia) also adopted Christianity through the agency of two Roman boys, Aedesius and Frumentius, who had been captured and made slaves of the king. Constantine probably worsened the situation of Christians in Persia, however, by writing a letter to Sapor I, reminding him of all the disasters that befell emperors who persecuted Christians, notably Valerian, who died as a prisoner of the Persians. Up to this point, Christians had been tolerated. Now they were suspected of being agents of the Romans. A few years before Constantine's death, Sapor opened hostilities and later started persecution. Constantine signed a friendly treaty with Armenia, the first Christian kingdom, and took up the offer of the Armenian nobility to rule their kingdom in exchange for defense against the Persians, who had occupied Armenia in 334. Constantine was preparing for a Persian war when he died.

A Mixed Blessing

Constantine's contribution to the evangelization of the Roman Empire and even beyond was an immense, but not an unmixed, blessing. The increasing assistance he supplied the churches tipped the scales for Christianity over against all competitors, even the syncretistic solar monotheism attractive to many of the emperors as they sought to unify their fragmented and far-flung empire. Constantine moved from tolerance of all cults to favoritism of Christianity to open intolerance and efforts to make Christianity the religion of the empire. Not only so, but he sought also to effect unity among Christians, since, in his view, the unity and well-being of the empire depended on the concord in common faith and worship of all of its citizens. Here he set Christianity on the track of persecution that has cast a shadow on its history ever since. Christians had themselves experienced

206

fearsome persecution at times, but even that did not equal the pain they inflicted on non-Christians and even on other Christians as they gave religious sanction to the state's coercive powers. By the time of Theodosius I, intolerance had become a public virtue.

The irony of the blessing Constantine bestowed is evident in his death-bed baptism. Exactly why he delayed baptism is uncertain. He may have done so for political reasons, to avoid offending the predominantly pagan populace; for personal reasons, because he felt unworthy and, early on, unsure of his faith; for theological reasons, wanting to be sure he would receive full remission of sins and not wanting to undergo the rigors of penance at this time; or for a combination of these. However that may be, when he fell ill shortly after Easter 337, he withdrew from Constantinople to a nearby spa with thermal springs and then to Helenopolis, where he prayed in the church his mother had built in honor of Lucian of Antioch and other martyrs. He then traveled to Nicomedia, where he convened a group of bishops and told them he had wanted to receive baptism in the Jordan River, but now he could not. He then asked for baptism and, donning the white robe of a catechumen, received baptism at the hands of Eusebius of Nicomedia, whom he had once sent into exile for Arian sympathies.

Constantine died at Pentecost. Although he was buried in Constantinople in the Church of the Apostles, the Roman Senate honored him by deification. It remained for his sons—Constans, Constantine II, and Constantius—to continue christianizing an empire already divided and only superficially touched by Christian faith.

CHAPTER NINETEEN

CHURCH AND STATE AFTER CONSTANTINE

Constantine inaugurated an era of bright hopes for the churches, and his sons followed the same policies. Only Emperor Julian seriously threatened to reverse the tide set in motion by Constantine's energies on behalf of the churches and against paganism. The brevity of his reign, however, diminished his efforts to supplant Christianity with a revived paganism. The next several successors, all Christians, resumed support and favors intended by Constantine. Although Jovian, Valentinian, and Valens exhibited considerable tolerance for paganism, they did not extend it to Christian sects. Gratian and Theodosius brought an end to all tolerance. Under Theodosius, the Catholic Church was defined legally in terms of communion with Damasus, the Bishop of Rome, and Peter, the Bishop of Alexandria. Constantine's vision had finally become reality.

Not all Christians, even those within the orthodox sphere, were unaware of the dangers lurking in Constantinianism. The churches would easily become a pawn of the powerful state. One of Constantine's own sons, the Arian-leaning Constantius, ruler in the East (337–361), pointed up the risks, as Constantine himself had, when a ruler cannot remain content with ecclesiastical decisions. For the West, therefore, there emerged a less optimistic and more realistic theory separating the spheres of church and state, articulated with particular force by Ambrose, Bishop of Milan, and Augustine, Bishop of Hippo.

Constantine's Sons and the Church, 337–361

After a three-month interregnum during which potential claimants to the throne were disposed of, the rule of the empire was divided among Constantine's three surviving sons. Constantine II, the oldest, ruled Britain, Gaul, and Spain and held a certain precedence; Constans took charge of the rest of the West as far as Thrace; Constantius II controlled the East. In 340, Constantine II, charging his younger brother with flouting his authority, invaded Italy and was killed at Aquileia, thus leaving two-thirds of the empire in the latter's hands. In January 350, Constans was overthrown by an officer of German descent named Magnentius. After obtaining support of Vetranio, another claimant crowned by his troops, Constantius defeated Magnentius at Mursa on September 28, 351, and, after Magnentius's final defeat in the summer of 353, reunited the empire under a single Augustus.

All three sons, reared as Christians, followed faithfully in the footsteps of their father, stepping up his late attacks on paganism, extending favors to the churches, and intervening at will in ecclesiastical affairs. As ruler in the West, where Nicene orthodoxy had strong support, Constans applied pressure on behalf of Nicaeans. In 342, he arranged the Council of Sardica, which cleared Athanasius, Marcellus of Ancyra, and Paul of Constantinople. In 345, he prevailed upon Constantius to reinstate Athanasius after the latter's second exile. He also used military force to crush Donatism, by this time a powerful socioeconomic rebel movement in North Africa.

In the East, where sympathy for Arianism was strong, Constantius leaned in a different direction on this divisive matter. He sought counsel of Eusebius, from Nicomedia and Constantinople, and later of Eudoxius, Bishop of Constantinople, as his court bishops. Although he did not favor the overtly Arian bishops who said the Son was "unlike" (*anomoios*) the Father, he sided with those who advocated abandonment of unbiblical terms, like *homoousios* ("of the same essence") or *homoiousios* ("of like essence"), and instead the use of the simple and biblical *homoios* ("like"). Accordingly, he intervened in the appointment or deposition of more and more bishops and summoned others to his court to browbeat them into conformity, as he did in the case of Tiberius, Bishop of Rome, and Hosius of Cordova. In 355, he transferred the Council of Milan from the church to his palace so as to force the bishops to choose between condemnation of Athanasius and their own exile. When the bishops protested that the emperor's action violated the church's canon, he replied, "My will is the canon," appealing to Arian bishops to sustain him (Athanasius *History of the Arians* 4.8). The culprit in Constantius's eyes was the intransigent Athanasius, who would not go along with a neutral, conciliatory formula such as *homoios*. Peace and harmony must take precedence over theological considerations. When the opponents objected, Constantius took refuge in his success: Had he not defeated the usurper Maxentius?

Both Constans and Constantius continued their father's war against paganism. In 341, Constans issued a law decreeing the cessation of all sacrifices. In 356, Constantius ordered the closing of temples and the cessation of sacrifices under penalty of death. Although some temples were closed, it would appear that authorities enforced these decrees rather lightly, for no pagans suffered martyrdom.

Constantius extended the privileges of the clergy, exempting them from all supplementary taxes and from requisition of animals for postal service.

Although the clergy were not satisfied with exemptions from regular taxes and asked for more, he granted immunity only for church lands, a concession revoked by Julian. Otherwise, he exempted from personal taxes only those clergy scraping out a bare living. He relaxed some rules of Constantine preventing ordination of men of curial family only if they surrendered their fortunes.

Julian and the Restoration of Paganism, 361–363

Whatever his early religious opinions, up to the death of Constantius on November 3, 361, Julian had been forced to hide them except on occasion among his troops. On his accession, he immediately ordered the opening of the temples, offering of sacrifices to the gods, and restoration of the pagan cultus. Assembling Christian bishops, he directed them to lay aside their differences and each observe his own beliefs in the conviction that freedom would increase dissension. Pagans exploded with joy. In Rome, the pagan party reestablished the Altar of Victory, ordered torn down by Constantius in 357. In many places, of course, the temples had never closed, but where they had, they now were quickly reopened and revived. Julian himself saw to it that a pagan temple and altar were erected in Constantinople and, with great pomp, imolated victims at the foot of a statue of Fortuna erected by Constantine in the chief basilica of the city. Reversing the favoritism of his predecessors, he restored pagan priests to their ancient honors, privileges, exemptions, and rents. Twenty years of Christian hegemony, however, had taken a toll of the priesthood, and Julian had a major challenge. Julian also sought to revive occult practices, himself assisting in a seance (Ammianus Marcellinus *History of Rome* 22.7).

Wise enough not merely to restore the pagan cults materially, Julian undertook a thoroughgoing reform. He developed a hierarchy in imitation of Christianity's, in effect founding a pagan church similar to the one planned by Maximin Daia (Eusebius *H.E.* 8.14; Lactantius *Deaths of Persecutors* 36). He installed a priest over each province, similar to a metropolitan, on whom the *flamen* in each city (a kind of bishop) would depend, and charged them to enroll priests and lower clergy. The emperor himself was the sovereign pontiff (*pontifex maximus*), having power to designate leading dignitaries, deprive and punish them, fix the law and theology, and design the religion. Julian himself wrote pastoral letters to his priests. The provincial priests not only offered sacrifices and presided over provincial assemblies or festivals, but they also governed the clergy of the province, deriving their authority from the *pontifex maximus*. Julian demanded that priests, their wives, their children, and their servants set "an example of respect toward the gods" or be deprived of their "sacred ministry" (*Ep.* 49). Under the provincial priest were priests in each city who supervised others serving local temples. On one point, Julian's plan differed from the Christian: admission of women to the priesthood to serve certain deities.

Julian organized temple activities along Christian lines also. He ordered prayers to be offered at set times, especially morning and evening. Psalms were sung, and musicians were trained in psalm singing. He appointed teachers and readers to give instruction in pagan doctrines and exhortations. A great weakness here, however, lay in a lack of scriptures or tradition to sustain preaching.

Julian introduced penitential discipline—although it is difficult to see how it could function effectively, given pagan mores. He evidently placed much emphasis on clerical morals, wanting his priests to rival the most exemplary members of Christian clergy in zeal and morality. He chose for the priesthood only persons of the most strict moral repute without regard to social class, whereas up to his day priests only guarded purity. While they served the altar, Julian considered them priests at all times and thus bound to be pure at all times. He instructed them to pray three times a day, offer sacrifices once a day, observe exact continence, nourish themselves by reading and philosophical meditation, and avoid contact with the public except in performance of ministry. He expected them not only to avoid evil, but also to avoid contemplating evil or engaging in doubtful pleasantries or reading literature offensive to the gods or frequenting the theater or taverns or circuses. In short, Julian propounded a puritan sense of behavior.

Julian paid Christianity another compliment in imitating its charities. He instructed his high priest in Galatia to establish numerous hostels in each village so that strangers could have the care they needed. The Jews take care of their own. Pagans take care of nobody. But "the impious Galileans [Christians] take care not only of their own but ours as well" (*Ep.* 49). Thus the latter win all the converts. To sustain his charities, Julian put the necessary funds at the disposal of the provincial priests, directing that a fifth be used for priests and the rest for strangers and the needy. Yet he realized that pagans themselves would need to learn how to give as Christians did. According to Sozomen (*H.E.* 5.16), Julian especially admired the letters bishops wrote to commend poor travelers to the care of other Christians. He also wanted the priests to match the church in burial of the dead, discerning in this again a key to Christianity's success. He even counseled his priests, with some reluctance, to assist prisoners.

Julian's revived cultus shocked well-educated pagans not only by the extent of sacrifices but by its occultism as well. Julian constantly searched entrails of sacrificed animals for clues to the gods' plans. He constructed a sanctuary dedicated to Mithra in the palace at Constantinople and participated in the mysteries there as a priest as well as a devotee. Yet he paid obeisance to all the gods—those of ancient mythology, the Asiatic deities, and the Egyptian deities Isis and Osiris. Above all, he considered himself "a servant of the Sun god" (*Oration* 4), whom he often identified with Jupiter. This allowed him to maintain a compromise between absolute polytheism and absolute monotheism and, at the same time, incorporate Platonism. The Supreme God created the universe and distributed control over various nations and cities to lesser gods. Thus we have differences of customs, laws, and moral codes.

Julian did not try to attack Christianity outright so much as he sought to disrupt it. Late in 361 or early in 362, he issued an edict recalling exiles banished by Constantius. Most of these were Nicaeans: Athanasius, Meletius of Antioch, Eusebius of Vercelli, and Lucifer of Cagliari. Some, however, were semi-Arians: Basil of Ancyra, Eleusis of Cyzicus, Silvanus of Tarsus, and Eustathius of Sebaste. Others included the Sabellian Photinus and the Arian Aetius. Under the guise of concern for freedom, Julian fanned the flames of controversy in the churches, favoring heretics where he could. Athanasius had scarcely returned in triumph to Alexandria before Julian exiled him again. When Alexandrians protested, Julian wrote a long dissuasive against Christianity and in behalf of his reform; yet he had some difficulty chasing Athanasius out of the city.

As another measure for restricting Christian influence, Julian excluded Christians from civil and military service and thus won some converts to his cause, for many held to Christianity by a thin thread anyway. He placed a great price on the conversion of scholars and people of letters. One such convert was Caesarius, brother of Gregory of Nazianzus and son of the bishop. At the same time, he barred Christians from teaching pagan literature, in effect, excluding them from the schools, since such literature comprised the curriculum, on the grounds that they could not do so honestly. Christians, however, could attend public schools. Thus Julian put parents in the difficult position of deciding whether they would give their children adequate education. He retracted exemptions from public duty granted to Christian clergy by his predecessors to dampen the appeal of ministry for the wealthy. Although he denied that he wished "Galileans" killed or harmed in any way, he declared unequivocally his preference for "the god-fearing"—that is, pagans. After riots in Edessa in 361 or 362, Julian confiscated ecclesiastical possessions and forbade further feuding.

Julian also composed a treatise *Against the Galileans*, published sometime early in 363. For his material, he turned to earlier polemicists, such as Celsus and Porphyry, pupil and successor of Plotinus. From what has survived, it is possible to see the main lines of his attack: discrepancies between the Old and New Testaments; Christian abandonment of Jewish customs; introduction of new customs, such as the cult of martyrs; the superiority of pagan savior-gods, such as Heracles or Asclepios, to Jesus; and Christian persecution of pagans and other Christians. Although Julian wanted this to be his greatest work, he did it hurriedly, and, due to his death a few months later, it made little impact.

Julian touched off a crisis in Antioch in October 362 when he ordered the remains of Babylas, a Bishop of Antioch, martyred during the persecution under Decius (249–251), removed from a church built in front of the temple of Apollo. A crowd of Christians gathered to sing psalms. A few made threatening gestures. Julian, losing control of himself, ordered the ringleaders arrested and punished. A few days later, the temple caught fire and burned. Julian retaliated by closing the Great Church of Antioch, which Constantine had built, and confiscating its golden vessels. Thereafter he stepped up his efforts to repress Christianity. He dealt with cities according to their Christian affiliation, depriving some persons of rights because they were Christian, granting others special favor because they showed zeal for the old religion. Once again he banished Athanasius, who had just returned to the city of Alexandria, thus raising the level of hatred for the emperor. Before he left Antioch in March 363, the city found itself at complete loggerheads with him.

Fortunately for Christianity, Julian did not live long enough to implement his plan to supplant Christianity with a revived syncretistic religion of the state. In the spring of 362, he evidently decided to resume the war on the eastern front, abandoned by Constantius. Inspired by the exploits of Alexander the Great, Julian led his army to the walls of the Persian capital, Ctesiphon. Unfortunately, by this time summer heat had set in, discouraging efforts to capture the city. Fearful lest the Persians seize his ships and use them against the Roman troops, Julian ordered them burned. He then had to lead a demoralized army overland. On June 25, 363, they engaged a large Persian force. Julian valiantly raced in and out among his troops to spur them on. Leaving himself so exposed, however, had fatal consequences, for a spear, whether Persian or Roman is uncertain, pierced his side and claimed his life a few hours later.

From Julian to Theodosius

The morning after Julian's death, his generals met to elect Jovian as his successor. When Jovian protested that he could not lead a largely pagan army because he was a Christian, the generals replied, "We are all Christians here." Jovian led the battle for several days until Shapur, fearful of a full-scale war with the Romans, opened the way for a thirty-year peace treaty. Part of the price of peace was the surrender of Arsaces, the King of Armenia, whom Shapur arrested and blinded. The Romans also ceded five provinces on the left bank of the Tigris. As they passed by Tarsus on the way west, they buried Julian's corpse just outside the city walls.

Jovian (363–364) inaugurated a period of toleration and noninterference, which his successor, Valentinian I, continued. According to pagan historian Ammianus Marcellinus, Jovian did not disturb anyone or cause any to worship this or that, or issue threatening edicts forcing others to worship as he did (Ammianus Marcellinus *H.E.* 30.9.5). He repulsed efforts of Arians to prevent the recall of Athansius to Alexandria.

Early in his reign, Valentinian (364–379) shared his rule with his brother Valens, consigning the East to him. Both feared religious practices that would work to their political disadvantage. Thus they forbade haruspicy (examination of bird entrails for signs) for harmful purposes, although they did not consider it criminal. Similarly, they forbade bloody sacrifices without putting a clamp down on other forms of pagan worship. Valens, however, did not maintain Jovian's policy of noninterference. He returned, rather, to a policy similar to that of Constantius, leaning toward a modified form of Arianism and threatening opponents with harassment and exile. Jointly, the emperors barred wealthy citizens from entering the priesthood to avoid public service.

Gratian, who began a joint rule with Valentinian and Valens in 367, did not pave the way for Theodosius. During his reign, he refused the title Pontifex Maximus, took away the endowment from the sacred colleges, and removed the Altar of Victory from the Senate house. Whether he did these things before Theodosius came to the throne, however, is unlikely. It appears that he did nothing spectacular against paganism until 379. The fact is that he continued Valentinian's policy of nonintervention in church matters so long as peace prevailed. In Africa, he confiscated the property of Donatists in 376. When confronted with Arianism for the first time in 378, he turned to Ambrose for advice. For a time thereafter, he continued his policy of toleration, banning only Eunomianism, Photinianism, and Manichaeism in an edict issued after Valens's death in 378. When bishops in a Roman synod asked him to exile a bishop condemned by the pope or by the synod and to free the pope from jurisdiction of any court except the emperor's, Gratian reluctantly granted the first request for bishops under the pope's jurisdiction but evaded the second with vague language.

A Fully Christian State

Theodosius himself, therefore, deserves credit for turning the empire into a fully Christian state. Invited by Gratian to share the rule in 379, he did not take long to act. In February 380, he issued the edict *Cunctos populos,* commanding all the peoples under his rule to follow the form of religion handed down by the apostle Peter to the Romans and followed by Damasus, Bishop of Rome, and Peter, Bishop of Alexandria. In sum, that would mean to believe in "the doctrine of Father, Son, and Holy Spirit, one deity of equal majesty and pious trinity." Those who adhered to such faith could call themselves Catholic Christians, but others must be designated demented and barbarian and heretical and be stricken first by divine vengeance and then by imperial action in accordance with the will of heaven (*Cod. Theod.* XVI.1.2.). Theodosius genuinely believed he had received power from heaven to establish the one true form of religion as represented by Rome and Alexandria. A Spaniard, he shared the Western views on Nicaea. Another experience, however, may have added to the vigor with which he pursued his pro-Nicene policy. While most emperors from Constantine on delayed their baptisms until their deathbed, an illness forced Theodosius to receive baptism at the hands of Ascholius, Bishop of Thessalonica, a Nicene with strongly Western affinities. Shortly after his arrival at Constantinople, at any rate, Emperor Theodosius began to remove Arians and replace them with bishops who accepted the Nicene Creed. In Constantinople itself, Arianism had gotten a strong grip, and Theodosius had to weather a popular storm against his replacement of Demophilus with Gregory of Nazianzus. Soldiers had to protect the saintly Gregory on his way to the Church of the Apostles. The empire, still unsettled by controversy between Arians and Nicenes, Theodosius convened the Second Ecumenical Council at Constantinople to ratify conclusions he had already reached. In a special rescript in January 381, he denied heretics any place to celebrate the mysteries and prohibited their assembly. The name of the one supreme God alone was to be celebrated everywhere in accordance with the Nicene faith. Photinians, Eunomians, and Arians were specifically condemned. The edict even defined Nicene faith. Any who disturbed the true churches were to be driven from the city so that the Catholic churches could again achieve unity in this faith (*Cod. Theod.* XVI.5.6).

The emperor proceeded with energy to stamp out heresy. In 372, Valentinian I had already forbidden Manichaean assemblies and ordered confiscation of their property. In 381, Theodosius tightened up further by ordering that no Manichaean of either sex could bequeath or inherit (*Cod. Theod.* XVI.5.7). He levied a death penalty against Encratites, Saccofori, and Hydroparastatae (*Cod. Theod.* XVI.5.9), the first time the death penalty was prescribed for heresy! The decree also introduced inquisitors and informers into the churches. By 383, laws against heresy reached a peak, as he summoned a synod to deal with all heresies. Only Novatians and Luciferians escaped.

Theodosius was evidently not hostile to paganism from the beginning of his reign, for legislation against it was mild until 391. The emperor did his best to protect legitimate rights of pagans, restraining the cutting of trees in sacred sites and protecting pagan artworks and temples. He played no part in its disestablishment. He even appointed pagans to high office. According to Libanius (*Oration* 30.18), Theodosius allowed libations but not sacrifices to be offered. Christians, however, used existing laws to rally against paganism. Cynegius, Praetorian Prefect of the East from 384 to 388, a crony of the emperor, led the attack. In February 391, Theodosius ordered an end to sacrifices, directing judges to fine even onlookers (*Cod. Theod.* XVI.10).

On June 16, 391, Theodosius signaled the beginning of a new era by the application of his decree of 380 against sacrifices. In this year, Christians destroyed the Serapeum in Alexandria, though not on imperial command. Official policy was to close but preserve edifices. In the West, the campaign against paganism sought to eradicate all traces. Eugenius, elevated to the imperial office after the death of Valentinian II in August 392, entered into an alliance with the pagan aristocracy of Rome. Later in the year, Theodosius openly attacked paganism by legal action, forbidding every type of pagan religious practice—blood sacrifice, incense, family devotion, and the like. Pagans rallied behind Eugenius, who crossed the Alps in 393 and joined in the effort to restore the Altar of Victory to the Senate. War was inevitable. Theodosius, accompanied by his two sons, left Constantinople in May 394 and reached enemy territory in September. Although victorious in an early engagement, he was nearly overwhelmed in a second. A sudden storm evidently arose and saved him and his army. Resistance collapsed. Eugenius was killed. Arbogast, a barbarian general, committed suicide. Thereafter, Theodosius inaugurated a full-blown anti-pagan policy in the West.

One incident during Theodosius' reign offers a good look at the emperor's commitment to the Catholic Church. In 390, citizens of Thessalonica rioted in protest of the imprisonment of a favorite charioteer and killed the Gothic officer named Butheric, whom the charioteer had tried to rape. In Milan, Theodosius immediately ordered a massacre. Before the troops arrived, he sent a second messenger to countermand the first command, but the message did not arrive in time to avert the slaying of thousands. Ambrose, Bishop of Milan, was horror-stricken when the news reached him. A week or so later, however, he dispatched a private letter to Theodosius, demanding that the emperor do penance, just as David had done after the killing of Uriah the Hittite. Although initially recalcitrant, Theodosius consented to his pastor's demand. For a whole year, he put on sackcloth and ashes and went through the process to be restored. Many viewed it as a victory of church over state, priest over king. Obviously, the emperor wanted to be convincingly Catholic.

Theodosius died January 17, 395, at the height of success. During his sixteen-year career, he brought closer to completion the christianization process inaugurated by Constantine. Unquestionably, the Nicene party in the church benefited the most, for Theodosius assured its triumph within the empire. The Apostle to the Goths, Ulfilas (311?–381), however, had planted the Arian seed well enough among barbarians that it would take centuries of mission effort and the help of numerous other rulers to secure the victory of orthodoxy. The churches would have been wise to take a closer look at Theodosius's gifts, however, for in subsequent centuries they would exact a high price, not the least part of which came in the form of persecution.

CHAPTER TWENTY

CHRISTIANIZING THE ROMAN EMPIRE AND EVANGELIZING THE WORLD

The conversion of Constantine, however interpreted, opened a new chapter in Christian history. Instead of representing a despised and persecuted minority, Christianity now became the fad, and Christian leaders found themselves with the enviable task of trying to christianize the masses who knocked on church doors trying to get in, erect new and grand buildings to replace those destroyed under Diocletian and his cohorts, and expand existing structures to reach into every nook and cranny of the empire with the gospel of Jesus Christ. Small wonder Eusebius and other Christians would think the millennium had arrived.

Church Structure and Conversion of the Empire

From this point on, there was a concerted effort, in councils of bishops as well as by observant missionary bishops like Ambrose of Milan, to increase the number of congregations and episcopates. Attentive leaders sensed the moment had arrived to bring the whole empire under the Christian banner in fact as well as in name. In Gaul, for instance, there is evidence for the existence of only a dozen episcopal sees before Constantine; by the end of the sixth century, they had grown to 119. In North Africa, although episcopates numbered nearly a hundred already at the time of Cyprian (248–258), by the fifth century the three provinces of Africa, Numidia, and Mauretania counted an estimated 632 to 768 bishops. Similar evidence could be cited for other parts of the empire.

Christianity expanded, as noted early, as an urban religion. Churches planted in the cities assumed responsibility for evangelizing the suburbs and, eventually, the surrounding countryside. Sometimes claims overlapped, creating tensions. As a consequence, councils of the Constantinian and post-Constantinian period decided to bring the jurisdictional areas into approximate line with the dioceses and provinces of the empire. In 325, the Council of Nicaea made the political province (equivalent to an American state) the basic unit for the churches' larger divisions. By 341, the Synod of

Antioch in Encaeniis, the Eastern churches had adopted the diocesan divisions (roughly equal to American counties) within a province as well. The Council of Constantinople in 380–381 strongly reaffirmed the diocesan and provincial patterns. A parochial system probably began to develop during the late fourth century also, perhaps first in Gaul, but the evidence is by no means clear. Expansion of urban churches to surrounding areas probably supplied the main impetus for the development of parishes, the actual implementation of which required several centuries.

The evangelizing of rural areas, so long neglected in the process, occurred in a more irregular manner than that of the cities. Planting of churches by the clergy usually followed several patterns: (1) Sometimes a bishop or group of bishops consecrated another bishop and sent him to evangelize and to organize a group of Christians into a church. For the period under study, for example, Eusebius of Nicomedia and other bishops consecrated the great Arian missionary Ulfilas in 341 and sent him to work among the Goths (Philostorgius *Church History* 2.5, 6). (2) Sometimes a bishop sent presbyters or deacons to start and organize a Christian community. After Constantine, the role of presbyters at the local level increased in significance in many areas. (3) Sometimes the bishop or bishops nearest at hand gathered with an already existing congregation and instructed them until they could elect a bishop or presbyter, who would be consecrated or ordained. (4) Sometimes a bishop himself evangelized and instructed converts until he had prepared a suitable candidate to carry on after him.

Local Communities and Conversions

Constantine, his mother, Helena, and other wealthy patrons increased markedly the appeal of Christianity through the erection of opulent edifices attractive to a cultured clientele. With nudgings of various kinds, inquirers came, many reluctantly and many willingly, to find out what Christianity offered. In the *First Catechetical Instruction*, composed at the request of a somewhat disheartened deacon assigned the task of talking to inquirers, Augustine outlined procedures he thought helpful. Catechists should examine the motives of those who came—whether from fear or love of God or for temporal advantages or to escape some personal loss. In response, they should accentuate love throughout their presentation. They should adapt their message—the history of salvation from Genesis to Revelation—to the hearers' capacity and powers of comprehension. Certain classes would require special handling, especially the well-educated and students. Catechists must treat them indulgently and patiently, like a mother hen tending her chicks, repeating when necessary and prodding the indifferent and slow learners. Indicative of the variety of persons coming at this time (about 400), they must adapt what they did to the needs of hearers.

Many who came from imperial insistence doubtless hesitated and only reluctantly opted for Christianity. In the time of Theodosius, many persons of the upper classes deferred baptism, perhaps following the example of the emperors themselves, but more likely resisting joining the church. The very demands of discipleship inhibited many. Some doubtless felt genuinely that the expectations were greater than they could meet, but the hesitancy of many others seems to have been more mundane. Baptism was an insurance of forgiveness of all past sins as they continued to live according to prevailing lifestyles. Persons of higher social station particularly faltered on the way to the baptistery, simply because they were not prepared to surrender many of the pleasures and privileges and duties that their wealth enabled them to enjoy or demanded that they discharge. Although Emperor Theodosius took away the option of not becoming a Christian, the wealthy and powerful could defer baptism until they stood at death's door and thus continue to enjoy life in a more secular mode. The clergy had to chide and cajole.

The Christian Argument and Appeal

Vast numbers, however, did find the appeal of Christianity strong enough to lure them into the churches. Apologists of this day, just as earlier ones, used a wide array of arguments to convince the unconverted. Some made much of the superiority of Christian baptism to Jewish baptism and circumcision. The latter were only "shadows" and "types" that wash away the filth of the body but do not cleanse the soul. They contrasted the weakness of Greek philosophy with the power of baptism to effect actual change in human lives. Such brash claims shocked educated pagans like the Neoplatonist philosopher Porphyry (ca. 232–ca. 303) and Emperor Julian (361–363). The latter caricatured the Christian appeal. At the same time, the emperor paid Christian baptismal procedures the high compliment of incorporating them into his plan for reviving paganism.

Apologists ridiculed the materialism of both pagan and Jewish worship and argued the superiority of Christian worship. According to Lactantius, a teacher of rhetoric appointed by Diocletian but converted around 300, pagans poured all their energies into temples, altars, sacrifices, libations, and images but gave little thought to manner of life (*Divine Institutes* 31). By contrast, Christian worship focused on one God without deference to subordinate creatures, even *divine* ones, and worshiped in a spiritual manner. Arnobius, Bishop of Sicca (d. 330), among many others, defended the spiritualization on the grounds that divine beings do not need physical temples, images, altars, shrines, sacrifices, incense, or libations; indeed, they are offended by such things. From another point of view, Eusebius contended that Christ's once-for-all sacrifice needed to be remembered in the "bloodless sacrifice" of the Eucharist. Ultimately, however, the apologists pointed to Christian charity and behavior as the final confirmation of authentic worship. Christians offer positive proof of the superiority of their worship by exhibiting justice, Lactantius insisted. Innocence toward God and mercy toward humankind satisfy the perfect justice of Plato.

Christian discipline supplied Christians with their strongest case, both in answering critics and in establishing the superiority of Christianity as a philosophy. By the fourth century, pagans rarely invoked the slanders they used earlier, such as cannibalism and incest, though they often blamed Christians for calamities that befell the empire. In his campaign to reestablish pagan religion, Emperor Julian did deride "the Galileans" as "impious" and "corrupt" and "depraved," but he meant by these epithets mainly their "atheism"—that is, their refusal to believe in the gods of Greece and Rome. He also put them down for drawing their converts "from the baser sort— shopkeepers, tax gatherers, dancers and libertines" (*Against the Galileans* 238E). Once again, however, he paid the high compliment of trying to imitate Christian discipline in his revived cult.

Christian apologists turned the tables on their enemies. They ridiculed the myths about the gods and the terrible moral examples they offered, which even the allegorical exposition of Homer could not rehabilitate. They treated philosophers more gently, for they could often enlist them, especially Stoics and Platonists, in their critique of pagan morality, religion, and life. Yet even the philosophers failed to live up to what they themselves taught. Although they lauded courage, justice, wisdom, and temperance— the cardinal virtues—Lactantius argued, they seldom practiced them (*Divine Institutes* 5.13-15). What distinguished Christians from philosophers was the way they lived: in the manner the philosophers said people should live. This argument attracted a considerable number of persons otherwise contemptuous of Christian thought, such as the noted Roman Neoplatonist Victorinus, whose conversion helped steer Augustine into the Christian fold. Another Neoplatonist, Alexander of Lycopolis, explained what exercised such a pull. As he saw it, Christianity "gives most of its attention to moral preparation" and presents its truths in such a simple way that the masses catch on (*Against Manichaean Views*). Alexander, who apparently did not become a Christian, objected to Christian reliance on scriptures rather than reason, but he admired Christian behavior.

Scriptures supplied apologists, evangelists, missionaries, and others their fundamental documents for defending and propagating the faith in this era as in earlier ones. Even though church and synagogue were irreparably divided by this time, apologists could not ignore the Jews. In some parts of the empire, Jews continued to represent a significant minority as Christianity toppled its competitors. Sadly, missionary bishops like Ambrose of Milan displayed no tolerance for them, and Christian exhortations often resulted in outbursts of violence and persecution. John Chrysostom and Augustine composed violent sermons and treatises against the Jews. The most basic contention was that scriptures predicted the cessation of the old law (Isa. 8:16-17) and covenant and the institution of a new law (Isa. 2:3-4; Mic. 4:2-3) and covenant (Jer. 31:31-32). The success of Christianity proved God's intention for the church. Jerusalem had fallen, the Temple was destroyed, and the Jews were scattered, while Christianity prospered and became a universal faith.

Use of scriptures in apology to Gentiles required greater subtlety than that to Jews, as apologists of this day recognized. Lactantius (*Divine Institutes* 5.4) gently rebuked those who tried to find prooftexts for their arguments from scriptures. Arnobius constructed his case *Against the Nations* almost exclusively from Hellenistic writings. Lactantius himself considered it best to give proofs from philosophers and historians and then add testimonies from scriptures. Where they cited scriptures, however, apologists allegorized in order to find in scriptures the best in Greek philosophy, poetry, or other literature. Like their predecessors, they still had to argue the superiority of truth found in scriptures based on inspiration and antiquity. Whatever truth the Greeks received, they got either through the divine Logos who spoke in the prophets or by plagiarizing from Moses, author of the Pentateuch and "the founder of all barbarian wisdom." In addition, the apologists argued that the scriptures offered greater consistency of content than the disparate corpus of Greek and Roman literature or even some of its commendable expositors such as Plato (Eusebius *Preparation for the Gospel* 14.4).

Such arguments posed obvious problems in the effort to reach both Jews and Gentiles, but, with imperial encouragements and enticements, they persuaded some. Ambrose recorded specific accounts of conversions among Jews in which he had played a role (*Explanation of the Psalms* 36.80; *Sermons on Luke* 6.65). In his treatise *Against Julian* (2.3-7), Gregory of Nazianzus related an apocryphal story of the conversion of many Palestinian Jews when some sort of miracle hindered their rebuilding of the Temple. The winning of Gentiles depended more heavily on clothing scriptures in a Hellenistic philosopher's toga by allegorical exegesis to overcome their alien character.

Christians and Persecution of Pagans

During their first three centuries, Christians had ample reason to cry out for toleration and did so eloquently. In the mid-second century, Justin

Martyr pleaded powerfully for the freedom to believe without restraint. Religious liberty, Tertullian insisted, "is a fundamental human right, a privilege of nature, that every person should worship according to his or her own convictions. One person's religion neither helps nor harms another person." He went on to say, "It is not in the nature of religion to coerce religion, which must be adopted freely and not by force" (*To Scapula* 2). Lactantius, tutor of Constantine's son Crispus, declared that "nothing is so much a matter of free will as religion, and no one can be required to worship what one does not will to worship. One can perhaps pretend, but one cannot will" (*Divine Institutes* 54).

As Constantine and his successors arranged a marriage between the church and the state, however, Christian memory of pleas for toleration faded. Even before, many were not prepared to extend the freedom they asked for themselves to those they considered heretics. Tertullian, for instance, insisted that "heretics may properly be compelled, not enticed, to duty. Obstinacy must be corrected, not coaxed" (*Scorpion's Sting* 2.1). Following Constantine's conversion, this kind of logic could be expanded as zealous Christians sought to impose their faith on everyone in the empire. Evidently because of their tenacity in adhering to their faith, Jews usually received less favorable consideration in sermons or treatises than did Gentiles. Ambrose, Bishop of Milan, for instance, lashed out at them for their unbelief, self-righteousness, and obstinacy. He called them "mindless," "worse than lepers," and spoke of Judaism as "the most empty Jewish superstition" and "the evil Jewish fire" that burns but does not warm. Chrysostom characterized the large Jewish populace of Antioch as "wretched" and "good-for-nothing." He counted them enough of a threat to the church to deliver a series of harsh sermons against them, as Augustine also did. Ambrose rebuked Emperor Theodosius when he forced the Christian citizens of Callinicum, a town on the Euphrates, to make reparations for a Jewish synagogue they had destroyed in a rage against "unbelievers."

Christians' tolerance of Gentiles decreased as their victories increased with imperial assistance. Preachers regularly exhorted the unconverted to respond with an openness and enthusiasm they could not have manifested before Constantine. Sometimes their zeal led to excesses. Augustine, for instance, let the ardor of the moment carry him away in a sermon delivered at Carthage in June 401. Against the background of a series of edicts by Honorius, he inflamed the passion of his hearers against idols. God had wished, ordered, and predicted the wiping out of every pagan superstition. The Romans had pulled down the idols in that stronghold of paganism. Would that Carthaginians would shout, "As in Rome, so also in Carthage!" If the Romans tore down the Roman gods, then why do they still stand here (*Sermon* 24.5-6)? Such incitements sometimes produced disasters for Christians as well as for pagans. In Sufes, Byzacena, probably in 399, pagans massacred sixty Christians as a reprisal for toppling a statue of Hercules.

In more reflective moments, the clergy cautioned against the use of violence and left the liquidation of paganism or heresy to the state. Although Chrysostom urged monks to destroy idol temples, he refused to coerce anyone to believe. Christians never made war on anyone; rather, they sought "to effect the salvation of persons by persuasion and word and mildness" (*Saint Babyla* 3). Quite clearly, however, something was happening to Christian perceptions as Christians smelled victory over all competitors. The churches demanded freedom for themselves that they would not think of conceding to others. When the Arian Empress Justina demanded use of one church building in Milan in which she might exercise her faith, Ambrose responded, "Palaces belong to the emperor, churches to the bishop" (*Letter* 20.19). At the same time, he constantly urged imperial action against heretics, schismatics, and pagans. Optatus, Bishop of Milevis (ca. 370), was the first to advocate the death penalty for Donatists. In 406, Augustine laid the foundation for the medieval inquisition as he justified the use of force against the latter.

Evangelizing the Empire

Evangelization of the Roman provinces proceeded at an uneven pace after Constantine's conversion. Antioch and Syria, Asia Minor, Alexandria and parts of Egypt, Rome and its environs, and parts of North Africa represented already strong Christian constituencies. Elsewhere, imperial encouragement notwithstanding, paganism offered stout resistance.

In parts of Syria and Palestine, Semitic faiths held on tenaciously. By this time, few Jews voluntarily accepted Christianity. In Phoenicia and sections of Syria, various Semitic cults did not disappear until the sixth century. Anti-Christian riots occurred during Julian's reign. When Marcellus, Bishop of Apamea, ordered the demolition of temples in the city and villages, a group of pagans seized him and burned him alive while soldiers he had enlisted were preoccupied with carrying out his command to destroy the temples (Sozomen *Church History* 7.15). Even in Antioch, perhaps the first large city to become predominantly Christian, paganism remained strong enough in the sixth century to claim a recognizable head. Throughout Asia Minor, moreover, pagans still constituted cults during the second half of the fourth century and as late as the sixth.

In Greece, Christianity overwhelmed the old faiths without struggle. Athens, however, was still viewed by Christians as a corrupter of youth. In 529, Emperor Justinian eliminated the last source of offense by closing the schools there. To the north of Greece, Christians carried on the christiani-zation process in Dalmatia and in the Danubian provinces.

Although Alexandria boasted a strong Christian contingent, even among non–Greek-speaking persons, by the time of Constantine, much remained to be done both there and in the rest of Egypt. During the late fourth century, an energetic and zealous bishop decided to flaunt the victory of Christianity over its competitors. Converting a temple of Dionysus into a church, he removed the statues and paraded objects used in the mysteries through the streets of the city. Pagans retaliated by killing many Christians, wounding others, and turning the Serapeion into a temporary fortress. They held out steadfastly and rallied enough public support that the emperor granted them a pardon in hopes that this would entice them to become Christians. Such clemency evidently convinced few, but the emperor proceeded thereafter to demolish all pagan edifices in the city (Sozomen *Church History* 7.15). Evangelization of the rest of Egypt took place gradually. Upper Egypt developed an inclusive episcopal organization during the fourth century. The bishop of Alexandria evidently directed the process of placing bishops in every important city in Egypt. Yet pagan cults still hung on in outlying areas well into the sixth century, as they did elsewhere.

In North Africa, a stronghold of Latin Christianity at the time of Con-stantine's conversion, Christianity extended its reach outward from impor-tant cities little by little. Paganism, however, held on tenaciously there too. First the Donatist controversy, which began in 311, and then Arianism, imported by the Vandals in the fifth century, weakened Christian witness noticeably. In Augustine's day (Bishop of Hippo 395–430), paganism still thrived. The temple of Caelestis in Carthage was not closed by imperial order until 391. Until 398, most rulers were pagan. Small wonder, then, that bishops like Augustine sometimes grew impatient and cried out for vigor-ous action.

As strong as Christianity became in Rome even before Constantine, pagan cults continued there long after this era. Many of the aristocracy risked much in defense of the ancient religions of Rome. Quintus Aurelius Symmachus (d. 410), a notable orator in a family prominent in public affairs for over a century, openly and vigorously opposed removal of the Altar of Victory from the Senate by Emperor Gratian. As Prefect of Rome, Symmachus headed a depu-tation of the Senate to Gratian in 382, a second to Valentinian II in 384, a third to Theodosius and Valentinian II in 392. All proved unsuccessful. Eugenius, in his brief reign, restored the altar, but Theodosius removed it again after defeating Eugenius and Arbogastes. Indicative of his tenacity, Symmachus tried again in 403 or 404. Ambrose lifted up a strong voice in opposition to restoration of the altar in a letter to Valentinian. Such an act could be conceived of as nothing less than a resumption of persecution of Christians by pagans and a sacrilege (*Letter* 17.9).

225

Outside of Rome, paganism persisted in the villages and countryside. Christianity registered its greatest success in northern Italy, where Ambrose pressed for the triumph. In Milan, he battled Empress Justina and the Arians for control of the area. In 396, he suggested that there were many churches, though pagan enclaves still dominated areas around Turin in the fifth century. A large part of the populace of Ravenna still remained faithful to the ancient deities. South of Rome, paganism survived at least until the time of Gregory the Great (590–604).

Although Christianity gained a stronghold in Spain early on, it overwhelmed paganism slowly. The Visigoths who invaded Spain during the fourth century brought an aggressively Arian faith, regarding it as the national Gothic faith, and attempted to win others to it. The Suevi, who invaded Spain in the fifth century, initially adopted the Catholic faith but then were converted to Arianism.

By the time of Constantine, Christianity had barely penetrated north of the Pyrenees and the Alps into the provinces of Gaul and Germany. After Constantine, however, it spread rapidly, especially in the cities, where many prominent members of the upper classes entered the church. The most heralded missionary was Martin of Tours (d. 397). Serving in the Roman army, he divided his cloak and gave half to a beggar on the road near Amien one day. A vision of Christ impelled Martin to receive baptism and take up the monastic life. After obtaining a discharge from the army, he traveled some and then in 360 joined Hilary, Bishop of Poitiers. Shortly afterward Martin founded the first monastery in Gaul at Ligugé. About 372, he became Bishop of Tours. There he encouraged the spread of monasticism and the building of churches around Tours, possibly introducing a rudimentary system of parishes. Victricius (ca. 330–ca. 407), Bishop of Rouen and also a soldier who had renounced his military profession, undertook mission work as far as Flanders, Hainault, and Brabant.

When and how Christianity developed in the British Isles is uncertain. Since most Roman contacts at this time came through Gaul, it is reasonable to infer that Christianity entered through such contacts. Substantial evidence exists for at least two lines, one Anglo-Saxon and the other Roman. The clash between the two reached a high level in the seventh century and resulted in a Roman victory. Precise data on Christianity in Britain do not appear until the fifth century.

Beyond the Boundaries of the Empire

Although the adoption of Christianity as the religion of the Roman Empire represented Christianity's most notable triumph, it did not stand

226

alone. The powerful missionary impulse of the first three centuries continued to propel it outward beyond the boundaries of the empire.

The northern barbarians began to enter the church in vast numbers, lured in part by admiration of all things Roman. The first barbarians to opt for Christianity in large numbers were the Goths. They probably heard of Christianity through captives they took as they laid waste to Moesia and raided the coasts of Greece and Asia Minor in the third century, then moved into Dacia, which the Romans had abandoned. Exposed initially to three types of Christianity—Catholic, Arian, and Audian—most became Arians as a consequence of the work of Ulfilas (ca. 311–383). Catholicism evidently reached the Goths first. Constantine himself overcame Gothic invaders, who then, terrified by their defeat, embraced the Christian religion (Socrates *Church History* 1.18). A Gothic bishop named Theophilus attended the Council of Nicaea (2.41). Audius, a Syrian bishop charged by fellow bishops with teaching anthropomorphism, won numerous converts among the Goths and developed an extensive organization with monasteries and bishops. Ulfilas, however, born among the Goths, was far better equipped to reach them than were other missionaries. Consecrated a bishop by Eusebius of Nicomedia about 341, he spent the remainder of his life among the Goths, at first outside the empire and then in Moesia II. He translated all of the Bible except the four books of Kings (1 and 2 Kings; 1 and 2 Chronicles) into Gothic, refusing to do these because they were too warlike.

Although Armenia formally opted for Christianity around 300, paganism there still survived in mountainous areas. During the fourth century, Armenian literature appeared, including an Armenian translation of the Bible and other religious books. Nerses (d. ca. 373), a direct descendant of Gregory the Illuminator, undertook to reform the Armenian Church after his election as Catholicos around 363. His criticisms of the monarchs, however, resulted in exile and then in his death. When Armenia fell under Persian rule in the fifth century, Christians were severely persecuted.

Christianity arrived in Georgia in the late third or early fourth century through the efforts of a Christian captive named Nino or Nonna. Nino won over the queen after performing a healing in the name of Christ. The king, Mirian, reputedly became convinced when he got lost during a hunting trip and found his way out by calling on the name of Christ. The people soon followed the king, who sent to Constantinople to ask for an alliance and for clergy (Socrates *Church History* 2.7). Mirian's son and successor zealously supported the church. Until the Persian invasion of the fifth century, Christianity continued to thrive.

Constantine's conversion did not prove a boon for Christianity in Persia. So long as it remained illegal in the Roman Empire, Persian authorities seldom molested the church. When Constantine adopted it, he wrote a letter to Sapor II (320–381), the Persian king, commending to him in strong terms the Christian religion and indicating his affectionate interest in Christians all over Persia (Eusebius *Church History* 4.13.9-13). Sapor, a Zoroastrian, evidently was alarmed by the note, for he soon initiated a pogrom throughout his kingdom that extended even to Armenia. Despite severe persecution, Christianity survived among the Syriac-speaking members of the population. Sapor first ordered Christians to pay double taxes collected by their bishops. When one bishop refused, he was martyred. In Julian's day, persecution diminished, but resumed under his Christian successors. Sapor's successors proved more tolerant.

Christianity may not have reached India and Ceylon until the fifth century, unless one accepts early legends about the apostle Thomas. Whenever it did reach India, it probably spilled over from Persia. One bishop at Nicaea signed himself "John the Persian of all Persia and Great India," but whether "India" refers to the present-day country or to southern Arabia is uncertain. Emperor Constantius sent a "Theophilus the Indian" on a mission to southern Arabia and Ethiopia. The same person proceeded to "other parts of India," but again this may have meant southern Arabia. Persecution in Persia may have caused Christians to flee to India.

By the reign of Valens, Christianity was represented among people east of the Jordan. A dowager ruler of the "Saracens" required the consecration of a monk of her choice as bishop as a condition for peace after her forces defeated the Romans. The monk, named Moses, informed the Romans that he knew well the Roman creed. He and others proceeded thence to win converts among this people. One of these was a tribal chieftain named Zocomus, impressed by the prayer of another monk that his wife would bear a child (Sozomen *Church History* 6.38). A synod meeting at Antioch in 363 or 364 included a "Bishop of the Arabs" (Socrates *Church History* 3.25). Christianity arrived early, too, in southern Arabia. Pantaenus's "India" may have meant southern Arabia; if so, it would confirm Christian presence there in the second century. The Theophilus dispatched by Constantius was reported to have worked among the Himyarites in southwest Arabia. Constantius supported his work even with gifts for native rulers and churches designed both for Roman travelers and traders and natives. Ordained a bishop, Theophilus erected three churches there (Philostorgius *Church History* 3.4-5). Refugees from Persia may have started other work there as well.

The earliest knowledge of Christianity in Abyssinia, or Ethiopia, is connected with the arrival of Frumentius and Edesius, two Roman youth taken captive. According to Sozomen, these youth were returning with their mentor Meropius, a philosopher of Tyre and also a relative, from "India" when they were taken captive at a port where they had stopped for water. The Abyssinian king made Edesius his cupbearer and Frumentius, the older boy, administrator of his house and treasures. Because they served him faithfully for long years, the king freed them. At the request of the king's son, however, they did not return to Tyre as they wished but remained behind to direct the affairs of the kingdom. Frumentius, on inquiring, discovered Christians in Abyssinia, assembled them, and built a church. When the prince attained adulthood, he granted Frumentius and Edesius freedom. Although Edesius returned to Tyre, Frumentius went to Alexandria, where he asked Athanasius to appoint a bishop over the Abyssinians. After consulting his clergy, Athanasius consecrated Frumentius himself, who spent the rest of his life evangelizing his adopted people (Sozomen *Church History* 2.24).

By the end of the fourth century, Christianity stood in a position very different from the one it held at the beginning of it. Within the Roman Empire, with imperial backing, it had become, at least nominally, the religion of the majority. The memory of persecutions had faded. Now other cults experienced the lash, most soon to pull a curtain of secrecy over their religious activities or abandon them altogether. Whereas Christianity survived three centuries of intermittent harassment and persecution, most others, Judaism excepted, faded fast. Beyond the boundaries of the empire, Christianity was also experiencing success. Outside, Armenia alone adopted Christianity as the state religion, but Christianity was registering smartly in virtually all areas contingent to the Roman Empire. To some extent, the conversion of the Roman colossus helped, for as Rome went, so went many other peoples living in Rome's shadow. In at least one area, Persia, however, Constantine's and his successors' intimations of their hopes for Christians led to persecution. Yet even that did not deter the remarkable advance of the Christian faith. What would hurt far more would be internal dissension and strife.

CHAPTER TWENTY-ONE

A PEOPLE RENT BY STRIFE

As noted concerning earlier periods, Christianity inherited diversity from its Jewish parent and added to it as it incorporated more and more diverse peoples. What astounded Christian watchers like Constantine was Christianity's ability to hold together, not only in spirit but visibly, so many divergent elements. However scholars may judge Constantine's conversion, he obviously discerned in Christianity a unitive capability that the solar monotheism of Mithraism or any of Christianity's other competitors could not claim. Although all of them boasted local societies that offered many of the same things Christianity did, none had an empire-wide network and structure that joined the local groups in a worldwide fellowship and mission. Constantine hoped earnestly and with reason that his newly adopted faith would cement together the whole sprawling colossus he governed in a manner never seen before. If he guaranteed peace and offered help, how could the church fail to assist him in the attainment of that goal?

Sad to say, the church soon became a disappointment. Anyone who had looked at its earlier record should not have been surprised or shocked, for it had experienced fragmentation almost from the beginning, as earlier chapters of this volume have made clear. The Donatist controversy greeted Constantine even before his conversion. Both parties vied for his favor. The Donatists, perhaps naive in invoking any kind of imperial help to promote their cause, lost. Constantine, at any rate, sustained the Catholic party, which had the support of Christians outside of North Africa and which, for that reason, would have been more likely to help him unite his empire. Constantine and his successors, therefore, with the exception of Julian, vigorously sought to herd the Donatists back into the Catholic fold.

On the heels of the Donatist controversy came a second one, precipitated by an Alexandrian deacon named Arius. Despite the feverish efforts of Constantine to impose a settlement that would preserve unity in both the church and the empire, this was only the beginning. At first focused on the relationship between Christ as the divine Logos and God the Creator and Father, it gradually shifted to a debate regarding the relationship between human and divine in the person of the Son, the incarnate Logos. Sectional or regional rivalries played a major role in the controversy. The "schools" in Alexandria and in Antioch approached the doctrine of Christ quite differently, with Alexandria doing it "from above"—that is, emphasizing the divine—and Antioch "from below"—that is, accentuating the human. Imperial efforts at reconciliation by force merely exacerbated the tensions; they did not diminish them. As a result, the Arian controversy and its sequel boomed thunder and lightning throughout the century.

Arius and His Teaching

According to Epiphanius (*Against Heresies* 69.1), Arius was born in Libya and was already an "old Man" (69.3) when the controversy erupted in about 318. Whether he studied under Lucian of Antioch or represented Antiochene theology is debatable. The first clear evidence for his story locates him in Alexandria as a presbyter and pastor of the church of Baucalis, where the remains of Mark were thought to have been interred, with a reputation for popularity as a preacher and for asceticism. He probably took that influential post about 313, the year Alexander assumed the episcopate, although Sozomen (*Church History* 1.15; 32.20–33.2) alleged that he took part in the Meletian schism in 306, a point not confirmed by other writers. The new bishop had his hands full with an ultra-ascetic group led by a certain Hieracas of Leontopolis, who questioned the doctrine of resurrection, urged celibacy, and denied that baptized children who died in infancy could enter heaven, since they had not done righteous works (Epiphanius, *Heresies* 67). Persecution also had left some aftereffects.

In the circumstances Alexander evidently acted with considerable suspicion toward his presbyters, demanding specimen sermons to see if they were orthodox. At this point, about 318, the conflict between Arius and Alexander came to the surface. Each publicly repudiated the other's theology, and Arius blithely rejected his bishop's authority. Alexander complained of Arian congregations' meeting for worship in the city. Among his fellow presbyters, Arius evidently had strong support, for some were already resisting the bishop for other reasons. Alexander's denunciations of Arius, therefore, did not have the desired effect of uniting a sorely divided clergy, but he did secure Arius's formal condemnation by an Alexandrian synod about 321.

Arius left Egypt, but he did not give up. He appealed to Eusebius, Bishop of Nicomedia, and perhaps also Eusebius of Caesarea. Synods in both Bithynia and Palestine rallied Arius's supporters. Alexander replied by issuing a series of letters setting forth not only the charges against him but also those against his followers, and then convened another synod in Alexandria in 323 to condemn the renegade presbyter, as the dispute reached its height. At this point, the emperor began to take an interest in the affair. He sent Hosius, Bishop of Cordova, to Alexandria in the winter of 324/5. Alexander welcomed this help in restoring some semblance of unity to the Alexandrian church. Hosius probably informed Constantine of actions he took, but the emperor had decided already to convene a general council to resolve the growing dispute. Bishops assembled in Antioch assumed the meeting would take place in Ancyra, but Constantine wanted it to occur close to his own watchful eye.

There is considerable uncertainty regarding Arius's own views, for his lengthy poem entitled *The Banquet* (*Thalia*) has survived only in part, and his opponents may have distorted what he said. Although scholars once assumed he drew his idea of Christ as a "created Logos" from Lucian of Antioch, the consensus now is that Arius was more Alexandrian than Antiochene. Following in the footsteps of Origen, he directed his salvos against an *Exposition of Faith* by Gregory Thaumaturgus. Arius had an intense concern about the *unity* of God. To safeguard the single rule (*monarche*) of God, he insisted on subordination of the Son not merely in role but in nature as well. Only the Father exists from all eternity. The Logos, therefore, is created. "There was a time when he was not," Arius insisted. To be sure, he existed before everything else, "the firstborn of all creation," yet he belongs to the order of creation. Like Apollinaris later, Arius believed that the Logos united with the flesh (*sarx*) of Christ, so that he did not have a human soul. The Logos took over the function of the rational soul, which would explain why Christ did not sin—that is, disobey God, whereas all other humans do.

The Council of Nicaea, 325

Constantine, alarmed by the disruption of the "peace" of the church, did not wait long to take action. He arranged for the bishops to travel to the council by imperial post and entertained them at his own expense. How many attended is uncertain, despite the traditional 318 cited by Athanasius. Recent research confirms only about two hundred names, so that Eusebius of Caesarea's estimate of 250 may be fairly accurate (*Life of Constantine* 3.8).

Arius had some supporters, though probably not as many as the twenty-two the Arian Philostorgius (*Church History* 1.8) claimed. He did have the backing of Bithynian bishops Eusebius of Nicomedia, Theognis, and Maris as well as Syro-Palestinian and Cilician bishops. Eusebius of Caesarea leaned toward Arian christology. Arius evidently felt enough support that he could state his position boldly at the outset. He had already taken a stand against the use of the term *homoousios*, "of the same substance or essence," in a letter he wrote to Alexander and in his *Thalia*. "For he is not equal to

God," he wrote, "nor yet is he of the same substance [*homoousios*]." Eusebius of Nicomedia backed him up on this contention.

The majority was not sympathetic. Eusebius of Nicomedia rashly began with what the Arians considered nonnegotiable and thus put themselves in an impossible position when the council settled on the disputed term. Eusebius of Caesarea attempted to make peace by proposing the use of a Palestinian baptismal confession. The majority rebuffed this, however, for the creed did not address the key issue—namely, whether the Son was "of the same essence" as the Father or was a lesser being, which in one fell swoop thrust aside the Arian clichés that the Son was "a thing made," "a creature," and that "there was a time when he was not" and that "he is mutable by nature" (Athanasius *Epistle to the Africans* 5). The Arians kept weaseling their way around all the other terms, but they could not escape the implications of this one. The original creed of Nicaea has not survived. What is usually cited as the Nicene Creed is the one adopted at Constantinople in 381.

The Arians entered one more protest, objecting that the term could not be found in scriptures. Constantine, however, settled the matter by defending the use of the term against their objections and interpreting it in such a way that even Eusebius of Nicomedia could accept. The council then proceeded to condemn Arius's views and person, excommunicate him, and degrade him from the presbyterate. He and three others—Secundus of Ptolemais, Theonas of Marmarica, and the deacon Euzoius—were sent into exile by Constantine. The combination of civil and religious penalties held ominous implications and sowed the seeds for years of bitter wrangling as emperors changed their minds on such matters.

The bishops assembled at Nicaea attended to some other matters of importance before they departed. As noted earlier, they resolved the controversy over Easter by adopting the Roman custom of observing it always on Sunday. The emperor himself reinforced the decision by circulating a letter applauding the decision to observe *one* day lest "in so holy a thing there should be any division" (Eusebius *Life of Constantine* 3.18-20). Not all Easterners, however, acceded to the decision. The council also condemned the Audians and Meletians and issued several rules relative to matters of discipline, including questions about readmission of Novatianists and members of other sects.

The Sequel to Nicaea

Tough as its actions were, the Council of Nicaea did not attain the unity the emperor desired so fervently. Immediately after the council, the Nicaeans retained Constantine's confidence. The emperor promptly removed

Eusebius of Nicomedia and Theognis of Nicaea, who had signed the statement about *homoousios* but refused to approve Arius's exile, when they approached him and admitted they had signed only for prudential reasons. He exiled them to Gaul. Continuing dissension in Egypt, perhaps from Libyan bishops, forced Constantine to meet again with them. Evidently, a local Egyptian synod approved the sentence against Eusebius and Theognis. In 326, however, Eustathius of Antioch got into a heated debate with Eusebius of Caesarea. Some tactless remarks he made during a visit by Constantine's mother, Helena, led to charges of heresy and immorality and his removal from office, probably in 327. Arians seized on this opportunity to plead for the return of Arius, Eusebius, and Theognis. In November 327, Constantine invited Arius to his court at Nicomedia. Arius and Euzoius presented a kind of noncommittal creed to the emperor and his advisers that was silent on *homoousios*, but it satisfied him. Constantine, backed up by a synod in Bithynia, then instructed Alexander, Bishop of Alexandria, to restore Arius to communion. Alexander refused. Eusebius of Nicomedia promptly assembled a synod in Nicomedia that confirmed the restoration of Arius and formally anathematized Eustathius and Alexander. On April 17, 328, before all of this happened, Alexander died.

Athanasius, elected to succeed Alexander despite substantial opposition, embarked on a stormy career as the leader of the Nicaeans. Eusebius of Nicomedia, restored to his see, led the Arians right up to the moment of his death in 341. The synod of Nicomedia appealed to Athanasius to reinstate Arius, but he refused and disregarded Constantine's threats. Meantime, by 330 the Meletians allied themselves with the Arians against Athanasius. United with Eusebius, they initiated a fierce campaign that dominated church affairs for the next ten years.

Born of non-Christian parents in Alexandria around 295, Athanasius converted to Christianity at an early age. Educated in the school of Alexandria, he became a deacon and a secretary to Alexander and attended the Council of Nicaea with him. Before 318, while still in his twenties, he composed his short treatise on *The Incarnation,* in which he explained how, by the incarnation of the divine Logos, God restored the image of God in fallen humanity and overcame death, the consequence of sin, by Jesus' death and resurrection. Hurled into the center of the Arian controversy at the beginning, Athanasius suffered exile five times as a result of his tenacious defense of the Nicene formula. He died May 2, 373.

Athanasius resisted all pressures to abandon the Nicene formula. In 332 or 333, Arius evidently feared his friends at court had abandoned him and boldly protested directly to the emperor. Emphasizing the strength of his support in Libya, he aroused the suspicion of Constantine that he was threatening schism, what the emperor most wanted to avoid. As a result, Constantine wrote an extraordinarily severe letter dissecting Arius's theology and finding it incompatible with Nicaea. He proceeded to order Arius's works burned, like those of the anti-Christian polemicist Porphyry. Anyone who refused to surrender copies was to be executed. The emperor concluded by inviting Arius to make a defense at court. Arius evidently did well enough in this to be invited to defend himself two years later at a major gathering of bishops in Jerusalem. Composed mostly of Syro-Palestinian and Cilician bishops sympathetic with Arius, the bishops met first at Tyre to condemn Athanasius. The synod of Jerusalem in September 335 proceeded to clear Arius and notified Athanasius of its action, together with Constantine's approval. Athanasius, before receiving this letter, set out secretly for Constantinople to appeal personally to the emperor. This turned out to be a disaster, resulting in his first exile in November 335. When Arius returned to Alexandria, he met a volatile reaction and was refused communion. Constantine summoned him back to the capital, where friends at court defended him before the emperor against charges of fomenting discord in Alexandria.

The position of the Nicene party continued to deteriorate. Arians capitalized on the refusal of Marcellus, Bishop of Ancyra and a strong Nicene supporter, to participate in the synod of Jerusalem. A new synod met in the summer of 336, deposed Marcellus on the charge of holding the heresy of Paul of Samosata, and demanded that Alexander, Bishop of Constantinople, admit Arius into communion in the capital. In a meeting with the emperor, Arius subscribed to the Nicene Creed. As a consequence, Constantine ordered Alexander to admit Arius to communion. As Arius proceeded to the Hagia Eirene Church, where he was to receive Communion, however, he stopped at a public toilet and died there of some kind of internal hemorrhage.

Arian Ascendancy, 335–361

Arius's misfortunes notwithstanding, thanks to the shift in Constantine's sentiments, Arians remained more or less ascendant from 335 until the death of Constantius in 361. At his death in 337, Constantine received baptism at the hands of Eusebius of Nicomedia. Athanasius returned from exile immediately, but he did not remain long. In 339, he had to flee to Rome, taking with him some monks and thus importing that institution to the West. By intervention of Constans, the Western emperor, Athanasius returned to Alexandria in 346 over the objections of Constantius. After the death of Constans, he was again vulnerable to Arian attacks. Consequently in 356 Constantius succeeded again in driving him from his see. He remained in hiding near Alexandria until Julian took the throne in 361, but

Julian sent him packing once more in 362. His last exile, under Valens, lasted only a few months (365–366).

Four different positions emerged during this period: (1) Nicaeans, led by Athanasius, insisted that the Son is "of the same essence" (*homoousios*) with the Father. If the Son were not true God and true man, Athanasius argued, then humankind would not have been restored again to the divine image. (2) On the opposite extreme, thoroughgoing Arians contended that the Son is "unlike" (*anomoios*) the Father. He is a created being, above humans but not truly God. Between these two positions stood (3) those who were prepared to say that the Son is "like" (*homoios*) the Father according to the scriptures but not "of the same essence," and (4) those who tiptoed toward the Nicene position by saying that the Son is "of *like* essence" (*homoiousios*) but would not go so far as to concede the Nicene position. Arians made much of the fact that the term *homoousios* cannot be found in scriptures. Athanasius replied by pointing out that, while not in scriptures per se, it expresses what scriptures intend.

During Constantius's reign, Nicaeans did not win many victories. In 341, bishops assembled at Antioch affirmed the Nicene formula but deposed Athanasius. In 343, a synod meeting in Sardica cleared Marcellus of Ancyra and Athanasius of charges of heresy, but a counter synod held at Philoppopolis repudiated its actions. Three synods convened at Sirmium (351, 357, 358) and others held at Arles (353), Milan (355), Antioch (358), Ancyra (358), Constantinople (360), and Alexandria (362) favored the Arian party. Arian ascendancy reached its peak in 357 at the second synod at Sirmium. This synod proscribed the use of terms like *ousia* ("essence"), *homoousion*, and *homoiousion* as unscriptural and distinctly denied the true divinity of the Son.

Apollinaris: Nicene Overkill

One of the most vigorous advocates of the Nicene formula and bitterest opponents of Arianism was Apollinaris (ca. 310–ca. 390), who became bishop of Laodicea in 360. A staunch ally of Athanasius, receiving him on his return from exile in 346, Apollinaris sought to give a definitive answer to the question, Why did Christ not sin, that is, disobey God, despite the fact that all human beings do so? The answer lay in the way the divine Logos united with the human. Whereas human beings consist of body, soul, and spirit or rational soul, in Christ the divine Logos replaced the spirit, thus making him incapable of moral error. Arius had thought of him as less than God; Apollinaris, reacting against this, thought of him as less than human.

In 362, a synod meeting in Alexandria condemned teaching similar to this. Apollinaris, however, explained himself to the satisfaction of other

Nicaeans. As his views became better known, he came to the attention of other synods. Roman synods condemned Apollinaris by name between 374 and 380. Both Apollinarianism and Arianism were condemned at the second ecumenical council held in Constantinople in 381.

The Great Cappadocians

The controversy grew increasingly complex, especially after the death of Constantius. Many sought a middle ground between the Nicene *homoousios* and the Arian *anomoios*. Basil of Ancyra, after about 356, gathered around him a group of bishops who favored the term *homoiousios* and received a favorable nod from the synod of Alexandria in 362 and from Athanasius. Strict Arians looked with much less favor on this. When Macedonius, successor of Eusebius of Nicomedia as Bishop of Constantinople (342–362), came out strongly on the side of Basil, the Arian-dominated Synod of Constantinople in 360 deposed him.

Meantime, a group known as *Pneumatomachoi*, who affirmed the full divinity of the Son but doubted that of the Holy Spirit, appeared. Possibly the Tropici mentioned by Athanasius in one of his letters written between 355 and 361, the Pneumatomachoi came to the forefront in 373 when Eustathius of Sebaste broke with his friend Basil of Neocaesarea (the Great). Pope Damasus condemned them in 374. They reached their peak about 380 on the eve of the Council of Constantinople, which condemned them along with Arians and Apollinarians.

Leadership out of this morass came from three bishops known today as "The Great Cappadocians": Basil of Neocaesarea (ca. 330–379); Gregory of Nyssa (ca. 330–ca. 395), Basil's brother; and Gregory of Nazianzus (329–389). Educated at Caesarea in Cappadocia, Constantinople, and Athens in the finest culture of the day, both pagan and Christian, Basil forsook the world and became a hermit in 358. In 364, he left his seclusion, after Emperor Julian had unsuccessfully tried to lure him to court, and took up a defense of the Nicene position against the Arian Emperor Valens. In 370, Basil became bishop of Neocaesarea, where he served the rest of his life. This brought him into the thick of the battle against the Arians, the Pneumatomachoi, as well as Damasus of Rome and Athanasius of Alexandria, who refused to recognize Meletius as Bishop of Antioch. Basil had unusual gifts as an organizer. He framed two rules for monks, which helped to draw monasticism closer to the institutional church, and he developed hospitals and hostels for care of the poor, for whom he organized a system of relief.

Gregory of Nyssa, Basil's younger brother, temporarily became a rhetorician but then entered a monastery founded by Basil. Consecrated Bishop of Nyssa around 371, Gregory supported the Nicene Creed warmly. Deposed by Arians during the reign of Valens (376–378), he returned to his see and played a major role in the Council of Constantinople in 381. A mystic and theologian of great originality, he was much in demand as a preacher.

Gregory of Nazianzus, son of the Bishop of Nazianzus, studied at Athens at the same time Basil did. He too took up the monastic life and only reluctantly accepted ordination as a priest in the village of Sasima about 372. He assisted his father at Nazianzus until the latter's death in 374, then retired to Seleucia in Isauria. In 379, Theodosius called him to Constantinople, where his eloquent preaching did much to establish the Nicene faith and to prepare for the Council of Constantinople. During the Council, he was appointed Bishop of Constantinople, but he withdrew after only one year and spent the remainder of his life at Nazianzus or on his own estate.

The Cappadocians came up with a redefinition of the Nicene formula that was acceptable to moderate Arians as well as to Nicaeans. Fear of Sabellianism or Modalism still possessed many who were convinced that the term *homoousios* would obscure the distinctness of persons within the Trinity. In response to this problem, the Cappadocians interpreted the word *homoousios* with the formula *Mia ousia kata treis hypostaseis* ("One substance in three persons"). Such an interpretation required a redefinition of the word *hypostasis*. Previously it had meant "substance." Basil explained the distinction between *ousia* and *hypostasis* by using an analogy. For Athanasius, Father, Son, and Spirit are one being living in a threefold form or in three relationships, as, for example, one person may be at the same time a father, a son, and a brother. For Basil, Father, Son, and Spirit are three like or equal beings sharing a common nature, as, for example, different persons share in the common nature of human beings. Both views conserved Christ's divinity. The East generally has followed the Cappadocians, the West Athanasius; the West has always tended toward Modalism.

The Council of Constantinople, 381

Theodosius I, the Great, an ardent supporter of Nicaea, convened the second ecumenical council at Constantinople in 381. Only 150 Nicene and 36 Arian bishops, all Easterners, attended. Meletius, Bishop of Antioch, opened the council but died during the course of it. Gregory of Nazianzus and then Nectarius of Constantinople succeeded him as presidents. Since the Nicene Creed was lost in the interim, the bishops had to draft an essentially new statement into which they inserted the *homoousios*. At the same time, they condemned a long list of "heretics": Eunomians or Anomoeans, Arians or Eudoxians, Semi-Arians, Pneumatomachians, Sabellians, Marcellians, Photinians, and Apollinarians. Against the Pneumatomachoi, the Council asserted the full divinity and elaborated on the doctrine of the Holy Spirit, barely mentioned in the Nicene Creed. The Council also established Constantinople as the second see after Rome "because it is new Rome" (Canon 2) and laid down some rules for receiving persons from various sects or factions (Arians, Macedonians, Sabbatians and Novatians, Tetradites—those observing Easter on the Jewish Passover— and Apollinarians to be received by laying on of hands; Eunomians, Montanists, and Sabellians to be rebaptized).

Further Controversy

Emperor Theodosius put his stamp of approval on the Council shortly after it concluded its business. He directed that all churches be surrendered to supporters of the Niceno-Constantinopolitan formula tested by communion with selected bishops (*Theodosian Code* 50.3). Even this powerful action, however, in no way ended the divisions and controversies. Arianism, it is true, no longer dominated within the empire thereafter, but it held sway among Goths, Vandals, Lombards, and Burgundians during the next couple of centuries, only gradually rooted out by the efforts of Catholic missionaries.

The martyr of the protracted controversy may have been Origen. Quoted by both Arians and Nicaeans, his teaching became the subject of controversy and eventually condemnation nearly three hundred years after his death. Even before the Arian controversy broke out, Methodius of Olympus, Bishop of Lycia (d. 311), attacked Origen's doctrines of creation and resurrection, maintaining the identity of the resurrected body with the earthly one. Pamphilus (ca. 304–309), a disciple of Origen and a later director of the school at Caesarea, prepared a defense of his mentor with the help of Eusebius of Caesarea during his imprisonment in the persecution of Maximinus Daza. Eusebius later supplemented this *Apology*.

Origen's followers included many of the notables of the fourth century. Besides Pamphilus and Eusebius of Caesarea, there were genuine Origenists like Didymus of Alexandria, Athanasius, the Great Cappadocians, Hilary of Poitiers, and, for a time, Jerome. There were also slavish Origenists like the "tall brothers," monks of Nitria. The main opposition to Origen came from the anthropomorphites, monks of the desert near Scete in Egypt headed by Pachomius, father of communal monasticism.

Epiphanius, Bishop of Salamis (ca. 315–403), touched off the fuse in 394 by condemning Origen publicly at Jerusalem. John of Jerusalem and Rufinus (ca. 345–410), translator and editor of many of Origen's works, defended him. Jerome, though previously a disciple heavily dependent on some of Origen's biblical works, now condemned him. The controversy grew so bitter that Rufinus had to flee Palestine and take refuge in Aquileia in northern Italy. Through free translation he sought to vindicate Origen and conserved many of his writings.

In Egypt, meanwhile, Theophilus, Patriarch of Alexandria (d. 412), inaugurated a fierce campaign against Origenism, which lasted from 399 until 403. When the "tall brothers" refused to deliver church funds to him, they had to flee to Chrysostom in Constantinople for protection. Theophilus then turned his guns toward Chrysostom, using the dissatisfaction of a group that included the Empress Eudoxia to have him condemned at "the Synod of the Oak" in 403 and again at Constantinople in 404. Although Chrysostom was cleared, the dispute over Origen continued.

CHAPTER TWENTY-TWO

CHANGING CHURCHES

Converts crowding to get in necessitated changes in the churches of the Roman Empire. The most obvious indication of the new era was the restoration and erection of buildings large enough to accommodate the influx of new members and grand enough to suit the tastes of wealthy and cultured persons who came with the flood. Less visible but no less important, the churches adjusted their practices in admission of new members, shortening the process to incorporate them more rapidly. They elaborated their liturgies so as to effect a higher level of culture and reinterpreted and restructured the ministry to mirror the prevailing social pattern in a hierarchical society. In the meantime, the incorporation of so many persons with such limited formation placed a heavy demand on the churches' disciplinary procedures.

Buildings! Buildings!

The persecution under Diocletian (303–311) left standing few Christian edifices that had been erected during the long reign of peace from Gallienus (260–268) to Diocletian. House churches, of course, often escaped, but others did not. After the conversion of Constantine, therefore, the churches had to build in frenzied fashion simply to provide for persons who were already members. Within a few years, they had to make room for vast numbers of new converts whom imperial pressures sent bounding in their direction. Cities that had heavy Christian constituencies, such as Rome, Antioch, Alexandria, Carthage, or Constantinople, and Jerusalem, which was revered for its history, soon became centers of church architecture, adorned with buildings constructed in the grandest possible style. On a smaller scale, as well, churches appeared everywhere.

Two styles prevailed: the rectangular basilica and the circular, convergent martyrium. The churches avoided the ornate style of temples adorning the typical Greek and Roman forum and imitated instead the common public buildings called basilicas. These buildings usually consisted of a rectangular room, divided into three sections by rows of columns parallel to the longer walls. At one end was a niche (apse), at the other the entrance.

The roof extended in tiers like a layer cake, with the higher part in the center and the lower part over each side aisle. Windows on both the upper and the lower levels allowed light to fill the sanctuary. This style dominated for several centuries.

Initially employed as memorial chapels enclosing the tombs of martyrs or hallowing places associated with Jesus, in the East the convergent style became popular for worship connected with the saints. During the late fourth and fifth centuries, Christians often erected grand martyria and relocated the relics of martyrs or saints. Notable in this style of building was the dome, like that in the Roman pantheon. These buildings resembled tombs. Many were built octagonally to symbolize the "eighth day"—the day of resurrection. Convergent churches normally consisted of two parts distinguished by a row of columns, a center and an aisle running around the walls. Like basilicas, they had a layered roof so that the dome would rise much higher than the roof over the aisle and windows on both tiers would allow light to illuminate the whole building. Saint Stefano Rotondo in Rome, one such church, dates from the fourth century.

From the mid-fourth century on, churches were constructed with the apses facing east, since prayers were said facing in that direction. This evidently represented a reversion to an earlier custom, attested in the "house church" at Dura-Europos. In the age of Constantine, churches had apses in the west end, probably as a consequence of Constantine's predilection for sun worship. Few churches, however, had a true east-west longitudinal axis.

Inside churches, the altar or communion table claimed the center of attention. In some it stood at the back of the apse; in others where the apse joined the sanctuary, and in yet others it was located near the center of the sanctuary. Altars were wooden tables of varying sizes and shapes upon which the people placed their "offerings." Gradually stone replaced wood and the Synod of Epaon in Gaul in 517 prohibited wooden altars altogether. As the focal point of worship, altars were often constructed of costly materials.

During the fourth century, churches also began to place canopies, called *ciboria* ("cups"), over the altar, once again enhancing its importance. Early on, too, five or six columns were placed around the altar to adorn the apse in which the presbyters sat. This feature later gave way to the iconostasis, the screen dividing the choir from the nave or sanctuary. The chair of the bishop, *cathedra*, stood at the back of the apse on a higher level than the benches for presbyters. Because its location made it difficult for people to hear, some bishops had portable chairs or else preached from the *ambo*, or pulpit, which stood nearer the congregation, sometimes in the middle of the nave. Ambos were often elaborately carved.

Churches usually had other buildings attached to them, such as a house for the clergy, a hostel to care for travelers, a bath, a *diaconia* where deacons distributed charities, and a baptistery. Early on, baptisms probably took place in streams or rivers or other bodies of water. The earliest mention of a separate building for baptisms concerns a new church erected at Tyre in 314. Like martyria, in the West baptisteries were usually octagonal or circular with an inner octagon of eight columns surrounding a sunken font and supporting a domed roof. In the East, baptisteries were rectangular or square. The font, normally recessed into the floor, was sometimes octagonal, sometimes cruciform. Since most baptisteries averaged only two to four feet in depth, effusion rather than immersion may have been practiced in most places. Indeed, catacomb art uniformly depicts the candidate standing in water just above the ankles having water poured on the head. Candidates also may have knelt and had their heads pushed face forward into the water. Because candidates for baptisms were nude, baptisteries usually had an adjoining dressing room; some had a whole complex of rooms.

By the end of the fourth century, Christians began to do something they had resisted earlier: convert pagan temples into Christian churches. Some obviously no longer felt a need to guard themselves against all things pagan as they had previously. Instead of razing the temples, therefore, they put them directly, with some modification, to Christian use. San Clemente in Rome, for instance, incorporated walls of what may have been a factory building and covered a sanctuary of the Mithra cult with its apse.

Art

Like architecture, Christian art took an upward turn during the fourth century as more affluent, cultured, and well-educated persons entered the church. In earlier centuries, of course, some Christians appreciated and used art, the earliest surviving specimens being drawings in the catacombs of Rome. Christians used the style of the declining cosmopolitan art of Rome, early on relying on pagan artists, but they shifted from the realistic to a symbolic style and drew themes from the Bible just as their Jewish forebears had. From the very first, catacomb art featured the theme of deliverance. The early gallery of the Catacomb Domitilla represented this with paintings of the good shepherd, Daniel between two lions, and Noah in the ark receiving the returning dove. Fourth-century painters added to these Moses smiting the rock to slake the thirst of the Israelites in the wilderness, the three Hebrews in the fiery furnace, Abraham being restrained from sacrificing Isaac, the healing of the woman with the hemorrhage, the healing of the paralytic, the three magi presenting the gifts to the

Christ child, and others. Among all of the catacomb drawings, the most popular was Jonah being tossed overboard, swallowed by a mythical sea monster, and luxuriating under a vine in Nineveh. Frequent, too, were symbolic depictions of baptism and the Lord's Supper, the sacraments of salvation. Alongside biblical scenes like these, artists depicted hope with symbols such as the anchor, the dove, the vine of immortality, and the orant—a person with hands uplifted in prayer. The paintings reveal clearly the reliance on popular Greco-Roman forms and Jewish-Christian stories.

Christians also adorned sarcophagi with art. In the West, they inherited from second- and third-century ancestors the frieze-type of coffin, on which they depicted a series of scenes without division by space, such as the raising of Lazarus; the healing of the blind man, the paralytic, and Jairus's daughter; or Old Testament subjects. In the East, after persecution ceased, Christians could bury their dead above ground in more elaborate tombs with vastly improved art. In these columnar sarcophagi, artists could separate scenes by panels and thus depict them with far greater effectiveness. One of the finest specimens is the sarcophagus of the Roman prefect Junius Bassus, who died in 359. In ten separate panels, the artist has depicted such central biblical scenes as Abraham's sacrifice of Isaac, Adam and Eve, Daniel in the lions' den, Jesus and the Samaritan woman at the well, the Zacchaeus story, and the arrest in the Garden of Gethsemane.

Christian art of the fourth century reflected clearly the process of accommodation to culture, which was taking place at the time. The earliest Christian vault and wall mosaics discovered thus far are located in a small mausoleum under St. Peter's in Rome. Built during the second century for the Julii family, the mosaics probably date from the middle of the third century and after. A mosaic in the center of the vault depicts Christ as the unconquered sun driving his chariot across the sky, with the nimbus around his head shooting out like the arms of the cross and bearing in his left hand an orb. The pagan sun god had been transformed into the risen Christ, triumphant over death and Lord of the universe!

Church art in this period did not achieve the splendor it attained in the next two centuries, but at Constantine's urging it improved rapidly. Constantine complained about the lack of artisans to do skilled work and directed that some youth be given leisure to learn their art. Although little of the art of Constantine's churches has survived, the *Liber Pontificalis* describes how the interior of St. Peter's looked. A gold mosaic decorated the apse. Gold and precious marbles adorned Peter's shrine. The altar was silver-gilt set with four hundred precious stones. On top of it was a solid gold cross. A large golden dish served as the offertory. Before the apostle's tomb was a crown of light and four large candlesticks. Thirty-two silver candelabra lit the sanctuary. The emperor wanted the churches, at least some of them, to assume some of the glamour of the imperial court.

Although St. Peter's held a special place among Christian shrines, its furnishings were not exceptional among churches in important urban centers.

Baptisteries, like churches, often had elegant furnishings and art. The well-preserved Orthodox Baptistery at Ravenna, constructed and furnished between 400 and 450, featured figures of prophets in each of the eight niches on its walls. On a second tier, friezes of sixteen minor prophets adorned the arcades on each side of the windows. The dome represented in three rings empty thrones and altars, apostles, and Christ's baptism. The mosaics were extraordinarily rich in color.

Wealthy Christians also brought Christian symbolism into their homes, depicting the story of faith on wall panels, vases, lamps, or other objects of art. Constantine and his mother, Helena, led the way in this christianization process.

The Liturgy

The dramatic change in the church's situation in the Roman world opened the way for significant additions to its worship. Like the edifices now erected with imperial support and sanction, the liturgy too grew more elaborate and took on some of the pomp and ceremony of the imperial court. No longer the despised and persecuted minority fighting for their lives, Christians could speak about their "mysteries" in language they formerly rejected as the language of the "world." Similarly, they took over calendar observances from that world and transformed them into Christian "moments" by some theological sleight of hand as they sought to christianize a vast new constituency.

The Sunday liturgy remained the mainstay of Christian worship in this era, and the first part, the service for catechumens, changed little. This service consisted still chiefly of prayers, readings from both the Old and the New Testaments, and the sermon as the key means of instructing converts. An added feature, influenced by Christian monasticism, was more and more extensive singing of psalms. As in earlier periods, sermons were mainly verse-by-verse expositions of scriptures but, as time passed, with greater rhetorical polish by persons like Ambrose, Gregory of Nazianzus, Augustine, or John Chrysostom, who were skilled in the art.

Hearers stood during sermons, which often were long. They also came and went and interacted with the preacher. In the absence of modern-day amplification systems, many persons doubtless had difficulty hearing unless preachers had well-developed voices; Augustine, although captivating as a speaker, had a weak voice.

The second part of the liturgy, the mass of the faithful, still reflected the regional diversity of early Christian worship, but there were pressures toward uniformity. Changes took the form chiefly of elaboration in the eucharistic rite by way of fixed forms. Egeria, a pilgrim who visited the East between 381 and 384, depicted for that city a much more elaborate celebration both daily and on Sunday. Morning worship on Sunday began at full daylight and lasted until about eleven o'clock in the Martyrium and then continued in the Church of the Resurrection, a practice reflective of the tendency to focus on sacred places and events. The Jerusalem liturgy influenced worship customs throughout the Roman Empire.

The Calendar

The Christian calendar underwent major development during the fourth century as the Holy Land once again opened for pilgrims. As converts poured into the churches by thousands, a calendar marking "great moments" in the history of salvation served a crucial educational function, enabling the newly baptized to "act out" in daily, weekly, or yearly observances the story they had chosen as their own. Some of these observances already had fixed places in the calendar, but many others were added at this time.

For daily worship, Constantine's conversion widened Christian options immensely. Where the faithful had once been forced to gather clandestinely in family or small groups, they could now flock to the churches for early morning hymns; minor prayer services at 9:00 A.M., noon, and 3:00 P.M.; and evening hymns. By the late fourth century, in many areas companies of monks set the standard of faithfulness by assembling before daylight to sing psalms and throughout the rest of the day to maintain the daily regimen of prayer.

The weekly calendar, already largely in place, became more fixed. Concerned to set themselves apart from Jews, especially in areas where the latter represented sizable minorities, Christians no longer hesitated to claim Sunday as their day of worship. They fasted on Wednesdays and Fridays, marking these days with afternoon Eucharists. They also held special Eucharists on Saturday mornings. Christians never fasted on Saturdays, even during Lent.

According to Egeria, whose depiction of the liturgy in Jerusalem reveals its future direction, the Easter cycle constituted the major feature of the Christian year. Candidates for baptism began daily instruction and all began fasting eight weeks before Easter. This culminated in Holy Week, the week just prior to Easter. Observance of Easter lasted seven full weeks, reaching its conclusion at Pentecost. Following Pentecost, the faithful resumed Wednesday and Friday fasts, which they had given up at Easter. At this time, Jerusalem observed only two other special days: Epiphany and the Dedication of the Church of the Holy Sepulchre. Other sources, however, recount a whole row of saints' days on which the churches celebrated the Lord's Supper.

In Egeria's time, Lent lasted eight weeks rather than the forty days that became traditional later on. During Lent, the faithful as well as catechumens fasted all day except Saturday and Sunday. They also attended a number of extra services added to the normal cycle, including a Friday night vigil that lasted until the celebration of the Saturday Eucharist before sunrise. The amount of preaching also increased. During Lent, fasters gave up not only oil and fruit but also bread. Some even maintained a complete fast from Sunday Eucharist until the breaking of the fast on the next Saturday, but such rigors were not required. Some persons ate each evening or at least at noon on Thursdays.

Holy Week began with a vigil on Friday evening a week before Easter Sunday. Observers proceeded on Saturday to Bethany, the house of Lazarus. On Sunday, they observed normal services in the morning. In the afternoon, however, they held special services at the Eleona and Imbomon on the Mount of Olives and then proceeded down the Mount of Olives carrying palm branches and made their way through the city to the Church of the Resurrection for evening prayers at a late hour. On Monday, Tuesday, and Wednesday the faithful observed the usual prayer services but added a four-hour service beginning at three in the afternoon in the Martyrium. On Thursday, they maintained the usual observances until noon. At two o'clock they began a continuous round of services that lasted until dawn the next day, save for a short break for an evening meal. These services focused on Judas' betrayal of Jesus. The nighttime services took place on the Mount of Olives. On Friday, people gathered at seven o'clock at Golgotha *behind* the cross and at noon proceeded to the *front* of the cross. That night the young and vigorous who had sufficient stamina kept a vigil at the Church of the Resurrection. On Saturday, there was no celebration of the Eucharist.

Easter was the center of the Christian calendar. The paschal vigil began on Saturday night. Candidates received baptism and shared in their first communion about midnight. The following week, the bishop instructed them each morning in the "mysteries," that is, baptism and Eucharist. On five of the eight days of Easter Week, Christians celebrated the Eucharist in buildings on Golgotha. On Wednesday, they observed it at the Eleona and on Friday at Sion.

The period from Easter to Pentecost differed from the rest of the year because of the absence of fasting, the whole period being a time of rejoicing. Filling out the biblical frame, the churches began to mark the ascension of

247

Jesus on the fortieth day after Easter. According to Egeria, this feast took place in Bethlehem rather than in Jerusalem. Pentecost, "fiftieth," continued the celebration of Easter. No all-night vigil preceded it. Rather, the festival entailed a full round of observances, lasting, in Jerusalem, until midnight.

The feasts of Encaenia, or Dedication, and Epiphany were also recognized in the late fourth century with eight-day celebrations that symbolized resurrection. The Feast of Dedication commemorated annually the erection of the Church of the Holy Sepulchre. Epiphany, January 6, involved a vigil at the Church of the Nativity in Bethlehem, a midnight celebration of the Eucharist, and then a trek to Jerusalem. The festival continued for eight days with daily Eucharists in various holy sites. The Presentation of Christ in the Temple was commemorated forty days after Epiphany, according to Egeria, with services similar to those observed at Easter.

Christmas entered the calendar in the West during this period, where Epiphany was unknown. The earliest evidence for the celebration of December 25 as the date of Christ's birth appeared in the Philocalian Calendar, drawn up at Rome in 336. According to John Chrysostom in a sermon delivered in 386, it was not introduced in Antioch until around 375. Egeria did not refer to it for Jerusalem, and Alexandria did not adopt it until about 430. At Constantine's urging, Westerners evidently christianized the Roman festival of the unconquered sun, December 25, by attaching it to a "great moment" in Christian history of salvation. This suited perfectly the emperor's strategy. As the custom moved eastward, it left a serious problem in that Epiphany, universally recognized in the East, also commemorated Christ's birth. The solution was to make January 6 represent the visit of the magi or the baptism of Jesus.

Celebrating the Saints

The cessation of persecution quickened interest in martyrs and saints. By the end of the fourth century, Christians had erected martyria all over the empire and lovingly transferred remains or relics of saints and martyrs there. Pilgrims traveled thousands of miles in the most difficult conditions to visit holy sites, first those in Palestine and then in other places consecrated by the blood of saints. The churches also expanded the calendar to commemorate these exemplary Christians who inspired others by their living and by their dying.

In a funeral oration preached for his brother, Basil of Caesarea, in 379, Gregory of Nyssa recalled festivals in honor of Stephen, Peter, James, John, and Paul during the period between Christmas and January 1. Numerous later sources confirm the custom in the East, but local calendars differed widely. Rome, for instance, honored only John in December, Peter and Paul in June. A festival in honor of Mary did not appear until the sixth century in Gaul, the seventh century in Rome.

Numerous other festivals began locally, primed by special interest. From a very early date, the churches remembered their martyrs with special celebrations. Later on, others adopted the same days and incorporated them into their calendars.

Christian Discipline

Beneficial as it was in many ways, the membership explosion that came with Constantine's conversion heavily taxed Christian discipline. Vast numbers now had minimal comprehension of what it meant to be Christian. The Synod of Elvira (Illiberris) in Spain in about 306 illustrated the breakdown of basic morality in its severe canons. After declaring themselves Christians, some persons continued to function as *flamines*, priests offering sacrifices as public officials, and to offer pagan sacrifices. Other canons dealt with murder, adultery, abandonment of spouses, using children as prostitutes, usury, lighting candles to placate spirits, incest, augury, sodomy, false witness, intermarriage with Jews or Gentiles, and gambling. A few years later, the Synod of Arles in Gaul indicted gladiators, charioteers, actors, usurers, and others who violated well-established Christian standards.

In some areas, the churches took strong and decisive action. Churches in the East developed what appears in retrospect to have been a highly legalistic system of discipline that eventually proved unworkable. Originally put together in response to the breakdown of Christian discipline in the late third century, it assumed more fixed features in the era of peace inaugurated by Constantine. Rather than excommunicating serious offenders permanently, bishops now graded penalties to fit the offense. As in the earlier period, they distinguished five grades: "mourners," "hearers," "fallers," by-standers," and "restored penitents." Penalties varied from synod to synod until some standardization occurred late in the fourth century. In 314, the Synod of Ancyra in Galatia, for instance, required persons forced to offer sacrifices and doing so willingly to spend one year as "hearers," three as "kneelers," and two as "by-standers" before being restored to communion. It required persons found guilty of bestiality (having sexual intercourse with animals), if under age twenty, to spend fifteen years as "fallers" and five as "by-standers"; if over twenty, to spend twenty-five years as "fallers" and five as "by-standers." It stipulated that persons indulging in magic or other pagan customs must do three years as "fallers" and two as "by-standers." In some cases, it levied penances without gradation—seven years for adultery, ten years for abortion or child exposure, five or seven years for unpremeditated murder, and lifetime excommunication for premeditated murder.

By the late fourth century, although the system remained in force, bishops quietly phased it out. Even with the threat of government enforcement hanging over their heads, many persons would not endure the humiliation of long penances. To avoid having to undergo them, they covered up and persuaded friends to cover up for them. In canonical letters written in 374 and 375, Basil of Caesarea threatened to place those who covered up for others under the same penalty the guilty party deserved (Canon 74). About the same time, John Chrysostom, realizing how difficult it was to impose discipline on the easygoing populace of Antioch and repulsed by the mechanical character of the whole system, openly opposed long years of discipline and developed several alternative modes of repentance. No sin, he declared, is outside God's mercy, and God accepts even imperfect repentance. Length of repentance doesn't matter a whit; what matters is sincerity. Repentance must be voluntary. It is enough to confess privately. "If you have condemned your sin, you have put off the burden of it" (*Lazarus* 4). Alternatives to the system, Chrysostom observed elsewhere, include simple confession, contrition, humility, almsgiving, prayer, and forgiveness of others (*The Devil as Tempter*, Hom. 2).

In the West, the churches never developed grades or degrees to differentiate offenses and penalties. As in earlier times, the *exhomologesis* (public confession) required public displays of remorse, such as weeping, disheveled hair, soiling of face and neck, and wearing sackcloth. Restoration as described by Jerome (*Dialogue Against the Luciferians* 5), entailed a priest's offering of an oblation, laying on of hands, invoking the return of the Holy Spirit, and inviting prayers of the people for restoration of the penitent. Catholics repudiated the rigors of the Novatianists or Donatists. The church, Ambrose insisted, has the power to forgive all sins. God has granted priests the power to forgive all. God, of course, does the forgiving; human beings only exercise the ministry of God's forgiveness. Yet, Ambrose went on to note, the rule of a single repentance following baptism still applies. He displayed the authority of a strong bishop to demand public confession in his excommunication of Emperor Theodosius for the slaughter of seven thousand citizens of Thessalonica. Only grave and notorious scandals necessitated public confessions; prayer sufficed for minor sins, Augustine said (*Sermon* 351, *Repentance*).

A Royal Priesthood

The rapid influx of new Christians created a crisis of leadership for the churches. Understandably but unfortunately, many Christian communities laid hands too hastily on some of the new and more cultured converts, indiscriminately ordaining neophytes, the lapsed, and persons of questionable reputation. Canon 2 of the Council of Nicaea summed up the dilemma succinctly, noting that "many things, either by necessity or otherwise by human pressures, happened contrary to the ecclesiastical rule, so that persons recently converted from Gentile life to the faith, after a very brief instruction, were baptized and almost immediately thereafter were promoted to the episcopate or presbyterate."

Such haste opened a Pandora's box of moral, educational, and theological maladies for which key leaders subsequently struggled to supply remedies. Many of the newly ordained, like Synesius of Cyrene, conscripted forcibly to be Bishop of Ptolemais and Metropolitan of the Pentapolis in 410 C.E., lacked both motivation for and understanding of their offices. Others had a poor sense of the boundaries that separated Christian from pagan, even on basic matters that did not involve subtle cultural distinctions. Fourth-century councils and other documents have left ample evidence of various kinds of debauchery that injured badly the church's reputation. The powerful jaws of superstition still held many clergy fast, for they indulged in sorcery, magic, and astrology and wore amulets and magical charms. Some dressed and acted like dandies. They indiscreetly frequented pubs, bathed with women in public baths, kept women in their houses, and acted carelessly in their relations with virgins and widows. Some continued to participate in pagan wedding rites, to attend the shows and games, and to share in such other customs as the churches had once uniformly denounced as idolatrous. Some sought and used their offices for the sake of personal gain—buying and selling offices, taking usury, always seeking better appointments, and engaging in secular enterprises on the side. Married clergy often let family problems damage their witness.

Many disciplinary canons of fourth-century councils addressed these problems head on. As a matter of prime importance, the bishops sought to halt indiscriminate ordinations by establishing certain age limits (fifty for bishops, thirty for priests), insisting on adequate training, careful examination of background and reputation, prohibition of clerical "tramps," issuing letters of commendation for both clergy and laity, and, in the East, eliminating popular elections. In line with increased care in selection, they turned increasingly to the monks as models of piety, conscripting many of them for the clerical ranks. The bishops also sought to remove or render innocuous in other ways unworthy or disreputable clergy. Since high views of ordination prevented outright withdrawal of orders, removal from duties was customary in the case of such serious offenses as lapsing in persecution, adultery or fornication, simony, usury, or other forms of avarice. The councils likewise laid down rules for clerical behavior in relations with women, attendance at public functions, and the like and absolutely banned all forms of sorcery, magic, and astrology.

The drive to sustain and improve the moral worthiness of the clergy in a lascivious age carried with it an additional impetus toward celibacy. Essentially the same factors that produced the monastic movement were at work here. Wiser heads tried to steer clear of extreme forms of asceticism, such as self-mutilation, but at the same time they sought to sound a clear note against the licentiousness and otherwise lax morality of the age. Specifically with reference to the clergy, concern for purity expressed itself in several ways. In both East and West nonmarriage *after* ordination became the general rule by the early fourth century. There was strong opposition to second marriages and to marriage to widows. Within marriage, clerical continence was practiced widely in both the East and the West, but it became a "binding rule" only in the West, first by order of Pope Siricius (384–399). Even there, some braved the papal wrath by opposing the view openly—Bonosus, Bishop of Sardica, and the layman Helvidius, condemned at Capua in 389; Jovinian, condemned at Milan in 390; and Vigilantius, condemned by Pope Innocent I (402–417). A celibate clergy, however, played a significant part in the evangelization of Europe.

In connection with the struggle to conserve integrity, the distinction between clergy and laity became more and more pronounced. In a treatise composed about 373 when the bishop of Antioch tried forcibly to ordain him, John Chrysostom placed the office well above mortal competence or worthiness. To preside over the church or to undertake the care of souls is so exalted that all women and the majority of men fail to qualify. This office, he wrote, may be "discharged on earth, but it ranks among heavenly ordinances" (*The Priesthood* 3.4). Priests, therefore, must be as pure as angels. In administering the Eucharist, they represent God to humankind and thence have an authority not given even to angels. In baptizing, they not merely pronounce the removal of spiritual uncleanness but "actually and absolutely take it away" (3.6). Even beyond baptism, they "have authority to forgive sins," and they bear fearsome responsibility to care for the needy and to teach and preach the gospel.

Not all carried so exalted an image of the office, and few could implement it. In this era, nonetheless, the clergy, especially bishops, often exercised immense social and political power. As a bishop, Ambrose of Milan (374–397), for instance, administered not only baptism, the Eucharist, and penance, but he in effect functioned as a public official as well. He superintended extensive church charities to relieve the poor, care for the sick and imprisoned, entertain strangers, pay debts of persons unable to meet their liabilities, maintain and educate orphans, and meet other needs. He defended widows and orphans against public seizure of their estates. He heard and adjudicated civil disputes. He confronted emperors and empresses regarding both their beliefs and their behavior. As metropolitan of northern Italy, he supervised the dioceses of the entire province of Aemilia-Liguria. He stood as a bulwark against Arianism, even that of Empress Justina. He played a significant role in urging on the final defeat or paganism throughout the empire.

Official investment of the episcopate with public responsibilities of necessity reshaped it. Whereas early on bishops presided over small flocks like shepherds, some, especially in areas where there were few episcopates, now became powerful executives whose main duty was to direct other clergy and to represent their churches in the public arena. Yet by the end of the fourth century many did exceedingly well in these new roles as Christianity became the public faith. Basil of Caesarea as well as Ambrose, for example, managed to combine pastoral and public duties with remarkable skill. This new cadre, drawn from the very best of society, lifted Christianity to a new plateau. Although it may have stumbled momentarily in its effort to assimilate vast numbers, it recovered its stride in this period and went on to become truly the religion of the empire.

CHAPTER TWENTY-THREE

THE CALL OF THE DESERT

What began as a trickle in the late third century became a flood in the fourth as thousands of young men and women fled to the desert. Many withdrew to escape from the intolerable burden of public taxes and service, but many others sought literally to fulfill the call of Christ to self-denial, cross bearing, and discipleship. The martyrs had inspired pagans and Christians alike by their example. Since the era of peace prevented actual martyrdom, some elected a martyrdom of fasting and prayer in battle against the forces of evil. They confronted demons in their main habitat: the desert.

Egypt was not the only locus for the monastic experiment. Monasticism may have developed independently in Syria, for Syrian monasticism assumed a character of its own, being far more austere than Egyptian monasticism. From these two places, the movement spread all over the Roman Empire, first in the East and then in the West. As it grew, it changed character. The hermitic type persisted, but it yielded ground to the less austere communal type of monasticism initiated by Pachomius. Wise ecclesiastical leaders, in the meantime, rescued it for the organized church by pulling the monks closer to the churches and putting them at the service of the church. Monasteries served as centers of charity, and monks sustained bishops in their theological battles. In the West, they bore the main burden for the evangelization of Europe.

Egypt

The rapidly increasing flow of hermits to certain parts of the Egyptian desert assured that they would not remain in isolation from one another very long. Associations of hermits developed at different locations. The first was at Pispir, not far from the Red Sea, where Anthony had fled to escape the crowds who wanted to imitate his holy life. Anthony left the privacy of his "Inner Mountain" about every five to twenty days to give them help and advice (*Life of Anthony* 89). Anthony's disciples included Hilarion, the founder of monasticism in Palestine (ca. 310); Macarius the Egyptian, who initiated a settlement at Scete (ca. 330); as well as others who remained at Pispir.

Associations sprang up elsewhere. At Chenoboskion, where the famous Gnostic library was discovered in 1947, a monk named Palaemon headed a group of hermits who lived nearby, shared his style of life, sought his advice, and cared for him in illness. The most famous of his pupils was Pachomius, usually regarded as the father of coenobite, or communal, monasticism. Pachomius remained at Palaemon's side until the latter died. After burying him, Pachomius founded the monastery at Tabennesis.

Huge bands of monks gathered in a valley about sixty miles south of Alexandria and established three communities. Monasticism at Nitria was initiated by Amoun, whose wealthy and cultured parents died when he was twenty-two. Already married, he persuaded his wife to lead a life of continence from the day of their marriage. After eighteen years they separated, and Amoun went to Mount Nitria (ca. 320–330), where he spent the remainder of his life. By the end of the fourth century, about five thousand monks, according to Palladius, inhabited the area. Monks here still lived under no rule and pursued the solitary life, working and praying alone but gathering on Saturdays and Sundays in the large church. They supported themselves by weaving linen, but they included physicians, confectioners, wine-sellers, and bakers. They attached great importance to memorization of scriptures, and some reputedly could quote all of both the Old and the New Testaments. They valued work and obliged even guests to join them in it after a limited time there.

Not far from Nitria, six hundred monks lived in a place called Cellia, "the cells" (Sozomen *Church History* 6.31). Like the hermits at Nitria, they also assembled on Saturdays and Sundays for worship, but they did not maintain close contact otherwise. They built their huts far enough apart that they could not see or hear one another. Among the most famous monks to reside there was Macarius the Alexandrian, who had cells also in Scete, Libya, and Nitria. He astonished even other monks by his fasting and lived to be nearly a hundred (d. ca. 393). Evagrius of Pontus in Cappadocia spent two years in Nitria and fourteen in Cellia. His writings on prayer influenced markedly Eastern theology and practice of prayer.

At Scete, a monastic colony sprang up under the leadership of Macarius the Egyptian, or the Great, about 330. A disciple of Anthony until that time, Macarius dug a tunnel a half mile long between his cell and a cave in order to escape visitors (Palladius *Lausiac History* 17). Many of his sermons, letters, and sayings have survived. Like monks at Nitria and Cellia, those at Scete attended faithfully on Saturdays and Sundays one of the four churches in the community. Life was harsh not only because of self-imposed austerities, but also because of lack of water and food. The community maintained a strict discipline. Like the monks at Nitria, they combined work and prayer, trying to memorize all of the scriptures. Cassian gained much of the material for his *Conferences* and *Institutions* at Scete from such famous monks as Paphnutius and Serapion.

Other colonies of hermits formed near Alexandria, Rhinoccorura, Babylon and Memphis, Heracleopolis, Phoenice, Oxyrhynchus, Achoris, the Arsinoite regions, and the Thebaid. Some of these numbered in the thousands. Palladius, for instance, counted two thousand in a colony near Alexandria (*Lausaic History* 7). All subsisted on simple diets, usually one meal a day, which they varied according to individual age and strength (Cassian *Conferences* 2.22). They tried to avoid extremes in asceticism. They slept only a short time before dawn (Ibid., 7.34). Younger monks confessed faults to older, more experienced monks.

Associations like these evolved naturally into the coenobite monasticism of Pachomius. A monk named Aotas had tried to establish a community but failed (*Life of Pachomius* 77). Pachomius, born about 292 of pagan parents in the Upper Thebaid, first came in contact with Christians while serving in the army raised by Constantine. There he witnessed the application of Christian charity in food and drink brought to soldiers by Christians, and thus he decided to become a Christian. Upon release from the army, he went to Chenoboskion to receive instruction in the faith and to be baptized in the village church. Hearing about Palaemon, Aotas joined him, sharing his dwelling and working with him. One day, he went to Tabennesis on the eastern bank of the Nile, where a celestial voice instructed him to remain and build a monastery (*Life* 7). With Palaemon's assistance, he built a cell there. His brother, John, soon joined him, but he wished to live as a hermit. Others, however, followed, and within a short time the community numbered a hundred. When the monastery at Tabennesis overflowed, he built another at Pabau or Proou, which also grew rapidly. Not only individuals but also colonies of monks came. Pachomius directed some of them to set up new communities at Chenoboskion, Monchosis, Thebeu, Tase, Tismenae, Panopolis, and Pachnoum. Pachomius himself changed his residence from Tabennesis to Pabau, which then became the head monastery of the Pachomian system. In 346, disease ravaged the monasteries, claiming the lives of over a hundred monks, including Pachomius. Before he died, Pachomius named Petronius, superior of Tismenae, to succeed him, but he died two months later. Petronius appointed Orsisius, superior of Chenoboskion, to succeed him. Under him, the Pachomian communities thrived, but their material prosperity led to controversy over management. In 350, Orsisius solved the problem by appointing Theodore as his coadjutor and leaving the control to him. Theodore ruled the complex of monasteries wisely for eighteen years. Little is known of the monasteries after Theodore's death except that they evidently continued to prosper and spread. According to Palladius, there were 3,000 monks during Pachomius's life and 7,000 when he wrote (around 420; *Lausiac History* 7).

Pachomius gradually developed rules for his monks that became more and more precise as the communities overflowed. At the beginning, Pachomius evidently admitted new monks after a preliminary examination. In time, however, he required a three-year probation and admitted strange monks with some caution. Pachomian communities consisted of numerous buildings within a walled enclosure: church, assembly hall, dining hall, library, kitchen, food pantry, bakery, infirmary, various workshops, and houses for members of the community. According to Jerome, they numbered from thirty to forty. Each dormitory housed twenty-two to forty monks in individual cells and contained a common meeting room. Near the monastery gate was a hospice for visitors, who included women.

A Superior-General, or Archimandrite, held supreme power over the monasteries. He appointed heads for each of them and visited them regularly. A superior and an assistant governed each monastery. Monks were assigned to houses usually according to their work and were ranked according to seniority; each house was ruled by a head and an assistant. Twice a year the monks gathered at Pabau to celebrate Easter and for administrative purposes on August 13. During the latter meeting, superiors reported on the work of their monasteries during the year and each monk forgave others for the wrongs they had done to him.

The Pachomians admitted all except a very few whose earlier lives made them unsuitable, requiring willingness to obey the rules of the community. Even children entered. New applicants remained outside for several days while doorkeepers taught them prayers, psalms, and the rules.

The monks gathered in their houses several times a day for prayer: at dawn, noon, evening, before they went to bed, and at night. On Saturdays and Sundays they celebrated the Eucharist. Twice a week, on fast days, monks received instruction in Christian doctrine and scriptures with emphasis on memorization. Those who could not read had to learn. Most monks wove mats and baskets, but some did more specialized work required by the communities. While working, monks observed the rule of silence and were expected to meditate constantly on scriptures. Pachomius recognized the importance of work not only to maintain the monasteries but also for its spiritual values. Monks normally ate two meals a day, at noon and in the evening, in silence. Food consisted of bread, cheese, herbs, olives, fruit, and certain green vegetables, but neither wine nor meat. Monks fasted on Wednesdays and Fridays. During Lent, they ate only uncooked food, and some ate only every two or five days. If monks fell ill, they were cared for in the infirmary, where they could take wine and eat meat. Monks could choose how long they wanted to sleep, but many tried to spend most of their time in prayer. They were not permitted to speak to one another after they had retired to their cells in the evening.

Monastic discipline was severe. Monks underwent constant surveillance and correction. If they spoke or laughed during psalmody or prayer, they were required to stand before the altar and be rebuked by the superior of the monastery. If they arrived late, they would undergo the same humiliation and stand during the next meal in the refectory. If they committed more serious offenses, such as lying or disobeying, the superior would determine their punishment. Repeated offenses could lead to demotion, corporal punishment, or expulsion. Yet Pachomian rules avoided excesses. Pachomius, for instance, allowed fires in cold weather and permitted monks to visit sick relatives, attend funerals, or receive visits from relatives. The main object of obedience was harmony and spiritual growth for the community.

Not far from the Pachomian community at Panopolis, Schenoudi developed a different type of cenobite monastery. As a young boy, he joined his maternal uncle Bgoul, head of the White Monastery, and earned such a reputation for piety that he succeeded his uncle as head of it, perhaps around 385. He remained in that position until his death around 451, reputedly at 118 years of age. The monastery grew rapidly, requiring him to add many buildings. He also established a monastery for women. Unlike Pachomius, Schenoudi was noted for strictness and harshness, once flogging a monk so severely that he died.

Early writings mention other coenobite monasteries besides these. Deserving of special mention are communities of women that developed alongside those for men. Some women as well as men lived as hermits. Palladius, for instance, reported that a serving woman named Alexandra left the city of Alexandria and lived in a tomb for ten years, spinning flax and praying or recalling scriptures (*Lausiac History* 5). Pachomius founded the first community. This began with a cell built for his sister, Mary, at Tabennesis. Soon many other women came and placed themselves under Mary's direction. Pachomius himself laid down the rules for the community, his monks did the building. When this community overflowed, Pachomius built a second one near the monastery at Tismenae. Later on, Theodore formed a third convent near Pabau. Palladius reported that one of the monasteries housed four hundred women (*Lausiac History* 33). The convent established by Schenoudi was still larger, reportedly consisting of eighteen hundred nuns. Convents appeared elsewhere, too; at Antinoe there were twelve, according to Palladius (*Lausiac History* 59), one with sixty nuns presided over by an eighty-year-old ascetic named Amma (mother) Talis. Chrysostom referred to associations of virgins in Egypt (*Hom. in Matt.* 8). The anonymous *History of the Monks* (5) reports that there were very many nuns at Oxyrhynchus.

Syria

Monasticism sprang up in Syria during the last quarter of the third century, evidently without direct connection with Egypt. The earliest known figure was Jacob, consecrated Bishop of Nisibis around 300, who took up the anchorite life about 280 or shortly before in the mountains of Nisibis. Still more famous was Juliana Saba, whose fifty-year career Ephrem Syrus celebrated with a poem. Since Saba died in 367, he must have taken up the life of a hermit about 317. Syrian monks lived in both Roman and Persian territories in Mesopotamia.

Syrian monasticism distinguished itself from monasticism elsewhere in its severity, primitivism, mortification, and individualism. Gregory of Nazianzus spoke with astonishment about Syrian monks who fasted for twenty days at a time, wore iron fetters, slept on the bare ground, and stood motionless with hands outstretched in prayer in the rain, wind, and snow (*Historic Poems*, col. 1455). Theodoret of Cyrus recorded that Jacob of Nisibis dwelt in the solitude of the highest mountaintops and in the thickets of the forests. During the summer, he sought no shelter; in the winter he lived in a cave. He wore no clothing, lit no fires, and built no dwelling. He rejected work and ate no food earned by work, sustaining himself by eating herbs and fruits (*Religious History*, col. 1293f.; Voobus, 1:151). A letter of Ephrem depicted a monasticism whose devotees abandoned their communities and assumed a life not far removed from that of animals. They lived with animals, ate grass, and perched on rocks like birds. They shunned work and spent their time exclusively in prayer. Contemptuous of life, they took no precautions against savage animals and snakes. A poem of Ephrem depicted emaciated persons as looking more like eagles than like human beings. In another writing, he noted several groups of monks unwilling to die a natural death and seeking either to starve themselves or to kill themselves by some kind of hideous torture.

When coenobitism reached Syria is uncertain. An inscription attests the existence of a monastery at al-Hit in Hauran in 354, and Ephrem Syrus (ca. 306–373) left hints of others in his poems. Manichaeism also had something to do with the founding of coenobite communities. According to Jerome, Hilarion, a discipline of Anthony, settled in Majuma about 306 (*Life of Hilarion*). Syria did not have any monasteries before that.

Ephrem Syrus deserves considerable credit for the shape and influence that monasticism took in northern Mesopotamia. Hearing the call in youth, he spent much of his life in the vicinity of Nisibis, moving to Edessa about ten years before he died. An admirer of Jacob of Nisibis, he favored anchoritism over coenobitism and a severe form over the milder Egyptian form. Through poems, sermons, and other writings he promoted the anchorite model vigorously. After him, however, the flux of youth toward solitude changed the character of the movement. Hermits established residences and moderated the wild features of Syrian monachism. The churches exerted pressures here, too, for many did not regard animalistic practices of some monks to be Christian. Even the government stepped in to put a stop to excesses. An inward consolidation gradually brought the monks into closer contact with Christian communities and effected further changes. Many monks became bishops.

Despite reservations of the earlier generations, therefore, coenobitism gradually increased. According to the *Acts of Ephrem* (10), Edessa had already become something of a center of monasteries before Ephrem arrived there around 357. *The Pilgrimage of Etheria*, however, shows that monasteries did not dominate the mountains around Edessa. Coenobite communities would have been small; Syrians established predominantly coenobitic communities in Armenia. When Theodoret composed his *Religious History* around 444, he reported that there were thousands of coenobite monasteries not only in Syria but in all of the East as well. By this time, the size of the communities also increased.

Palestine

The Holy Land had drawn pilgrims from at least the third century on. The conversion of Constantine increased opportunities for people to make pilgrimages. The holy sites especially attracted hermits who wanted to spend their lives near them.

Monasticism in Palestine began with Hilarion. Born of pagan parents about 291 near Gaza, he was converted and educated in Alexandria. Attracted to the Egyptian desert by the example of Anthony, he returned at age fifteen to Palestine, gave away his inheritance, and settled down to a solitary life near Majuma, south of Gaza, on the Egyptian model. About 330 others joined him in the founding of a monastery. To escape the crowds that flocked to him on account of his reputation and miraculous gifts, he returned to Egypt around 353. Later, he moved to Libya, Sicily, and finally to Cyprus, where he died in 371. His disciples included Epiphanius (ca. 315–403), who founded a monastery near Eleutheropolis, halfway between Jerusalem and Gaza, around 335. In 367, however, the bishops of Cyprus consecrated him their metropolitan as Bishop of Salamis. In that capacity, he played a major role in theological controversies in support of the Council of Nicaea.

A new wave of enthusiasm for the monastic vocation followed the return of Athanasius from exile in 346 and the publication of his *Life of Anthony* in 356. Basil of Caesarea, baptized in 357, toured monastic sites in Palestine and Egypt. Hilary of Poitiers (ca. 315–367) and Eusebius of Vercellae (d.

371) carried stories about the Egyptian monks to the West. Rufinus (ca. 345–410) visited the monks of Egypt about 372. There he met Melania the Elder (ca. 342–ca. 410), an aristocratic Roman woman who brought three hundred pounds of silver for Pambo, Abbot of the Pachomian monastery in Nitria. After six years at Nitria, Rufinus proceeded to Palestine in 381 and, with Melania's help, founded a monastery for men like the one she had founded in 373 for women on the Mount of Olives. He returned to Italy in 392.

Palestine's most famous monk was Jerome (ca. 342–420). Born at Strido near Aquileia in Italy, he studied in Rome and received baptism there. He then returned to Aquileia to devote himself to an ascetic life. About 374 he set out for Palestine but stopped on the way in Antioch. He then spent four or five years as a hermit in the desert of Chalkis. Ordained a presbyter at Antioch, he spent some time in Constantinople and returned to Rome, where he served as secretary to Pope Damasus and taught scriptures and fostered asceticism especially among wealthy and cultured Roman women. Forced to leave Rome after the death of Damasus in 385, he toured Antioch, Palestine, and Egypt with Paula and Eustochium, two women of the Aventine Circle he had met with in Rome. Finally, in 386 he settled at Bethlehem, where he spent the remainder of his life, studying and presiding over a monastery. Funding for the monastery came from the wealthy Roman matron Paula, who, with her daughter Eustochium, took up residence in Bethlehem also in 386.

John Cassian (ca. 360–435), one of the chief architects of Western monasticism, joined a monastery at Bethlehem as a young man, but he left it about 385 to study monasticism in Egypt.

Sinai

The desert around Mount Sinai became one of the choicest spots for monks because of its connection with Moses. When Etheria visited Sinai in the late fourth century, she found a flourishing community of anchorites not only on the mountain but also all around it. Monks constructed a church on top of the mountain and at the site of the burning bush, where the monastery St. Catherine's now stands. The monks delighted in guiding pilgrims and were amply rewarded for it.

Prominent in the development of monasticism in Sinai was Silvanus, a Palestinian who had headed a community at Scete before moving to Sinai about 380. Living first at Sinai, he later founded a large monastery in the Wadi Ghezzeh, near Gerara, in the Gaza area. His disciple Zacharias succeeded him about 415 as leader of the community there (Sozomen *Church History* 6:32).

Cappadocia

By the late fourth century, the monastic seed was planted in virtually every area where Christianity penetrated. In Cappadocia, Macrina (ca. 372–379) and her brother Basil of Caesarea (ca. 330–379) took the lead. Macrina exerted a major influence over both Basil and Gregory of Nyssa, another of the brothers in this eminent family. She lured Basil away from a promising secular career to the Christian priesthood and toward the monastic life. With her mother, she established a monastery for women on the family estate in Pontus. With former servants, they practiced *koinonia* in goods and work. In his *Life of Macrina,* Gregory reports that Macrina gave away all of her possessions and followed the rule of apostolic poverty. She gained quite a reputation for healing miracles.

After receiving the best classical education possible at Caesarea, Constantinople, and Athens, Basil responded, at the urging of Macrina, to the monastic call. He visited monks in Syria and Egypt in 357 and then assumed the role of a hermit on the Iris River near Neocaesarea. He framed the monastic Rule that bears his name between 358 and 364. Set out in a shorter (55 items) and a longer (313 items) form, Basil's Rule avoided the extreme asceticism of the hermits. He preferred the model of Eustathius, Bishop of Sebaste, to the Egyptian or Syrian models. Asceticism as a means to perfect service of God can be attained in communal life under obedience. Basil clearly preferred the communal to the anchorite type of life. The main objective of the monk is to love God and neighbor; it is better achieved in community. Monks too should seek to unite in the one Body of Christ, for the communal life is far safer and more practical. Questions posed and answered by the Rule point up the social context that contributed to the call of persons to the monastic life. Married persons, slaves, and children were among the applicants; Basil favored the entrance of children because they were more pliable. Unlike some hermits who tried to devote themselves exclusively to prayer, Basil required a combination of prayer and labor. Monks should choose trades that would allow for a tranquil life and aim at simplicity and frugality; farming, perhaps, was preferred. Monks should perform services for those who are in need. Decisions about vocation, however, should be made by the community and not by the individual, who must obey these decisions.

Basil probably saved monasticism by putting it into the service of the church. Stripped of some of its severity, especially in the Syrian model, and equipped with broader purposes, it attracted some of the brightest youth, including Basil's brother, Gregory of Nyssa (ca. 330–ca. 395), who entered a monastery founded by Basil. Consecrated Bishop of Nyssa around 371, Gregory took an active role in supporting the Nicene faith. In addition to numerous theological treatises, Gregory composed many works on spirituality: a treatise on Christian perfection, entitled *The Life of Moses*; sermons on the Song of Songs, the Lord's Prayer, and the Beatitudes; treatises on virginity; and a *Life of Macrina*, his sister. In *The Life of Moses*, he depicts the mystical journey as a progression from light to darkness and lays the foundation for apophatic (negative way) theology, characteristic of Orthodoxy. We can only say who God is not; we cannot say directly who God is.

Basil also drew Gregory of Nazianzus (329–389) toward the monastic life. Son of the Bishop of Nazianzus in Cappadocia, Gregory met Basil at the university in Athens. Soon thereafter, Gregory opted for the contemplative life. Ordained against his will, he was installed in the see of Sasima around 372. He served as an associate (suffragans) to his father until the latter's death in 374 and then withdrew to a hermitage in Seleucia in Isauria. In 381, he was appointed Bishop of Constantinople, but he resigned after less than a year and retired first to Nazianzus and then to his own estate.

The West

The West had its ascetics in earlier centuries, but it turned its gaze eastward in earnest when Athanasius brought two Egyptian monks to Rome during his first exile. Later he went to Trier and Gaul. His *Life of Anthony*, composed in 356, soon circulated in a Latin translation in the West. By the late fourth century, the names of the most famous Egyptian monks had become household words in Rome. Women especially played a seminal role in the development of asceticism there.

At the center of the women ascetics in Rome stood Marcella (325–410). After the untimely death of her husband, she took up a life of devotion. In her palace on the Aventine Hill, she gathered other notable women—her sister Asella, Fabiola, Lea, Paula, Eustochium—for intensive study of scriptures, charitable activities, and prayer. Her mother, Albina, joined the circle of pious women who gathered around her. When Jerome came to Rome in 382, she enlisted him to assist in the study of scriptures. By his own admission, she constantly pressed him to go deeper in his interpretation of them. When Jerome and others took flight to Palestine in 385, she remained in Rome at the helm of the movement. She died in 410 as a consequence of abuse suffered at the hands of the Gothic invaders of Rome.

On the death of her husband and two sons, Melania the Elder, a wealthy Roman aristocrat, took up the ascetic life at age twenty-two. In 372, she placed her only surviving child in the care of Christian friends and set out for Egypt, where she visited monks in the Thebaid, Nitria, and Scete and left rich gifts. She defended orthodox (Nicene) monks in court against Arian accusers and, when many of them were banished to Palestine, followed them there. With the help of Rufinus, she founded a double monastery on the Mount of Olives. At the height of the Origenist controversy, which pitted Rufinus against Jerome, she returned to Italy about 399 or 400. When the Goths invaded Italy in 408, she fled with other members of her family and returned to Jerusalem, where she died around 410.

Paula (347–404), another eminent member of the Aventine Circle, took up the ascetic life at age thirty-three following the death of her husband. According to Jerome, she could trace her lineage back to Agamemnon and her husband's back to Aeneas. Two daughters, Blesilla and Eustochium (ca. 370–419), joined her in her devout life; but Blesilla died, possibly as a result of excessive austerities. Jerome's letter to Eustochium, then only fifteen, on virginity created such a storm that she and her mother fled the city behind Jerome. When they finally arrived in Bethlehem, Paula and Eustochium founded a monastery for men and a much larger one for women, which Paula ruled. Subsequently a granddaughter named Paula joined her grandmother and aunt to be reared under her grandmother's direction. Eustochium succeeded Paula as head of the monastery.

Another distinguished member of the Aventine Circle was Fabiola (d. 399). A member of the famous *gens Fabia,* she had violated church custom by divorcing her first husband and remarrying. After the death of her second husband, she distributed much of her immense wealth to the poor and devoted herself to care of the sick. In 395, she joined Paula and Eustochium in Bethlehem, but she returned to Rome on account of her discomfort with the Origenist controversy, the isolation of the monastery, and the threat of invasion of Palestine by the Huns. There she joined Pammachius, son-in-law of Paula, in erecting a hospital in Portus.

Many males in these powerful Roman families resented and opposed the contemplative life. So, too, did the masses. In 384, they blamed the death of Paula's daughter Blesilla on the monks and called for their expulsion from Rome. The poet Rutilius Namatianus ridiculed monks for their "fear of the evils of fortune." Yet some of the nobility dared to offer support. Pammachius (ca. 340–410), a Roman senator of the Furian family and husband of Paulina, another of Paula's daughters, admired Jerome. After Paulina's death, he embraced the monastic life and devoted the fortune he had inherited from her to care for the indigent. Among other things, with Fabiola he erected a hospital for pilgrims at Portus and the Church of St. Giovanni e Paolo. What he found offensive was excesses and not the ascetic life itself. Although Jerome dedicated several works to him, Pammachius did not hesitate to criticize Jerome's intemperance in his attacks on Jovinian because of the latter's views on virginity and on Rufinus because of his support for Origen. Pammachius died during the Gothic invasion of Rome in 410.

Challenges to the ideal of virginity evoked sharp replies from Jerome, Ambrose, and Augustine. A Latin theologian named Helvidius, evidently concerned to defend marriage against growing preference for celibacy, met vigorous opposition from Jerome for denying the perpetual virginity of Mary. Jovinian (d. ca. 405), a monk, was attacked by both Jerome and Augustine and condemned by synods at Rome and Milan for denying that virginity was a higher level of Christian life than marriage and that abstinence as such was better than eating. In 402, Pope Innocent I made celibacy an "indissoluble rule" for the clergy.

The monastic life also caught on in Gaul. Hilary of Poitiers (ca. 315–367) and Eusebius of Vercellae (d. 371) got a taste of it during their exile to Phrygia (356–360) and passed on some of their enthusiasm to Martin of Tours (d. 397). A soldier in the Roman army and already a catechumen, Martin had a vision of Christ, which impelled him to receive baptism and take up the religious life. In 360, after resigning his commission, he joined Hilary of Poitiers and founded the first monastery in Gaul at Ligugé. Later he established the famous monastery at Marmoutier. After his appointment as Bishop of Tours about 372, he promoted the spread of monasticism throughout Gaul as a means of evangelization.

Looking to the Future

As twilight settled over the West, the ascetics prepared themselves for the immense challenges that lay ahead. No longer marginal to church and society, as the early hermits had been, the monastic tradition had taken sufficient institutional shape to equip monasticism not only to survive but also to serve the churches in remarkable ways. In the East, Basil's Rule assured that the monasteries would help the churches, administering relief to the poor, operating a hospital for lepers, visiting the sick, and educating the deprived. In the West, Cassian's Rule, although favoring the Egyptian model, also guaranteed a more amenable working relationship between church and cloister. So, too, would a model developing at Lérins. In the traumatic times that followed, the churches turned to the monks to see how Christians should respond when their world crashed around them. In both East and West they prevailed on monks like Basil, the Gregorys, Martin, Paulinus, and a host of others to assume the highest offices of the church. The most crucial days, however, lay ahead for the monks as they carried the Christian message to the barbarians pressing south into the Roman Empire. Theirs would be the strategic role in the evangelization of Europe.

PART FIVE

DIVIDING WORLDS 400–600 C.E.

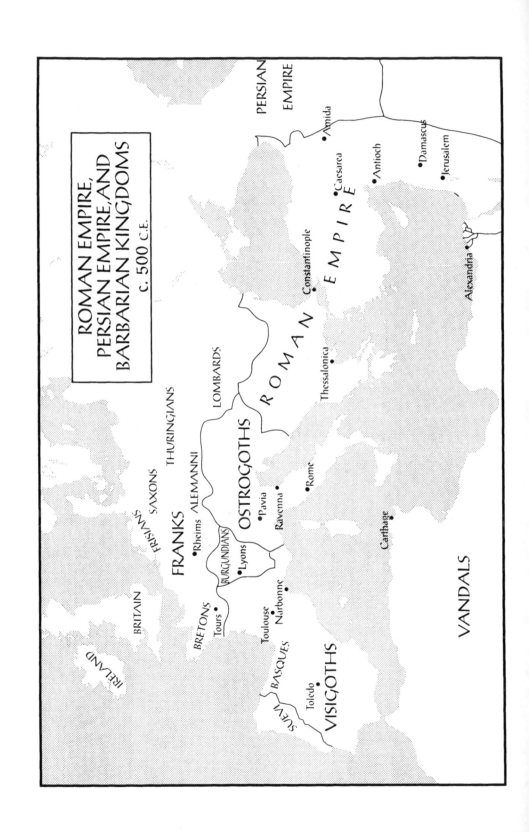

ROMAN EMPIRE,
PERSIAN EMPIRE, AND
BARBARIAN KINGDOMS
c. 500 C.E.

PERSIAN EMPIRE

Amida
Damascus
Antioch
Jerusalem
Caesarea
Constantinople
ROMAN EMPIRE
Alexandria
Thessalonica
LOMBARDS
THURINGIANS
SAXONS
FRISIANS
FRANKS
ALEMANNI
Rheims
OSTROGOTHS
BURGUNDIANS
Pavia
Lyons
Rome
Ravenna
Carthage
BRITAIN
BRETONS
Tours
Toulouse
Narbonne
VANDALS
IRELAND
SUEVI
BASQUES
Toledo
VISIGOTHS

CHAPTER TWENTY-FOUR

THE BARBARIAN "INVASIONS"

What we usually refer to today as the barbarian "invasions" had little resemblance to what we would call invasions. They represented, rather, gradual migrations south until the "barbarians" finally controlled most of the territory that had belonged to the western part of the Roman Empire. During the third century, the Romans managed to hold back the tide of northern Europeans who constantly pressed south, seeking warmer climates and more hospitable places to live. They invited some to settle as *coloni*, farmers, within the confines of the vast empire. Pressures persisted, however, as more and more tribes sought the benefits of living within the Roman Empire. Meantime, internal decay rendered Roman resistance increasingly ineffective. As early as Constantine, removal of the capital from Rome to the East represented growing alarm at the decline of the western empire. Diocletian planned to move the capital to Nicomedia. Constantine simply selected the obscure village of Byzantium, a site he could christianize more readily. By the late fourth century, the emperors had virtually abandoned the West, turning control of the army over to a succession of barbarians. In 476, Odovacer, no longer willing to serve the emperor's lackey in the West, Julius Nepos, returned the symbols of office to Emperor Zeno (474–491). For a long time already, Western leaders had not been able to stem the tide of incursions by first one and then another tribe.

The churches suffered severely on the extremities of the empire, in some areas virtually disappearing altogether. In Rome, Vandals and others notwithstanding, things did not change radically, partly because, as Augustine pointed out, many of the barbarians had already been converted to Christianity. What began to occur was a gradual process of cultural deterioration, which the churches helped to retard but could not prevent altogether. The barbarians envied Roman culture, but they lacked the means to conserve what they admired. The one institution that possessed some capability for holding on to the past and giving directions for the future was the Roman Church. Skillful popes managed to step into the political and cultural vacuum created by the "invasions" and enhance the influence of the church. The so-called *Donation of Constantine,* composed in the eighth century as Frankish rulers challenged papal claims, was fictitious but not entirely erroneous in depicting the bishops of Rome as the successors of Constantine in the West. From about the mid-fifth until the mid-eighth century, the bishops of Rome functioned in fact as the major political and religious leaders in the West. The barbarians were too divided among themselves to establish the kind of hegemony the Carolingians would later hold.

The Barbarian Migrations

The initial wave pressing southward consisted of German peoples east of the Rhine and north of the Danube. Slavs came later, during the sixth century. Originally located in southern Scandinavia, Denmark, and adjacent lands, the German tribes drove the Celts, who occupied lands west of the Elbe to the Rhine, farther and farther westward. By about 200 B.C.E., western Germans had pushed the Celts to the Rhine and as far south as the Main. A century later, they had occupied southern Germany and had attempted to flood Gaul, only to be halted by Julius Caesar. Subsequently, another migration followed from Scandinavia. It consisted of a different group of Germans, usually designated eastern Germans. Whereas by the early Christian era the western Germans evolved from a race of hunters and shepherds to one of farmers, the eastern Germans remained nomadic. Pressures from the easterners forced the western Germans to seek settlements in Roman territory. The major western tribes included the Alemanni, a composite of Suevian tribes, who settled along the upper Rhine; the Franks, who settled along the lower Rhine; the Saxons, who were located between the Weser and the Elbe; and the Thuringians, who settled south of the Saxons. During the fifth century, the eastern Germans, consisting of the Goths, the Vandals, the Gepids, the Burgundians, and the Lombards, effected the occupation of the Roman Empire in the West. By the third and fourth centuries, they had already moved south as far as the Black Sea and the Danube.

Christians in the Barbarian Migrations

The migrations of peoples during this period obviously radically changed the situation of the Roman Empire and its people, including Christians. It is well known that Christianity gradually won over the migrants. Although this may seem somewhat surprising, Christianity had several factors in its favor for doing exactly that. In his *History of the*

Expansion of Christianity, Kenneth Scott Latourette lists four: First, the migrants admired Roman civilization and culture and adopted many of its features, including Christianity. Second, the religions most of the invaders espoused offered feeble opposition to more advanced religions, such as Christianity and, later, Islam. Third, Christianity had already accommodated itself to Greco-Roman culture in ways that would make it attractive and helpful to the barbarians, above all, in the battle against the powers of evil. Fourth, Christianity contained within itself a powerful missionary vitality not dampened by the invasions. As Latourette points out, however, in this period "professional" missionaries figured far more prominently. Initially, Arian Christianity dominated among the Goths and, through them, other barbarian peoples. Later on, thanks especially to the Franks, Nicene Christianity gained ascendancy.

The effects of the barbarian migrations varied markedly from area to area. On the edges of the empire, where Christianity had not had the opportunity to become deeply rooted, the invasions virtually obliterated the churches, necessitating reevangelization. The Romans had developed Pannonia (modern Hungary), Noricum (modern Switzerland and Austria), and Rhaetia (modern Bavaria) mainly to buffer the northern boundaries of the empire. In such places, Christianity had to be brought back by missionary activity from the seventh century onward. Christianity also nearly went out of existence in the Flemish plain (modern Holland) and the British Isles.

Closer to the center of the empire, the churches suffered less severely. In most of Gaul, for instance, the invasions disorganized the life of the churches, but they did not obliterate them. Modern ecclesiastical archaeology has turned up evidence of continuing Christian activities at Strasbourg, Treves or Mainz, and Xanten. Thus it would be difficult to overestimate the importance of monastic communities and leaders who could negotiate with the barbarians.

The invasions had their least effect in some other areas where activities continued much as they had before the invasions. Families carried on as they had in the fourth century, not as in the heyday of the empire but in its diminishing years. They held steadfastly to their Christian heritage as an integral part of their cultural inheritance. In Italy, the Ostrogoths conserved the Roman legacy when they conquered it (489–493). The Visigoths did much the same in South Gaul (413–507) and later in Spain. The Burgundians gained a reputation for gentleness. Even the Vandals left the western part of Africa unconquered, and while the region lapsed into barbarism, Christianity did not disappear. The Vandals envied Roman society and hence romanized. Few of the conquerors, as a matter of fact, escaped christianization of some sort. The chief struggle had to do with the brand of Christianity they were to adopt—Arian or Nicene. Arians attempted to impose the Arian faith, Nicenes the Nicene. The Vandal kings Genseric, Huneric, and Thrasamund rallied people to Arianism and fiercely persecuted dissenters. In Carthage, Genseric drove Quodvultdeus from his see and kept it vacant for twenty-four years (456–480). Such policies finally failed, however, increasing Catholic hostility and determination rather than diminishing it. Africans welcomed Byzantine troops under Belisarius as liberators in 533. Unfortunately, the controversy as well as the invasions greatly weakened African Christianity. On the Catholic side, Clovis became the champion after his baptism, imposing the Catholic faith on the Visigoths in 507, the Burgundians in 532–534, and the Ostrogoths in 536.

Many bishops played significant roles in mediating with the invaders to avert far worse consequences than would have occurred otherwise. Although feats claimed for bishops have suffered from embellishment, some have the ring of truth. During the Visigothic invasion of Gaul under Wallia in 406, for instance, Exuperius played a major role in the defense of Toulouse as the invaders ravaged one city after another. Germanus, Bishop of Auxerre (418–448), led a contingent of Britons threatened by a combined raid of Saxons and Celts from Scotland. His enthusiasm inspired them to victory. In 451, Leo I (440–461) served as an emissary to negotiate with Attila, although the latter's withdrawal probably was inspired by other pressures. The most effective protector was doubtless Severinus, the apostle of the Danube, whose devout life and miraculous powers awed Rugians, Alemanni, Thuringians, Heruls, and other invaders of Noricum in the late fifth century. After spending some years as a monk in the East, Severinus came to Noricum about 453 and established two monasteries. Although never consecrated as bishop, he gained the confidence of Odovacer. His influence at least tempered some of the cruelty of the invaders. The intercessions of Genevieve of Paris (422–502) were believed to have diverted the Huns from the city in 451.

The churches themselves offered sanctuary to the frightened citizens. Although the invaders did not always honor sanctuaries, most of the barbarians had undergone sufficient christianization to respect Christian places and things. Gregory of Tours, for instance, recorded that when Clovis defeated Syagrius at Soissons, Remigius of Rheims sent a plea that he preserve a beautiful vessel belonging to him. Clovis, not yet a convert, gave orders to save it, but one of his soldiers, declaring that the king should not have more than his legal share, smashed it to pieces. Clovis did not immediately retaliate. Later, however, when reviewing his troops, he found fault with that soldier's arms and threw one of his weapons to the ground. As the soldier stooped over to retrieve it, Clovis smashed his head with an axe, saying, "So you did to the vessel of Soissons." A century later, Lombard law included recognition of sanctuary in the churches.

Twilight in the West

Civilization diminished slowly as a consequence of the barbarian "invasions" and not suddenly as has often been assumed. Cities like Ravenna illustrate the continuance of art and architecture of commendable quality. Galla Placidia (423–450) also chose Ravenna, the imperial residence from 402–404, as her official residence. The Ostrogoth Theodoric and his successors made it the capital of Italy from 493 to 535. After 540, it came again under Byzantine rule. Rome, repeated sackings notwithstanding, still continued to build impressive churches and to furbish them with fine mosaics and frescoes under popes Sixtus III (432–440) and Felix IV (526–530).

The Western churches went on with the task of evangelization. The fall of Rome in 410 revived oft-repeated charges that Christianity was responsible for the calamities because Christians had abandoned the gods who had made Rome great. Augustine spent thirteen years (413–426) writing his classic apology, *The City of God*, in response to these claims. Pope Gelasius had to protest the revival of the Lupercalia about 495, and pagans constantly threatened to revive past celebrations as popular anxieties mounted with new threats.

Much depended on leadership of dedicated clergy and monks. In Gaul, outstanding bishops like Caesarius, Bishop of Arles from 503–543, assisted in the transition. Caesarius exercised most of his ministry under Arian Gothic kings in a city and country where the population included Catholics, Arians, Jews, and pagans. In his sermons, he addressed a wide array of people interested in the good life. He left no aspect of life untouched by his criticisms as superinspector, and he urged memorization of the scriptures, their letters from heaven. He depicted life as a battle between Christ and the devil. Each person must decide which way to go. The devil uses paganism to lure them away from Christ. Traps included ritual bathing on St. John's day, bacchanalian orgies among rural people, vows to trees, prayers to fountains, pagan altars and idols, women refusing to weave on Thursday because of deference to Jove, and consultation with soothsayers and healers about omens—all customs well known in antiquity. Caesarius warned against taking drugs to aid or prevent pregnancy, buffoonery in daily life, and selfish use of money. He appealed to the charity of his flock. He expected to exercise control over the lives of his people that he could not have, but the Franks discerned accurately the importance of dealing with bishops like Caesarius. Bishops such as he forged Christian communities that Clovis and others could use as a basis for holding their kingdoms together. Their work, at any rate, supplied the foundation on which medieval Europe would be built.

CHAPTER TWENTY-FIVE

THE ONGOING TASK

Christianity had made great strides within the Roman Empire during the fourth century. The whole Mediterranean sphere covered by the Roman Empire had become Christian in name if not in fact. The church had organized by provinces and dioceses to assure that every nook and cranny would have some kind of Christian witness. Grand new edifices dotted the landscape once graced by pagan temples, statues, and other reminders of a devout religious past. Masses of people crowded into the churches and martyria and joined with enthusiasm in the worship of the cult that had survived centuries of intermittent persecution.

However significant this progress, nonetheless in 400 C.E. much remained to be done to effect major changes in the lives of individuals and in the shape and character of a whole society. Perusal of the sermons or letters of John Chrysostom in the East or Augustine in the West will show that Christianity had not supplanted the old cultus or the oriental mysteries or the philosophical religion of the Roman people. It had registered its most noteworthy success in the cities, the target of its first mission efforts. Yet even there, the old religion held on in cities like Rome, especially among the Roman aristocracy. The upper classes did not yield readily even to imperial pressures to convert to Christianity. In rural areas, moreover, paganism held on tenaciously during the next two centuries, for Benedict of Nursia and Gregory the Great both complained about the remnants of it in Italy. The word *pagan*, as a matter of fact, derives from the Latin word *paganus*, meaning "farmer." If the survival of ancient religious commitments did not cause enough problems in and of itself, the Germanic "invasions" confronted the church with an added challenge. Although most of the invaders had been exposed to some sort of Christianity, they knew it in the form of Arianism, which, in some ways, better suited their polytheism, for Arianism implicitly gave encouragement to belief in multiple divine beings. Much of the missionary task, therefore, focused on winning Arians to the Nicene faith of the Catholic Church.

The Eastern Roman Empire

Already by the time of Constantine the vital center of the Roman Empire had shifted to the East. Constantine's removal of the capital to Byzantium simply took note of reality and gave in to the inevitable. Although the Romans continued some kind of nominal rule in the West, the empire itself existed in the East, and it was there that Christianity steadily embraced the entire body politic or was embraced by it. Since the East was more Greek than Roman, it is best to speak about the development of a Hellenistic Christian society, for Christianity took on the form of Greek *paideia* ("culture").

With the exception of Julian (361–363), emperors after Constantine (d. 337) believed that God had entrusted to them the task of christianizing the Roman Empire. Theodosius I (379–395) brought Constantine's vision of a Christian empire to a new level when, in 391, he ordered the Praetorian Prefect to prohibit all sacrifices and visiting of pagan holy places, declared marriage of Christians to Jews a form of adultery, and deprived apostates from Christianity of all honors and hereditary rank as well as the right of inheritance and of bequests of property. Theodosius's sons, Arcadius in the East (395–408) and Honorius in the West (393–423), were much less resolute than their father, and they ran into roadblocks. In the East, Arcadius renewed prohibition of ancient holidays in the calendar, proscribed the visiting of temples and the celebration of sacrifices, withdrew privileges enjoyed by pagan priests, and ordered destruction of temples still standing in rural areas. In the West, Honorius, still very young, had to yield to Stilicho, the Vandal who headed the army and who became his father-in-law. Although Stilicho did not rescind statutes against paganism, he treated them lightly. The Roman aristocracy, led by Senator Symmachus, held out strongly for the old religion and blamed Christianity for the fall of Rome. Stilicho permitted pagan gatherings and the continuance of temples in Africa. He did, however, burn the Sibylline books. In 410, Rome fell into the hands of Alaric and the Goths. Alaric, although professing Christian faith, set up Attalus as a rival to Honorius for a time, but he soon withdrew support, opening the way for the demise of pagan political power in Italy. After Stilicho was executed in 408, Honorius stiffened the policies of the government in the West. He ordered the income of pagan temples devoted to the army, remaining images destroyed, the temples devoted to public purposes, and pagans excluded from civil offices and the army. Had it not been for the barbarian migrations, Christianity might have had the same success in the West that it had in the East.

Bishops deserve credit for the zeal with which their flocks sought to make Christianity the sole religion of the empire. In the East, John Chrysostom, Bishop of Constantinople from 398 to 404, constantly urged his people to live lives of such commendable piety that others would want to imitate them by becoming Christian. He discouraged the use of coercion. If Christians lived as they should, he claimed, they would not have to force conversions. In sermons addressed to members of his flock in Antioch, however, he overstated the Christian case *Against the Jews* in ways that laid the foundation for persecution in later centuries. Like most others of this period, he was caught up in a mass movement to victory and did not see where boundaries needed to be set. Without such zeal, however, it is hard to explain how Christianity could have won the eastern Roman Empire as it did.

The persistence of legislation against paganism as late as Justinian (527–565) demonstrates that the old cults had not ceased by that time. Although the authorities registered greater concern about heretical Christian groups, they could not ignore the pull of paganism. Legislation of this period forbade bequests for maintenance of pagan cults, prescribed the death penalty for baptized Christians engaging in pagan rites, ordered pagans to go to churches for instruction, exiled and confiscated the property of those who refused baptism, required baptism of pagan children, and confiscated property of pagans who had received baptism in order to serve in the army but had made no effort to convert their families. Such strong legislation, requiring baptism of all adherents of the old cults, confirms that the battle for religious commitment remained vigorous. As Justinian directed his energies to the imposition of uniformity of belief, he made a virtue of intolerance. Christianity did not persecute pagans as severely as the latter had persecuted Christians in the first three centuries, but persecution did occur. In the main, Christian violence toward competing cults took the form of destruction of temples and idols or, in the case of Jews, synagogues, and repressive legislation.

The Western Roman Empire

Although the same legislation applied to both East and West, the winning of the western Roman Empire proved far more difficult than the winning of the East. During the career of Ambrose as Bishop of Milan (373–397), four types of pagan religion still exerted appeal: the traditional public religion, the animism prevalent in rural areas, the mystery religions, and Neoplatonism as the religion of the educated. Although it is debatable how strong the appeal of the old state cultus was generally, the Roman Senate kept it alive. The Pontifical College still carried on as it had in the past. The Vestal Virgins still occupied their place at the foot of the Palatine. The temples still stood open to the public and performed their customary sacrifices to the gods. Many pagan festivals still went on as usual. Statues of the Olympian and other gods dotted the Forum. The Romans, convinced that Rome had become great not merely because of the gods but also because of the people's *devotion* to the gods, did not surrender the ancient worship easily. The strength of the old religion became manifest in the battle that three distinguished Roman nobles—Praetextatus, Symmachus, and Flavian—fought to save the Altar of Victory in the Senate House.

The old religion held on still more tenaciously in small towns and rural areas that were usually untouched by the authorities. The tenaciousness of the old religion in such areas was clearly manifest in Africa during Augustine's day. On June 1, 408, Honorius issued stern edicts intended to eliminate the last vestiges of the old religion. Shortly afterward, as reported by Augustine, the citizens of Calama held a pagan festival "without interference from anyone." Pagan dancers paraded in front of the church right up to the door and, when the clergy tried to stop the performance, stoned the church. A week later, after the bishop of Calama had informed the authorities about the violation of the imperial edicts, pagans stoned the church a second time. The next day they struck again, this time not only stoning the church but also setting it afire and killing one of the clergy. The mob raged from 4:00 P.M. until late at night, forcing the bishop to hide in order to save his life. None of the authorities intervened. The only person who offered Christians help was a stranger. When Augustine himself went to Calama, he had little success in securing amendment or conversion. As a matter of fact, a former official named Nectarius wrote to Augustine to entreat him to intercede for the offenders whom he thought the authorities punished too severely (Augustine, *Ep.* 90). Eight months later, not convinced by the Bishop of Hippo's response, he wrote again to protest the penalty (*Ep.* 103).

The task of evangelizing the western part of the empire was complicated immensely by the barbarian invasions, as Augustine's career attests quite well. Himself a convert from Manichaeism, a dualistic sect with strong appeal in North Africa, Augustine took the same strong stand against paganism that his mentor Ambrose of Milan had taken. Although early in his career as Bishop of Hippo Augustine had opposed the use of coercion, he discovered in the case of the Donatists that force worked; consequently, after about 406 he favored it as the means of christianizing the empire, specifically the portion over which he himself had special responsibility. In his response to the pleas of Nectarius of Calama, he made light of any effort to defend the old religion. How could one argue the morality of the old when it painted, carved, wrote, danced, and sang of Jupiter's adulteries? If Nectarius really wanted to help his "fatherland," as he claimed, then he would let people "be converted to the worship of the true God and to a chaste and religious life." Christians, after all, had acted with mildness. He, as bishop, had always tried to prevent too severe a penalty. He strove to obtain pardon not only for Christians' sins but for those of others as well, but pardon cannot be obtained without amendment of life, and amendment can come only by conversion.

The sacking of Rome by the Goths, led by Alaric in 410, complicated the Christian apologetic task. Christians had been arguing the superiority of their religion on the basis of the victories it had secured. The fall of Rome, the Eternal City, proved what many pagans and reluctant converts to Christianity had suspected all along: Abandonment of devotion to the gods who had made Rome great had caused earthquakes, floods, and other disasters. Now it brought the worst of all disasters: the fall of Rome. On the heels of this catastrophe came the Vandal invasion of North Africa. In 413, Augustine began what many consider to be his greatest work, *The City of God*, in response to this charge. In 417, he urged Paulus Orosius, a native of Braga in Spain who had migrated to Africa ahead of the Vandals, to write his *Seven Books Against the Pagans*. In *The City of God*, completed in 426, Augustine first reviewed history to show that the world had not gotten worse because of the advent of Christianity. The fact that the Goths were Christians had caused them to mitigate the harsh treatment barbarians meted out in pre-Christian times. Contrary to what pagans thought, moreover, Rome had not become great because of the gods. Its expansion had occurred through the use of brute force. The gods had proved to be impotent, for instance, in preventing the sack of Troy. It is the true God who determines who will win and who will lose. An eternal struggle has existed between the earthly and the heavenly cities.

The Vandals were laying siege to Hippo during the last months of Augustine's life (d. 430). The Donatist schism had weakened Christianity in North Africa, and many Donatists evidently joined the Arian Vandals against Catholics. The Vandals expropriated Catholic churches, exiled clergy and lay leaders, and sentenced some bishops to hard labor in the interior. Not until Belisarius, the Byzantine general, recaptured North Africa in 533 and 534 could Catholics again relax. Thereafter, Catholics proceeded to apply repressive measures against Arians and Donatists. Christianity made some progress among the native Berbers, but it must not have had a firm grip, for it disappeared when Islam swept across North Africa early in the seventh century.

In parts of Italy, the old religion still remained vital during the fifth and sixth centuries. Despite Ambrose's effective work in the provinces of Aemilia and Liguria, many educated persons still honored the old gods in Turin during the fifth century. According to Maximus of Turin (d. 408–423), moreover, paganism dominated the surrounding countryside. When Benedict of Nursia went to Monte Cassino around 529, he found a temple to Apollo with its statue and altar on which people still placed their offerings. Gregory the Great complained that paganism survived in Sicily,

Sardinia, and Corsica at the end of the sixth century. Arianism, however, posed a more serious challenge than did the remnants of a dying paganism.

In Spain, the Synod of Toledo in 589 lamented growing idolatry. As in Italy, however, Arianism offered more competition. The Suevi converted from paganism to Catholicism and then to Arianism. The Visigoths were Arians. Usually tolerant of Catholics, in 580 King Leovigild convened a council at Toledo and persuaded it to convert Catholics, accepting them without rebaptism. A year before, his son Hermenegild married a Catholic woman and converted, but he was killed in an insurrection against his father, supported by Spanish-Romans. Under another of Leovigild's sons, Recared, Catholicism triumphed. In 589, Recared declared himself a Catholic, and eight Arian bishops, many Arian priests, and a number of nobles followed in his train. Others, however, refused and rebelled. Although Recared succeeded in suppressing the opposition, his successor died in an Arian rebellion.

In Gaul, Christianity had taken huge strides during the fourth century, especially in the cities. Martin of Tours (d. 397) contributed significantly to this development, as did other bishops, such as Victricius of Rouen (ca. 330–ca. 407), like Martin a former soldier. In the late fourth and early fifth centuries, prominent members of the Gallo-Roman upper classes entered the church and advanced its cause. Among the most eminent was Paulinus (353/4–431), who became bishop of Nola in 409. Born into a noble and wealthy family of Bordeaux, he received a good education. After a brief public career and a few years of leisure, he received baptism at the hands of Elphinus, Bishop of Bordeaux, in 390 and, with his Spanish wife, Therasia, took up the ascetic and contemplative life and began to distribute his fortune to the church and to the poor. Ordained a priest at Barcelona in 394, he and his wife founded a home for monks and the poor at Nola and lived lives of great austerity. He corresponded with some of the most eminent churchmen of his day—Martin of Tours, Ambrose, Augustine, and Pope Anastasius I—and is ranked alongside Prudentius as one of the foremost Christian poets of the patristic period.

Thanks to the organized effort of Martin of Tours, Victricius, Paulinus, and others, Christianity reached into the countryside of Gaul, where the invasion by barbarians had less impact than it did in the cities. Attila and the Huns left great devastation when they swept through Gaul early in the fifth century. Although romanized, other barbarians did the same. Nonetheless, Christianity survived as some bishops courageously rallied their flocks. Lupus held together the see of Troyes for more than fifty years (427–479). Sidonius Apollinaris (ca. 423–ca. 480), a member of an aristocratic family of Lyons and son-in-law of Emperor Avitus (455–456), was elected Bishop of Clermont in 469, probably while still a layperson, to protect the city against the Goths. He exerted himself strenuously but unsuccessfully to avert the occupation of Clermont by the Visigoths under Euric in 475. After a period of imprisonment, he returned to his episcopate, where he spent the last few years of his life writing letters. Despite the disruption, the conversion of Gaul continued. In the mid-fifth century, a synod at Arles labeled bishops neglectful if they had not stamped out worship of idols in their territory and legislated penalties for landowners who permitted idolatry on their lands.

Although the barbarian invasions disrupted the churches in Gaul as they did other aspects of civilization, they did not obliterate it. Monasteries such as that at Lérins survived and produced a succession of notable bishops for churches throughout southern Gaul. In many parts of Gaul, Arian Christianity dominated with the entry of the Goths. Burgundians who moved south of the Rhine adopted the Catholic faith that they found in that area, but they then converted to Arianism. The Franks under Clovis (ca. 466–511), however, chose the Catholic faith and helped to expand it throughout Gaul by the sword. Nonetheless, if Gregory of Tours (ca. 540–594) reported accurately, the level of Gallic Christianity at the end of the sixth century (591) had fallen rather low. What helped it was an infusion of new blood with the migration of the Celtic peoples from southwest Britain to Armorica, on the coast of Gaul. The immigrants brought with them the more disciplined Christianity of the British Isles and Celtic monasticism.

The British Isles

Evidence of Christianity prior to the Anglo-Saxon invasion of the British Isles is slim. By the end of the fourth century, many leading families in Roman Britain had accepted Christianity. According to Theodoret, Christianity in the Isles was Catholic, the most likely source of which was Gaul. In 429, two Gallic bishops, Germanus of Auxerre and Lupus of Troyes, went to Britain to dampen the influence of Pelagianism. There Germanus preached to considerable crowds in churches and elsewhere. Although Christianity spread rapidly throughout the islands during the fifth century, the Angles and the Saxons began to establish permanent settlements and virtually to obliterate all traces of Christianity in the east during the last half of the century. The churches survived in the western part, into which the invaders did not penetrate. From the west, especially from Ireland, emerged a powerful impetus for the winning of the Anglo-Saxons and the reevangelization of the continent.

A major figure in the survival and spread of Christianity was Patrick (ca. 390–ca. 460), "the Apostle of Ireland." Born in Britain and reared as a Christian, Patrick was captured at age sixteen by Celtic pirates and spent six years as a pig herder in a district of Ireland called Tirawley. He escaped, made his way to the southeast coast of Ireland, and persuaded sailors to give him passage to Gaul, where he spent some time in the monastery at Lérins, founded shortly before by Honoratus. Returning to his family, he dedicated himself to the church. He undertook training for the ministry, however, at Auxerre in Gaul, from whence he was sent to Ireland, where he spent the rest of his life as a kind of itinerant bishop evangelizing local chieftains, educating their children, ordaining clergy, and establishing monasteries for men and women.

Another person of major importance for the evangelization of the British Isles was Ninian (ca. 360–ca. 432). Son of a converted chieftain of the Cumbrian Britons, Ninian received instruction in Rome as a youth. Consecrated a bishop in 394, probably by Siricius I (385–399), he returned to Scotland by way of Tours, where he met Martin, to whom he dedicated the church he founded at Whithorn, called Candida Casa. The latter became a center from which Ninian and his monks set out to convert the Britons and Picts and a seat of training for Welsh and Irish missionaries.

Celtic Christianity had a quite different character from that found on the continent during this period. It lacked territorial organization under diocesan bishops and featured a strongly monastic character. Bishops often played subordinate roles to abbots. Celtic Christianity also differed from Roman in such customs as the date of celebrating Easter and the form of the tonsure. In the sixth century, Irish monasteries had a reputation for scholarship and religious vitality, around which developed a Christian Celtic culture, which they carried to other peoples.

The most famous and influential of the Irish missionaries was Columban (ca. 543–615). Born about 543 in southeast Ireland, now Leinster County, and reared by a devout mother, Columban heard early on the call to an ascetic life and, despite his mother's pleas, left home to pursue it. After studying scriptures with a certain Sinell, he entered the monastic community of Bangor in Ulster County. Several years later, around 590, he led a band of twelve to Brittany and into Merovingian territory. Eventually, he and his companions took up residence in a ruined castle at Annegray in the Vosges. The attraction of many to the community forced Columban to find another place for a monastery, a former fort, Luxeuil. Still expanding, the monastery established another at Fontaines. Columban's monasteries followed a rule much more severe than Benedict's. The rule called for absolute obedience to the head of the monastery, as much silence as possible, a minimum of food, early rising, and more rigorous penance for sins. The alien character of this form of Christianity aroused strong opposition. Columban had to defend himself before a Gallican synod in 603 and at Rome. Although the bishops did not close the monastery, Columban aroused the hostility of Brunhilda, grandmother of the Burgundian King Theuderich, in whose territory he resided. Theuderich proceeded to force

Columban's deportation in 610. The monks began work at Bregenz on Lake Constance among the Alemanni, but in 612 the Burgundian king extended his dominions to that area also and forced further migration. Columban and his followers then settled in Bobbio, Italy, where they established a community noted for its learning. Columban died in 615.

Although forced out of Gaul, Columban's stern monasticism made a deep impression on the Merovingian lands in the way of Christian ideals. Eventually the custom of imposing specific penances for individual sins became a part of accepted Gallic practice. From the point of view of Christian missions, the boost Columban's monasteries gave to evangelization was of still greater importance. From Luxeuil, missionaries proceeded north. The most famous of his companions was Gall, whose name was given to the town near the head of Lake Zürich, where he worked with zeal in destroying pagan idols.

Ireland sent numerous other *peregrini* (itinerant missionaries) besides Columban to carry out the evangelization of Europe. Another seminal figure was Columba (ca. 521–ca. 597), founder of a kind of missionary training center on the island of Iona. Born of royal parentage in Donegal, Ireland, in 521, Columba received his early education under Bishop Finnio. Early on, Columba dedicated his life to a monastic vocation. Although ordained a priest, he was never appointed bishop. In 562 or 563, he took twelve companions to Iona, where they built a monastery in which they could train missionaries. From Iona, Columba ventured many times into Scotland as a missionary to non-Christians, witnessing and winning Picts, Druids, and others. Although Ninian and Kentigern (d. 603) may have won over many of the Picts and Scots in the preceding period, contemporary evidence seems to indicate that Columba had plenty to do.

The Barbarians

The evangelization of the Germanic peoples immigrating into the Roman Empire has been mentioned numerous times already in discussing the conversion of the empire. The fact is that it proceeded in somewhat the same gradual way the invasions themselves occurred. Since most of the barbarians admired Roman culture, they tended to take over all things Roman, including religion, but they did not assimilate either culture or religion without adapting it to their own needs and outlook. Barbarians recruited for the Roman army took over the faith that dominated the army, but, at the same time, they changed it. Thence, there remained a considerable task of deepening and strengthening the understanding of Christianity.

The first of the invaders to adopt the Christian faith in considerable numbers were the Goths. Some of them opted for the Catholic faith first, for, according to Socrates, one Gothic bishop attended the Council of Nicaea. Augustine reported persecution of Gothic Catholics, and John Chrysostom strove hard to win converts among the Goths, consecrating a bishop to send to them. Other Goths became Audians, who formed a separate rigorous sect in Syria led by Audius, a person of commendable piety but questionable theological views. Constantine banished them to Scythia. During the mid-fourth century, Audius won many converts among the Goths, but the latter suffered severe persecution at the hands of the pagan Goths about 370. Most Goths, however, became Arians as a result of the extraordinary mission work of Ulfilas (ca. 311–383). During Ulfilas's lifetime, the Christian Goths suffered severe persecution at the hands of Athanaric, a native chieftain, evidently in revenge for mistreatment by the Romans. Another chieftain, Frithigern, solicited Roman help and defeated Athanaric and then adopted Christianity, the faith of the Romans, which at the time was Arian in the court of Constantius II. When harassed by the Huns, Frithigern and his followers obtained permission to cross the Danube. A dispute erupted between this mass of settlers and the peoples of the area and led to a conflict. The Goths defeated imperial forces at the battle of Adrianople in 378. Nevertheless, they seem to have passed on their faith to the Ostrogoths, the Gepids, and the Vandals, although evidence on this is conflicting.

As strong as Arianism was among the Goths, it did not have an equally strong chance of winning the battle of faiths, even in the West. The majority of Westerners were Catholic. The Catholic Church had far stronger organization, a fact that even the invaders admired. Gothic rulers, moreover, were not as intense in their loyalty to the Arian faith as were Catholic rulers. Not many of them, at any rate, persecuted Catholics. With the conversion of Recared in Spain in 589, the last of the Gothic Arians officially went over to the Catholic faith. The Franks soon assured the triumph of the Catholic faith over Arianism in the heart of Europe.

Outside the Empire

Christianity continued to spread not merely within the Roman Empire but beyond its boundaries as well during the fifth and sixth centuries. As a matter of fact, the chief factor in slowing or halting its advance to the East was the rise of Islam in 622. Nestorian Christianity came to dominate the church in the Persian Empire toward the close of the fifth century. Monophysite Christianity spread rapidly in the East during the sixth.

In Armenia, the first nation to adopt Christianity officially, the instruction of the populace in Christian faith continued steadily throughout the fourth century. The Bible was translated into Armenian near the end of the fourth or beginning of the fifth century. Under Nerses (d. ca. 373), the sixth Catholicos of the Armenian Church, a reform took place that deepened the Christian impact on the country. In the fifth century, however, Armenia fell under the control of the Persian Empire. Although Persian rulers at first seemed satisfied to interfere in and control church affairs, later they propagated Zoroastrianism and persecuted Christians as a hereditary enemy. The persecution did not let up until near the end of the century.

In Georgia, Christianity arrived late in the third or early in the fourth century. As in Armenia, Georgian Christianity also suffered from Persian dominance after making steady progress during the fourth century. In the second half of the fifth century, however, Vakhtang I (446–499) drove the Persians out, purged the country of Zoroastrianism, built churches, and established bishoprics. Whereas Armenian Christianity chose the Monophysite tradition, Georgians remained Chalcedonian except for a brief period during the sixth century. Originally dependent on the patriarchate of Antioch, the Georgian Church became autocephalous during the eighth century.

In the Persian Empire, as indicated in an earlier chapter, Christians became suspect when Constantine adopted Christianity as the religion of the Roman Empire and tried to obtain favorable standing for Christians in Persia. With strong centers in Edessa and Adiabene, Christianity extended itself throughout the Mesopotamian area over which the Persians extended their control. During the fifth century, Christians carried the faith to the east of the Tigris-Euphrates Valley. Severe persecution in Persia lasted throughout the long reign of Sapor II (310–379) but subsided under Sapor III (383–388), Bahram IV (388–399), and Yazdegerd I (399–420). The change of policy opened the way for the conversion of prominent nobles. In 410, Christians formed a national organization headed by the Bishop of Selenica-Ctesiphon (the capital city), who received state recognition. The Catholicos was made responsible for the behavior of the people. The state tolerated Christianity and gave it a certain national recognition, which tempered suspicions, but it did not prevent occasional persecution. After the condemnation of Nestorius, a strong Nestorian tradition developed at Edessa under the leadership of Ibas. Following the Council of Chalcedon in 451, harassment and persecution caused many Nestorians to migrate to Persia, where a school at Nisibis gradually supplanted the one at Edessa as a Nestorian center. Several Persian rulers from the mid-fifth century on, especially Peroz (457–484), actively supported them. Severance of ties with the Roman Empire after their expulsion from Edessa by Emperor Zeno in 489 helped to improve their situation in Persia. The Nestorian Church distinguished itself from the early sixth century on by its mission work in Arabia, India, and east Asia.

How early Christianity arrived in India is uncertain, but the evidence for it is strong by the end of the fifth century. Cosmas Indicopleustes reported in the middle of the sixth century the existence of Christians on what is thought to have been Sri Lanka, in inner India, in Male, and in Kallina, the last two probably on the west coast of India. Christians in Kallina, he said, were led by a bishop consecrated in Persia. Commercial contacts with India may have led to the planting of Christianity in a number of locations, including southern Arabia and Persia.

Evidence for Christianity in Arabia is fragmentary but more definite than that for India. By 500, Christianity spread itself widely, coming chiefly from the Roman Empire and Mesopotamia through merchants, officials, professional missionaries, and hermits who sought refuge in the deserts of northern Arabia. It owed much also to contacts with Abyssinia or Ethiopia. Although the emergence of Islam put a stop to Christian expansion in the area, the ruler of Hira, southwest of Babylon near the Arabian edge of Mesopotamia, may have been a Christian in the last part of the sixth century. Cosmas Indicopleustes reported the presence of Christians in Arabia Felix and among the "Homerites" (Himyarites?).

Christianity also spread extensively to the north of Persia, east of the Caspian Sea and west and east of the Oxus River. Although it never had great strength in the area, Merv (in northern Persia) had a bishop from 334 through the fifth and sixth centuries and a metropolitan in the sixth, tenth, and eleventh centuries. Herat (on the Ochus River in Persia) had a bishop in the sixth century. Christians existed among the Hephthalite Huns and Turks toward the close of the fifth century.

In summary, Christianity continued its vital mission thrust during the fifth and sixth centuries. Within the Roman Empire, a now highly organized church continued the task of converting the unconverted. Although vestiges of the old religious cults and practices remained throughout the period, the appeal of the old diminished as imperial legislation increasingly worked in the church's favor against competitors. The countryside yielded last. As this process continued, however, the Germanic invasions posed a new challenge, not so much to conversion to Christianity as to which brand, Arian or Orthodox, would be chosen. Since most barbarians had been exposed first to Arianism, the Catholic Church, especially in the West, had to work hard to gain the upper hand in areas colonized by those of Arian persuasion. In this instance, greater zeal for Nicene orthodoxy worked in its favor as it won first one and then another of the barbarian leaders. A tragic sidelight of Christianity's success was growth of intolerance to pagans, Jews, and other Christians, which would result in violence as a style of mission that reached its consummation in the crusades of the Middle Ages.

The connection of Christianity with the Roman Empire doubtless aided it immensely in winning the barbarians, most of whom envied Roman culture. Although the invaders often wreaked havoc on the cities and peoples they conquered, they absorbed much of the culture and with it the religion. In consequence, Christianity not only survived the transition from Roman to barbarian influence, it gained from it. In some other areas, however, the Roman connection proved a disadvantage for Christianity. In many areas of the East, it perhaps gave an alien cast that impeded evangelization. Yet even in these areas Christianity planted its seed and saw plants sprout and grow. Few areas bordering on the land of Christianity's birth lacked a Christian witness by the year 600.

CHAPTER TWENTY-SIX

SOLITUDE THE RAGE

During the fifth and sixth centuries, the contemplative life became the rage in both East and West. Husbands and wives, sometimes entire families, and the best and brightest youth took up the ascetic way as the ideal philosophical/religious life. The reasons for the popularity of the monastic vocation would have differed in the two areas. In the East, monasticism rode the wave set in motion during the preceding century, first in the form of hermitic and then in that of coenobitic (communal) solitude. Although both types remained vital, Basil of Caesarea assured the triumph of the coenobitic type and, with his Rule, corralled the monastic movement for the institutional church. Monasteries dotted the landscape. So many developed in cities like Constantinople and Antioch that some emperors went on the attack to disperse them. The monks, however, won the battle and played significant roles in the theological controversies that wracked the Eastern churches during these two centuries and in the iconoclastic controversy in later centuries.

In the West, monasticism, carried westward by several routes, started late but caught fire immediately in an age of extreme cultural disruption brought on by the Germanic invasions. People witnessing the end of civilization as they had known it found in the hermitic or coenobitic life a means of survival. The contemplative way conditioned them for repeated shock waves and prepared them for death. The nobility in Italy, Gaul, Ireland, and elsewhere got caught up in a movement of detachment from this world and contemplation of the world to come. In Ireland, a more disciplined monasticism emphasizing *peregrinatio* ("exile") ignited a movement for the evangelization of the British Isles and the continent of Europe. Monks and monasteries took on an immensely important social role as kings and princes, especially in Merovigian Gaul after the conversion of Clovis (ca. 496), promoted and used them not only to christianize their realms but also to effect order.

The East

Eastern monachism had reached maturity by about 400 and underwent little significant change thereafter. Some extreme forms of hermitism still existed, especially in Syria. The Boskoi grazed like cattle. Dendrites lived in trees. Catenati loaded themselves down with chains to prove the triumph of mind over body. The Stylites erected pillars and raised them higher and higher toward heaven. First and most famous of the Stylites was Simeon (ca. 390–459), who was also a catenatus. Born on the Syrian border of Cilicia, he first lived the life of an anchorite in the monastery of Eusebona (between Antioch and Aleppo) and then at Telanissos, which was nearby. After several years Simeon built a pillar and gradually raised it to a height of sixty feet. There he lived more than thirty years, fascinating admirers with athletic feats such as standing all night motionless with his hands raised upward to heaven or touching his forehead with his feet 1,244 times in succession. He attracted a stream of pilgrims and inspired many imitators. According to his admiring biographer, he exerted much influence— converting pagans, advising kings and princes, reconciling enemies, and upholding the cause of Chalcedon.

Thanks to the influence of Basil of Caesarea's Rule, drafted in two forms between 358 and 364, the majority of monks in the East opted for the communal (coenobite) style of monasticism. Drawn from the Pachomian pattern in Egypt, the Rule eliminated many of the extremes of hermitic monasticism, although it was still severe. It put asceticism to work in communal obedience. It established set hours for liturgical prayer, manual labor, and other tasks and imposed the rule of poverty and chastity similar to that adopted later in the West. Basil's Rule also arranged for education of children and for care of the indigent in connection with the monastery.

Lauras (convents) sprang up in great numbers all over the Byzantine world. In Egypt, the cradle of monasticism, strong communities composed of hundreds of monks—both men and women—continued at Nitria, Scetis, Oxyrhynchus, Faou, Tabennesis, and Thebes. The Gnostic library uncovered in the 1940s belonged to a monastery at Chenoboskion, or Nag Hammadi.

Near what was thought to have been the location of Mount Sinai, monks formed a community at Wadi Faran, an oasis well supplied with water. Faran was an episcopal see in the fourth century. About 389, Etheria found a considerable number of men and a church at the foot of Jebel Musa on what they thought to be the site of the burning bush. In the sixth century, some of these monks appealed to Emperor Justinian (527–565) for protection against Bedouin tribes. Always interested in securing the boundaries of his empire, the emperor erected the cloister, which still stands there, and sent troops to protect it. In the tenth or eleventh century the relics of St. Catherine, an Alexandrian saint martyred early in the fourth century, were brought to the monastery and her name attached to it.

In Palestine, monasteries continued to spring up near many of the holy sites. The two monasteries erected by the Roman matron Paula (347–404) continued under the direction of her daughter Eustochium (370–ca. 419) and then her granddaughter Paula (d. 439) at Bethlehem. Sabas (439–532), a native of Mutalaska in Cappadocia, founded a large laura (the present Mar Saba) in 478 in the desolate Wadi en-Nar, between Jerusalem and the Dead Sea. In 492, the Patriarch of Jerusalem made him superior of all the hermits in Palestine.

The monastic life had great appeal in the East. The diocese of Constantinople had sixty-eight and that of Chalcedon forty monasteries during Justinian's day. The power of the monks and their independence troubled the Byzantine emperors. This monastic independence must also have troubled bishops during the theological controversies of the fifth and sixth centuries. Egyptian monks favored the doctrine of one nature in Christ (monophysitism), monks of Palestine and Constantinople that of two natures (dyophysitism). As proposed by Emperor Marcian (450–457), a Chalcedonian, the Council of Chalcedon ruled that monasteries were not to be built thenceforth without the approval of the bishop of a diocese and that monks, whether in town or country, should submit to episcopal authority under penalty of excommunication. Monks, however, must not have taken the decrees too seriously because later councils had to reiterate the threat.

Monks played a role in the condemnation of Nestorius at the Council of Ephesus (431–433) and at Chalcedon (451). When he became Patriarch of Constantinople in 428, Nestorius disputed the term "Mother of God" (*Theotokos*) as applied to Mary. The extreme reverence in which monks held Mary led immediately to attacks on Nestorius. Their substantial numbers carried great weight, and they readily enlisted the support of the Patriarch of Alexandria, Cyril (412–444), always ready to recoup some prestige lost to upstart Constantinople.

The West

The savaging of Rome early in the fifth century resulted in the relocation of the center of Western monasticism. Many fled to Africa and to Palestine ahead of the Goths and Vandals. When Melania the Elder fled Rome in 408, her daughter, Albina; her granddaughter, Melania the Younger and her husband, Pinian, accompanied her on her flight from Italy. The wealthy ascetic couple founded two monasteries at Tagaste, Augustine's home town, where they remained for seven years. Later they entered convents at Bethlehem founded by Paula and Eustochium. After Pinian's death in 431, Melania the Younger founded another monastery on the Mount of Olives.

In the West, monasticism found stout defenders and promoters in Ambrose (ca. 339–397) and Augustine (354–430). Ambrose lauded monastic self-denial and supported a monastery on the outskirts of Milan. At the request of his sister Marcellina (ca. 330–ca. 398), he composed the treatise *The Virgins*, in which he sought to allay parental fears of the ascetic life.

Africa

Doubtless, Augustine had more to do with the monks' becoming models for the clergy in the West than anyone else. At Cassiciacum near Milan, before his conversion, he already participated in a quasi-monastic group, one certainly interested in asceticism. The crucial experience leading to conversion was the narration by Ponticianus of a story about two young Roman noblemen who left their fiancés and became hermits after hearing the story of Anthony of Egypt. On his return to Africa, he formed an ascetic community. After his ordination at Hippo, he established a monastery. Although he cannot be credited for the rule that bears his name, he set an example that later generations returned to repeatedly by founding a monastic community for the clergy of his diocese.

The monasteries of Africa, as was the case with other aspects of church life, suffered severely as a consequence of the Vandal invasions. The experience of Fulgentius (468–533 or ca. 462–527), Bishop of Ruspe and a devoted Augustinian, was probably a common one in the fifth and sixth centuries. A Roman civil servant, he took up the monastic vocation in which he suffered constant persecution at the hands of the Vandal King Thrasamund, an Arian. Soon after his installation as Bishop of Ruspe, around 502 or 507, Fulgentius was banished to Sardinia with about sixty other Catholic bishops. Although allowed to return about 510–515, he was banished a second time two years later. After the death of Thrasamund in 523, Hilderic permitted Fulgentius to return. Persecution later drove many monks from North Africa to Spain.

Gaul

Monasticism had more lasting success in Gaul. From a seed planted there by Athanasius during his exile in Trier in 336, monasticism grew into a thriving plant. The person largely responsible for popularizing it everywhere in Gaul was Martin of Tours (d. 397). Sulpicius Severus (ca. 360–ca. 420), an Aquitanian noble converted to the ascetic life about 394 by the example of Paulinus of Nola (353/4–431), popularized Martin as the model monk, bishop, and missionary even before he died. The contribution of monasticism to the evangelization of Gaul enhanced its place in the Frankish kingdom during the fifth and sixth centuries.

The ascetic movement appealed to many of the nobility. Two monasteries in particular—Lérins and St. Victor at Marseilles—attracted eminent persons who then played a major role in shaping the Frankish Church. The monastery of Lérins was founded by Honoratus, later Archbishop of Arles, about 410. A member of a consular family, Honoratus (ca. 350–429) had set out after his conversion to visit holy sites in Syria and Egypt. Following the death of his brother Venantius in Achaia, Martin took the advice of Leontius, the Bishop of Frejus, and settled on the island of Lérins. He continued to direct the monastery even after his election as Archbishop of Arles in 426. Hilary (403–489), a relative of Honoratus, succeeded him as Abbot of Lérins and Archbishop of Arles.

Lérins laid claim to numerous other eminent figures in this period. Vincent (d. before 450) framed the often-quoted definition of Catholic faith as "what has been believed always, everywhere, and by all." Salvian (ca. 400–ca. 480), whose name is usually associated with Marseilles, came originally to Lérins from a noble family of Cologne. Eucherius (d. ca. 449) left a wife and family to enter Lérins and later served as Bishop of Lyon (from 434 on). He actively promoted the ascetic life. Lupus (ca. 383–479), Bishop of Troyes (429–479), entered Lérins after seven years of marriage to Pimeniola, sister of Hilary of Arles. Caesarius (ca. 407–542), Archbishop of Arles (502–542), entered Lérins in 489. With the help of Alaric II and Theodoric the Great, the Gothic rulers, he succeeded in making Arles the primatial see of Gaul.

Rivaling Lérins in influence during the fifth and sixth centuries was the Abbey of St. Victor at Marseilles, founded by John Cassian in 415. Western monasticism owes its shape in great part to Cassian. Born in either Provence or, more likely, Dobrudja, Scythia Minor of the Roman Empire, Cassian (ca. 360–435) entered a monastery in 382 near the cave of the nativity at Bethlehem, accompanied by Germanus. In 385, he and Germanus moved to Egypt in search of "perfection" and soon became enamored of Egyptian hermitic ideals. Thereafter, neither felt comfortable any longer in Bethlehem.

They spent time at three different locations: the salt marshes near Panephysis, the desert of Scete, and the region of Diolcos and Panephysis. At Scete they joined a community headed by Macarius (ca. 300–ca. 390), who was then over ninety years old. In 399 or 400 they had to bring their stay to an abrupt halt when the Origenist controversy erupted. Breaking a pledge to return to Bethlehem, Cassian turned up next in Constantinople, probably because of his Origenism. John Chrysostom welcomed Origenists, one of several things alienating him from the clergy of the city.

Sent by Chrysostom on an embassy to Pope Innocent I (402–417) around 405, Cassian developed a friendship with Leo, later Pope Leo I (440–461). Some years later, he founded twin monasteries at Marseilles, one for women and one for men, dedicated to the martyr Victor. The barbarian invasions provided a kind of apocalyptic stimulus to the monastic movement. Within a short time, St. Victor and other houses associated with it claimed 5,000 monks. Cassian supplied the guidance that the movement needed through the publication of his *Institutes* and *Conferences* between 425 and 430. He died in 435.

In some contrast to Basil of Caesarea, Cassian looked upon the hermitic as the most mature form of monasticism; the coenobium, he thought, was for beginners, the hermitage for the mature. He did not depend on Pachomius for his rule, advising rather than ordering and differing in many details. His special contribution lay in the development of the daily hours of prayer. In Egypt, according to his own account, the monks observed two formal prayer times—nocturns and vespers—in which they chanted twelve psalms and kept the rest of the day for silent meditation. Cassian felt that monks needed more prayer and added three other times of prayer traditionally observed in the churches: the third, sixth, and ninth hours. In the sixth century, Benedict of Nursia added three more. Monks in Cassian's monasteries lived a moderately austere life. They slept three or four hours a day. Their diet consisted of two large buns, soaked beans, and fresh vegetables. On Saturdays and Sundays they received more cooked food. A group of elders governed the monastery. Younger monks were to obey older ones and confess to them.

Cassian derived many of his ideas from Evagrius Ponticus (346–399), whom he met at Nitria, although he made critical changes. Evagrius devised the classification later known as the "seven deadly sins" (anger, lust, avarice, envy, gluttony, accidie, and vainglory or pride) and explained how monks could fight them through recitation of psalms, study of the scriptures, manual labor, and remaining in one's cell. Eventually monks can attain *apatheia* (lack of desire), the key Stoic virtue. *Apatheia* produces charity, and charity leads to *gnosis*. Cassian opposed excessive mortification. He emphasized scriptures, understood first literally and then spiritually, as the key source for filling and conditioning the mind. The goal is purity of heart, which can be attained by praying without ceasing. Cassian depended to some extent on Augustine for his doctrine of grace, but he shared the Eastern concern for free will.

During the turbulent and unsettled period of incursions by the Goths, Burgundians, and Franks, monasteries sprang up throughout Gaul. Germanus (ca. 378–448) may have founded the abbey that bore his name at Auxerre. Moutier St. Jean, son of a senator of Dijon, founded the Abbey of Reome, which later bore his name, about 450. Two brothers, Romain and Lupicin, founded Condat high in the Alps at Jura on the border between France and Switzerland, also in the middle of the fifth century. Condat affected an Eastern style. Under its fourth abbot, Eugende (496–510), it developed a school that supplied education to the people of the area. The monastery had considerable influence on the Burgundians as they extended their rule to the area. The Burgundian King Sigismund, after renouncing Arianism, rebuilt the monastery at Aguane and brought monks from Condat and Lérins to inhabit it between 515 and 522.

The Merovingian line, which began with Clovis, took an active interest in the promotion of monasticism. Although Clovis (ca. 466–511) himself did not found any monasteries, he gave large gifts to the monasteries of Martin of Tours and Hilary of Poitiers (ca. 315–367). The next two generations of Merovingians established and endowed numerous monasteries. Childebert I was a friend of monks, and Chlotar I, though by no means a saintly person, was associated with Radegundis in the founding of St. Croix.

Queen Radegundis (518–587), daughter of a prince of Thuringia, had married Chlotar around 540 rather reluctantly. When the latter murdered her brother about ten years later, she fled and persuaded Medard, Bishop of Noyon, to ordain her as a deaconess. Shortly thereafter, she founded a monastery for women outside Poitiers and spent the last thirty years of her life in it. Adopting the rule framed by Caesarius of Arles, she emphasized charity and peace and urged her nuns to pray for all rather than be preoccupied with their own salvation. Merovingian monasteries evidently did not make too much use of the Rule of the Benedict at this period.

Why did people of power and wealth found monasteries? Some did so out of the hope of winning salvation through relief of poverty, the good work of good works. Others wanted to ensure perpetual prayer on their behalf and for their families. Others valued the fact that the monasteries guarded relics of martyrs and holy persons, and those that could claim important relics prospered—Tours, Poitiers, Lyon, Trier, Autun. Some others recognized in the founding of monasteries a way to save family properties, otherwise easily seized or lost, and continued to exert some influence over their use. Individuals entered monasteries, of course, to find salvation, to have more security than the world offered, and to give themselves to the life of prayer.

Ireland

In Ireland, monasticism assumed a character quite distinct from earlier forms. Although it antedated his arrival in 432, its development depended heavily on the work of Patrick. As noted in an earlier chapter, Patrick fostered monasticism in his evangelization of Ireland. In Ireland, as a matter of fact, monastic institutions overrode episcopal organization and captured the imagination of the people. When kings or chieftains converted, they often became monks and abbots of monasteries, which sometimes numbered in the thousands.

Women also got caught up in the ascetic movement. The most famous of the Irish monastic founders was Bride, or Brigid (d. ca. 523), credited with founding the first women's convent at Kildare.

What especially distinguished Celtic monasticism was its austerity. Love of God, in the Celtic view, required "application and toil." Physical penances, such as fasting and plunging into cold water, were encouraged to kindle service to God. Key figures in defining Celtic monasticism were Columba (ca. 521–597) and Columban (ca. 543–615). Columban's rule called for moral perfection achieved by thorough self-scrutiny, confession, and doing appropriate penance. Penance was therapeutic rather than punitive. Accordingly, Columban required private confessions before eating and going to bed.

Italy

By the sixth century, monasteries were scattered all over Europe, poised to carry out the task of evangelizing and reevangelizing. Although they shared a common heritage, they existed in great variety, often determined by their founders. No rule dominated in the way Basil of Caesarea's Rule prevailed in Eastern monasticism. Only larger monasteries would have had copies of that Rule in Rufinus's translation or the Rule of Pachomius in Jerome's or Cassian's *Conferences* and *Institutes*. The solution to the problem came from Italy in the concise, temperate, and appropriate form framed by Benedict of Nursia. Although Benedict's Rule did not gain immediate widespread acceptance, it gradually caught on and overwhelmed all competitors, including the influential but more stringent Rule of Columban.

Benedict's background is obscure. Born at Nursia around 480, he was educated at Rome. The licentiousness of the city, however, caused him to withdraw about 500 and take up a hermit's life in a cave at Subiaco. A community gradually formed around him, and he established twelve monasteries with twelve monks each. The jealousy of some monks, however, caused him to flee Subiaco. Around 525 he took a small group of monks to Monte Cassino, where he remained until he died, probably in 547. Here he composed his first Rule.

Benedict's Rule addressed one of the central problems of the turbulent sixth century in Italy as first the Ostrogoths and then the armies of Justinian and later the Lombards wreaked havoc. In the midst of such an insecure situation, the Rule focused on stability and orderliness. It provided for a community ruled by an abbot elected for life and supported by agriculture. Within the walls of its enclosure, the monks could raise all of the food the community required and provide for all other necessities. The community existed for nothing else than to arrange an orderly life for those within it, although, like other families, it did extend hospitality to outsiders and relieve the needs of the people around it. The monks wanted simply to serve God without distractions from the world.

Under the Rule of Benedict, monks ordered their day around three activities. They spent about four hours a day in liturgical prayer, four in meditative reading (*lectio divina*), and six or more in manual labor of some kind. Benedict wanted nothing to take precedence over the *Opus Dei*, "Work of God." Seven times a day, usually beginning about 2:00 A.M., the monks gathered to recite psalms. Whereas some desert monks sought to recite all 150 Psalms every day, Benedict arranged for their recitation once a week. The spiritual reading consisted solely of scriptures, early monastic literature, and the writings of the Church Fathers, although, in three or four hours a day, monks may have ventured beyond that diet from time to time. Manual labor would not have consisted only of farm activities, because Benedictine monasteries employed *coloni* to do heavy manual labor. Monks, therefore, probably engaged in domestic arts and crafts.

The monastic movement also drew women. Benedict's twin sister, Scholastica (ca. 480–ca. 543), established a convent at Plombariola, a few miles from Monte Cassino. According to Gregory the Great, brother and sister met annually outside the monastery to compare notes. Scholastica died just before Benedict and was buried in the tomb he had prepared for himself. He was later buried beside her.

The Rule of Benedict gained ground slowly after the death of its framer. Cassiodorus (ca. 485–ca. 580), a Roman senator who eased tensions between Romans and Goths, founded two monasteries along Benedictine lines at Vivarium and became a monk in one of them around 540. After trying in vain to establish a school at Rome along lines of the Alexandrian, he turned his monastery into a kind of academy that encouraged both secular and religious learning. He collected a huge library and required the monks to spend time in study. A disciple of Benedict, Placidus, the son of a wealthy senator, founded a Benedictine monastery at Messina in Sicily around 534. Shortly thereafter, he and his sister Flavia and two monks were slain by Moorish pirates. In Sicily, most monasteries followed the rule of Basil. Martyrdom of monks assisted in the dissemination of the movement.

The most ardent advocate and promoter of Benedictinism, however, was Pope Gregory I (590–604), the Great, who, in his *Dialogues,* turned Benedict into a legend and set an example for others in living the monastic life. The son of a Roman senator, in 573 he relinquished his role as prefect of the city of Rome, sold his vast properties, and distributed much of his wealth to the poor. He founded seven monasteries, six in Sicily and one in Rome—the Monastery of St. Andrew, into which he himself entered. After serving seven years as *apocrisarius* (ambassador) to the court at Constantinople (578–585), he became abbot of St. Andrew's. Reluctantly, he assumed the papacy in 590. About 593, he composed the *Dialogues,* which highlighted the lives of Benedict and other early Latin saints. Although it is not certain that even the Monastery of St. Andrew followed the Rule of Benedict in Gregory's time, his promotion of Benedict as the saint par excellence obviously weighted the scales in favor of the Rule thereafter.

With Gregory, Western monasticism stood at the threshold of its golden age. He valued the monastic vocation in itself, not simply as a means to an end. He exempted certain monasteries from episcopal control. He sharply separated the monastic from the clerical life and insisted that clergy give up clerical functions when they entered monasteries. He did his best to raise the monastic life to its highest possible level, and he vigorously opposed Emperor Maurice's (582–602) prohibition of soldiers' or public officials' entering monastic communities. He entrusted monks, such as Augustine, head of St. Andrew's in Rome, with the task of evangelizing the British Isles. From this point on, the monks would play an increasingly important role in the life of the church.

CHAPTER TWENTY-SEVEN

EAST IS EAST AND WEST IS WEST

One of the striking developments of the fifth and sixth centuries was the expansion of the rift between the East and the West. The barbarian invasions consummated in the fifth century hastened and widened the breach, for they constricted exchanges between the two areas. The separation, however, had more basic roots even than barbarian control of the West. The two areas had different histories and cultures. Although differences in language would have been an obvious sign of separation, they signaled something deeper in cultural differences. The Roman East was not, after all, really Roman. Actually it was not Greek either, even though Hellenism spread widely throughout the ancient world. The course of several controversies shows that the East was not homogeneous. There was a Greek East, to be sure, but there were also an Egyptian East and a Syrian East. Consequently, the emperors had constantly to struggle to hold a disparate people together. All of these areas inherited and sought to live by some of the same ideas, but they appropriated and applied them differently.

The divergencies appeared in a number of areas. For one, Easterners and Westerners developed different models for the relation of church and state. Although heirs of the same liturgies, Easterners and Westerners had quite different concepts of worship and used different styles and liturgies. In this period of transition, which was so significant for shaping the Western church, furthermore, Christian culture underwent a "barbarization" not experienced in the East. The "Dark Ages" did not descend on the East as on the West.

Contrasting Temperaments

Formally the East and the West maintained their historic ties up to 1054, except during the brief Acacian schism (484–528) and during the Photian schism (869–879). It does not require special insight, however, to see the widening of the distance between the two halves of Christendom. The truth of the matter is that Easterners and Westerners had fundamentally different temperaments. Easterners were imbued far more deeply with the spirit of Hellenism than were Westerners. Easterners used the Greek language, while even cultivated Westerners such as Augustine scarcely knew or desired to know it. Easterners delighted in speculative thought just as the ancient Greeks had. By this period, certainly, the average Easterner had a better education than his or her Western counterpart, enabling laypersons as well as clergy or monks to take an active part in theological discussion and debate. Although this had a downside in a near obsession for theological precision, it precluded the dominance of theology by ecclesiastical authorities such as happened in the West. From it, moreover, derived the Eastern preference for a conciliar approach to settling matters of debate. This approach, unfortunately, did lend itself to wrangling and division, for minorities seldom conceded the majority opinion in theological matters.

Westerners, on the other hand, had a more practical bent than Easterners. Trying to survive in these turbulent centuries, they could not afford the luxury of speculative thought in which Easterners engaged so heartily. The number of Western bishops who participated in the first seven ecumenical councils could be counted on two hands. How to help the faithful overcome temptation, sin, and guilt was of far greater moment than whether Christ was *homoousios, homoiousios, homoios,* or *anomoios* with the Father. Consequently, Westerners expended far more of their energies fashioning a system of pastoral guidance than they did engaging in speculative theology. The barbarian invasions increased the penchant for the practical. It is not surprising that it was Celtic monks who fashioned the penitential system as a means of introducing converts to the bare rudiments of Christian life.

Church and State

East and West quite clearly went in different directions in their understanding and acting out of the relationship between church and state. Constantine set the pattern for the East, or, perhaps more accurately stated, perpetuated the ancient Roman pattern. Eusebius, as Constantine's *alter ego*, envisioned the emperor as God's representative in all affairs of the empire, including religious affairs. Although the church may assist him in discovering God's will, he alone has universal authority and is the ultimate reference in religious matters. To disobey the emperor would be to disobey God. Confirmation of the theory can be found in Constantine's handling of the Donatist and Arian controversies. Except for Julian, Constantine's successors followed in his footsteps. In the fifth century, the emperors increased their use of the church for political purposes. This tendency reached its peak in the sixth century under Justinian.

Justinian not only summoned councils, but he also took control of each step of the proceedings. When he learned that African bishops opposed his condemnation of the "Three Chapters," he excluded them from the Fifth Ecumencial Council in 553, designed to effect that goal. His wife, Theodora, who leaned toward Monophysitism, secured the removal and possibly the death of Pope Silverius (536–538) and the installation of Vigilius (538–555) on the basis of a promise that he would help negotiate the condemnation of Chalcedon. Justinian then forced Vigilius, against conscience, to condemn the "Three Chapters." Although some scholars have objected to the characterization of Eastern church/state concepts as caesaropapist, in Justinian's case this would seem appropriate.

Justinian dealt harshly with persons not considered orthodox. He deposed, excommunicated, and sometimes banished Nestorians and Eutychians. Depending on political circumstances, he vacillated in his treatment of Arians, being somewhat lenient until his forces won Africa from the Vandals in 534. He placed Manichaeans under the death penalty and took harsh action against Montanists and Gnostics. He placed Samaritans and Jews under severe restrictions, albeit not as repressive as those against heretics. His legislation punished apostasy from Christianity with death and required baptism of all citizens. They also denied pagans the right to education and forbade their public worship. On closing the school at Athens in 529, Justinian offered professors the option of baptism or exile. Seven chose exile.

Justinian's *Code* even legislated the theology, worship, and structure of the church. One title included four laws "On the Highest Trinity and on the Catholic Faith and That no one dare debate about these matters publicly." Others dealt with legacies to churches, bishops and the clergy, heresy, apostasy, repression of paganism, sanctuary, and manumission. The later "Novels" focused on such specific matters as the number of clergy who could minister in Hagia Sophia, disposal of land belonging to the Church of the Resurrection in Jerusalem, erection of a see at Justinian's birthplace, clerical discipline, and regulation of monasteries. In a "Novel" issued March 16, 535, Justinian stated his own theory of church and state. Priests and emperors should work in harmony, the priests offering prayers and the emperors ruling.

In practice, Justinian followed the arrangement set up by Marcian at the Council of Chalcedon in 451 to assure a free imperial hand in the guidance of the whole Eastern church through the Patriarch of Constantinople. "New Rome" was "to have the same advantages in the ecclesiastical order" as Old Rome "and be second to it." Patriarchs thereafter spoke often of themselves as "ecumenical" patriarchs. When John the Faster tried to formalize it, Pope Gregory I (590–604) indignantly denounced the idea. The emperor, likewise, took pains to assure control of monasteries.

What made many wary of the Constantinian model of a Christian empire was the Arianism of Constantius II (337–361), successor of Constantine in the East. Athanasius quickly learned that he would have to pay a price for steadfastness in adhering to Nicene orthodoxy. It was the Western church and not the Eastern, however, that came to his aid. When the emperors Constans and Constantius jointly convened the Council of Sardica around 343 to settle the issue of Athanasius's orthodoxy, Eastern bishops refused to attend on the ground that Westerners regarded Athanasius as a member of the assembly. Westerners met anyway under leadership of Hosius of Cordova and cleared Athanasius. A letter from Western bishops to the Emperor Constantius subtly questioned the use of secular force against orthodox bishops and suggested that the emperor's task was to ensure "most precious liberty" to all his subjects. Hilary of Poitiers (ca. 315–367), who preserved the letter, went on to develop the principle of freedom in religion: God does not ask for and will refuse a coerced confession. The Western Council of Sardica (Can. 3) sought to buttress its position by constituting the bishop of Rome as a court of appeal for bishops in certain cases.

With the backing of Constans, the Council of Sardica brought temporary relief for Nicene supporters in the East and even the restoration of Athanasius. Ironically, however, in the meantime Constans persecuted Donatists, evoking from Donatus the query, "What has the emperor to do with the church?" After the death of Constans in 350, Constantius resumed his repression of Nicene bishops. When Western bishops insisted at the Council of Milan in 355 that they would violate canon law if they obeyed his directives, he declared that the imperial will was the same as canon law! He also sent for Pope Liberius (352–366) and forced him to break with Athanasius. When Liberius refused, Constantius banished him from Rome until he signed an Arian formula. When Hosius of Cordova (ca. 257–357), then nearly a hundred, declined to sign a statement against Athanasius, Contantius banished him to Sirmium. Hosius penned a courageous letter propounding a two-kingdoms theory: God has entrusted the earthly kingdom to the emperor but the church to the bishops; so Constantius had better watch out lest he offend God. At the Council of Sirmium in 357, nevertheless, the emperor forced the aged Hosius to sign the "Blasphemy," an agreement to communicate with Arians, before he could return to Cordova. Before he died, Hosius retracted his signing.

The firmness of the Constantinian model's grip on Eastern thinking is evident in the hesitancy of Athanasius to speak other than obediently and respectfully of Constantius. Not until 358, in his *History of the Arians*, did he break that pattern. Some emperors—Jovian and Valentinian I—professed the dualistic theory, but it came to its most forceful expression in Martin of Tours (d. 397) and Ambrose of Milan (ca. 339–397). Martin argued against the trial of Priscillian, a Spanish bishop who founded an aberrant ascetic sect that went by his name, in the imperial court at Trier on a charge of witchcraft, a capital offense. A secular judge should not try an ecclesiastical case, he insisted. After Martin left the city, Priscillian was tried and executed.

Ambrose, as noted in an earlier chapter, pressed the theory of separate jurisdictions to the maximum in 385 in his conflict with the Empress Justina over the use of the basilicas of Milan for Arian worship. "Palaces belong to the Emperor, churches to the bishop," he declared. Ambrose, however, did not contend for completely separate realms. The emperor has the *duty* to suppress paganism and heresy and can call and ratify councils, of course, at the request of the church. Here, Ambrose tended toward a theory of church ascendancy over the state.

From this point on in the West, the papacy became the bulwark for the liberty of the church. The Council of Sardica had pointed in the direction in which the popes from Damasus on (366–384) would steadily move. As will be seen subsequently, the confused political situation in the West aided the papacy in its struggle to emancipate itself from dominance by the emperors. Yet where the church obtained too many favors from the established powers, whether in East or West, it ran the risk of subordination to them. Like Ambrose, the popes tried to guard against this risk by placing the church in the ascendant position. In the West this policy had a certain feasibility in the fifth and sixth centuries as the invasions created a power vacuum. Bishops intervened in cases of capital punishment. They received appointment as financial officers of cities. They sat in judgment on the morality of emperors and other officials, as Ambrose had in requiring Theodosius I (379–395) to do penance for the massacre of the citizens of Thessalonica in 388.

In 494, Pope Gelasius I stated the two-kingdoms theory in its classical form in a letter to Emperor Anastasius I (491–518). Of the two realms, the priestly is the more weighty, for the priest must render an account to God in the judgment. In actual practice, however, neither the emperors nor the rising Frankish kings in the West took that doctrine seriously. Frankish kings played about the same hand as the emperors did. In 549, the Council of Orleans recognized as much when it laid down the rule that bishops would be elected "with the consent of the king (*cum voluntate regis*)." Although a pope as powerful as Gregory the Great (590–604) often objected to imperial decrees, he taught that to offend God's anointed was to offend God. When Emperor Maurice (582–602) ruled that soldiers could not become monks, his objections notwithstanding, Gregory obeyed the ruling. Subsequent history is full of tales of the church's struggle, both Western and Eastern, to liberate itself from secular control.

301

Worship

East and West also took different paths in the evolution of their worship practices during the fifth and sixth centuries as Christian worship entered the third major phase of its development. In this phase, beginning in the late fourth century, Christian worship in the East felt keenly the impact of monasticism. At the heart of the monastic devotional regimen was the chanting of psalms. Since the people looked to the monks as teachers, spiritual guides, and guardians of orthodoxy, it is not surprising to see a blending of the monastic devotional routine with the liturgy current in the great sees—Constantinople, Antioch, Alexandria, and Jerusalem—where monasteries abounded. In the West, the monastic impact came later after the liturgies had solidified, but it was telling there too.

Up to the fourth century, the liturgy retained a uniform outline throughout Christendom, but it was still fluid and subject to alteration in details. By the second half of the fourth century, fluid uniformity had given way to fixed liturgies representing different geographical areas. The fixing of worship forms was doubtless necessitated by growth in the size of congregations and the demand for greater splendor to suit the tastes of more cultured and affluent constituencies. In addition, constantly increasing concern for theological precision, especially in the East, mandated more exact formulation of prayers and other elements of the service. Certain centers, especially the patriarchal sees, crystallized local liturgies and set the pattern for the churches in their sphere of influence. Variations in language in different regions, moreover, assured that the liturgies of East and West would diverge still further.

Language accounts for one of the most self-evident ways in which Eastern and Western worship differed. In the West, Latin quickly established itself as the language of the liturgy, and the liturgy was not translated into other languages. In the East, although Greek was the common language of the empire and thus spread over a wide sphere, the churches did not fix Greek as the liturgical language but rather encouraged translation into the vernacular. Early on, Syriac-speaking Christians fashioned their own liturgy, which later came under influence of the Greek liturgy of Antioch. In the patriarchate of Antioch, the Greek liturgy was also translated into Syriac, the prevailing popular language. Elsewhere the Greek liturgy appeared in the language of the people—Coptic in Egypt with some admixture of Greek, Armenian, Georgian, and, later, other languages.

More basic in distinguishing the worship of East and West was the relative importance of the liturgy in the two areas. The liturgy had much greater significance in the lives of Christians in the Byzantine sphere than it did in the lives of Western Christians. It was the central expression of church life, far more important than the sermon, catechetical instruction, almsgiving, or any other organized church activity. To participate in the liturgy was to take part in the drama of salvation with the saints of all the ages and the heavenly hierarchies. The writings of Pseudo-Dionysius, probably composed in Syria about 500, gave eloquent expression to the mythology of the liturgy. According to Pseudo-Dionysius, the liturgy of the church models itself, in Platonic fashion, on the heavenly. God in essence, the Godhead, cannot be known, for God is "beyond essence" and "beyond knowing." Christ, however, God incarnate, can communicate Light to us through the heavenly hierarchies in a kind of downward spiral. The hierarchy is a "sacred order" whose goal is "to enable beings to be as like God as possible and to be one with God" (*Celestial Hierarchies* 3.2). Thus the higher ranks (seraphim, cherubim, and thrones) transmit wisdom to the middle (dominions, powers, and authorities), and the middle to lower (principalities, archangels, and angels). At this level the celestial hierarchy matches up with the ecclesiastical hierarchy, which also has three levels. The ecclesiastical hierarchy communicates the divine revelation through the mysteries (sacraments)—baptism (called the Illumination), eucharist, ordination, and anointing of the dead. Just as Jesus communicates through the celestial hierarchy, so also he, as it were, assimilates the earthly hierarchy "to his own light" (*Ecclesiastical Hierarchies* 1.1) and bestows the power of the sacred priesthood. This hierarchy belongs, therefore, to the noumenal and not merely to the phenomenal world. Because by its nature it encompasses all sacred elements in itself, it can be the means of divinization and, as the ultimate goal, union with God.

By way of contrast, Western Christians made far more of the reception of the eucharist or mass itself. In the East, the eucharist took place only as the people assembled for worship, and churches thus had only one altar. In the West, as the number of priests multiplied in monasteries to serve the needs of people for forgiveness of sin and masses for the dead, the number of altars in the churches multiplied, usually by creating altars in the side aisles.

Paralleling differences in liturgy were differences in church architecture in the three major geographical areas of Christendom—the Latin West, the Greek East, and the Syriac-speaking area from Palestine eastward. Byzantine church architecture took a major turn during the reign of Justinian (527–565). Up to this time, the basilica had dominated in both East and West, and it would continue to prevail in the West. In the East, however, Justinian deliberately broke with tradition in favor of vaulted, centrally planned church buildings used since the third or fourth century in palace halls, funerary structures, baths, garden buildings, and, to a limited extent, churches or martyria. Although this type of edifice appeared more frequently around 500, not until Justinian did architects make it the rule, thus deliberately setting out in a different direction from the West. The major impetus for the change probably came from the liturgy, for the centrally planned structure was ideally suited to performance of a service wherein the liturgy dominated everything else. Foremost of Justinian's churches was Hagia Sophia in Constantinople, constructed between 532 and 537 after the original basilica erected in 360 was burned in the Nike revolt. Outside Constantinople itself, however, only San Vitale in Ravenna, completed between 546 and 548, imitated the plan of Hagia Sophia closely. As the imperial capital in the West, of course, San Vitale stood within the court circle, and Justinian and Theodora attended the dedication. Elsewhere the style was more sober and less daring, based on older architectural principles.

Culture

Christian culture declined in both the East and the West during the fifth and sixth centuries but for quite different reasons. In the East, theological disputes consumed the energies of the best scholars and, in time, created a climate of intimidation in which they feared to express themselves. In the sixth century, Emperor Justinian was the boldest theologian as well as the fashioner of a political and cultural renaissance, for he was one of few who did not have to fear his own censure. In the West, the barbarian invasions took their toll. It is possible, nevertheless, to cite some outstanding examples of continuing cultural vitality in some ways stronger than in the East.

The "Golden Age" of Greek Christian literature came to an end during the first half of the fifth century. Besides the copious polemical literature written in the heat of combat over christology by advocates of Monophysite and dyophysite traditions, the Antiochenes produced some outstanding exegetical works—John Chrysostom's (347–407) homilies and Theodore of Mopsuestia's (d. 428) commentaries being notable examples. Socrates Scholasticus (ca. 380–450), Sozomen (early fifth century), and Theodoret of Cyrus (ca. 393–ca. 466) extended the *Church History* of Eusebius, which ended in 323, into the early fifth century. The most creative literature, however, came from the pens of ascetics, such as Hesychius of Jerusalem (d. after 450), Nilus of Ancyra (d. ca. 430), Diadochus of Photice in Epirus (mid-fifth century), and Pseudo-Dionysius (ca. 500). The last, as noted earlier in discussion of the liturgy, exerted massive influence on Christian spirituality of both East and West in subsequent centuries. Although early use by Monophysites aroused some opposition to the writings, acceptance by Leontius of Byzantium in the first half of the sixth century, Gregory the Great, Sophronius of Jerusalem (d. 638), and Maximus the Confessor (d. 662) banished fear of them.

Justinian also encouraged literary arts. The most noted writer was the historian Procopius, author of a *History*, a treatise on *Buildings*, and *Anecdota*, which satirized Justinian, Theodora, and practically all other persons of importance in Constantinople. Leontius of Byzantium ranked high as champion of Chalcedonian orthodoxy against Nestorianism and Eutychianism (ca. 543–544). John of Ephesus (ca. 507–586) represented the Monophysite cause in his *Ecclesiastical History* and *Lives of Eastern Saints*. Evagrius Scholasticus (ca. 536–600), a lawyer by profession, preserved valuable sources in his *Ecclesiastical History*, covering the period from the Council of Ephesus in 431 to 593.

Better indexes of the renaissance that occurred under Justinian were his contributions to art and law. After the Nike revolt destroyed the public buildings in Constantinople, Justinian rebuilt the city on a more lavish scale than Constantine had originally planned. He sought to make works of art not only of churches but also of palaces, the senate, monasteries, public baths, theaters, the aqueduct, and even fortifications. Outside the capital, he had erected at the foot of the traditional site of Mount Sinai the famous monastery later devoted to St. Catherine, and he scattered mosaics all across the Roman world, the most notable being in Ravenna. Unfortunately, Justinian's extravagances in war and in building nearly bankrupted the imperial treasury.

Justinian's famous *Codex*, issued first in 529 and reissued in 534, compiled, harmonized, and christianized the laws of the Roman Empire. In his legislation, Justinian sought to achieve what he attempted to do everywhere: to make the whole conform to the ideals of a Christian commonwealth. Accordingly, the Code began with a confession of faith and anathemas against heretics. Other legislation tried to humanize, for example, by improving the lot of slaves—although it did not prohibit slavery.

After Justinian's death in 565, the external security of the empire deteriorated rapidly. The barbarians grew bolder. Meantime, pressure from Turkish tribes caused the Slavs to seek settlements within the empire. First settling on the north coast of the Black Sea and possibly to the south of the Danube by 300, they stood ready in the sixth century to move into the Balkans. In 562, the Avars launched their first attack on the empire. Thereafter, Slav and Avar raids occurred frequently, almost exterminating the old population north of the Balkans. Meantime, a more dangerous and damaging threat rose in the East. In 608, the Persians conquered Syria and Palestine and ravaged Armenia, Cappadocia, and Galatia. In 619, they captured Egypt. Imperial policy framed by Justinian had so offended Syrians and Egyptians that they either offered no resistance or else aided the Persians. Heraclius recovered Syria and Egypt, but at tremendous cost. He had to obtain a loan from the church to finance his Persian expedition. Meanwhile, he failed to see the Islamic threat on the horizon, which would soon sweep away all the Eastern and North African lands still held by the empire. Had it not been for its sea power, the Byzantine Empire might have disintegrated all at once.

Although the West experienced this radical disruption far sooner, it would be erroneous to posit a complete break with the Latin past and a total disintegration of culture. The Germanic invasions dealt a devastating blow to culture and learning on the edges of the empire, but even there they survived, thanks especially to the monasteries and the churches. Monks copied and illuminated precious manuscripts. Monasteries built up libraries to preserve the treasures of the past, both classical and Christian. Monastic schools perpetuated the tradition of learning. At the beginning of the sixth century, cathedral or episcopal schools appeared. Caesarius of Arles conducted one in Provence during his episcopate (503–542). In 527, a Spanish council at Toledo set out careful plans for episcopal schools, and the institution spread thereafter. Steady barbarization led the second Council of Vaison in 529, the year Justinian closed the school at Athens, to direct the churches to give Christian education to young children admitted as readers. This type of school spread rapidly because of pressing need.

Quite clearly, there was a downward spiral in the West from the early fifth until the renaissance of learning in the eighth century. In the first half of the fifth century, the West boasted some of its most illustrious names. Jerome (ca. 342–420) had no peer even in the East in biblical scholarship. Augustine (354–430), though not apt at biblical languages, excelled as a theologian. Through his *Conferences* and *Institutes,* John Cassian (ca. 360–435) made a contribution to Western monasticism, exceeded only by Benedict of Nursia's *Rule.* In one area, poetry, the West surpassed the Greek East, which produced no important poet other than Gregory Nazianzus, although the Syrian Church excelled also in poetry. Latin poetry flowered in the fourth century with the Spanish priest Juvencus (ca. 330), the noble Roman woman Proba (ca. 360), and the nominal convert to Christianity Ausonius (ca. 310–ca. 395), teacher of Paulinus of Nola (353/4–431). Paulinus composed thirty-five poems, but they lacked creative power. Greatest of the Latin Christian poets was Prudentius (348–ca. 410), a lawyer who had a distinguished career in civil administration.

From the late fifth century on, Westerners had to struggle to conserve the remains of their classical heritage as the invasions took their toll. Yet even here, in Italy and Gaul, both classical and Christian traditions survived throughout the sixth century. In Italy, Boethius (ca. 480–ca. 574), the son of a Roman consul, became a friend and adviser of Theodoric, the Ostrogothic chief, and, in 510, himself a consul. He planned to translate all of Plato and Aristotle into Latin, but his premature death prevented realization of that task. He wrote commentaries on several of Aristotle's works and on Victorinus Afer's translation of Porphyry's *Isagoge.* Boethius composed original works on arithmetic, geometry, and music for the quadrivium. Extended debate on his relationship to Christianity has recently settled in the affirmative with the authentication of a treatise he composed *On the Holy Trinity*. He penned his most famous work, *The Consolation of Philosophy*, during his imprisonment, awaiting execution for treason, a charge incurred during his defense of an ex-consul named Albinus on the same charge. *The Consolation* became very popular in the Middle Ages; King Alfred translated it into Old English, and Chaucer into Middle English.

Cassiodorous (ca. 485–ca. 580) was, like Boethius, a member of a noble Roman family. He held several high civil offices—quaestor (507), consul (514), chief of civil service (526), and praetorian prefect (533). In 540 he founded two monasteries under the Rule of Benedict at Vivarium and retired there. His writings included *The Institutions of Divine and Secular Letters,* in which he urged a union of sacred and profane studies in Christian education, and the *Historia Ecclesiastica Tripartita*, which combined the histories of Socrates, Sozomen, and Theodoret. The latter served as the chief textbook of church history in the West during the Middle Ages.

Rome's worst days probably came when Justinian re-established Roman rule over Italy. The Ostrogoths resisted the Byzantine advance fiercely for twenty years (535–555). When King Totila realized he could no longer hold Rome, he deported the entire population to Campania. For forty days the city remained desolate. The Lombard invasion followed in 568 close on the heels of this devastating experience. Yet, although the Lombards threatened, they did not take Rome itself, and it seemed somehow to come back from the dead each time. Its vitality in this arduous time can be seen in the life and work of Gregory the Great. Gregory could not match Boethius or Cassiodorus in scholarship. By his own confession, he knew no Greek, which is perplexing by virtue of his years in Constantinople. He also lacked their knowledge and appreciation of classical culture. Where he excelled was in personal piety and practical wisdom. As a popularizer and transmitter of Augustine, he laid the foundations of medieval Western theology. Although he understood his mentor imperfectly, he handed on his central teachings in a lucid style that people of limited education could grasp. More important, he set a noble standard for his office as *servus servorum Dei* ("servant of the servants of God") and stabilized the church in one of its most trying eras.

In Gaul as in Italy, the classical tradition was decreasing as the Bible, the Fathers (especially Augustine), and hagiography were increasing. One would err to conclude from this, however, that learning ceased and culture vanished. As noted earlier, great monasteries like those at Lérins and Marseilles were turning out a succession of outstanding leaders of high intelligence, good family background, and substantial education who were creating a new cultural synthesis. Gregory of Tours and Venantius Fortunatus reflect in their writings how at the end of the sixth century the shift was taking place.

Gregory (ca. 540–594) belonged to a Gallo-Roman senatorial family that produced several bishops. Elected Bishop of Tours in 573, he, like others of the same era, preached and wrote, above all, to encourage faith. In that pursuit it is not surprising to find a mixing of fact and fantasy. In his chief hagiographical work, *Eight Books of Miracles,* he displayed extreme credulity and said little of real historical value. In his *History of the Franks,* which he began in 576, by contrast, he depicted accurately the parts of the story on which he had firsthand information. As earlier chroniclers had done, he began with a confession of faith and sketched history from creation to 397. In Books II–IV he related Frankish history to 575, based on well-selected sources. In the main part of the work, Books V–IX, he narrated events as they happened between 575 and 591. Without his account, historians could scarcely reconstruct the history of the period.

Venantius Fortunatus (ca. 530–ca. 610) was not a native of Gaul but of Treviso (near Venice) in Italy. Educated at Ravenna, where Eastern influence still lingered, about 565 he undertook a pilgrimage to the shrine of Martin of Tours in appreciation for the cure of an eye ailment. Flattering poetry won him a good reception at the court of Sigebert of Austrasia at Metz, where he stayed until 567. As the Lombards overran northern Italy, he decided to stay at Poitiers. There he became acquainted with Radegunde, the former queen who had by then become a nun, and Agnes, abbess of the monastery. Meantime, he befriended Gregory of Tours, who encouraged him to publish his poetry. In the late sixth century, Venantius was elected Bishop of Poitiers. Educated in classical form and style, he is remembered chiefly for his long metrical life of Martin of Tours, but he also composed prose lives of Hilary of Poitiers, Germanus of Paris, Radegunde, and other notables. Some have characterized him as "the first of the medieval poets."

Especially noteworthy in this period of transition was the substitution of hagiography for history. In the circumstances, it is not hard to understand why this happened. The first concern had to be to give people overwhelmed by tragedy some sign of hope. Biblical miracles lived again in the saints, bishops, monks, and, here and there, rulers who sometimes did something extraordinary. The church produced retellings of saints' lives that could offer examples not so much of what had been as of what ought to be. Local holy persons set a living example of a pattern called for by the Bible.

Christianity has often been criticized for what happened here, and some criticism is doubtless deserved. In reaching for some straw of hope, Westerners simply papered over reality by restoring hagiography, which often must have misled those it was designed to help. Admitting that point, however, one must recognize that the churches were the only Western institutions stable enough to do anything in a time of severe crisis. They may have undertaken too much when they tried to fill the enormous void created by the Germanic invasions. The maintenance of civilization was a subordinate part of the church's task of spreading the gospel, converting, and christianizing. It took time for enough of the latter task to be achieved that the churches could contribute more to the broader aspects of society.

CHAPTER TWENTY-EIGHT

IMPERIAL POWER AND RIGHT DOCTRINE

Imperial intrusion into ecclesiastical affairs routinized by Constantine and his successors proved increasingly costly in subsequent centuries. The more the emperors tried to effect unity by imperial mandate, the more they drove wedges between the churches and the peoples of the empire, and the wider they made the gap between East and West. The East developed an obsession for orthodoxy, as if the mystery of God might somehow be encompassed in a neat formula. The monks were especially inflexible. "God is an exacting Judge who demands adherence to the appropriate formulas. Anathema on those who don't agree!" In consequence, bitter wrangling shattered the empire itself, with the Egyptians heading in one direction, the Syrians in another, and the Greeks in yet another.

John Chrysostom

Nothing illustrates better the costliness of misguided imperial politics than John Chrysostom's battles with the Empress Eudoxia during his brief tenure as Bishop of Constantinople (398–407). Elected to the office over his own protest, he immediately undertook the daunting task of reforming the court, the clergy, and the people of Constantinople, a task his easygoing predecessor Nectarius (381–397) had left untouched. Zealous that Christianity present an attractive front to a still unconverted society, Chrysostom rebuked pride in wealth, wanton luxury, profligate spending, pagan customs at weddings and funerals, superstitious reliance on amulets and magic charms, lack of seriousness about baptism, and numerous other popular vices. The empress, unfortunately for their relationship as pastor and parishioner, interpreted much of his preaching as a personal affront. His clergy, too, whose level of commitment had sagged badly under Nectarius, resented his efforts to upgrade their performance by deposing two deacons and refusing communion to other clergy as well as preaching reform. As he proceeded to take active measures to reform churches under his patriarchate, he ruffled other feathers. Three bishops in the latter group finally found a leader in Theophilus of Alexandria (385–412), who had consecrated Chrysostom to the see of Constantinople but who had himself coveted the office. The club Theophilus used to strike was Chrysostom's support of Origen and protection he offered Origenists.

In 401, three of the "Tall Brothers," Origenist monks from Egypt, and about fifty other Origenists sought refuge in Constantinople. Chrysostom received them with caution, writing to Theophilus to check their standing. In 403, however, Epiphanius, Bishop of Salamis and bitter anti-Origenist, appeared in the capital and refused to commune with Chrysostom unless he condemned Origen and expelled the Tall Brothers. Chrysostom replied that he would leave the matter to a synod already scheduled. Epiphanius abruptly left Constantinople on May 16 and died en route home. A month later, Theophilus, knowing he had Eudoxia's support and that of many other clergy, arrived with an Egyptian entourage determined to depose John. The synod of thirty-six bishops assembled at the Oak, a suburb of Chalcedon, in July 403 and, after hearing twenty-nine charges against Chrysostom, deposed him. In a letter to the emperor the bishops urged his banishment for treason in calling the empress a Jezebel. His exile, however, lasted only a few days, for the people of Constantinople mobbed the imperial palace and demanded his recall. As he returned, they hoisted him triumphantly on their shoulders, carried him back to his episcopal throne, and would not leave until he had preached a sermon *ex tempore.* A rival council composed of sixty bishops gathered later to annul the proceedings of the Synod of the Oak. Patriarch and empress lavished compliments on each other.

The reconciliation, however, did not last long. Within two months, another occasion arose for the great preacher to offend his powerful parishioner. When licentious dancing accompanied the erection of a silver statue in honor of Eudoxia, he could not refrain from criticism that quickly reached the empress's ears. His old enemies proceeded to convoke another synod at the end of 403. This synod dragged on for some time until Chrysostom's opponents persuaded the emperor to prevent him from celebrating the Easter rites on April 16, 404, on the grounds that he had unlawfully returned to his see. As he prepared to baptize about 3,000 candidates, troops attacked the congregation, arrested him, and confined him to his palace. This time, even the outcry of the people failed to prevent his exile first at Nicaea and then at Cucusus in Lesser Armenian, where he died on September 14, 407. In his place, Emperor Arcadius appointed first Arsacius (404–405) and then Atticus (406–426), the two who had taken the lead in plotting against Chrysostom. In his exile, he received comfort from a noble matron and deaconess named Olympias, with whom he shared a special friendship during the time he resided in Constantinople. Olympias did not allow imperial threat of confiscation of her property to interfere with her faithfulness to a friend.

Nestorianism

The liability of imperial intrusion is visible also in the continuing competition between the sees of Alexandria and Antioch and their christologies. Both the *Logos-sarx* christology of Alexandria and the *Logos-anthropos* christology of Antioch had valid points to make, the former doing christology from above (emphasizing divinity) and the latter from below (emphasizing humanity). Imperial anxiety to force a common formula on all, however, created a rigidity that denied the validity of alternate views and encouraged constant criticism and one-upsmanship, a tendency clearly illustrated by the christological controversies of the fifth and sixth centuries.

The condemnation of both Arius and Apollinarius in the first two ecumenical councils had exposed the weakness of Alexandrian *Logos-sarx* christology, its inclination toward effacement of the human nature by the divine. Although Apollinarius meant to correct Arius's subordination of the Logos-Son to the Father in his essential nature, he fell into the same trap as Arius when it came to the human nature, for both attributed Christ's sinlessness to the Logos's replacement of the human mind. Christ could not have sinned—that is, disobeyed God—as we do, because he did not have a human mind, the source of such disobedience. It was precisely the devaluing of the human that most concerned the Antiochenes and their *Logos-anthropos* christology, surfacing especially when Nestorius, himself a heresy hunter, became Patriarch of Constantinople in 427.

Behind Nestorius stood Diodore, head of the so-called school of Antioch and Bishop of Tarsus from 378 to 394, and Theodore, Bishop of Mopsuestia in Cilicia (392–428). Diodore was both anti-Arian and anti-Apollinarian. Concerned to preserve Christ's complete human nature, he emphasized strongly the distinctiveness of divine and human. The Logos should not be thought of as Son of Mary. Rather, the Logos, born of the Father, made a temple for himself of the man born of Mary. Although Diodore verbally maintained the unity of the person of Christ, he came fearfully close to the separation of persons charged, probably unfairly, to Nestorius. The Son of God only *indwelt* the son of David. Although a far more astute and discerning theologian, Theodore leaned in the same direction. A friend and fellow student of Chrysostom, he shared the Antiochene concern to safeguard the human nature. In Jesus, God dwells "as a Son," which means that the human and divine natures remain distinct but are united in will and operation so as to remain indissoluble. In correcting Apollinarius, Theodore too came near to propounding a doctrine of two persons. His analogy for the union of natures was the biblical image of the conjugal union of husband and wife, two persons united as "one flesh." In his scheme, Mary could be called *Theotokos*, "Mother of God," only insofar as she was the mother of the man assumed by God.

The deficiency of Antiochene christology came out clearly in the theology of Nestorius. The first to deny publicly that Mary was *Theotokos* was not Nestorius but his domestic chaplain, Anastasius, whom Nestorius brought with him from Antioch. In a sermon preached in the capital on November 22, 428, Anastasius argued that, since Mary is only human, she could not be Mother of God, for "it is impossible for God to be born of humankind" (Socrates *H.E.* 7.32.2). The sermon aroused such a storm that, on Christmas day, Nestorius launched a series of sermons in support of Anastasius. The imperial court stood by Nestorius, but monks, clergy, and most of the people either opposed him or stood by in silence as a lawyer named Eusebius, later Bishop of Dorylaeum (ca. 448–451), led the protest. When the archimandrite Basil brought a group of monks to the episcopal palace to remonstrate, Nestorius had them remanded to prison.

The opposition, however, increased. On Lady Day (March 24), 429, Proclus, Bishop of Cyzicus, delivered a panegyric "On the Virgin Mother of God" in which he contended that salvation required that God be born of a woman. Nestorius, who was present, asserted his right as the patriarch to reply. Although Proclus succeeded him as Archbishop of Constantinople, at this point a more formidable opponent appeared in the person of Cyril, Patriarch of Alexandria (412–444) and nephew of Theophilus, nemesis of John Chrysostom.

Anxious like his uncle to make the most of every opportunity to put Constantinople in its place, Cyril first responded to the sermons of Nestorius against the *Theotokos* in an encyclical: *To the Monks in Egypt,* written about Easter 429. For him it was a simple question as to whether Mary's Son was God or not. In June, Cyril wrote Nestorius his first letter, informing him that inquiries of Pope Caelestine and complaints of the churches forced him to seek Nestorius's correction. Early in 430, Cyril sent a second letter reinforcing his case against Nestorius. Nestorius replied to both, contending still that *Theotokos* was "pagan" and that it was better to call Mary *Christotokos.* He ended his second letter by noting that their imperial majesties were happy with what was being taught in the capital. Cyril, quick to pick up on the last point, proceeded to address a treatise to Theodosius II (408–450), *On Right Faith*; a second to his sisters Arcadia and Marina; and a third to Pulcheria and Eudocia, the elder sister and wife of Theodosius. On this he miscalculated, for the imperial household prided itself on its orthodoxy. However, Cyril gained help from another direction, Pope Caelestine (422–432).

Caelestine had written Cyril early in 429, immediately after receiving copies of Nestorius's Christmas sermons, which attacked the use of *Theotokos*, asking Cyril whether they really were Nestorius's. After he had received letters and a treatise from Nestorius, he had them translated into Latin and turned them over to Cassian (360–435) for a reply. Cassian responded with a treatise *On the Incarnation of the Lord Against the Nestorians* (430–431), contending that Pelagianism naturally leads to Nestorianism, that Mary must be called *Theotokos* rather than *Christotokos*, and that there must be an essential rather than a moral union. In April 430, in the meantime, Cyril replied to Caelestine's inquiries and sent further writings against Nestorius. He also tried to enlist other supporters in the East, but he found reactions mixed because John, the Patriarch of Antioch (428–441), did not wish to worsen the controversy involving his friend Nestorius, even though he agreed about *Theotokos*.

Councils in both Rome and Alexandria in 430 sought to secure the submission of Nestorius. After the Synod of Rome, Caelestine wrote seven letters. In one addressed to Cyril, he asked him to act as his proxy, but not, as sometimes thought, at the Third Ecumenical Council, plans for which had not yet formed. In a letter to Nestorius, he threatened separation from the college of bishops and excommunication if Nestorius did not conform to Cyril's teaching. In the other letters—to the clergy and people of Constantinople and to Eastern bishops—he warned of Nestorius's teaching. Nestorius, however, simply stiffened his resolution, confident of imperial backing.

In November 430, Cyril assembled the Synod of Alexandria to execute the commission of Caelestine. The synod demanded that Nestorius anathematize his "impious tenets." After reviewing the theological points in question, the bishops appended a list of *Twelve Anathemas* to which Nestorius was to assent. The Apollinarian cast of the latter enabled Nestorius to effect a breach between Cyril and John of Antioch. When the four bishops bearing the letter and anathematisms arrived in Constantinople on December 5, 430, they learned that the emperors Theodosius and Valentinian III had summoned a universal council to convene at Ephesus by Pentecost 431. The Emperor Theodosius intervened because the welfare of the empire, in his mind, was "bound up with the worship of God." He blamed Cyril for fomenting the troubles, but he was ready to forgive, he said, if Cyril would hurry to the council.

Both Nestorius and Cyril rallied their forces in anticipation of the council. Nestorius's main allies included John of Antioch; Andrew, Bishop of Samosata (431–434); and Theodoret, Bishop of Cyrus (423–458), one of the notable apologists of the Antiochene school and author of an *Ecclesiastical History* covering the period from Eusebius to the outbreak of the Nestorian controversy (323–428). Both Andrew and Theodoret composed critiques of

Cyril's *Anathemas.* Cyril countered Andrew in an *Apology Against the Orientals,* Theodoret in an *Apology Against Theodoret in Behalf of the Twelve Chapters,* and Nestorius in a treatise *Against the Blasphemies of Nestorius.* He also wrote Caelestine to ask whether the council should accept Nestorius's recantation, if offered. During the fortnight before the council opened (June 7-21, 431), Cyril busied himself with the strengthening of his support. Meanwhile, some of Nestorius's supporters tried, without success, to get him to concede.

Unfortunately for Nestorius and the conduct of the council, John of Antioch and the pro-Nestorian contingent did not arrive until after the council opened. Cyril refused to delay any longer, since he knew he had a clear majority in his favor. This decision proved costly, for it overrode the will of the imperial High Commissioner, Count Candidian, as well as Nestorius's supporters. The 198 assembled bishops presided over by Cyril, claiming to represent Pope Caelestine, quickly arrived at their decision—to depose and excommunicate Nestorius. On June 26, however, John and the Orientals arrived. Without taking time to change clothes, they convened a second council composed of forty-three bishops and, after hearing Candidian's report on what had transpired, deposed Cyril and his main supporter, Memnon, Bishop of Ephesus, and excommunicated all of their adherents unless they should repudiate the *Twelve Anathemas.*

Although the belated arrival of papal legates with instructions to support Cyril shifted support in the capital to his side momentarily, he did not have long to celebrate. Count Candidian and the Nestorians blocked the access of Cyrillians to the imperial court for a time. As now one and then the other party gained Theodosius's ear, the emperor finally decided to treat Cyril, Memnon, and Nestorius as alike deposed and sent a new commissioner, John, to the council. In August 431, the new commissioner arrived at the council with a letter from Theodosius, noting that he had accepted the deposition of the three prelates "as intimated to us by your piety." The commissioner placed Cyril and Nestorius and later Memnon under arrest.

The Council of Ephesus did not itself arrive at a doctrinal statement acceptable to those who attended. What is known as the *Formula of Reunion* originated, rather, with the Orientals and was largely the work of Theodoret of Cyprus. Although it affirmed the use of *Theotokos,* the statement favored the Antiochene rather than the Cyrillian position. Theodosius finally dissolved the council, sending Nestorius to a monastery in Antioch and Cyril back to Alexandria. He appointed an old friend of John Chrysostom, Maximian, patriarch in place of Nestorius (431–434). There remained still, however, the task of reconciling the two camps headed by John of Antioch and Cyril. Skillful negotiations on the part of John led in 433 to acceptance of the *Formula of Reunion* by Cyril with the proviso that Nesto-

315

rius would be sent into exile. This agreement rankled many. Theodore, for instance, refused to consent to Nestorius's deposition. Alexander, his metropolitan, would neither accept the latter nor communicate with Cyril. The hierarchy in Cilicia excommunicated Cyril and withdrew from communion with Antioch.

After four peaceful years in Antioch, Nestorius was banished to Petra and then to Egypt, where he finally died about June 451. When his writings were banned, his followers circulated those of Diodore of Tarsus and Theodore of Mopsuestia, translated into Syriac, Armenian, and Persian. Harsh imperial action against the Nestorian school in Edessa forced the exile of most Nestorians to Persia.

Eutychianism

The imperial solution to the christological controversy that swirled around Nestorius did not pacify supporters of Cyril either, exile of Nestorius notwithstanding. Cyril himself had to make far too many concessions to Antiochene thinking to put at ease the anxieties of his followers who still clung to the formula "one incarnate nature of God the Logos." In their minds the *Formula of Reunion* of 433 was dyophysite—that is, it emphasized two natures in the incarnate Christ. They could say that there were two natures *before* the union, but they insisted that there was only one *after* it. At Alexandria, the Monophysites were led by the ambitious Dioscurus, Cyril's successor (444–451); at Constantinople by Eutyches, for thirty years archimandrite of a large monastery near Constantinople, and his godson Chrysaphius, minister of Theodosius. The influence of the eunuch Chrysaphius along with Theodosius from 441 until the latter's death as a result of a fall from a horse on July 28, 450, assured for a time the triumph of Eutyches.

Leading the opposition to Eutychianism was Theodoret of Cyprus. In a work written in 446–447, *The Beggar or Polymorph,* Theodoret described the Eutychian theology as a collection of old Gnostic rags and argued (1) the unchangeable character of the Lord's divinity, (2) the nonmixture of divinity and humanity, and (3) the impassibility of his divinity. The Eutychians soon responded with a counterblast against Irenaeus, Bishop of Tyre and friend of Nestorius; against Ibas, Bishop of Edessa (435–457), who had interpreted Cyril's acceptance of the *Formula* as a retraction and blasted his own bishop, Rabbula, as a tyrant and turncoat; and against Theodoret. Through connections at court, the Eutychians secured the deposition of Irenaeus and consecration of Photius in his place as Bishop of Tyre (448–451); the deposition and banishment of Ibas with imprisonment in as many as twenty different places; and the confinement of Theodoret to his own diocese—all by imperial decree.

The tide began to turn against Eutyches soon thereafter, however. In November 448, he was hailed before Flavian, Archbishop of Constantinople, at a synod on charges brought by Eusebius, Bishop of Dorylaeum (448–451) and the leader of the opposition to Nestorius twenty years earlier. Eusebius had tried to divert his friend Eutyches from the path of error but had failed. At first Eutyches declined to attend the synod but sent a letter in which he confessed his belief in "one nature" of God incarnate and argued that a doctrine of "two natures in one Person" could not be found in the Fathers and, even if it could, he would not believe it. When he did finally attend, he refused to admit two natures in the incarnate Lord. The synod proceeded to condemn him not only for Apollinarianism but also for Valentinianism. He then appealed to the synods of Rome, Alexandria, Jerusalem, and Thessalonica.

Although Eutyches did not delay in appealing to Rome, Flavian did. In the meantime, Eutyches used his court connections to advantage, and on March 30, 449, Theodosius summoned a council to meet at Ephesus on August 1, which has gone down in history as the "Robbers' Synod." Pope Leo was a bit late in issuing his *Tome* to head off a council that he considered unnecessary, and the *Tome* and his legates received a very rough and impolite treatment at the council.

As a prelude to the council, the Emperor Theodosius ordered Flavian to produce a written statement of his faith. Flavian complied willingly, affirming his agreement with Nicaea, Constantinople, and Ephesus and acknowledging belief in "two natures in one person" after the incarnation. Meantime, Chrysaphius and Eutyches invited Dioscurus to attack Flavian. Chrysaphius also made sure the council would consist of as few opponents of Eutyches as possible. Theodosius himself assured Dioscurus that Theodoret would not attend. He summoned Pope Leo I, who sent three legates bearing the *Tome,* which favored the dyophysite views of the *Formula of Reunion* and Flavian.

Meeting in the same church the earlier Council of Ephesus had met in under the presidency of Dioscurus, the "Robbers' Synod" proceeded in predictable fashion. Dioscurus relegated forty-two prelates who had taken part in the condemnation of Eutyches to the status of spectators. He refused to allow the papal legates to read Leo's *Tome.* When the council heard the minutes of the council, which the condemned Eutyches read, they cried out for the burning of Eusebius of Dorylaeum, his accuser, and acclaimed Eutyches' confession of one nature in the incarnation. They reaffirmed Eutyches' orthodoxy and restored him to his office as presbyter and archimandrite. They then proceeded to depose Flavian and Domnus, Archbishop of Antioch. Troops rushed to force signatures against Flavian and to arrest Flavian and Eusebius. Flavian later died as a result of kicks and blows he received from some of the monks. The bishops then reinforced imperial decisions against Irenaeus, Ibas, and Theodoret and ratified Cyril's *Twelve Anathemas.*

Reaction against the proceedings set in immediately. Theodoret, Flavian, and Eusebius of Dorylaeum all appealed to Rome. Receiving these appeals at a synod in Rome celebrating the anniversary of his consecration, September 29, 449, Leo wrote seven letters of protest against the "Robbers' Synod," urging Easterners to "stand fast" against this injustice. He persuaded the Western Emperor Valentinian III; his mother, Galla Placidia; and his wife, Eudoxia, to intercede with Theodosius. Theodosius, however, ignored all entreaties, and the situation did not change until he died on July 28, 450. His sister Pulcheria (450–453) and her husband, Marcian, turned the tide against the Monophysites.

Chalcedon

Pulcheria's first act was to have the eunuch Chrysaphius, who had exerted such strong influence over her brother, put to death, thus depriving the Eutychians of their chief secular support. She then wed Marcian, a senator and soldier held in high esteem and as committed to the dyophysite position as she was. Together the monarchs proceeded to reverse the effects of the Synod of Ephesus in 449, bringing Flavian's body back to Constantinople, recalling Theodoret and other exiles and restoring relations with Rome. Before responding to letters from Leo, placing blame for the situation on Dioscurus and other bishops who aided him and suggesting how the issue could now be dealt with, the regents issued a summons to the bishops on May 17, 451, to meet in an ecumenical council at Nicaea on September 1. Although Leo still did not favor a council, he appointed two legates on June 24 and supplied them with a copy of his *Tome* and other instructions. He also sent letters addressed to the Emperor Marcian, the Patriarch Anatolius, Julian of Cos, and the council. Leo's main concern was the restoration of those deposed for faithful adherence to the Catholic faith as set forth in his *Tome.*

Although the emperor originally designated Nicaea, he had to shift the site closer to the capital, the suburb of Chalcedon, for fear of the Huns in Illyrica. When many of the 520 bishops, all Easterners except the two papal legates and two Africans, hesitated lest the monks of the capital disrupt their proceedings, Marcian issued a decree forbidding disturbances. The Empress Pulcheria added to this a letter expelling all monks, clergy, or laypersons in the vicinity except those present by imperial orders or to aid their bishops. Thus secured, the council opened at Chalcedon on October

8 and lasted until November 1. Imperial Commissioners headed by the Patriarch Anatolius took charge in the absence of "the believing Emperors" who "presided for the sake of order."

As the council opened, supporters of Dioscurus, Juvenal of Jerusalem, and Anastasius of Thessalonica—bishops of Egypt, Palestine, and Illyricum—lined up on one side and supporters of Leo on the other, to the left and right of the nineteen imperial commissioners. The commissioners ordered Dioscurus to defend himself and directed that Theodoret, excluded from the "Robbers' Synod," be invited in. The appearance of Theodoret as the accuser along with Eusebius of Dorylaeum set off a round of cheers from backers of Leo and a chorus of boos from backers of Dioscurus. The commissioners had to take a firm hand to silence the raucous assembly. When secretaries reviewed the proceedings of the "Robbers' Synod"—how it had forbidden the reading of Leo's *Tome*, rehabilitated Eutyches, and condemned Flavian—many bishops present at that meeting hastened to offer excuses and apologies for their part in it. Review of the minutes of Flavian's Council of Constantinople and his declaration of faith brought forth a general exclamation that he had "rightly explained the faith." At this point Juvenal, the Patriarch of Jerusalem, and all of the bishops of Palestine crossed over to the Leonine side. Next followed the bishops of Illyricum, except for Atticus, Bishop of Nicopolis (446–451) and Metropolitan of Epirus Vetus, who claimed illness and left the hall, and even four Egyptian bishops. Dioscurus remained almost alone save for the rest of the Egyptians. Before concluding the first day's session, the bishops attributed the evils of Ephesus in 449 to Dioscurus, Juvenal, Thalassius, Eusebius of Ancyra, Eustathius of Berytus, and Basil of Seleucia and declared them deposed.

Two days later, at the second session, without Dioscurus and the deposed bishops present, the bishops set about the task of framing a satisfactory doctrinal statement. In turn, they reviewed the creeds of Nicaea and Constantinople, Cyril's second letter to Nestorius and his letter to John of Antioch, the *Tome*, and some extracts Leo had collected from Hilary of Poitiers, Gregory of Nazianzus, Ambrose, Chrysostom, Augustine, and Cyril. The *Tome* forcefully argued against Eutyches the doctrine of two natures without confusion in one person. The majority of the assembly simply ignored the *Twelve Anathemas* of Cyril and acclaimed the *Tome*, saying, "Peter has spoken through Leo." Some, however, found three passages in the *Tome* sounding a bit too Nestorian. At the request of Atticus of Nicopolis, who had now returned, the commissioners granted a five-day recess to allow a committee headed by Anatolius to examine the *Tome* and prepare a response to the doubters.

After reaffirming the deposition of Dioscurus in a session he refused to attend, in its fourth session the council reiterated its acceptance of Nicaea, Constantinople, Ephesus (431–433), and Leo's *Tome* as "in harmony with

319

the Creed." The imperial government, however, pressed for a precise doctrinal formula acceptable to all. A statement drawn up by the committee headed by Anatolius sounded acceptable to some but not to others. When the commissioners inquired of the emperors how to break the deadlock, they were instructed (1) to put the committee back to work, or (2) to let each bishop, one by one, express his belief through his metropolitan, or (3) to hold a synod in the West. Since the last two options were unthinkable, the bishops declared their determination to come up with a definition. The committee, therefore, went to work once more and came out with the formula of Chalcedon. The critical clause affirmed *Theotokos* while rejecting both Eutychianism and Nestorianism.

Although the language was Cyrillian, the substance was basically Antiochene and Leonine. Discerning observers could easily foresee disaster looming on the horizon.

In the first place, the emperors pressed for a more precise formula than the six hundred plus signers could subscribe to in good conscience. Just as Constantine had done at Nicaea, moreover, they forced acceptance of a Western formula when, in fact, nearly all of the signers were Easterners. The majority doubtless favored Cyril's and not Theodoret's or Leo's definition. The only happy subscribers, therefore, were either the adherents of the imperial court or Nestorians, who hailed the definition as a vindication of their exiled leader. Armenians, Syrians, and Egyptians, never comfortably a part of the empire anyway, returned home convinced Monophysites. As if this were not enough by itself, Marcian laid a heavy hand on the churches by proposing three canons designed to limit the growing assertiveness of the monks, the increasing secularity of clergy and monks, and clerical migration and by insisting on elevation of the status of the patriarchate of Constantinople to a jurisdictional level equal to that of Rome in the West. The latter proved extremely offensive to the papacy, but the assembled bishops chose not to pay serious attention to the protests of the papal legates. Leo did his best to have the canon overturned, but he finally had to approve the council's decision regarding faith without withdrawing his protest about Canon 28. The Emperor Marcian himself had his hands full defending the theological formula. On February 7, 452, he issued a decree making it illegal for "cleric or soldier or person of any condition" to raise disputes in religious matters. Few, however, paid any attention to that or several other decrees designed to quiet the opposition to Chalcedon.

Monophysitism

The Cyrillians soon displayed their numbers and strength in Palestine, Egypt, and Syria. Dropping Eutyches' doctrine, which suggested absorption of the human nature by the divine in the incarnation, the Monophysites now proposed, in line with Cyril, a coalescence of divine and human natures in a single theanthropic ("divine/human") nature. They saw in Leo's resistance to Canon 28 of Chalcedon a glimmer of hope that he, too, might reject the council's decisions, but that hope proved false.

In Palestine, a former monk named Theodosius stirred up the large body of monks there against the Council of Chalcedon as having rehabilitated Nestorius and defamed Cyril by deposing his successor, Dioscurus. Theodosius did not find it difficult to rally the support of such illustrious pilgrims as the Empress Eudocia, widow of Theodosius II, whose definitive council was the so-called Robbers' Synod of Ephesus in 449. When Juvenal of Jerusalem returned to his see, he found the gates of the city closed to him and had to flee to Constantinople as Theodosius proceeded to place Monophysites in the bishoprics of Palestine. The emperors first wrote to the monks to defend Chalcedon and then took action to arrest Theodosius, who fled to Mount Sinai, and to restore Juvenal. Leo also sought further information and wrote to the monks to explain the *Tome* and to Empress Eudocia to point out that Chalcedon opposed both Nestorianism and Eutychianism. Tragedies in her family evidently encouraged the empress to return to the Catholic fold. The capture of Theodosius by imperial police and his death in a monastery in Constantinople in 457 put an end to the Monophysite rebellion in Palestine.

In Egypt, the Monophysites mounted a more determined and permanent challenge. Although the Alexandrian populace regarded Dioscurus as their patriarch until he died on in September 4, 454, the Prefect of Egypt proceeded to install Proterius immediately after the Council of Chalcedon on orders from the Emperor Marcian. Mob riots broke out against Byzantine imperialism and had to be suppressed by troops dispatched from Constantinople. On the death of Marcian and election of Leo I (457–474) as his successor in 457, Timothy Aelurus ("the Cat") seized on the occasion of the absence of the general in command to take control of the patriarchate. When Proterius secured a measure of revenge by having the general remove Timothy, his partisans hunted him down, murdered him in the church baptistery and dragged his remains around the city and burned them, reputedly after cannibalizing them. They then appealed to Emperor Leo to overturn Chalcedon. Prompted by Pope Leo I, who declared the proposal to be a work of the Antichrist, the emperor exiled Timothy "the Cat" to Gangra and ultimately to the Crimea, where he remained until after the emperor's death. The Chalcedonians elected another Timothy, Salofaciolus ("the Little Capmaker"), to replace him (459–482). Pope Leo wrote his last three extant letters to the Patriarch Timothy Salofaciolus.

Timothy Aelurus, however, was not finished. After the accession of Leo (474–491), the usurper Basiliscus (475–477) bid for the support of the

Monophysites of Egypt by recalling Timothy from the Crimea after eighteen years of exile (458–476). In a decree called the *Encyclical*, he sanctioned the two councils of Ephesus (431–433 and 449) and denounced both the errors of Eutyches and the "novelties" of Chalcedon. He required all bishops to sign, making deposition the penalty for refusal. Timothy got a cold shoulder from the Patriarch Acacius in Constantinople, but he repaid him by summoning a synod at Ephesus to reinstate Paul, a bishop whom Acacius had deposed. He had no trouble returning to Alexandria carrying the remains of Dioscurus in a silver casket. Timothy Salofaciolus retired to a Pachomian monastery.

In Syria, Monophysitism also had a strong supporter in Maximus, an ardent Cyrillian. To the faithful throughout Syria, Monophysitism alone could guarantee the divinity of Christ. The leader of the Monophysite forces was Peter the Fuller, who had once belonged to the community of Acoemetae, ardent Chalcedonians, but had split with them and become head of a monastery at Chalcedon. In 468 he accompanied Zeno to Antioch, where he served as commander-in-chief of "the East." There he led the Monophysites in driving out Martyrius, Patriarch of Antioch (460–470), and succeeded in having himself installed as Martyrius's successor. Martyrius appealed to Gennadius, Patriarch of Constantinople (460–471), and secured Peter's exile. Basiliscus restored him to the throne of Antioch (475–476), but Zeno banished him once more when he regained control of the empire in 477. Monophysites murdered the Chalcedonian Stephen (478–482). Acacius installed Calandion as a compromise candidate (482–485), but Peter the Fuller ascended the throne a third time (485–488).

The Monophysites reached the pinnacle of their power under Basiliscus, who obtained the signatures of three of the four Eastern patriarchs—Alexandria, Antioch, and Jerusalem—to his *Encyclical*. Only Acacius of Constantinople held out, drawing support from the monks of the capital, especially the Stylite Daniel, who descended from his pillar to rouse the populace in support of Chalcedon and to predict the return of Zeno. The prediction so overawed Basilicus that he issued an *Anti-Encyclical* negating the *Encyclical*, but the move did not save him. Zeno reentered Constantinople in July 477 and restored the status quo as it had existed before Basiliscus. Receiving congratulations from Pope Simplicius (468–483), the emperor and the patriarch quickly proceeded to remove Timothy Aelurus, Paul of Ephesus, Peter the Fuller, and his protégé John of Apamea. In Egypt, however, the removal of Timothy did not end the schism, for Monophysites replaced him with one of their own, Peter Mongus ("the Stammerer" 477–490), despite the fact that the Catholic Patriarch Timothy Salofaciolus was still living. Zeno sent orders to the Prefect of Egypt to put Peter Mongus to death, but Timothy interceded to have the sentence commuted to exile. Timothy ruled five years (477–482). By virtue of a political *faux pas* on the part of John

Talaia, Timothy's elected successor, however, that offended the Patriarch Acacius, Peter Mongus returned to the throne. Zeno sent instructions to banish John Talaia. He also addressed to the bishops of Egypt the *Henoticon*, which he intended to resolve the controversy by shifting imperial favor to the Monophysites.

Shifting Balances

The objective of Emperor Zeno's issuing the *Henoticon* is quite clear: Hopes for recovery of the West being extremely dim after Odovacer returned the symbols of the office in 476, Zeno needed to concentrate on uniting the populace in the East, most of whom favored Monophysitism. Deliberately sidestepping the issue of Chalcedon's legitimacy, the *Henoticon* focused on the Creed of Nicaea, reaffirmed at Constantinople and at Ephesus by those who opposed Nestorius, as an adequate basis for union. It denounced Eutyches, approved Cyril's *Twelve Anathemas,* and, summarizing the faith in an unexceptionable way, anathematized all who believed anything to the contrary. Zeno's successor, Anastasius (491–518), pursued the same policy in hopes of conciliating Syria and Egypt. In 496 he secured confirmation of the *Henoticon* at a Council of Constantinople. He removed Euphemius from the patriarchate of Constantinople and installed Macedonius II (496–511), who, though Chalcedonian, did not quibble about the *Henoticon* for a time; when he did, Anastasius replaced him with Timothy, a Monophysite.

No real change of policy occurred under Justin (518–527) and his able nephew Justinian (527–565). The *Henoticon,* although not formally revoked, was allowed quietly to disappear. Immediately after Justin's accession on July 15, 518, the populace of Constantinople cried out for confirmation of Chalcedon, expulsion of the Monophysite Severus from the patriarchate of Antioch, and reconciliation with Rome, but they could not force a major shift. Justinian made only a token turn toward Chalcedon, for he needed still to unite the empire. The Empress Theodora, moreover, favored Monophysitism.

Justinian, an astute lay theologian, took a keen interest in theological matters. Three controversies gave him an opportunity to shape the doctrine of the churches—Theopaschitism, 519–533; Origenism, 531–543; and the "Three Chapters," 544–553. The Theopaschite controversy originated from an addition of the phrase "who was crucified for us" to the Trisagion: "Holy God, Holy strong, Holy immortal, *who was crucified for us,* have mercy on us." A Monophysite clause emphasizing the doctrine of one nature in Christ, its addition precipitated riots in Constantinople when it was introduced on November 6, 512, by the Monophysite Patriarch Timothy. Later, however, with the backing of the emperor, a modified form, "One of the Trinity was crucified in the flesh," became acceptable, notwithstanding the opposition of radical Chalcedonians such as the Acoemetae. By its use, Justinian hoped both to dissociate himself from Nestorianizers and to aid understanding of Monophysites. The phrase not only received approval at the Fifth Ecumenical Council in 553, but Justinian himself embodied it in a hymn as well. He argued that if one of the Trinity did not suffer in the flesh, He could not have been born in the flesh and Mary could not be called *Theotokos.*

Origenism, so hotly contested about 400, again became an object of debate early in Justinian's reign when the New Laura near Jerusalem secretly became the center for Origenism, triggering the wrath of Saba, Abbot of the Old Laura. In 531, Saba went to Constantinople to demand that Justinian expel the Origenists. Saba died in 532 before Justinian could take any action. Subsequently, however, two monks of the New Laura gained the emperor's ear and, in 537, appointment to important sees, so that it was not until 543 that the papal *apocrisarius* at the imperial court, Pelagius, managed to turn Justinian's opinion. In 543, Justinian issued an edict or letter to Menas, Patriarch of Constantinople (536–552), condemning the Origenists. Soon afterward, the Home Synod under Menas gave spiritual sanction to the condemnation. Included in the errors of Origen were his overstatement of the subordination of the Son, his theory of the pre-existence and fall of souls, his universalism, and his doctrine of successive worlds. In 553, the Fifth Ecumenical Council included Origen in the list of persons condemned for heresy. Thereafter, Eustochius, Patriarch of Jerusalem (552–564), quickly put an end to Origenism in the monasteries of Palestine.

Justinian's condemnation of the "Three Chapters" arose out of a suggestion of the Empress Theodora that the Monophysites might be more conciliatory if he were to condemn the Nestorianizers. In 544, Justinian issued an edict condemning the "Three Chapters," which originally meant certain propositions, but later came to mean the person of Theodore of Mopsuestia; the letter of Ibas of Edessa to Maris; and the writings of Theodoret of Cyrus. Somewhat reluctantly, the Eastern bishops subscribed to the condemnation. Pope Vigilius (538–555), however, resisted until he was brought to Constantinople and was browbeaten for a year; even then, Western bishops repudiated him for capitulating. Byzantine recovery of Rome from the Ostrogoths at precisely this time, however, left the pope without options, and Justinian would let no one stand in his way.

The Council of Constantinople, opening May 5, 553, brought Justinian's main theological concerns together for final disposition. So anxious was he to get on with it that he published in anticipation in 551 a *Confession of Right Faith Against the Three Chapters,* thus breaching his agreement with Pope

Vigilius. At the Council, Vigilius bravely declined to condemn Theodore, although he agreed to censure his language, or to dishonor Theodoret and Ibas. Justinian exploded. He revealed the secret oath Vigilius had taken to aid in the condemnation of the "Three Chapters" and ordered his name removed from the diptychs on the grounds that he had revealed himself a Nestorian by refusing to condemn them. The assembled bishops had only to assent to Justinian's will in the matter. All 164 signed. The pope's capitulation led to a rift with Western bishops that, in some cases, lasted a century and a half. He could hardly have done otherwise.

Justinian's successors deviated from the conciliatory route he had taken. Justin II (565–578) and Tiberius II (578–582) both favored Chalcedon and persecuted Monophysites. In both instances, the patriarchs—John III Scholasticus (566–577) and Eutychius (577–582)—played a strong role in determining ecclesiastical policy under weak monarchs. With the support of Justin and Sophia, John III launched a severe persecution of Monophysites in 571. Eutychius began to persecute them in 580. Maurice (582–602), although not super-Orthodox, aligned himself with John the Faster, Patriarch of Constantinople from 582–595, in his quest to make the see of Constantinople an "ecumenical patriarchate" equal to Rome. Once more, doctrine conceded to politics without solving a problem. Compromise and coercion could quell dissent momentarily, but they could not effect unity of either the church or the empire.

CHAPTER TWENTY-NINE

BEING CHRISTIAN IN A COLLAPSING WORLD

In the West, Christians confronted a radically different world in which they had to live out their faith under far more strenuous circumstances than Easterners knew. During the fifth and sixth centuries, they had to wrestle with the reality of life and death in a collapsing world. Beset by matters much more urgent, they wanted to have some *raison d'être* for the fall of the Eternal City and to hear some word of encouragement when the very wrath of heaven seemed unleashed against them.

Two quite different sets of answers came to their ears, one from the monk Pelagius and the other from the Bishop of Hippo, Augustine. Pelagius gave an answer for the few, the strong: Augustine for the many, the weak. This evil, Pelagius insisted, was a consequence of humans' failure to live up to their God-given potential. Consequently, the answer lay in discipline, doing the good that nature equips us to do. For Augustine, long one of the weak himself, such an answer failed to take into account the awesome power of evil and the frailty of humanity. People needed more than self-discipline, strong wills; they needed supernatural grace, the Holy Spirit, God's presence and power to strengthen them in their weakness.

Over the long run, neither Pelagius nor Augustine won the debate, although Pelagius's reputation suffered far more damage than Augustine's. Christians of the West claimed Augustine as their theologian *par excellence*, and his thought shaped Western thinking more than any other. Nevertheless, it would be naive indeed to assume that a rapidly barbarized civilization understood and appropriated his ideas without significant alteration. Far from it. While acclaiming him, they also modified what they took from him, tempering his thought to fit their own experience and point of view. In a society on its way to domination by monks like Pelagius, the Synod of Orange in 529 sprinkled Augustine with a few dashes of modified Pelagianism to make him more savory to medieval tastes.

Augustine

Augustine's own life (354–430) and work mirror in many ways the tumultuous times through which Western civilization was passing. A child of ambitious middle-class parents, he received the best education their meager resources would allow—first at Thagaste, then at nearby Madaura, and finally at Carthage. As a matter of fact, he had to delay his study at Carthage one year while his father, Patricius, found money to send him there. Although his parents agreed about education, they did not agree about religion. Patricius was pagan until converted near the end of his life, Monica a devout and puritanical Christian. Their conflicting desires in religion for their son probably had much to do with an extended and tortuous process of conversion.

At Carthage, the seventeen-year-old Augustine abandoned what little Christianity he possessed. "In love with love" (*Conf.* 3.1.1.) he entered into a common-law marriage that lasted fifteen years to a woman he never named in his writings, but who bore him a son named Adeodatus ("Given by God"). At age nineteen, Augustine experienced what some have labeled his "first conversion" on reading Cicero's *Hortensius*. The *Hortensius* changed his "feelings" and directed his energies toward God and a search for wisdom for its own sake. He turned to the Bible to find wisdom, but its crude style disappointed someone so geared to style. It may also have heightened a sense of guilt kept ever before his mind by his mother, Monica, for he turned to the Manichaean sect, then attractive to so many students. The Manichaeans helped him to overcome the crudeness of scriptures by rejecting the Old Testament and allegorizing what they did accept and by explaining that evil was an eternal, and thus unavoidable, substance. He was doing what he was doing because he *had* to and should not feel bad about it. He remained a Manichaean "hearer," equivalent to a catechumen in the Catholic Church, for nine years.

Tragedy, however, broke the grip of Manichaeism on Augustine's life, in the death of a dear friend. Manichaean theology could neither account for the tragedy nor assuage the grief and pain Augustine felt. Grief overwhelmed him. He could think of nothing but death. So he tried the geographical solution and went back to Carthage.

At Carthage, Augustine experienced success as a teacher of rhetoric, but he found the students rowdy and undisciplined. By 382, moreover, he had grown disillusioned with Manichaeism, after a conference with Faustus, the leading Manichaean theologian, failed to solve his theological conundrum. Encouraged by his friend Alypius, an administrative lawyer who had gone on ahead of him, he decided to go to Rome. Guilt at deceiving his mother by slipping away without her, an illness, and students who did not pay their tuition shortened Augustine's stay in Rome, and he welcomed the Prefect Symmachus's invitation to become professor of rhetoric in Milan, site of the imperial court in the West and, more important, the bishopric of Ambrose. Monica, not easily put aside, later joined him at Milan.

Augustine initially went to hear the famous Bishop Ambrose out of curiosity regarding the latter's rhetorical skills. Open to being taught at this critical juncture of his life, however, he gradually reached beyond rhetoric to substance. Through allegorical exposition, Ambrose helped the struggling catechumen to transcend the rough exterior of scriptures and to discover there the wisdom for which he longed. Ambrose was less "soothing and entertaining" than Faustus, but "far more learned" (*Conf.* 5.12.23); he could defend the Old Testament against the Manichaeans. When Monica arrived, she reinforced her son's growing reliance on Ambrose as a spiritual guide.

More prominent at this juncture than Ambrose, however, was a circle of friends, ten in all, who rallied around Augustine in Milan. They loved Augustine enough to pool their resources to support the search for truth in which they engaged. They became the midwives of his rebirth.

The first stage in the process, in the summer of 386, entailed a transition from what remained of Manichaean thought to Platonic, particularly on the question of evil. Whereas Manichaeism propounded a radical dualism, ascribing to evil an eternal existence, Neoplatonism taught that evil is the absence or perversion of good. For Augustine, this translated into a radically different explanation for his seeming inability to control his sex drive. He was not doing what he was doing because he *had* to, as the Manichaeans said, but because he *wanted* to, as the Neoplatonists said. He had free will, and he must exercise it.

It was precisely at this point, however, that Augustine would see the need to go beyond Platonism and would, in the future, make a signal contribution to Western thought. Although in his mind he agreed with the Platonists, he still found himself a captive of two wills, so that, like the apostle Paul, he still did not do the good he wanted to do. And it was in Paul, over whose writings Augustine had been poring, that he found the answer: the grace of God. Hearing from his Platonist friends about the conversion of Victorinus, a noted Neoplatonist philosopher, eased his mind. If Victorinus found Christianity respectable, Augustine, too, could find it so. But he still had to face up to himself.

Self-confrontation occurred at Cassiciacum, a villa near Lake Como, where the little band had gathered to pursue wisdom, in a strange way but one perfectly suited to Augustine's struggle of soul. Ponticianus, an imperial agent visiting Cassiciacum, related the story of the conversion of two young Roman noblemen who, on hearing the story of Anthony of Egypt's conversion, left their fiancées and took up the ascetic life. The story struck

Augustine at the core of his being. As he graphically depicted his experience, through it God took him from behind his own back and made him look at himself, how vile and deformed and unclean he was. The voice of continence kept challenging. More and more distressed, he tore himself away from Alypius's side and threw himself down in a flood of tears. There he heard a child's voice urging, "Take up and read. Take up and read." Interpreting this as a divine command, he returned to where Alypius was sitting and picked up the scriptures he had thrown down in exasperation. They fell open to Romans 13:13. He did not need to read further.

In September 386, abandoning plans for marriage, Augustine took up a semimonastic "leisure" at Cassiciacum under patronage of Romanianus, to whom he dedicated a treatise *On the Happy Life*, to sort out his Christian philosophy. Unlike Ambrose and many Christians of earlier generations, he did not regard philosophy negatively, and he needed time to heal. By the end of his stay he was searching deep within himself for answers. "Teach me to know myself. Teach me to know You," was the urgent entreaty of the *Soliloquies*. He was discovering both the God of the philosophers and the God of Paul, the God of grace. He received baptism at the hands of Ambrose on Easter (April 25), 387.

Shortly thereafter, Augustine, his mother, Adeodatus, and his friend Evodius headed back to Africa. Monica died at Ostia before they set sail for Carthage, but not before she and her "son of tears" shared a vision of Wisdom together (*Conf.* 9.10.23-25), a remarkable mystical experience. After returning to Rome for a time to wait for the lifting of a blockade of the port, Augustine finally arrived in Carthage late in 388.

On his return to Africa, Augustine formed around himself once again a semimonastic community on the family estates in Thagaste, where Alypius later became bishop. Very soon, he had to take up the pen against the sect of Manichaeans. He wrote first a commentary *On Genesis* against them and then summarized his position in a treatise *On True Religion*. Subsequently in a treatise *On Free Will* he set forth a Neoplatonic view that Pelagius would later cite in support of the central tenet of his own system. Augustine's thinking gradually shifted, however, from a rational to a dogmatic stance.

Making a signal contribution to the African Church in his anti-Manichaean writings, he found himself pulled increasingly into its official life. In 391, having recently lost his friend Nebridius and his son Adeodatus, he went to Hippo Regius in search of a site for a monastery. As he stood in the congregation, the bishop, Valerius, spoke of the urgent needs of the church for priests. The congregation turned to Augustine and pushed him toward the apse, where the bishop and priests sat. A Greek who could not speak Latin well, Valerius tiptoed around custom to insist that Augustine preach. In 395 he asked the Primate of Carthage to consecrate Augustine as his coadjutor, also in violation of church canons, this time Nicaea's. With

Valerius's blessing, Augustine secured the monastery he had sought, but for the clergy of Hippo rather than for a circle of select friends.

Very soon, Augustine found himself engaging not only the Manichaeans but also the powerful Donatists. Donatism had had great success in Numidia, particularly in small towns and the countryside, and was in Augustine's day the established church. One Donatist, Tyconius, was the leading African exegete from whom Augustine himself borrowed heavily, though eventually excommunicated from his own church. Drawing on the discontent of people in rural areas, the Donatists, especially the most radical group called the *Circumcelliones,* employed violence against Catholics and fostered violence in return. Augustine viewed his role of bishop as protector of the people. Accordingly, he dealt with Donatists heavy handedly and became the recognized leader in the push to put down the Donatist revolt. When Augustine arrived in Hippo, Catholics were a minority, so the vigor with which he preached against Donatism was understandable. He showed none of the tolerance for which other Catholic bishops were known, caricaturing Donatists in popular tracts. He applauded imperial efforts of Honorius, a devout Catholic, to put an end to the schism as well as suppress paganism. In his long treatise *Against the Epistle of Parmenian,* he argued early on that a Christian emperor had a right to punish impieties. When in 405 the Emperor Honorius issued the *Edict of Unity,* branding Donatism a heresy, the Bishop of Hippo viewed it as an act of providence. Seeing that force worked, thereafter he developed a full justification for the state's suppression of non-Catholics. Fallen human beings require constraint, *disciplina,* he argued. After 405 he busied himself disposing of property of Donatist churches, drawing up lists of Donatists, receiving Donatist converts, and seeing that laws were enforced. In June 411 he personally headed the Catholic bishops at Carthage in the final confrontation with Donatist bishops. The imperial legate, Flavius Marcellinus, a devout Catholic, ruled that the Donatists had no case against imposition of the *Edict of Unity* of Honorius. Thenceforward, Donatism was repressed, although some vestiges survived underground until the seventh century.

The sack of Rome on August 24, 410, by the Goths under Alaric opened a new phase in Augustine's eventful life. Rome, symbol of civilization and of the endurance of civilized society, had fallen. Immediately the great bishop addressed lengthy sermons to the fears, griefs, and anxieties of his people and wrote letters to leading refugees, many of whom fled to Africa ahead of the invaders. He had to help them make some sense of the political collapse that had taken them by surprise and to find in it some ray of hope. His answer, spun out over thirteen years, became his indisputably greatest work: *The City of God,* a response to renewal of pagan charges blaming Christians for the fall of Rome. The word of hope on which he drew this work to a close was that, amid evils all around, there still flows, "as in a vast, racing river" (*City of God* 22.24.11), a wealth of good—in the human body, in human intellect, in nature—that reminds us of the greater good of eternity.

This same tragic set of events furnished the setting for the advent of Pelagius and the controversy that would occupy so much of Augustine's energies during his last years and held a central place in later impressions of the theology of Augustine. Because the controversy will receive extended treatment below, however, brief note should be taken of Augustine's remaining years. He continued, of course, to fulfill the increasingly important role of bishop. He not only tended the faithful in his own flock, but he also exercised a paternal care for the body politic to which they belonged. He kept pressure on public officials to extirpate the last vestiges of paganism and heresy and to unify Christians in the Catholic Church. In his last years after the fall of Rome he had to minister also to an array of prominent refugees—such as Melania the Younger and her husband Pinian, who fled Rome ahead of the Goths—and to answer inquiries of notables—such as Paulinus of Nola and his wife, Therasia—on how best to live the Christian life in such circumstances. Augustine's significance as a theologian, of course, brought him to the notice of scholars like Jerome, who could point up the great African's deficiencies in biblical interpretation even as Augustine could point up Jerome's as a theologian.

On September 26, 426, Augustine appointed his successor, Heraclius. Although preoccupation with the Pelagian controversy had caused him to neglect intellectual matters at home, he composed his treatise *On Christian Doctrine* at this time. As he aged, he modified some earlier views. Whereas in 390 in his treatise *On True Religion* he had negated continuance of miracles after the apostolic age, in the last book of *The City of God* he gathered a panoply of miracle stories. He made room for the unexpected. His health failing, he had to stand by helpless as he watched Roman Africa give way to the Vandals. In the spring of 430 they overran Mauretania and Numidia. In August of that year, Augustine fell seriously ill and died on August 28. Shortly afterward, the Vandals laid siege to the city, which was evacuated and partly burned. Fortunately, his library escaped.

Pelagianism

Little is known about Pelagius apart from the controversy he precipitated. According to early accounts, he was a British monk noted for his learning and piety; he spoke both Latin and Greek. He arrived in Rome at least as early as the pontificate of Anastasius I (399–401) and was held in high esteem by the group Jerome had shepherded in the 380s. Around 405 he made contact with Easterners, who shared his more optimistic view of human nature. He may have been influenced by Theodore of Mopsuestia (392–428), "the Interpreter," in writing his commentary on Romans. His own views, however, were shaped chiefly in reaction against Manichaeism and in debate with Augustine.

About 405, Pelagius became indignant when he heard a bishop quote with approval a statement from Augustine's *Confessions* (10.40): "Lord, you have commanded continence. Give what you command, and command what you will." Pelagius concluded that this kind of deterministic thinking was the source of moral laxity among Roman Christians. In his mind, all that was required was the exercise of human capacity for free will, *natural grace.*

Pelagius began to gather disciples, the most notable of whom was Caelestius, who equalled Pelagius in ability and exceeded him in outspokenness. More emphatically than Pelagius, Caelestius rejected the idea of a "fall" of humankind. Human beings in every age are in the same state as Adam at creation. They are free to will or not to will the good.

Pelagius and Caelestius might never have come to the attention of Augustine had it not been for the Gothic invasion of Italy. About 409, as the Goths approached Rome, they departed for Sicily and Africa. Staying in Sicily only long enough to plant some seeds of their theology, they proceeded to Hippo and then to Carthage, where, in 411, Augustine occupied himself with the Donatists. Pelagius pushed on toward Palestine, but Caelestius remained in Carthage, where, on seeking ordination, he found himself accused of heresy before Bishop Aurelius, by the then deacon Paulinus, who later became Bishop of Nola; he was in Carthage as an agent of the Church of Milan and there wrote a biography of Ambrose.

In 411–412, Aurelius summoned a council and Paulinus outlined Caelestius's errors: (1) Adam was created mortal and would have died whether he had sinned or not. (2) Adam's sin injured only himself and not the whole human race. (3) Newborn infants are in the same state as Adam before he sinned. (4) Adam's sin and death did not cause the death of all humankind, nor does Christ's resurrection cause the resurrection of all. (5) The law brings people into the kingdom of God just as the gospel does. (6) Even before Christ came, there were those who did not sin. In the course of the examination, Caelestius insisted in reference to the second point that the transmission of sin was an open issue, but on the third point he claimed that he had always affirmed that infants needed baptism "for forgiveness of sins." The council condemned him, and he proceeded to Ephesus, where he again sought ordination.

Although Augustine did not attend the council, he soon entered the fray with sermons and treatises intended to refute Caelestius's views as destructive of the doctrine of redemption. At the request of Marcellinus, the

Emperor Honorius's High Commissioner, Augustine wrote in 412 his first major anti-Pelagian treatise, *On Merits and the Forgiveness of Sins and the Baptism of Infants.* Yes, he admitted, Adam was created mortal, but he would not have died had he not sinned. Here already he seized on the mistranslation of Romans 5:12, "Adam, in whom [*in quo*] all sinned," to make the point that Adam's sin afflicted all of his descendants. Sin is more than imitation of Adam. Infants would not require baptism unless they were spiritually sick. In baptism they received forgiveness of original sin and not of their own misdeeds. Although by the grace of God and our free will we can be without sin, no one save Christ ever lived a sinless life.

As he completed this response, Pelagius's *Commentary on Romans* came into his hands with a further argument against original sin—that is, that if Adam's sin works against those who do not sin, Christ's righteousness is efficacious for those who do not believe. In a letter to Marcellinus, Augustine replied that infants, too, are believers and benefit from what parents and sponsors do for them. When Marcellinus had trouble understanding how, if it were possible to be without sin, as Augustine conceded, none had been sinless, Augustine wrote another treatise, *On the Spirit and the Letter*, pointing out that scriptures cite many examples of things God can do that have never happened. To live without sin depends on grace, that is, the Holy Spirit working in the soul, and not on free will. The will is set free only by grace.

The views of Pelagius and Caelestius found ready acceptance in Africa. Their appeal prompted Augustine to deliver a stern warning to a Carthaginian congregation on June 25, 413, about the novelty of saying that infants are baptized in order to enter the kingdom rather than to have sins forgiven. Unbaptized infants, he echoed Cyprian, are damned. One of the notables attracted to Pelagius was Demetrias, daughter of Olybrius, Consul in 395, who had fled to Carthage with her mother, Juliana, and her grandmother Proba as the Goths approached Rome. Her wealthy mother and grandmother arranged a marriage for her to an affluent protector in exile; but on the eve of the wedding Demetrias chose the life of virginity, gave her possessions to the poor, and took the veil. Jerome wrote to congratulate and encourage her and to give advice. So, too, did Pelagius in 414. In his letter, he emphasized the "strength" of human nature characterized especially by free will. Even non-Christians have done good deeds; how much more should Christians, trained to better things and aided by divine grace. Many—Abel, Joseph, Job—lived saintly lives under the law; how much more worthily should we live under grace. Everything turns on the will. We can merit grace! Augustine wrote to Juliana in 417 or 418 to warn lest Demetrias think she could attain spiritual riches by her own merits.

Early in 415, Augustine responded to Pelagius's treatise *On Nature* at the request of two youths of good birth and education, Timasius and James, whom Pelagius had persuaded to take up the ascetic life and to embrace his views, with a work entitled *On Nature and Grace*. Against Pelagius's theory of the sufficiency of the "grace of nature," the Bishop of Hippo argued a case for supernatural grace. Grace is not contrary to nature, but nature, vitiated by sin, must be delivered and governed by grace.

By this time, the center of attention shifted from Africa to Palestine, where Jerome was already doing battle with Pelagius, who had gained the ear of John, the Patriarch of Jerusalem (386–417). In a letter to an inquirer and in his *Dialogues Against the Pelagians* (415), Jerome argued much as Augustine had against the Pelagian concept of natural grace by which one can live sinlessly. In the meantime, John invited Orosius, a young Spanish refugee from Bragada in Gallaecia, to relate what he knew of the Pelagian controversy to the diocesan synod of Jerusalem on July 28. When Orosius concluded, the patriarch invited Pelagius in and asked him if he held the opinions that Augustine, Jerome, and others attributed to him. To the surprise of Orosius, when he said yes, the patriarch did not let that become a cause of condemnation. Instead, he asked whether Orosius and his fellow presbyters wanted to file a formal charge. When they declined, finding it increasingly difficult to communicate because of language barriers, John accepted Orosius's suggestion that the matter was Latin and should be referred to Pope Innocent I (402–417). Several weeks later, when Orosius went to pay his respects to John, the latter accused him of saying that no one could live without sin even with God's help. To clear himself, Orosius wrote his *Apologetic Book on Free Will*, which he addressed to the priests of Jerusalem.

Subsequently two refugee bishops from Gaul, Heros of Arles (409–412) and Lazarus of Aix (409–412), drew up formal charges against Pelagius and presented them to Eulogius, Bishop of Caesarea (404–417) and Metropolitan of Palestina I. Eulogius summoned the Synod of Diospolis to meet on December 20, 415, at Lydda. Thirteen bishops, including John of Jerusalem, attended, but Heros and Lazarus did not because one of them was ill. With a decided advantage in Greek language, Pelagius easily defended himself on the propositions cited before a panel of Eastern bishops, inclined, like John Chrysostom, to emphasize free will themselves. The synod acquitted him, and Pelagius now set about to repay Jerome. In a treatise *In Behalf of Free Will*, addressed to Jerome, Pelagius acknowledged the need for grace, but, as Augustine charged, he never accorded it its full Pauline significance. It meant: (1) nature with free will, (2) forgiveness of sins, (3) law and teaching, (4) inward illumination, (5) baptismal adoption, and (6) eternal life, but not the Holy Spirit present to empower. A year later, Pelagius received a major boost from Theodore of Mopsuestia's five books *Against Those Who Say People Sin by Nature and Not by Their Own Will*, directed at

Jerome. Some Pelagian thugs also raided Jerome's monastery at Bethlehem, and he barely escaped with his life.

The scene shifted after this (416–418), to Rome and Africa. In the summer of 416, Orosius, returning to Africa, delivered a letter of Heros and Lazarus to a council of Carthage, presided over by Aurelius. The council addressed a letter to Pope Innocent I asking him to place the weight of the Apostolic See behind their condemnation of Pelagius and Caelestius. A council at Mileve in Numidia, with Augustine among the sixty-one bishops present, seconded the request. Augustine and four other bishops backed this up with a private letter to the pope, revealing the level of anxiety in Africa about Rome's handling of the cause in view of known sympathies in Rome for Pelagius and Caelestius. The Synod of Diospolis, they explained, cleared Pelagius only because he admitted grace, but it did not realize that he had not accorded it its full meaning—the help of the Holy Spirit. Innocent replied to each of the letters, indicating that he had excommunicated Pelagius and Caelestius for having denied the need of grace and expressing his own doubts about the Synod of Diospolis. The pope's replies, among his very last acts, brought great joy to the Africans.

The rejoicing, however, did not last long. In 417, Caelestius reappeared in Rome, where he obtained clearance from Innocent's successor, Zosimus (417–418), a Greek, by presenting a confession of faith that glossed over the points of dispute. At a local synod in September 417, Caelestius deftly persuaded the gullible Zosimus of his own orthodoxy and of the haste of the Africans in condemning him. Zosimus assured Aurelius of Carthage that Caelestius's faith was "completely satisfactory" (*Ep.* 2.6). Pelagius also obtained the pope's approval, sending a doctrinal statement and letters from himself and Praylius, Patriarch of Jerusalem (416–425), who had succeeded John. Zosimus did not have sufficient theological acumen to catch in Pelagius's letter the subtle point that Christians, "by using their free will correctly, *merit the grace of God* and keep His commandments," a point Augustine noted immediately. It was not enough for him to say, "We confess free will but hold at the same time that we stand continually in need of the divine assistance." The question was, "What kind of assistance?" Zosimus summoned another synod to clear Pelagius, blaming Heros and Lazarus for fomenting trouble. He also directed Paulinus of Nola to come to Rome and defend his accusations against Caelestius, but he declined on the grounds that the judge had already declared for his adversary.

Aurelius of Carthage quickly assembled a few bishops at Carthage who proposed that Zosimus leave things stand as they had been under Innocent, "until he should become better informed about the case." In November 417, 214 bishops gathered and sent a second letter reiterating that they would adhere to Innocent's decision against Pelagius and Caelestius until they should come to the proper understanding of grace. Zosimus backpedaled.

While boasting that his decisions were not subject to review, he conceded the need for further deliberation and assured the Africans that things would stand as they were under Innocent. Meantime, the Africans turned to the imperial court, where they obtained a rescript from Honorius banishing Pelagius and Caelestius from Rome and threatening confiscation and exile for their followers. In 418, a council convened at Carthage, with 215 bishops representing all five African provinces, to lay down the Catholic doctrine of original sin and the need of grace. Zosimus had no option but to condemn Pelagius and Caelestius. Surprisingly, the contorted handling of the case did not lead to a breach with Augustine or the Africans. Rome smoothed the ruffled feelings of the Africans with letters to Valerius and Augustine composed by the Presbyter (later Pope) Sixtus and carried by the Acolyte (later Pope) Leo.

Pelagius's Friends

The victory at Carthage in 418 did not signal the demise of Pelagianism. Pelagius still had prominent and influential friends, including Roman exiles to Africa—Pinian; his wife, Melania; and her mother, Albina. They tried to persuade Pelagius to condemn the propositions alleged against him. In a letter he assured them that he believed in the necessity of grace and in "baptism of infants for forgiveness of sins." A bit suspicious of his assurances, Pinian consulted Augustine. The Bishop of Hippo replied in two treatises, *On the Grace of Christ* and *On Original Sin*, calling attention to the subtle way in which Pelagius steered around the main point. He affirmed grace with reference to the possibility of *choosing* good or evil but not with reference to *willing* or *being* good or evil. In his view, grace is *natural* and not *super*natural. He was really a masterful advocate of free will. At the same time, he contradicted himself when he spoke of baptism of infants for forgiveness of sins and yet denied that Adam's sin affected the whole human race. Augustine assured Pinian that Pelagius and Caelestius merited the condemnations they had received.

What must have troubled thoughtful laypersons as well as monks and clergy about Augustine's views is evident in a long letter (*Ep.* 194) Augustine wrote to the Presbyter Sixtus, later Pope Sixtus III (432–440), late in 418. The chief problem was the obvious arbitrariness of God's actions. Augustine's replies, defending the "inscrutable will of God," anticipated the uncompromising stand he took in treatises written in 426–427: *On Grace and Free Will* and *On Reproach and Grace*. In these, Augustine stopped just short of double predestination—that is, God's choice of some persons for salvation and of others for damnation. Because all humankind is a "condemned lump," God must have condemned all. By grace, however, God elected some for salvation. This grace is irresistible, as certain as the end to which it points.

The leader of the opposition to Augustine's more pronounced anti-Pelagian views was Julian, Bishop of Eclanum (417–454), whose family had once had close ties with Augustine. Immediately after the death of Innocent I, who had consecrated him, Julian took up the cudgels against views he feared would be fatal to divine justice and human responsibility and would alienate cultured people by superficial piety. He first attacked Pope Zosimus (417–418), then Augustine, and finally Pope Boniface (418–422).

In 418, Zosimus sent his *Tractoria*, condemning Pelagius and Caelestius, to all the principal sees of both East and West. Although none in Africa refused to sign, nineteen bishops in Italy led by Julian did and added a memorial in which they set forth the Semi-Pelagian position: The grace of Christ cooperates with free will and "will not follow those who refuse it." Whether one person is good and another bad is due to that person and not to the will of God. Both grace and baptism are necessary. Yet there is no "natural (original) sin." In disagreement with Pelagius, however, the document affirmed that the whole human race died in Adam and has been raised in Christ. In one of two letters he sent to Zosimus, Julian repudiated three propositions attributed to Pelagius and Caelestius: that humankind did not die in Adam or rise again in Christ, that newborn infants are in the same state as Adam, and that Adam was created mortal and would have died whether he had sinned or not. Zosimus excommunicated and deposed all nineteen bishops. The Emperor Honorius banished them. Undaunted by this action, Julian and his friends sought a new synod to rehear their case. When blocked in that, they turned to Rufus, Bishop of Thessalonica (410–431), and Atticus, Patriarch of Constantinople (406–426), for help. From there they tried to gain a hearing at Alexandria, Antioch, and Jerusalem, but in vain. Only Theodore of Mopsuestia, who was of the same mind, offered refuge in about 423.

Julian, a self-confident and haughty person, next took up the pen against Augustine, whom he, like Pelagius, suspected of Manichaeism. Augustine supplied the occasion with the first book of a treatise he wrote, *On Marriage and Concupiscence*, in 419 in reply to a Pelagian cavil that he implicitly condemned marriage as the means of transmission of sin. In this treatise, he affirmed that marriage is good, but noted that concupiscence entered into it by way of Adam's sin and is the reason why even those born in wedlock from Christian parents are not born children of God and thus need grace. Concupiscence remains in the baptized, though not its guilt, so that they are still inclined to sin. Julian attacked Augustine's doctrine in "four thick books" (Augustine *Against Julian* 1.2). Augustine responded hastily to some inaccurate extracts of Julian's work in the second book of *On Marriage and Concupiscence* and when it came into his hands, in the full-length treatise *Against Julian the Pelagian* in 422. In the latter, among other things, he gave his rejoinder to the five Pelagian arguments against the doctrine of original sin: (1) It makes the devil the author of human birth. (2) It condemns marriage. (3) It denies that all sins were forgiven in baptism. (4) It charges God with injustice. (5) It makes human beings despair of perfection. Around 424, Julian retaliated with a lengthy critique of the second book of Augustine's *On Marriage and Concupiscence*. Augustine began but did not live to complete a further response to Julian in 429–430. Although Julian handled opponents such as Augustine so crudely that he did not find many personal sympathizers, some of the extreme aspects of Augustinianism (for example, the condemnation of unbaptized infants and the irresistibility of grace) made his protest quite intelligible.

Julian also came to the attention of Pope Boniface I in 420 through two letters, one Julian himself addressed to Rome charging Catholics with Manichaeism and the other he and the eighteen exiles directed to Rufus, Bishop of Thessalonica (410–431), seeking help. At the insistence of the pope, Augustine wrote a substantial treatise, *Against the Two Epistles of the Pelagians*, defending (his own) Catholic teaching. From this point on, the Pelagians lost ground. Atticus drove Julian and his cohorts out of Constantinople. In 424, Theodotus of Antioch banished Pelagius from Jerusalem. Pope Caelestine exiled Caelestius from Italy, and in 429 he was forced out of Constantinople. The Council of Ephesus in 431 condemned both Pelagius and Caelestius. Julian, hounded from town to town, finally ended up teaching at a school in Sicily, where he died in 454.

Semi-Pelagianism/Augustinianism

Revered and respected as Augustine was, questions about the more extreme forms of his teaching persisted, especially in monastic communities, for his emphasis on grace seemed to undercut the life of prayer to which monks devoted themselves. In 426, African monks of Hadrumentum, reading Augustine's letter to Sixtus for the first time, thought it annihilated free will and sought clarification from Augustine himself. In response, he sent them his treatise *On Grace and Free Will* (427), in which he affirmed the need for preserving both but depicted the will as so debilitated by the Fall that only supernatural grace can overcome its effects. The monks understandably raised the question as to why they should be censured for wrongdoing if they had no more freedom than Augustine allowed. When Augustine learned of their objection, he sent them the treatise *On Reproach and Grace*. In it he answered that they deserved reproach because of their depravity as a part of the "condemned lump," just as unbaptized infants did. The elect persevere because they have been predestined to do so. Why they are elect belongs to God's inscrutable will. Although all should receive instruction because we do not know who is among the predestinated, the elect need and receive more help than Adam—the help of *irresistible* grace.

As this exchange was taking place, the original Pelagianism experienced some revival in Gaul and in the British Isles. In Gaul a monk named Leporius combined Pelagian and Nestorian emphases on free will to depict Jesus as an ordinary man who used his free will to live a sinless life. Gallic bishops forced Leporius to flee Gaul and take up refuge in Africa, where he came under Augustine's influence and retracted his views. In Britain, homeland of Pelagius, Pelagius's ideas found fallow soil among the laity. In 429 a large synod in Gaul sent Germanus, Bishop of Auxerre (418–448), and Lupus, Bishop of Troyes (427–479), to the British Isles to combat Pelagianism. A major confrontation took place at Verulamium (now St. Albans). The fact that Germanus returned in 447, accompanied by Severus, Bishop of Treves (446–455), to finish the job, attests the tenacity of Pelagian ideas among laypersons there.

More subtle and difficult to counteract, the modified form of thought was known as Semi-Pelagianism. As originally defined by a Carthaginian monk named Vitalis, Semi-Pelagianism ascribed the initial act of faith to the movement of the will unaided by grace, but necessary thereafter. It insisted on the need of grace thereafter. In an extended response (*Ep.* 217), Augustine countered that, if Vitalis's view was true, the church should stop praying for conversion of the unconverted, regeneration of catechumens, and perseverance of believers, for prayer depends on the grace of God taking initiative preveniently. If we don't believe that when we pray, we only pretend to pray. Only when the will is transformed by grace does it become free. In short, God effects through grace what we will. Whether Vitalis discerned his "error" and subscribed to the "Twelve Articles" of Catholic teaching Augustine outlined for him is unknown, but Augustine did not convince the monks at the two leading centers in south Gaul, Lérins and Marseilles.

Cassian, founder of the two monasteries at Marseilles, thought Augustine pressed too far the idea of prevenient grace. Hilary, Abbot of Lérins and Bishop of Arles (429–449), agreed with Cassian in this criticism. Both believed that Augustine's theology undermined human responsibility. Therefore, they stressed that nature can take the first steps toward its own recovery without the aid of grace. Although underscoring the need of grace, they differed from Augustine at two points: denial of the need for prevenient grace and the concept of irresistible grace. Informed by Prosper of Aquitaine (ca. 390–ca. 463), an ardent Augustinian, and a monk named Hilary about the situation in Gaul, Augustine composed his treatises *On the Predestination of the Saints* and *On the Gift of Perseverance* in 428 and 429, setting forth his views in their most pronounced form. In his treatise *On the*

Predestination of the Saints, Augustine took note of the difference between Semi-Pelagians and Pelagians: the Semi-Pelagians' emphasis on unaided free will only in the *initial* step of faith. In the supplementary *On the Gift of Perseverance,* Augustine sought to prove that perseverance is also a gift of God. As proof, he invoked the Lord's prayer and the prayers of the church for faithfulness. These were Augustine's last words in the Pelagian controversy except for a brief summary in his treatise *On Heresies,* an unfinished work.

Post-Augustinianism

Although Augustine's last treatises satisfied Prosper and Hilary, they exasperated the Semi-Pelagians, who circulated excerpts from them. After a futile attempt to defend his hero, Prosper took refuge in Rome around 431. In Rome, however, he found little sympathy for pronounced Augustinianism, for both Caelestine (422–432) and Leo (440–461) held Semi-Pelagians in high esteem. Leo, as a matter of fact, called on Cassian to reply to the Nestorians in 430–431. Try as he might, Prosper could not evoke from Caelestine or Sixtus III (432–440) or Leo a denunciation of Semi-Pelagians. Although Cassian declined to let Prosper draw him into a battle over his thirteenth *Conference* in 433–434, Vincent of Lérins did take up the challenge in his *Commonitorium* in 434. Under Leo, both as archdeacon and as pope, a whole series of writings emerged from Rome praising Augustine and yet repudiating extremes of Augustinianism. These agreed with Augustine's emphasis on the need for supernatural grace, but they either rejected or remained silent regarding his doctrines of predestination and irresistible grace.

The controversy remained muted until it flared up again about 475 under the leadership of Faustus, Bishop of Riez (459–ca. 490). When one of his clergy, Lucidus, began to teach Augustine's doctrine of predestination, Faustus forced him to retract his teaching. At the request of the Synod of Lyon in 474, he wrote also *Two Books on Grace,* in which he argued vehemently against the doctrine of prevenient grace.

The long-contorted issue was finally resolved at the Synod of Orange in 529 through the skillful guidance of Caesarius, Archbishop of Arles (502–542), the most outstanding preacher of the Latin Church at the time. Even though educated at Lérins and thus well acquainted with the distaste for Augustinianism, Caesarius had learned to love Augustine's "Catholic sentiments." His preaching of grace aroused the suspicion of some fellow bishops in south Gaul, and they invited him to clear himself before the Synod of Valence (527–528). Illness prevented him from attending, but he sent a message by Cyprian, Bishop of Toulon (524–549), emphasizing the need for prevenient grace. Immediately thereafter, he secured the approval of Pope Felix IV (528–530) of a series of propositions, which he presented for approval at the Synod of Orange on July 3, 529. Although only fourteen bishops attended, the added approval of the pope assured its unusual importance in history.

The Synod of Orange essentially upheld the Augustinian viewpoint. In its first two canons, it affirmed Augustine's doctrine of the Fall against Pelagianism. The Fall affected human nature as a whole, soul as well as body; not only death but also sin was transmitted to the human race through the Fall. In canons 3 through 8, the Synod rejected Semi-Pelagianism, insisting on the need for prevenient grace. Grace evokes prayer, prepares the will, initiates faith, encourages seeking, and aids our weakened nature. The remaining canons (9-25) also underlined the importance of grace, but they made no mention of predestination or the irresistibility of grace. Augustine's central teachings, but not his extremes, had survived. Monasticism, so significant already in the churches of Gaul, did not lose its *raison d'être*. Quite to the contrary, the foundations of the Middle Ages were well laid.

CHAPTER THIRTY

THE EMERGENCE OF THE PAPACY

Rome attained special importance in the church at a very early date because it was the capital of the empire and because it was there that both Peter, the apostle to the circumcision, and Paul, the apostle to the Gentiles, had died. The eagerness of the apostle Paul to go to Rome and to be sent by the Roman Christians to Spain (Rom. 15:24) indicates the importance he attached to the Roman Church. At the end of the first century, the Roman presbyters assumed that they had not only a prerogative but also a responsibility to offer fraternal counsel to the Corinthians who had risen up and deposed their elders. In his letter to the Romans, Ignatius, on the way to martyrdom in Rome, bore witness to the prestige of the Roman Church, addressing it as one "which presides in the place of the region of the Romans" and describing this as "a presidency of love." As Dionysius of Corinth noted in a letter to Soter, the Bishop of Rome from 175 to 182, Rome attained distinction for its charities "to many churches in every city" (Eusebius *H.E.* 4.23.10). Clement (96 C.E.) and Ignatius (110–117), moreover, both cited Rome's connection with Peter and Paul. Toward the end of the second century, Irenaeus carried this a step further when he spoke of Rome as "the greatest and most ancient and universally known church, founded and established at Rome by the two most glorious apostles Peter and Paul" (*Adv. haer.* 3.3.1) and proceeded to cite the list of Roman bishops up to his own day with the comment that "every church must agree [*convenire*] with this church on account of its greater pre-eminence [*principalitatem*]" (*Adv. haer.* 3.3.2). Although Irenaeus's main point was that churches of apostolic foundation, like that of Rome, should serve as measuring rods for all of the churches, the very fact that he cited the Roman list rather than that of other churches attests Rome's special importance.

Rome took a giant step forward in the early third century with the appearance of the theory that the city derived its authority from the bishop of Rome as Peter's successor. Curiously the idea manifested itself with the brilliant renegade Tertullian. Borrowing Irenaeus's succession theory, Tertullian demanded that heretics produce their lists as Smyrna or Rome could, proving respectively that John appointed Polycarp and that Peter appointed Clement. Here Irenaeus's distinction between the apostles and their successors gave way to the establishment of Roman primacy by citing Peter as the first bishop of Rome. The two rivals for the Roman episcopate in 217, Callistus and Hippolytus, relied on this theory and backed it up by citing Matthew 16:18-19. Neither, however, claimed *papal* but only *episcopal* authority.

That step was taken by Stephen (254–257) in his debate with Cyprian of Carthage over the question of heretical baptisms. Cyprian took the position that heretics and schismatics could not administer baptism at all because they did not possess the Spirit and, therefore, had to receive baptism. Stephen claimed that they needed only to have hands laid on them. He appealed to the Petrine text as the basis of his authority and, according to Cyprian (*Epistle* 75.17), "boasts of the seat of his episcopate and contends that he holds the succession from Peter, on whom the foundations of the Church were laid." Although Cyprian evidently acknowledged the special role of the bishop of Rome, he maintained strongly that all bishops are successors of Peter. When African synods took Cyprian's side, Stephen warned against "innovations" and threatened excommunication. He not only claimed authority for the Roman usage but also magnified his office as successor of Peter and occupant of Peter's chair, which, he insisted, gave the bishop of Rome authority over other bishops.

During the late third and fourth centuries, the churches centralized around several great sees—Rome, Alexandria, Antioch, and later Constantinople. Dionysius, Bishop of Rome (259–268), after consulting with a Roman synod, issued a mild rebuke to his namesake in Alexandria regarding his tendency to subordinate the Son to the Father too much. Of great importance here was the fact that Dionysius was responding to an appeal from Dionysius of Alexandria's opponents, initiating the custom exploited to advantage by Roman bishops in subsequent centuries. In 325 the Council of Nicaea (Canon 6) specifically mentioned, however, the rights of Rome in Italy, Alexandria in Egypt, and Antioch in the East. The emperors, moreover, strongly asserted their authority in ecclesiastical matters in ways that limited the claims of the bishops of Rome. First Constantine and then his sons, especially Constantius, exercised the role of the Roman Pontifex Maximus. Under Liberius (352–366) the Roman episcopate recovered some of its prestige in conflict with Constantius II. Constantius, an Arian, forced an Arian settlement on the synods of Arles (353) and Milan (355). When Liberius refused to acknowledge their decision, Constantius tried bribes and threats and then banishment to Beroea. Liberius did yield, but the intemperance of the Arians turned sympathies in favor of supporters of Nicaea. Liberius led the repentance of Western bishops. The major leader, however, was Athanasius, Bishop of Alexandria, so that Liberius stood chiefly as the leader of Nicene orthodoxy in the West.

Damasus

Roman primacy took another major step during the pontificate of Damasus (366–384). Damasus had to fight to gain control of the see to which he was elected on September 24, 366. Rapid growth in the wealth of the Roman Church made leadership of it a special prize worth seizing. Consequently, a minority gathered the same day and elected and consecrated Ursinus. Followers of Damasus, who was not yet consecrated, attacked the followers of Ursinus in Santa Maria Maggiore and killed 137 of them. Although the claim of Damasus was upheld, Ursinus continued to pursue the case until Gratian (375–383) intervened and banished him to Cologne and cleared Damasus. Damasus convened a Roman council in May and June 382 that made two requests of the emperor: that he confirm the privilege of the bishop of Rome to try cases of recalcitrant bishops so that no bishop would have to appear before a secular court, hearing both cases of the first instance and appeals, and that he shelter the bishop of Rome from accusers. In response, Gratian extended two new powers to the Roman see: He made the pope master of the process for trying all accused metropolitans throughout the West, and he provided for appeals to the pope for bishops tried by local synods. None of this, however, extended beyond the West, and Damasus and his successor framed a theory that would support its extension to the East as well. The attitude of bishops such as Basil of Caesarea (370–379) was disdainful. In the Meletian schism, Basil and most Eastern bishops supported Meletius as bishop of Antioch against Paulinus, whom Damasus and Athanasius upheld.

Damasus did not have an easy time establishing Roman primacy during the reign of the Emperor Theodosius (379–395). The emperor himself recognized two centers of Christianity—Rome and Alexandria—in his edict *Cunctos populos*, issued in February 380. At the Council of Constantinople in 381, later recognized as an ecumenical council, moreover, upstart Constantinople was accorded a rank just after Rome as "new Rome" and ahead of Alexandria, Antioch, and Jerusalem. Damasus responded by convening a Roman synod that, among other things, set forth the first official definition of papal claims. With obvious reference to Constantinople, the synod based Roman claims "on no synodal decisions" but on Christ's promise to Peter recorded in Matthew 16. It proceeded thence to establish a Petrine hierarchy without Constantinople—Rome, Alexandria, and Antioch. Although the theory has obvious weaknesses, it was taken for granted by the successors of Damasus and put in classic form by Leo the Great (440–461).

From Damasus to Leo

Papal primacy did not reach beyond the West during the pontificates of Damasus's successors. Siricius (384–399) extended his authority over Spain, Illyria, Italy, and Africa. In a decree addressed to Himerius, Bishop of Tarragona, February 10, 385, he urged circulation of his judgments to the bishops of Carthagena, Baetica, Lusitania, Gallaecia, and neighboring provinces and added, "No bishop is at liberty to ignore the decisions of the Apostolic See, or the venerable decrees of the canons." In other letters he threatened excommunication of any bishop who ordained priests without the knowledge of the Apostolic See of the Primate of Africa. At this juncture, Rome obviously placed itself above the episcopate, but the East still went its own way, not worried about being out of communion with the West, as the case of Flavian, Bishop of Antioch from 381 to 398, indicates. Although Western bishops accorded Rome special recognition, they also held Milan in high regard during Ambrose's time (374–397). Rufinus, in a letter to Anastasius (399–401), declared his consensus in faith with Rome, Alexandria, his own church at Aquileia, and Jerusalem.

Innocent I (402–417) clearly asserted Rome's authority, but his letters indicate some of the same restrictions placed on it. Although the West generally acknowledged Roman primacy, Africa expressed some reservations. Chrysostom welcomed Roman help in his defense, but he relied too on the decisions of Nicaea. In the West, Innocent confirmed Anysius (388–410), and his successor Rufus (410–431), Bishop of Thessalonica, as his vicar throughout the provinces of Illyria, checking a pull toward Constantinople. He handed out advice to Victricius, Bishop of Rouen (395–415), and Exuperius, Bishop of Toulouse (405–415), cultivating referral to Rome. In a letter to Decentius, Bishop of Eugubium (Gubbio), Innocent expressed shock at the intrusion of non-Roman liturgical practice into his metropolitanate and insisted on observance of Roman customs "everywhere" throughout Italy, Gaul, Spain, Africa, Sicily, and the neighboring islands. To follow foreign customs is to desert the head of the church.

During the Pelagian controversy, Africans sent Innocent three letters asking his support. In the first of his replies, addressed to the Council of Carthage (416), Innocent congratulated the council for referring the matter to the judgment of his see, "the source of the whole episcopate." He made similar assertions in reply to the Synod of Mileve and to a letter from Augustine and fellow bishops. At this point, the Africans rejoiced at the support they received from the pope. The statement "Rome has spoken, the case is settled," ascribed to Augustine, does not represent his response accurately, however. What he actually said was that reports of the two councils (Carthage and Mileve) had been sent to the Apostolic See and that Rome had sent rescripts so that the case was settled. African independence would shine through clearly when later popes glossed over the Pelagian problem.

Chrysostom's appeal to Rome should not be overstated either, for he sent identical letters to Venerius, Bishop of Milan, in 408 and to Chromatius, Bishop of Aquileia, in 407. Not only Rome but also Milan and Aquileia represented leading prelates. Innocent replied to appeals from both Theophilus of Alexandria and Chrysostom saying that he would require a council to settle the matter, meantime maintaining relations with both. Obviously, Innocent had not yet elevated his claims to the level of a general council, a view Chrysostom would have held also.

Zosimus (417–418) blundered badly in trying to assert his authority. His most serious error was his patronage of Caelestius and Pelagius, and African bishops did not hesitate to challenge him.

Boniface I (418–422) did not make the same mistake regarding the Pelagians, and he had occasion to advance further the claims of Rome. When the bishops of Illyricum refused to confirm the election of Perigenes as bishop—despite popular approval and Boniface's confirmation—and obtained a decree from the Emperor Theodosius II in which he directed that such matters could be settled by an assembly of bishops but not without the intervention of the bishop of Constantinople, Boniface leaped forward to defend the authority of his see against this "innovation." In the first of three letters, he appealed to the authority of Peter personified in his see. In the second, addressed to the bishops of Thessaly, he reiterated the Petrine claims and appealed to the Council of Nicaea's affirmation of Roman primacy and to the words of Jesus in Matthew 16. In the third letter he added an appeal to precedent: Once Rome has decided, what other bishop would need to call an assembly? Here he corrected Cyprian by saying that, while all bishops hold the same episcopal office, they must recognize the need for subordination for the sake of ecclesiastical discipline. Boniface stood in easy reach of Leo's concept of the papacy.

Coelestine (422–432) had little difficulty maintaining Roman authority in areas where it was already unquestioned, for instance, in Illyricum, but he had problems in areas less directly under his control and where conciliar organization was better developed, as in Africa and the East. Especially damaging to Roman standing in Africa was the case of Apiarius, a priest of Sicca Veneria in Proconsular Africa, whose bishop, Urbanus, had deposed and excommunicated him around 417. Apiarius went to Rome and obtained help from Zosimus, who threatened Urbanus with deposition if he did not restore Apiarius and sent three legates to settle the issue. Legates were an innovation borrowed from imperial practice; before they arrived, a council met at Carthage on May 1, 418, and forbade appeals from "presbyters, deacons, and inferior clergy." At a small synod held at Caesarea Maurentania on September 30, 418, the legates upheld the right of appeal to Rome by bishops and to "neighboring bishops" by "presbyters and deacons" and directed that Urbanus be excommunicated or sent to Rome if he would not cancel his decision against Apiarius. To back up his *commonitorium*, Zosimus mistakenly cited the fifth and fourteenth canons of the Council of Sardica as canons of Nicaea. The issue remained unresolved when Zosimus died. When the synod resumed under Boniface I at the Council of Carthage on May 25, 419, the Africans affirmed their acceptance of Nicaea and, in a letter to the pontiff, indicated that they would abide by such canons if proven Nicene and observed in Italy, but they objected to the arrogance of the papal legate Faustinus.

In the meantime, Apiarius had assumed a position at Tabraca, near Hippo, reputedly because of conduct that had led to his deposition and was excommunicated again. When he appealed to Rome, Coelestine restored Apiarius to communion without hearing his accusers and sent him back to Africa accompanied by Faustinus, the overbearing legate despised by the Africans. In a council held at Carthage around 426, the latter pressed for acceptance of the pope's decisions on the basis of "the privileges of the Roman Church." The Africans, however, after three days of inquiry, obtained a full confession from Apiarius and proceeded to entreat the pope to make fuller inquiry before restoring someone like Apiarius to communion and to point out that hearing cases of lower clergy violates the canons of Nicaea, which granted this right to local bishops. They were willing to recognize Roman primacy but not a primacy of jurisdiction.

Coelestine ran into similar resistance in the East in the Nestorian controversy. Eastern bishops resorted to Roman primacy when it suited them, but they could ignore it when they found it convenient to do so. At the Council of Ephesus in 431, Cyril of Alexandria presided, "holding also the place of the archbishop of the church of the Romans." When the Roman legates arrived, the assembled bishops heard and acclaimed Coelestine's letter. They placed Cyril and Coelestine on the same level, hailing the latter "as of one mind with the Council." The legates reversed the interpretation, that the bishops adhered to their head; but the bishops paid no attention. Cyril also ignored the assertion of papal claims by the legate Philip and asked the legates, "as representing the Apostolic See and the bishops of the West," to subscribe to the decree against Nestorius. Coelestine's successor, Sixtus III (432–440), was left the task of reconciling the see of Antioch. This happened without too much papal involvement, however, in the agreement of Cyril of Alexandria and John of Antioch to the Formulary of Reunion of April 433.

Leo

Leo I (440–461), the Great, laid down the theoretical base and established the primacy of the Roman see. In a series of sermons preached to bishops of his metropolitanate on the anniversary of his consecration and in several letters, he put forth a clear and comprehensive statement that the papacy has since operated on with little alteration. (1) Jesus bestowed supreme authority on Peter, as Matthew 16:18-19; Luke 22:31-32; and John 21:15-17 prove. (2) Peter was the first bishop of Rome. (3) Peter's authority has been perpetuated in his successors. (4) This authority is enhanced by the continuing mystical presence of Peter in the see of Rome. (5) Thence, the authority of other bishops does not derive directly from Christ but is mediated to them through Peter and Peter's successors. (6) Further, while other bishops' authority is limited to their own dioceses, the bishop of Rome has a *plenitudo potestatis* ("fullness of power") over the whole church and a responsibility to govern it.

Leo had much greater success in implementing these claims than did most of his predecessors. His bold leadership during the Hunnic invasions doubtless added to his personal mystique. Once again, however, the West acknowledged Roman primacy much more readily than did the East. In the West, even Africa now accepted Leo's authority as the synodical structure collapsed in the wake of the Vandal invasions. In Gaul, however, Leo ran into stiff resistance when he tried to discipline Hilary, Archbishop of Arles (429–449). Hilary, accompanied by Germanus of Auxerre (418–448), had assembled a council and removed Celidonius from the bishopric of Besançon because of two irregularities—marrying a widow while he was a layman and giving judgment in capital cases. Celidonius appealed to Rome and obtained Leo's support. Hilary crossed the Alps in midwinter to protest, insisting that the Roman see had no right to review decisions of a Gallic synod, the point made earlier in the case of Apiarius by African bishops. Leo, annoyed, dismissed charges against Celidonius and restored him to his see. He then wrote a letter to bishops of the province of Vienne, stating the prerogatives of the Apostolic See, condemning Hilary's arrogance and rude language, his encroachment on provinces not under him, and his recourse to the secular arm. Leo then declared Hilary deposed and his rights transferred to the bishop of Vienne; he also procured a rescript from Valentinian III, dated July 8, 445, which decreed that it was unlawful for bishops of Gaul or other provinces "to do anything without the authority of the Venerable Pope of the Eternal City." In short, the pope created a papal autocracy in the West. Hilary sought to conciliate Leo somewhat after a time, but in the end he remained as inflexible as Leo until his death on May 5, 449. Relations with Rome improved under Hilary's successor Ravennius (449–455) as Leo sought to rally Western backing for his *Tome*.

Eastern reaction to the *Tome* reflects quite clearly the continuance of Eastern Christian reservations about Roman claims. Both Eutyches and his opponents appealed to Leo for support. Leo sought further information from Flavian, Patriarch of Constantinople (447–449), and the Emperor Theodosius II (408–450) for more information. Flavian obliged, and on June 13, 449, Leo dispatched the *Tome*. It had hardly left Leo's hand before Flavian sent a second letter negating a council and saying that the matter only required Leo's "weight and support." Leo agreed, but the council later known as the "Robbers' Synod" was already set to meet at Ephesus in August 449 by order of Theodosius. Leo appointed three legates and sent with them a batch of letters, including the *Tome*. Dominated by Dioscurus, the Monophysite Patriarch of Alexandria (444–451), with an armed force at his disposal, the synod set aside the papal letters, reinstated Eutyches, and deposed Flavian. The legate Hilary barely escaped to return to Rome and give Leo a report. Flavian; Eusebius of Dorylaeum, who had also been deposed; and Theodoret of Cyrus all made appeals to Rome, but not in the language Leo himself would have used. In fact, Theodoret based his plea on Rome as the locus of the tombs of "our common fathers and teachers of the truth, Peter and Paul." Receiving the letters during a synod in Rome, September 29, Leo wrote seven letters to protest the proceedings at Ephesus and enlisted the Western Emperor Valentinian III; his mother, Galla Placidia; and his wife, Eudoxia, to write to the Eastern rulers. All based their claims for Rome on the Council of Nicaea. Theodosius II, however, sent cold rebuffs to all, saying essentially that the Easterners could look after their own affairs.

What turned the situation in Leo's favor was Theodosius's death on July 28, 450, when he was thrown from his horse. His successor, Marcian (450–457), zealously supported the position of Leo in the *Tome*. With the backing of both Western and Eastern emperors, Leo acquiesced to Marcian's summoning of a council for the fall of 451. At the first session of the Council of Chalcedon, the Roman legates presided, dealing with procedural matters. At the second session, on October 10, the assembled bishops acclaimed the *Tome*, crying, "Peter has spoken through Leo"; but Cyrillians found traces of what they thought was Nestorianism, which they asked some time to consider. When the council reconvened five days later, it deposed Dioscurus. In the next session, October 17, the bishops assented to the statement of the legate Paschasinus, which confirmed "the rule of faith as contained in the Creed of Nicaea, confirmed by the Council of Constantinople, expounded at Ephesus under Cyril, and set forth in the letter of Pope Leo when he condemned the heresy of Nestorius and Eutyches." As they construed it, Leo's *Tome* was in accord with the Nicene Creed. Over the determined opposition of the Roman legates, moreover, on November 1, the council reaffirmed the decision of Constantinople in

381 concerning the privileges of the Patriarchate of Constantinople, as second only to Rome, and decreed that the Patriarch of Constantinople would consecrate metropolitans for Pontus, Asia, and Thrace. Although this was not an innovation but a statement of current practice, it offended the legates, but they tried in vain to block it. Honorific titles and flattering letters to Leo did not appease him on this point. He feared a rival to his own see and foresaw subordination of the church to the state. He based his appeal on the decision of Nicaea—Rome, Alexandria, Antioch—but it fell on deaf ears. He finally had to declare his acceptance of the faith of Chalcedon without being required to withdraw his protest over the departure from Nicaea.

The Struggle for Integrity

From the Council of Chalcedon on, the papacy struggled to preserve its integrity against encroachments by the patriarchs in Constantinople and dominance by the emperors. Elevation of Constantinople at Chalcedon represented an imperial effort to assure that they would have more direct control over the entire church. Leo's successors resisted mightily. Ironically, two rather tragic happenings intruded to liberate them from Constantinople. One was the Lombard invasion of Italy in 568, which brought an end to Justinian's reestablishment of Roman control in Italy. From this point on, popes had to negotiate with other secular powers, eventually establishing an alliance with the Franks. The other was the Islamic invasion of Palestine and North Africa, which began in 632 and finally came to a halt a century later at the battle of Tours. The struggle that the papacy went through during this period gave it the basic shape that it retained throughout the Middle Ages.

The first major test for the papacy as defined by Leo arose soon after his death during the pontificates of Simplicius I (468–483) and Felix III (483–492), when the Emperor Zeno issued the *Henotikon* in 482, an edict whose object was to restore religious unity throughout the Byzantine Empire. The intentional vagueness of the decree offended both Monophysites and Chalcedonians. Apprised of the problem by the Patriarch Talaja of Alexandria, who had been deposed because he refused to acknowledge the *Henotikon*, Felix immediately demanded recognition of the Council of Chalcedon. Unfortunately, his legates sent to Constantinople permitted themselves to be intimidated and entered into communion with the Patriarch Acacius, adviser to Zeno in the affair, and with other Monophysites. At a synod in Rome, Felix deposed his legates and excommunicated Acacius, who promptly retaliated by removing the pope's name from the diptychs and severing all connections with Rome. Although his successors attempted repeatedly to restore connections, the schism lasted from 484 until 519.

Felix III was the first pope who had not ascended from the lower classes and thus knew the mind-set of the ruling classes. He also benefited from the able assistance of Gelasius as head of the chancery. Together Felix and Gelasius, who succeeded him as pope (492–496), challenged the policy pursued by the imperial government in Constantinople. During his brief pontificate, Gelasius continued the policy he had helped Felix III frame to clarify the function and standing of the emperor within the church. In a letter addressed to the Emperor Anastasius (491–518), Gelasius set forth a doctrine of two powers: priestly and royal. The priestly power is more weighty, he said, for priests have to take responsibility at the judgment even for kings. Moreover, even the emperor, though ruling humankind, had to bow his head and receive the eucharistic salvation from the hands of priests. If priests submit to the emperor in the civil realm, lest they obstruct the course of secular affairs, then the emperor should submit to them in religious matters. If such obedience is owed ordinary priests, how much more obedience is owed "the bishop of that see which the Most High ordained to be above all others"? In 495 a Roman synod elaborated the main point: "The apostolic See holds the *principatus* over the whole Church as the Lord Christ delegates it." The emperor's function in a Christian society is to learn, not to teach, what is Christian. He must find out from those who are qualified what is Christian—that is, from the pope, who alone holds the *principatus* over the divine community. The pope's powers are the same as Peter's. Emperors, therefore, should not order priests about but submit their actions to ecclesiastical superiors. Those who do so merit the title "Catholic." In a somewhat indirect fashion, Gelasius was telling Anastasius that the part he played in the Acacian Schism severed him from the church, a bold position in a time of burgeoning caesaropapism.

Two important pieces of literature supplemented the Gelasian scheme of papal monarchy. One was the writings of Pseudo-Dionysius, entitled *The Heavenly Hierarchies,* in which the unknown author depicted a divinely ordained order of ranks in ecclesiastical and heavenly societies necessitating different faculties and functions. The other was the fictitious *Legend of St. Silvester,* composed around 480 to 490, which stood behind the eighth-century *Donation of Constantine.* The *Legend* detailed the conversion of Constantine and explained how he had moved the imperial capital to Constantinople. The main point was to highlight Constantine's contrition before Sylvester, prostrating himself to receive the pope's forgiveness and to be reinvested with his imperial symbols and garments.

Although it did not bear fruit immediately for the papacy, the conversion of Clovis, probably in 496, was to have immense importance in the eventual liberation of the papacy from imperial control. In the West, Clovis and his successors played the role that Constantine had played within the Roman Empire and within the church. By the time of Pippin III (751–768), the Franks had become the vital instruments for protecting and assisting the papacy without posing the threat to its integrity that the Byzantine emperors posed.

At the very time that daylight began to break through in understanding relationships between church and state, however, the papacy itself was shaken by factions in the election of a successor to Anastasius II (496–498). A majority favored Symmachus (498–514), who advocated strict adherence to the principles laid down by Leo and Gelasius. A minority of some size, however, backed Laurentius, who wanted to accommodate the imperial viewpoint and who was not entirely opposed to a modified *Henotikon* as a means of restoring unity within the church. Both parties appealed to the Gothic King Theodoric the Great, an Arian, who declared Symmachus pope. When Laurentians made serious charges against Symmachus, Theodoric convened a council that investigated the charges and concluded as he had. Of special significance, the council ended with the declaration that the apostolic see could be judged by no one. Yet it took the firm hand of Theodoric to deliver all Roman churches to Symmachus's charge and to end the schism. A whole row of forgeries appeared to back Symmachus's claims and to place the papacy above criticism. The *Liber Pontificalis* ("Papal Book") also began to appear at this time, mixing narrative and interpretation of papal history up to the time of writing. Entries preceding the pontificate of Anastasius II have little correspondence to what actually happened, but those made after about 500 reflect growing self-awareness of the papacy itself.

Relationships between Rome and Constantinople remained strained throughout the reign of Anastasius (491–518) because of his severe attitude and acts of violence against supporters of Chalcedon until a rebellion led by Vitalian forced him to open negotiations with Hormisdas (514–523). Because Anastasius refused to condemn Acacius, however, the negotiations proved fruitless until Justin, an ardent supporter of Chalcedon, ascended the throne in 518. Justin received papal legates with honor, accepted the papal formula for unity, and struck the names of Acacius, the emperors Zeno and Anastasius, and other Monophysites from the diptychs. The improvement of relations with the East, however, aroused the suspicions of Theodoric, whose hegemony had already suffered a blow by the alliance of the Vandals with Byzantium after the death of their ruler, his brother-in-law Thrasamund. Theodoric tried a number of Roman nobles, including the scholar Boethius, for treason. When Justin revived the ancient laws against heretics to extirpate all traces of paganism and Arianism, Theodoric hailed John I (523–526) to his palace in Ravenna and forced him to lead a delegation to Constantinople to demand revocation of violent measures against Arians. The first pope to set foot in the imperial capital, John received a warm welcome, "as though he were Saint Peter himself." Justin backed away from some measures, allowing Arians to retain their churches, but this did not pacify Theodoric. He ordered John I imprisoned, where he died a few days later on May 18, 526.

The Formula of Union ending the Acacian Schism in 519 referred to the Roman Church as the one apostolic church that, according to Christ's promise in Matthew 16:18-19, had always preserved the true and pure catholic faith. Although this seemed like a victory for the papacy, it represented a well-calculated move by Justinian, who already guided his uncle Justin. In his mind, the Roman Church had an integral role to play within the empire under his own direction. In a revived Roman Empire, the city of Rome would rank higher than other cities and, correspondingly, the bishop of Rome would rank higher than other patriarchs. But Justinian never intended for the pope to hold jurisdiction. When he ascended the throne in 527, Justinian soon made clear that he would not tolerate any other ruler to claim final authority in matters he considered necessary for the well-being of the empire. His was a refurbished, christianized Roman imperial concept in which the emperor would hold responsibility for religious matters because these are a part of public law. During Justinian's long reign (527–565), the papacy faced a real challenge to its integrity, for the whole Eastern Church fully supported the imperial viewpoint. At Constantinople in 535, the assembled bishops declared that nothing could happen in the church without the consent and approval of the emperor himself.

The papacy did not have a happy experience with Justinian. In 536, Silverius (536–538?) was charged with treasonable liaison with the Ostrogoths when he tried to negotiate with them to prevent unnecessary bloodshed; he was deposed and sent into exile by a military court. He died shortly after resigning his office as a consequence of deprivations suffered during his exile. Vigilius (538–555), elevated to the office by Belisarius, Byzantine conqueror of Italy, ran afoul of the Empress Theodora, a Monophysite, when he stated his adherence to the formula adopted at Chalcedon and repeated the condemnation of the Monophysite Patriarch Anthimus. He also incurred the disfavor of the Emperor Justinian when he refused to condemn the "Three Chapters." To compel Western acceptance, the emperor ordered Vigilius removed and brought to Constantinople, where, under pressure, he acquiesced in the action and then vacillated as the West raised a storm of protest. He died on the way back to Rome in June 555. This celebrated case was a clear sign that the Byzantine government would go to any lengths to secure the agreement of the Roman Church in favor of "Roman" policy.

Dominance of the papacy by Justinian continued under Vigilius's successor, Pelagius I (556–561), chosen after an interval with Justinian's approval. Papal *apocrisarius* to the imperial court under Agapetus (535–536), he served as Vigilius's vicar at Rome during the latter's trip to Constantinople. He voluntarily sacrificed his personal fortune during Totila's siege of the city to relieve the famine of the inhabitants. He held the Western view about the "Three Chapters," and at Constantinople in 551 he persuaded Vigilius to oppose condemnation of them. From prison he vehemently attacked Vigilius's vacillation, but, in the end, he too capitulated to the emperor and approved their condemnation, perhaps because of his prospect of being elected pope. His wavering alienated many in the West and caused him to issue a solemn declaration of his commitment to the first four ecumenical councils, especially Chalcedon, and to take an oath that he had not been responsible for the harsh treatment and death of his predecessor. Although these acts reassured the bishops of Gaul and King Childebert of Paris, they did not satisfy the bishops of Milan, Aquileia, and Ravenna.

The Byzantine control dropped precipitously as a result of the Lombard invasion of Italy in 568, and the papacy now found itself in a position to reconsider its own Roman past and to reassert itself. Once the exarch took up residence in Ravenna, the emperor had little power and authority to direct the Roman Church. The popes now had to act as intermediaries between the Lombards and Constantinople, and, where they had to, they often negotiated independently with the invading armies with little fear of interference from Constantinople. Unlike earlier Germanic conquerors, the Lombards did not envy the Roman Empire. Rather, they sought to destroy it and to replace imperial administration with their own. They founded duchies in both north and south and looked on Rome itself as a duchy nominally related, like Naples and Sicily in the south, to the Byzantine Empire. Although most were originally pagans, by the eighth century they had accepted the Catholic faith. Meanwhile, the papacy collected patrimonies all over Italy and in Dalmatia, Gaul, Africa, Sardinia, and Corsica to become by the end of the sixth century the largest single landowner in Western Europe. All of these it governed after the Roman model. They furnished revenues to support the impoverished population of Rome as well as monasteries and the papal household itself.

Gregory I, the Great

As the sixth century came to a close, the Roman Church found itself in a very different position than the one that existed in the time of Justinian. The church now served as a link between diverse peoples and not just the constituency of the Roman Empire. The Visigoths in Spain, the Franks in

Gaul, and the Lombards in Italy all figured prominently in the larger picture and opened the way for some adjustments in the theory of the papacy.

Insight concerning this came from Spain, where in 589 the Visigothic King Recared had converted to the Catholic faith. Isidore, Archbishop of Seville (ca. 600–636), whose brother, Leander, had become an intimate friend of Gregory during their stay in Constantinople, perceived a way to forge a link between the Roman and Germanic nations through the church. He contended that, since the church is the one Body of Christ, it is composed of a plurality of nations within which the different princes function. Because there is only one Body, there can be only one rule: the pope's. The king's function, as a member of the church, was to strengthen priestly directives—that is, to use "princely terror" to support the word of priests. The king must use coercion to assure a just society. He assisted where the priestly word proved inadequate.

Gregory I (590–604) united the Gelasian and Isidorean theories. His predecessor, Pelagius II (579–590), had already had to protest assumption of the title of "universal patriarch" by the Patriarch John IV (582–595). Gregory reiterated the protest, noting the claim imposed on the Roman *principatus*. Rome alone, he argued, held the *principatus* over the People of God, the society of the Christian republic. This society was composed of nations outside the frame of the Eastern empire. Rome would provide the basis for the unity of the diverse peoples of the West. Although Gregory addressed the emperor in a quite different tone from Western rulers—the emperor as *dominus*, or lord, and the others as "sons"—he went on to insist that priests are superior to laypersons. Only if this is recognized can Christendom assume some kind of order. Just as heaven is hierarchical, so also is the society of the Christian republic.

Gregory is rightly acclaimed for the farsightedness of his policy. He recognized better than any of his predecessors the importance of the Germanic peoples to the future of the church. He had spent enough years in Constantinople as the *apocrisarius* to know the dangers posed by the emperors. Certainly he could see that Rome could expect no help from the struggling Eastern empire. Taking office just after the conversion of Recared, on the other hand, he could exploit his friendship with Leander, Bishop of Seville (ca. 584–ca. 600), to cultivate relationships with the now Catholic Goths. In Gaul he established regular communication with the Merovingians and with the bishops, making the Bishop of Arles his vicar. In Italy he maintained pleasant relations with the Lombard Queen Theodelinda, laying the groundwork for the eventual conversion of her people. To England he dispatched Augustine, Abbot of St. Andrew's monastery in Rome, in 596 to win the Anglo-Saxons. He already had a point of contact through Bertha, wife of the King of Kent and daughter of Charibert, King of the Franks.

CONCLUSION

Germanic "invasions" notwithstanding, the story of early Christianity is a remarkable one. It began in a "corner" of the empire among a people considered alien by the Romans. Its founder was crucified as a common criminal, its first constituents were virtually illiterate. It was one of many sects within Judaism, persecuted almost from the start—not a formula for survival, much less for success. Yet Christianity not only survived but also prospered. At first hesitantly but then more confidently, it spread from Jerusalem throughout Judea and, little by little, throughout the Roman Empire and beyond. Thanks to Constantine and his successors, persecution ceased and Christianity became the established religion of the Roman Empire. How can one explain this remarkable development?

From their Jewish ancestors Christians have learned to look for a divine hand at work in history, especially their history. Christ came "in the fullness of time," when everything was ready, to fulfill Jewish hopes and longings. Rejection by his own people opened the way for his "good news" to go to the Gentiles. The success of Christianity "proved" that it was of God.

Historians cannot be content with an explanation quite that simple. In some ways, however, it rings true. People of the Roman Empire and beyond lived with expectancy of an age of fulfillment. Emperor Octavian had that hope memorialized on the *Ara Pacis* beside the Tiber river in Rome. Animals and humans lived in harmony under the *Pax Romana*. At the same time Judaism had tilled the field, planting communities that gathered regularly for worship all over the ancient world, inculcating monotheism, fostering an admirable ethic, and pointing people toward the goal of history. Other oriental religions were making their way westward at the same time, attracting masses of followers, so that Christianity was able to ride the crest of their wave.

Why Christianity and not Judaism or the other religions? That, too, is a difficult question to answer. Historians are quick to point to Constantine. However one interprets his motives for adopting Christianity, no one can doubt the growing clarity of his desire to make Christianity the religion of Rome. When he opted for Christianity rather than the solar monotheism of Mithra, Christianity could claim only about 10 percent of the population of the Roman Empire. By the end of the fourth century, Theodosius I ruled it illegal not to be a Christian, certainly a boon to evangelism.

As much as Constantine and his successors deserve credit for the success of Christianity from the early fourth century on, we must still explain how

356

Christianity not only survived three centuries of intermittent harassment and persecution but grew as well. In answer to this question, I have pointed to Christianity's corporate life—catechumenate and baptism, worship centering in the eucharist, discipline, ministry and organization, scriptures—as the means through which early Christianity preserved its identity as a covenant missionary people as it incorporated the syncretistic peoples of the Roman Empire. Christianity inherited its most central and salient ideas from its parent, Judaism, including the conviction that it should propagate monotheism. The conviction of early Christians that covenant hopes had been fulfilled in the life, death, and resurrection of Jesus, however, intensified the missionary thrust. Once Christians, under Paul's leadership, broke free from the strictures connected with observance of the Law, they could accommodate to other cultures in ways Jews found unacceptable, becoming "all things to all people." Christianity could compete with other popular religions such as the Great Mother, Isis and Osiris, and Mithra in adapting itself to the cultures of the empire. Too much inclusiveness, however, would have undercut the motive for mission, and Christianity counterbalanced inclusivism with an exclusivism based on absolute commitment to God revealed in Jesus Christ and forged in the catechumenate and baptism.

Not even imperial assistance, moreover, assured that Christians would win the peoples of the Roman Empire to their faith. Commitment to the ancient deities of Greece and Rome or the oriental deities remained strong throughout the centuries dealt with in this book. The wealthy, cultured, and powerful resisted forcible efforts at their own conversion or the elimination of the last vestiges of the ancestral religions. Meantime, the Roman Empire, especially in the West, eroded inwardly as Germanic peoples threatened invasion from the north and Persians from the east. The unity Constantine hoped to gain from the Christian religion proved difficult to attain, for Christians were divided over doctrine. When Rome itself fell in 410 to Alaric and the Goths, the devotees of the ancient religions again cried, "Christians are responsible for the calamities befalling Rome! They deserted the gods who made Rome great, and now you see the consequences."

The German "invasions" put Christianity at risk once more and forced it to prove its resilience all over again. In the east, of course, the empire and Christianity remained strong. In the west, however, the Germanic peoples little by little resettled the empire. Fortunately, they admired all things Roman, including the Christian religion, and Christians had already carried the faith beyond the boundaries of the Roman Empire. Bishops such as Ambrose of Milan, Victricius of Rouen, Martin of Tours, and Hilary of Poitiers steadied their people during these invasions and continued to evangelize the invaders. In the fourth century and later, monasticism took wing, and monks soon were playing a central role in the evangelization of the Germanic peoples. They established monasteries and churches as centers of civilization. Ireland produced a new breed of monks who thought of themselves as itinerant missionaries (*peregrini*).

Throughout the period covered by this study of the early church we have seen Christianity engaging different cultures and effecting new relationships with them. Initially Christianity addressed itself to a predominantly Palestinian Jewish culture but almost as soon to Hellenistic Jewish culture. Then, as it incorporated more and more persons of Greek and Roman background, it accommodated itself to those cultures, at first cautiously but then more boldly by the fourth century. As it moved beyond the confines of the Roman Empire, it packaged itself to attract persons of other cultural backgrounds—Armenian, Persian, Germanic, Egyptian. Protestants have often looked on such accommodation as a "fall" of the Church with Christianity losing its pristine purity. While admitting the riskiness of accommodation, I have interpreted it as a sign of Christianity's missionary vitality counterbalanced by continuing inculcation of the church's covenant identity through its corporate activities, especially baptism and eucharist as the covenant rites par excellence.

Every generation of Christians faces the challenge of being faithful to the gospel in their own setting. Far from deserving censure, Christians of the first centuries C.E. merit commendation for their effort to hold on to the treasure entrusted to them. To be sure, each generation can be criticized for failing to live up to Christian principles. Persecutions, power struggles, and divisions did not honor the Christian faith, then, any more then they honor the faith today. On the positive side, however, we need in fairness to note that, in these centuries, there were always those who tried to achieve a higher standard of faithfulness to Christ—devout women and men ready to pay the ultimate price. Are we doing better?

BIBLIOGRAPHY

Secondary Works Cited in the Text Only

Bauer, Walther. *Orthodoxy and Heresy in Earliest Christianity.* Translated by Philadelphia Seminar on Christian Origins. Edited by Robert A. Kraft and Gerhard Krodel. Philadelphia: Fortress Press, 1971.

Chadwick, Henry. *Early Christian Thought and the Classical Tradition.* New York: Oxford University Press, 1966.

Corwin, Virginia. *St. Ignatius and Christianity in Antioch.* New Haven: Yale University Press, 1960.

Dodd, Charles Harold. *The Parables of the Kingdom.* Rev. ed. New York: Scribner's, 1961.

Frend, W. H. C. *The Donatist Church.* Oxford: Clarendon Press, 1952.

Harnack, Adolf. *History of Dogma.* Translated by Neil Buchanan. 7 vols. New York: Dover Publications, Inc.; reprint of 3rd German ed., 1900.

Latourette, Kenneth Scott. *A History of the Expansion of Christianity.* 7 vols. London: Eyre & Spottiswoode, 1938–45.

Loisy, Alfred. *The Birth of the Christian Religion.* Translated by L. P. Jacks. London: G. Allen & Unwin, 1948.

Manson, William. *The Epistle to the Hebrews.* London: Hodder & Stoughton, 1966.

Robinson, James M., ed. *The Nag Hammadi Library.* New York: Harper & Row, 1977.

Schweitzer, Albert. *The Quest of the Historical Jesus.* Translated by W. Montgomery. London: Adam & Charles Black, 1910.

Strauss, David Friedrich. *The Christ of Faith and the Jesus of History.* Translated and ed. by Leander Keck. Philadelphia: Fortress Press, 1977.

Turner. H. E. W. *The Pattern of Christian Truth.* London: A. R. Mowbray & Co., Ltd., 1954.

Walzer, R. *Galen on Jews and Christians.* London: Oxford University Press, 1949.

Primary Sources

Acts of Ephrem
Acts of Saint Cyprian
Acts of Saint Perpetua
Acts of Thomas
Alexander of Lycopolis, *Against Manichaean Views*
Ambrose, *Explanation of the Psalms*
———. *Sermons on Luke*
———. *The Virgins*
Ammianus Marcellinus, *History of Rome*
Apocalypse of Adam
Apology of Aristides
Ariso of Pella, *The Christian Dialogue*
Arius, *The Banquet*

359

Arnobius, *Against the Nations*
Athenagoras, *Embassy*
Athanasius, *Apology Against the Arians*
———. *Epistle to the Africans*
———. *History of the Arians*
———. *Incarnation of the Word*
———. *Life of Anthony*
Augustine, *Against Cresconius*
———. *Against the Epistle of Parmenian*
———. *Against Julian the Pelagian*
———. *Against the Two Epistles of the Pelagians*
———. *The City of God*
———. *Confessions*
———. *First Catechetical Instruction*
———. *Harmony of the Gospels*
———. *On Christian Doctrine*
———. *On Free Will*
———. *On Genesis*
———. *On the Gift of Perseverance*
———. *On the Grace of Christ*
———. *On Grace and Free Will*
———. *On the Happy Life*
———. *On Heresies*
———. *On Marriage and Concupiscence*
———. *On Merits and the Forgiveness of Sins and the Baptism of Infants*
———. *On Nature and Grace*
———. *On Original Sin*
———. *On the Predestination of the Saints*
———. *On Reproach and Grace*
———. *On the Spirit and the Letter*
———. *On True Religion*
———. *Sermon 351, Repentance*
———. *Soliloquies*
Basiliscus, *Anti-Encyclical*
———. *The Encyclical*
Boethius, *The Consolation of Philosophy*
———. *On the Holy Trinity*
Cassian, *Conferences*
———. *Institutions*
———. *On the Incarnation of the Lord Against the Nestorians*
Cassiodorus, *Historia Ecclesiastica Tripartita*
———. *The Institution of Divine and Secular Letters*
Celsus, *True Discourse*
Chronicle of Arbela
Chrysostom, *Against the Jews*
———. *The Devil as Tempter*
———. *Homilies on Matthew*
———. *The Priesthood*
———. *Saint Babylas*
Cicero, *Hortensius*
Clement of Alexandria, *Address to the Greeks* (*Protrepticus*)

————. *How the Rich Can Be Saved*
————. *The Instructor (Paedagogos)*
————. *Stromateis*
Cyprian, *Exhortation to Martyrdom*
Codex Justinianus
Codex Theodosianus
Corpus Hermeticum
Cyprian, *The Lapsed*
————. *To Donatus*
————. *The Unity of the Church*
————. *Work and Almsgiving*
Cyril of Alexandria, *Against the Blasphemies of Nestorius*
————. *Apology Against the Orientals*
————. *Apology Against Theodoret in Behalf of the Twelve Chapters*
————. *On Right Faith*
————. *To the Monks of Egypt*
————. *Twelve Anathemas*
Damascus Document
Didache
Didascalia Apostolorum
Doctrine of Addai
Donation of Constantine
Egeria, *The Pilgrimage of Egeria*
Epictetus, *Diatribes*
Epiphanius, *Against Heresies*
Epistle of Barnabas
Epistle to Diognetus
Eusebius, *Church History*
————. *Life of Constantine*
————. *Martyrs of Palestine*
————. *The Pascal Observance*
————. *Preparation for the Gospel*
Eutropius, *Compendium of Roman History*
Faustus of Riez, *Two Books on Grace*
Formula of Reunion
Galen, *Opera*
Gospel of Thomas
Gospel of Truth
Gregory I, the Great, *Dialogues*
Gregory of Nazianzus, *Against Julian*
————. *Historic Poems*
Gregory of Nyssa, *The Life of Macrina*
————. *The Life of Moses*
Gregory of Tours, *Eight Books of Miracles*
————. *History of the Franks*
Gregory Thaumaturgus, *Exposition of Faith*
Hegesippus, *Memoirs*
Heracleon, *Commentary on the Gospel of John*
Hippolytus, *Apostolic Tradition*
————. *Chronicle*
————. *Commentary on Daniel*

————. *Philosophumena* or *Refutation of All Heresies*
History of the Monks
Honorius I, *Edict of Unity*
Ignatius of Antioch, *Epistles to the Ephesians, Magnesians, Philadelphians, Romans, Trallians*
Irenaeus, *Against Heresies*
————. *Proof of the Apostolic Preaching*
Jerome, *Commentary on Matthew*
————. *Dialogue Against the Luciferians*
————. *Dialogues Against the Pelagians*
————. *Epistle to Marcella*
————. *Life of Hilarion*
————. *On Illustrious Men*
John of Ephesus, *Ecclesiastical History*
————. *Lives of Eastern Saints*
Julian, *Against the Galileans*
————. *Oration 4*
Justin, *Dialogue with Trypho*
————. *First and Second Apology*
Justinian, *Against the Three Chapters*
————. *Confession of Right Faith*
Lactantius, *Divine Institutions*
————. *On the Deaths of Persecutors*
Lampadius, *Alexander Severus*
Legend of St. Sylvester
Leo I, the Great, *The Tome*
Letter of Pliny to the Emperor Trajan
Liber Pontificalis
Life of Pachomius
Lucian, *Alexander Abonuteichos*
————. *Metamorphoses* or *The Golden Ass*
————. *Peregrinus*
Marcion, *Antitheses*
Marcus Aurelius, *Meditations*
Martyrdom of Polycarp
Melito of Sardis, *Apology*
Novatian, *The Good of Modesty*
————. *Jewish Foods*
————. *The Shows*
————. *The Trinity*
Optatus, *Against the Donatists*
Origen, *Against Celsus*
————. *Commentary on John*
————. *Commentary on Romans*
————. *Commentary on the Song of Songs*
————. *Dialogue with Heracleides*
————. *Exhortation to Martyrdom*
————. *First Principles*
————. *Hexapla*
————. *Homilies on Isaiah*
————. *Homilies on Joshua*

———. *Homilies on Leviticus*
———. *Homilies on Luke*
———. *On Prayer*
———. *Sermons on Judges*
Orosius, *Apologetic Book on Free Will*
———. *Seven Books Against the Pagans*
Palladius, *Lausiac History*
Pelagius, *Commentary on Romans*
———. *In Behalf of Free Will*
Philostorgius, *Church History*
Philostratus, *Life of Apollonius of Tyana*
Plotinus, *Enneads*
Pontius, *Life of Cyprian*
Porphyry, *Against the Christians*
———. *Isagoge*
———. *Philosophy from Oracles*
Preaching of Peter
Prudentius, *On the Crown* (Peristephanon)
Pseudo-Dionysius, *Celestial Hierarchies*
Ptolemaeus, *Letter to Flora*
Shepherd of Hermas
Socrates, *Church History*
Sozomen, *Church History*
Spartian, *Severus*
Tatian, *Address to the Greeks*
———. *Diatessaron*
Tertullian, *Against the Jews*
———. *The Apparel of Women*
———. *Apology*
———. *Baptism*
———. *Exhortation to Chastity*
———. *On the Crown of the Soldier*
———. *On the Dress of Women*
———. *On Idolatry*
———. *On Fasting*
———. *On Flight in Persecution*
———. *On Modesty*
———. *On Patience*
———. *On Prayer*
———. *On Purity*
———. *On Repentance*
———. *On the Shows*
———. *On the Soul*
———. *Prescriptions Against Heretics*
———. *Testimony of the Soul*
———. *To the Martyrs*
———. *To the Nations*
———. *To His Wife*
———. *To Scapula*
———. *The Scorpion's Sting*
———. *The Veiling of Virgins*

Theodore of Mopsuestia, *Against Those Who Say People Sin by Nature and Not by Their Own Will*
Theodoret of Cyrus, *The Beggar or Polymorph*
———. *Church History*
———. *Religious History*
Theophilus of Antioch, *To Autolycus*
Trimorphic Protennoia
Vincent of Lérins, *Commonitorium*
Zeno, *The Henoticon*
Zosimus, *Tractoria*
Zostianus and Allogenes

ABBREVIATIONS

Ad Scap.   Tertullian, *Ad Scapulan (To Scapula)*

Adv. haer.   Irenaeus, *Adversus Haereses (Against Heresies)*

Adv. Jud.   Tertullian, *Adversus Judaeos (Against the Jews)*

Alex. Abon.   Lucian of Samosata, *Alexander Abonuteichos*

1, 2 Apol.   Justin Martyr, *First and Second Apology*; Tertullian, *Apologeticum*

A.T.   Hippolytus, *Apostolic Tradition*

Barn.   *The Epistle of Barnabas*

1, 2 Clem.   *1, 2 Clement*

Codex Just.   *Codex Justinianum (Code of Justinian)*

Codex Theod.   *Codex Theodosionum (Code of Theodotian)*

Comm.   *Commentary*

Conf.   Augustine, *Confessions*

Dam. Doc.   Qumran *Damascus Document*

Dial.   Justin Martyr, *Dialogue with Trypho*

Diatr.   Epictetus, *Diatribes*

Did.   *Didache (Teaching of the Apostles)*

Ep.; Epp.   *Epistle; Epistles*

Eph.   Ignatius, *Epistle to the Ephesians*

H.E.   Eusebius, Socrates, Sozomen, *Historia Ecclesiastica (Church History)*

Hom.   *Homily*

Mand.   Hermas, *Mandates*

Mar. Pol.   *The Martyrdom of Polycarp*

Medit.   Marcus Aurelius, *Meditations*

Paed.   Clement of Alexandria, *Paedagogos (Instructor)*

Pereg.   Lucian of Samosata, *Peregrinus*

Smyrn.   Ignatius, *Epistle to the Smyrnaeans*

Vis.   Hermas, *Visions*

INDEX

Abgar, King of Edessa, 111
Abitina, 150
Abram, Abraham, 15, 120-21, 155, 197, 243
Abyssinia (Ethiopia, Axum), 206, 228-29, 285
Acacian Schism, 297, 350-51, 353
Acacius, Patriarch of Constantinople, 322, 350, 352
Achaia, 73, 291
Achilius Glabrio, 72
Achoris, 256
Acoemitae, 322, 323
Adeodatus, son of Augustine, 327, 329
Adiabene, 284
Adoptionism. *See* Monarchianism
Adrianople (Hadrianople), 283
Aedesius (Edesius), 206, 228-29
Aegae, 203
Aelia Capitolina (Jerusalem), 60, 109
Aemilia-Liguria, 114, 253, 278
Aemilian, Prefect of Egypt, 126, 128
Aetius (Arian leader), 212
Africa (province) 63, 73, 115, 120, 123, 127, 130, 131, 146, 148, 149, 173, 189, 199, 214, 272, 277, 289, 290, 298, 299, 329-32, 334-39, 345, 346, 348, 354
Agape meal, 54-55, 65, 172
Agapetus, Pope, 354
Agrippinus, Numidian Bishop, 116
Agnes, Abbess of monastery near Poitiers, 308
Aguane monastery, 293
Alaric I, Gothic King, 275, 278, 330, 357
Alaric II, Gothic King, 291
Albina, daughter of Melania the Elder and mother of Melania the Younger, 289, 336
Albina, mother of Marcella, 263
Alcibiades of Apamea, 156
Alemanni, 107, 270, 272, 282
Alexander of Abonoteichos, 66
Alexander, Bishop of Alexandria, 156, 204, 206, 231, 232, 234

Alexander, Bishop of Jerusalem, 110, 112, 191
Alexander, Metropolitan of Cilicia, 315
Alexander the Great, 120, 213
Alexander of Lycopolis, 221
Alexander Severus, Emperor, 120-21
Alexandra, woman monk of Alexandria, 258
Alexandria, 22, 23, 42, 45, 53, 63, 65, 67, 86, 88, 89, 91, 104, 109, 110, 116, 117, 119, 121, 123, 124, 128, 167, 171, 176-78, 180, 190, 191, 202, 205, 212-15, 224, 225, 229-32, 234-37, 241, 248, 255, 256, 289, 295, 302, 312, 315-17, 321, 322, 337, 343-45, 347, 350
Alfred, King of England, 307
Allegorical interpretation, 185-86, 187, 191
Alms, almsgiving. *See* Charity, Christian
Alogoi. See Monarchianism
Altar of Victory, 210, 214, 216, 225, 277
Alypius, friend of Augustine and Bishop of Thagaste, 327, 329
Amasia, 11
Amastris, 61
Ambrose, Bishop of Milan, 114, 192, 208, 214, 216, 218, 222, 223, 226, 245, 250, 252-53, 264, 276, 277, 279, 289, 300, 301, 319, 328, 329, 332, 345, 357
Ambrose, patron of Origen, 118, 121, 144
Amien, 226
Amma Talis, Egyptian monk, 258
Ammianus Marcellinus, 114, 214
Ammonius Saccas, 108, 168, 192
Amoun, monk of Nitria, 255
Amphion, Bishop of Nicomedia, 204
Ananias and Sapphira, 43
Anastasius, Bishop of Thessalonica, 319
Anastasius, chaplain of Nestorius, 313
Anastasius I, Emperor, 301, 323, 351, 352

LaVergne, TN USA
11 December 2009
166678LV00004B/307/P